LOUIS AGASSIZ

BOOKS BY CHRISTOPH IRMSCHER

Louis Agassiz: Creator of American Science

Public Poet, Private Man:
Henry Wadsworth Longfellow at 200

Longfellow Redux

John James Audubon, Writings and Drawings (editor)

The Poetics of Natural History: From John Bartram
to William James

LOUIS AGASSIZ

CREATOR OF
AMERICAN SCIENCE

Christoph Irmscher

HOUGHTON MIFFLIN HARCOURT
BOSTON   NEW YORK
2013

www.hmhbooks.com

Library of Congress Cataloging-in-Publication Data
Irmscher, Christoph.
Louis Agassiz: creator of American science / Christoph Irmscher.
p. cm.
Includes bibliographical references and index.
ISBN 978-0-547-57767-8
1. Agassiz, Louis, 1807–1873. 2. Agassiz, Louis, 1807–1873—Influence. 3. Naturalists—
United States—Biography. 4. Natural history—United States—History—19th century.
I. Title.
QH31.A2147 2013
508.092—dc23
[B]
2012014225

Book design by Brian Moore

Printed in the United States of America
DOC 10 9 8 7 6 5 4 3 2 1

For Daniel Aaron
On the occasion of his one hundredth birthday
With love

Contents

List of Illustrations

LOUIS AGASSIZ

Introduction

IN SEPTEMBER 1866, the American consul to Mauritius, fresh off the boat, paid a visit to the Boston publisher James T. Fields. He carried precious cargo with him, though it was not intended for Fields, but rather for the man known as America's greatest naturalist, the man everyone wanted to see when they came to Cambridge: Louis Agassiz. In the consul's luggage were two complete skeletons of the extinct flightless bird known as the dodo. Fields made sure that Agassiz received the bones forthwith. They were not perfect skeletons, Agassiz decided, but it was good to have them anyway. When Fields, making conversation, asked if "the Dodo were good enough to eat," Agassiz's face lit up. "Yes, indeed!" he said, in his French-inflected English. "What a peety we could not have the Dodo at our club. A good dinner is humanity's greatest blessing!" Unfortunately, the Dutch had beaten them on that score and killed all the dodos. But at least there were the bones. Agassiz put them in his museum.[1]

Surely Agassiz was joking in that response to Fields. The image of the illustrious members of the Saturday Club—among them the poet and publisher Fields, the poet and doctor Oliver Wendell Holmes, the poet and professor James Russell Lowell, and the philosopher Ralph Waldo Emerson—feasting on dodo at the dinner table at Boston's Parker Hotel is absurd enough, and Annie Fields likely had some fun including this passage in her postmortem biography of James Fields.

And yet the anecdote says much about the appeal Agassiz had for his fellow Americans: an expert on all manner of things living and dead, he kept his mind firmly trained on the enjoyment of life. In Agassiz, Americans had found the "lusty laugh that the Puritan forgot,"[2] Oliver Wendell Holmes once said. Agassiz was a bon vivant. He worked hard, harder than anyone these New England literati had ever known, but he also knew how to live life to the fullest. And a well-stocked dinner table defined Agassiz's world in more than one way. In a later conversation, Fields asked Agassiz if he thought man would ever figure out the mystery of life and death. Agassiz pointed at the food they were about to eat: "I am sure he will," he replied. "The time will come when these things will be made as clear as the table spread out before us."[3] We are still waiting for that time, it seems. Ironically, in a sense the dodo has outlived Agassiz, its would-be consumer: its skeleton (or at least the skeleton of *some* dodo) even today greets the visitor to Agassiz's museum, still known as the Museum of Comparative Zoology.

The story of the consul from Mauritius, with his dodo skeletons destined for Agassiz's museum, illustrates well the worldwide fame Louis Agassiz enjoyed. The details of his fabulous life had become the stuff of legend. Popularizer of the ice age, climber of mountain peaks, dredger of the deep seas, describer of fossil fish and jellyfish, taxonomist of turtles—Agassiz had done it all. He had given America its greatest science museum at the time, and he founded, on Penikese Island off the coast of Massachusetts, the first serious summer school in natural history, actively welcoming women as participants. At Harvard, he assembled around him the best and brightest young men of his time, thus creating, arguably, the first American graduate school. Born in full view of the stately snow-clad mountains of Switzerland, on the shores of lac de Neuchâtel, where he had first taught science to schoolchildren, Agassiz was mentored by the great naturalists Georges Cuvier and Alexander von Humboldt. When he came to the United States in 1846, not even forty years old, it seemed as if the New World had always been waiting for him.

Agassiz took to America like a fish to water. His unorthodox religious views resonated with New England Unitarianism, but he brought to them a scientific rigor and an uncompromising seriousness that his new friends, among them Ralph Waldo Emerson and James Russell Lowell, could only dream about. Agassiz's God, James Russell Lowell once said, in a poem dripping with admiration, was "very God."[4] Agassiz was never an orthodox believer or churchgoer, but his science was infused with the presence of the divine, which he found wherever he went: in Swiss glaciers, American lakes, and the Amazonian rain forest.

Industrious he certainly was: Agassiz published over four hundred scientific books and papers in his lifetime, most of which "could be consulted productively today by workers in the field," according to David C. Smith and Harold W. Borns of the University of Maine's Climate Change Institute.[5] A few years ago, a massive volume containing interviews with over fifty scientists gave tribute to what the book's very title identified as *Agassiz's Legacy*.[6] Many of those interviews had taken place at the Woods Hole Oceanographic Institution on Cape Cod, not far from Penikese Island, where Agassiz had founded his Anderson School of Natural History, seen by many as the direct ancestor of Woods Hole. Agassiz had taught his students to find, observe, and ask questions about creatures in their own environments, and this is precisely what, according to the interviews, biology professors are still doing today, at Woods Hole as well as at Stanford University's Hopkins Marine Station, which was the creation of Agassiz's former student David Starr Jordan. The photograph on the cover of *Agassiz's Legacy* shows a scene Agassiz would have enjoyed. The biologist Don Abbott and a young female student (Gabrielle Nevitt, who would later teach at the University of California–Davis) are gathering sponges in an intertidal zone off Hopkins Marine Station. Abbott, white-haired and distinguished-looking, is up to his knees in an intertidal pool, gazing at an open jar in his hand, while his student, kneeling on the slippery rocks, is about to close hers. This kind of intimacy—with nature, students, other scientists—was what Agassiz craved more than anything else. Fieldwork, for Agassiz, was an affair of the senses. It meant delighting in the present moment: the things we see, the sounds we hear, the air we feel, and the surfaces we touch. It meant passing on such delight to others, his students.

There were, to be sure, distinctly undelightful sides to Louis Agassiz: his shabby treatment of his first wife, whom he left behind when he traveled to the New World; his relentless resistance to Darwinism; and, perhaps most of all, his reprehensible belief that America belonged to the whites only.[7] In fact, people who are not working scientists tend to think of Agassiz as a misguided, opportunistic bigot. Even in his own Cambridge he has become a liability. Several years ago, an eighth-grader at the Agassiz School, a stone's throw from Agassiz's Museum of Comparative Zoology, came across a summary of Agassiz's racial views in the biologist Stephen Jay Gould's book *The Mismeasure of Man*. Horrified, he suggested that the school change its name. Which it did. In 2004, an official ceremony celebrated the renaming of the Agassiz School to honor its first African American principal, Maria Baldwin. And there's more to rename. In a recent broadcast of *Living on Earth*, the producer Bruce Gellerman, interviewing the Darwin biographer James Moore, referred to Agassiz with evident disgust, adding, "We're not far from Harvard University right here from our studios and many things are named after him." I wouldn't be surprised if the pothole-riddled Cambridge street that bears Agassiz's name was someday given a new identity too. And what about Mount Agassiz in New Hampshire or, for that matter, in California, one of the tallest peaks in the Sierras?[8]

Modern historians generally agree that the cosmopolitan Harvard professor Agassiz lost his battle against the reclusive British country squire Darwin, and rather dramatically so: "His science wasn't theoretical and his theory wasn't scientific," writes Louis Menand. "Darwin's ideas are devices for generating data. Darwin's theory opens possibilities for inquiry; Agassiz's closes them."[9] His God might have been "very God," as Lowell insisted, but Agassiz's attempt to yoke science and religion seems at best quaint or, more likely, dangerous today. Darwin, Agassiz's great nemesis, got his science right, or mostly right, and as part of the bargain, he seems much easier to write about too, as the flurry of publications associated with the bicentennial of his birth proved once again. Biographers have given much attention to Darwin's personal struggles, his sheer courage, and his determination to carry on with his work, even as his constantly ailing body, subjected to a variety of medical treatments ranging from amyl nitrite and arsenic to tartar emetic ointments, was refusing to come along for the ride. Adrian Desmond and James Moore, in their much-discussed book *Darwin's Sacred Cause*,[10] pointed to one of the catalysts for Darwin's lifelong suffering: the suffering of others. They argued that when Darwin, "a caring, compassionate man," resolved to come up with ways of proving the common origin of all living things, he was in fact hoping to refute, on the basis of science, all those who were still defending a certain type of human difference and thus slavery. Desmond and Moore recount a powerfully uplifting version of Darwin's story, and they tell it well. We are inclined to believe them when they attribute much of the impetus behind Darwin's emerging theory to the cries of a tortured Brazilian slave he overheard as a young man. In fact, we find it easy to imagine that the man for whom we care so much would have cared much for others too. Darwin gives us a story ready for the telling. If it is true that Darwin loves us, to modify the title of a recent book by George Levine, it is equally true that we love—or at least should try to love—Darwin.[11]

But can we love *Agassiz?* I would be the first to admit that the story of Agassiz the incorrigible racist commissioning photographs of Southern slaves while he was also working to give us the first modern description of a jellyfish's nervous system is a challenging one to tell. The last person to try his hand at it was the historian Edward Lurie, who over fifty years ago published a biography focused mostly on the details of Agassiz's tangled scientific involvements.[12] But Agassiz's story far exceeds the boundaries of his scientific investments. It is a story riven with the contradictions of a man who wanted to come across as both rigorously professional and unrelentingly popular, a man who believed that science practiced with due diligence could clear up not only the little problems that confound the specialists but also the whole cosmic puzzle itself. Agassiz was one of the first to establish science as a collective enterprise. Yet he insisted on putting his own personal stamp on anything that came out of the museum he had founded and forbade his assistants to claim credit for any part of their own research done on company time. He was a self-proclaimed advocate of abolition, yet he also believed in the racial inferiority of blacks. How on earth can we reconcile Agassiz the humble observer, reverently holding a moon snail in his hand, wondering at the beauty of God's world and eager to share it with others, with the authoritarian Professor Agassiz, who saw himself at the top of the chain of subordinates (students, other scientists, the public) and tolerated no disagreements? Brilliant scientist and craven racist, cutting-edge practitioner of fieldwork and industrious simplifier of scientific truths, caring mentor and callous despot—one is never done with Louis Agassiz. To be sure, we cannot today replicate the enthusiasm nineteenth-century Americans felt for him. But as any student of the period can attest, Louis Agassiz won't go away quietly either, won't let himself be replaced so easily with more unambiguously benign figures.

While Charles Darwin remained holed up in his country estate in Kent, preferring to receive letters rather than people at Down House and watching the unfolding controversy about his science from the sidelines, the relentlessly extroverted Agassiz constantly surrounded himself with other people: assistants, students, illustrators. Their voices, opinions, and ideas were frequently inseparable from his. This remained true even when they finally tried to detach themselves from Agassiz, as many of them did, more or less, sooner or later. If Agassiz's contemporaries kept diaries or composed their autobiographies—a typical activity of Victorians everywhere—Agassiz wrote letters, countless ones, in which he cajoled, cautioned, or condemned, but never confessed. For a biographer hoping to find clues as to how Agassiz "really felt" about an issue, how his private thoughts might have differed from his public pronouncements, or from what other people had claimed he felt, the search often proves futile. Although there are many pages of sparkling prose—unforgettable descriptions of jellyfish drifting in the sunset or glittering glaciers extending farther than the human eye can see—there is no such thing as a "great" Agassiz letter, a letter that makes all the elusive details of his personal life and scientific ambitions fall into place. By contrast, I can think of several letters by Charles Darwin, to his wife Emma or to his American friend Asa Gray, that would warrant such a description.

Thus, while Darwin often revealed his innermost thoughts, especially during his daughter Annie's final illness, Agassiz left many of the major events in his personal life—the death of his father, the dramatic separation from his wife Cecilie, the climactic confrontation with his adversary Gray on a train from New Haven—uncommented upon, as if they hadn't actually happened. Over and over again, his public voice drowns out his private one. Finally, even his public voice dwindled. Although Agassiz's name was attached to many books and hundreds of papers and although he continued to give lectures until the end of his life, he became increasingly content to let others do the talking and, in the case of his wife Elizabeth, the writing for him. Thus, even though as a scientist he descended into near silence, he in fact never stopped talking, if increasingly through the words of others: the people who loved or loathed him. There is no evidence that this would have bothered him or that he thought he was lacking anything. Even his last words, as chapter 1 shows, were most likely invented by others.

One thing is clear: Agassiz will not sit still for his portrait. Unlike the skeleton of the dodo at the Agassiz museum, he resists labeling even today. The story that is told in the following pages will take us to three continents and through at least three different languages, and it will often require us to see Louis Agassiz through the eyes of others, since, completely preoccupied with that beautiful moon snail in his hand or that promise of money for his museum from a new donor, he so rarely stopped to look at himself.

My book begins with Agassiz's very public death (chapter 1), which was in fact an astonishing kind of apotheosis. Fittingly for someone who so much believed in the power of science, this apotheosis took the form of an autopsy, the results of which were announced publicly. The great Agassiz's death left a whole country bereft, and the ensuing chapters will re-create the journey that brought this son of a Swiss country minister to such fame that news about his health regularly appeared on the front page of the *New York Times*. Chapter 2 takes us back to where it all began, the glaciers of Switzerland (which Agassiz's science caused to move again, if only before the geologist's inner eye) and his failed marriage to the beautiful, remarkably gifted Cecilie. Agassiz's intense relationship with the world's most famous scientist, Alexander von Humboldt, set the stage for his subsequent attempt to cast himself as Humboldt's American heir, the subject of chapter 3. The next chapter re-creates the ongoing battle waged, during the 1860s, between Agassiz and two estimable opponents—his Harvard colleague Asa Gray and his British competitor Charles Darwin—during which Agassiz played, or was forced to play, jellyfish to Darwin's barnacle. Agassiz's tortured dealings with his favorite student, Henry James Clark, as seen through Clark's eyes (chapter 5), and his unfortunate attempt to elevate himself as an expert on racial matters in the United States (chapter 6) prepare the reader for chapter 7, in which we see his second wife, the gifted writer Elizabeth Cary, insert herself into Agassiz's career in science to lend his ideas the popular appeal and relevance he craved. Finally, chapter 8 takes us to the place where Darwin's science began and Agassiz's ingloriously ended, the Galápagos Islands.

· 1 ·

AGASSIZ AT REST

O N DECEMBER 6, 1873, a chilly Saturday morning, Louis
Agassiz, professor of zoology and geology at the Lawrence
Scientific School of Harvard University, left his house at
36 Quincy Street.[1] Walking more slowly than usual, he paused frequently as he descended the broad granite steps. Professor Agassiz
was tired. The night before, he had helped celebrate the fifty-first
birthday of his wife, Elizabeth, in the company of family and friends.
He had even smoked one of those delicious cigars the doctors had forbidden him. Regardless, he now had to check on his museum, as was
his custom, even on weekends. Agassiz didn't have far to walk. As he
was crossing Broadway and then Cambridge Street, he would have
glanced briefly at the new building on his left, Memorial Hall, Harvard's "buttressed, cloistered, turreted" tribute to its Civil War dead,
also a sign of the power and wealth of the institution at which Agassiz had taught for over twenty years.[2] On Kirkland Street, Agassiz
turned left. He was on Divinity Avenue now, named after Divinity
Hall, the place where Harvard trained its young men for the minis-
try and where the Concord sage Ralph Waldo Emerson, now a good
friend, had once told his fellow Americans to "acquaint" themselves
"at first hand with Deity" and to "live with the privilege of the im-
measurable mind."[3]

Feel your call in throbs of desire and hope, Emerson had encouraged his audience then, and this is how Agassiz had lived his life too, always to the fullest. Agassiz wasn't like Henry Eustis, his dean, whose house he had just passed, a mediocre engineering professor who, befuddled by opium, had performed abysmally in the war and now stayed out of the limelight. A more cheerful sight was the plain, functional building on Agassiz's right, Zoological Hall, surely one of the first dorms for graduate students in the United States. Joel Asaph Allen, Agassiz's curator of birds, lived there, as did young William Brooks, who had become Agassiz's student just that summer. Not too long ago, Louis François de Pourtalès, a marine biologist and former student of vaguely aristocratic origins, had moved in too. He had followed Agassiz from Switzerland to the United States and, after working for the U.S. Coast Survey, a federal agency originally created to chart the entire coast of the United States, was now finally back with his old master.[4]

But in his mind's eye, Agassiz had already entered his temple, the only church of which he was a member, his glorious, specimen-filled Museum of Comparative Zoology, the large brick building that was waiting for him at the end of Divinity Avenue. It towered over the nearly five acres of land Harvard had given the great Agassiz so that he could build this spectacular home for his continually expanding collections: fish from Brazil, shells from the Pacific coast, birds from the Isthmus of Panama, mammals from the Rockies, spiders from the Himalayas, and fossils from Virginia, North and South Carolina, Georgia, Alabama, and Mississippi. New packages of specimens were arriving daily by train, mail, or personal messenger. Agassiz's empire extended throughout the North American continent—in his 1871 report to the museum's trustees he rendered thanks to the Union Pacific, Kansas, Denver, Hannibal & St. Joseph, Chicago Burlington & Quincy, and the Michigan Central railroads, as well as to Wells Fargo and Company and the American Merchants' Express Company—and far beyond, into every known corner of the globe.[5] Agassiz's students, earnest young men who could produce a good drawing even while peering through a microscope, would describe and classify what they could, while his devoted female assistants would thoroughly clean, mount, and label the specimens. At any given moment,

Louis Agassiz on the steps of his house at 36 Quincy Street. Undated stereoscopic card. Photograph by DeLos Barnum.

the place was bustling with activity, and Agassiz looked forward every day to being right in the middle of it all. This was his pleasure dome.

Agassiz had made this stroll—pleasant even on a damp New England winter day—so many times that he knew every inch of the way, each one of the maples lining the streets. There were no sidewalks in that part of the city yet, but Agassiz, never a natty dresser, bravely stepped where he had to. Passers-by, if there were any that Saturday morning, would have recognized "the Prof" (as he was known) instantly: the robust, square body of the epicure, the massive head perched atop the broad shoulders, the long hair under the soft hat, the small, quick feet. Above average in height, Agassiz, a capable swimmer and mountain climber when he was young, looked strong even from a distance. Now in his sixties, he was still a "capital pedestrian," in the words of one of his biographers. Like the German poet Goethe, whom he admired, he never used a cane, though he would occasionally be seen wielding an alpenstock.[6] In Boston and Cambridge, he was a presence both exotic and familiar, *ein Europäer*, a European through and through, as the writer William Dean Howells once observed, but one who radiated contentment "with his position and environment in New England."[7] A Harvard Divinity School student later remembered how he had run into Agassiz on a previous morning in Cambridge. The student was headed in the opposite direction when he noticed how some unearthly glow seemed to be illuminating an otherwise typically dreary New England day. Strangely, the light wasn't coming from the maple trees, "yellow with decay," but from the person he saw walking with determination toward him. He recognized Agassiz's round, pleasant face, unmistakable in its "diffused kindliness." Though Agassiz did not know the student personally, he gave him a pleasant nod, "for that was the way of Professor Agassiz." Everybody loved him, the student added, the educated people as well as the common folks, for there was "something Christ-like" in his devotion to the truth, "his unselfish desire that all should see as clearly as he saw it."[8]

The student's rapt recollection reflects the glorification of Louis Agassiz that had taken place, at least in the minds of his American admirers, long before his death, to the considerable annoyance of those who would not agree that he had drunk the milk of Paradise. The issue was not merely Agassiz's resistance to Darwinism. The sheer expansiveness of Agassiz's desires, the way he presumed to contribute to all areas of scientific knowledge, made the German naturalist Ernst Haeckel denounce him "the most ingenious and active confidence man in the entire field of natural history."[9] Ordinary people, though, didn't care. Agassiz remained a favorite with the farmers, whose tales of breeding cattle and horses keenly interested him, the fishermen, who traveled long distances to bring him their buckets with specimens for identification, and the children, who knew that he liked to carry strange and wonderful stuff in his pockets.[10] With his boylike enthusiasm for the world around him, Agassiz had an intuitive grasp of things other adults simply didn't or couldn't see. "It very rarely happens," enthused Oliver Wendell Holmes, the physician and poet, "that the same person can take at once the largest and deepest scientific views and come down without apparent effort to the level of popular intelligence." His scientific detractors notwithstanding, Agassiz had gained the hearts of all Americans. "This is," Holmes told him, "what singularly fits you for our country."[11] James T. Fields, Agassiz's publisher at Ticknor and Fields, liked to repeat the story of the farmer who showed up at his office to add something to an article by "Mr. Agashy" that had appeared in the *Atlantic Monthly* — not because he wanted to set him right, but because Agassiz had told him that his opinion mattered. Mr. Agassiz, said the farmer, was "a real good, queer man."[12]

The air in Agassiz's museum—never fresh, thanks to the mingled smells of alcohol, rotting specimens, dust, and tobacco—perhaps seemed particularly thick, even stifling, that Saturday morning. His many admirers imagined Agassiz as constantly up and doing: opening boxes, touching specimens; measuring, labeling, and storing them; drawing a quick sketch on a piece of paper, looking over a shoulder of a student charged with an important task. Maybe he was peering at the bones of the pterodactyl he had acquired two months ago or at the spawning salmon that Spencer Fullerton Baird of the Smithsonian Institution had just sent him, carefully packed in ice and sawdust.[13] Suddenly, though, Agassiz began to perspire "freely." (That is at least how a local newspaper, the *Boston Advertiser*, reported it the next day.) Soon after, he fell ill and had to be "carried to his home, about a quarter of a mile distant," not an easy task, since he was a big man. Back at his house on Quincy Street, "the Prof" collapsed. Agassiz wanted to do only one thing—sleep. He was never to get up again.[14] His family rallied to his side: his American wife of twenty-three years, Elizabeth "Lizzie" Agassiz, a partner in life as well as in science, and the children from his first marriage, to Cecilie Braun—his son, Alexander, who had helped him run his museum over the past decade or so; his daughter Ida, married to the Boston banker Henry Lee Higginson; and his youngest child, Pauline, wife of the wealthy philanthropist Quincy Adams Shaw. Alexander's young wife, the beautiful Anna Russell, daughter of an old Boston Brahmin family, selflessly stepped in too and was constantly by her father-in-law's side, providing whatever relief she could. Agassiz's marriage to Elizabeth had opened the doors of blue-blood Boston to him and his children, and blue-blood Boston now rushed to help him.

Word was sent right away to Dr. Charles-Édouard Brown-Séquard in New York, one of the world's foremost neurologists, with a career even more expansive than his name and a well-earned reputation for helping celebrities when their health was in crisis. In 1858, for example, he had treated Charles Sumner after Preston Brooks had beaten him senseless on the floor of the U.S. Senate. Brown-Séquard commanded considerable star power himself, and public awe and interest followed his activities. After the Prussian siege of Paris in 1870–1871, Brown-Séquard had fled to the States and settled in Cambridge, Massachusetts, for a few years, in a house with a garden where he could keep animals for his experiments. The easily impressed poet Henry Wadsworth Longfellow reported that the French doctor owned a thousand guinea pigs, with which he did what he pleased, "having this or that nerve severed."[15] Agassiz's family had consulted Brown-Séquard more than three years earlier, when the first signs of the current trouble had manifested themselves. In September 1869, Agassiz suffered a cerebral hemorrhage, which sent him into what Longfellow called "a year's eclipse" and required that he spend part of the next year away from his museum in the village of Deerfield, Massachusetts, under his wife's constant care. It was then that Brown-Séquard, who suspected hypertension, recommended that Agassiz quit his cigar smoking, advice that apparently had been ignored.

While Brown-Séquard packed his bags, Agassiz's own local doctor, Morrill Wyman, rushed over to Quincy Street. The older brother of the great anatomist Jeffries Wyman, the thick-set Morrill was a familiar sight in the streets of Cambridge, a family physician of the old school who despised the "city doctors" and their constantly rising rates; he never charged more than three dollars a visit. Despite his folksiness, Wyman had retained a keen interest in medical research. Among his accomplishments were the development of a procedure, known as thoracentesis, to remove fluid from the pleural cavity and the discovery of the link between hay fever and ragweed, which helped many of his suffering contemporaries find relief in the pollen-free mountains of New Hampshire.[16]

Agassiz was, as Wyman and Brown-Séquard noticed immediately, seriously ill. When, four days after his collapse, he still hadn't improved, worried friends and admirers congregated in front of his house. In fact, so many showed up that it became necessary to muffle the doorbell. Bulletins were displayed at the door of the Professor's residence so that visitors could get the latest update on his condition. "The anxiety is widespread," reported the *New York Times*.[17] Stunned into speechlessness, Longfellow, one of Agassiz's closest friends,[18] simply cut out an article about Agassiz's illness from the *Boston Ad-*

vertiser, pasted it on the back of a one-penny U.S. postal card, and mailed it to his friend George Washington Greene in Rhode Island.[19] He stopped by the house every day but, since there didn't seem to be any good news, never dared go in.

Agassiz had lived his life on the public stage, and it seems fitting that frenzied media speculation would accompany its final act. Frequent newspaper bulletins worked up interest in his illness to a fever pitch. They also, only too accurately, conveyed the doctors' puzzlement, which alternately alarmed and comforted the public. The language the papers used to describe Agassiz the patient resembled the scientific vocabulary of Agassiz the scientist: "Though the brain is affected and greatly weakened, the difficulty, in its present development, is not of a nature to cause delirium or destroy consciousness, and during the whole period the mental faculties have not been affected." In other words, the physicians weren't really sure what was going on: "They did not say that the Professor will, if he does not die, live the remainder of his days a shattered incurable, (as some dispatches have intimated,) but, on the contrary, express their belief that his entire recovery is just possible."[20] Such vague language didn't reassure James Fields. He wrote in his journal, "Agassiz is . . . probably dying. What a different world it will be to us without him. Such a rich, expansive, loving nature."[21]

Arguably, what was happening to the great Agassiz wasn't fair. Alexander von Humboldt, the hero of his youth, had lived to the ripe old age of ninety-five, and Agassiz, who never had any problems in the confidence department, thought that he should have more time left too. After the onset of his first neurological crisis, a few years earlier, he wrote to his assistant, Nathaniel Southgate Shaler, in a letter filled with instructions, "As long as I breathe I mean to look after everything. It is in my nature never to give up."[22] People who met Agassiz for the first time were usually struck by his energy and the sheer delight he took in life. Numerous photographic portraits, or cartes de visite, showed Agassiz visibly pleased with himself. In a particularly memorable salt-print photograph, he can be seen smiling broadly, radiating a satisfaction not often found in the subjects of early photography.[23] Or we encounter him self-consciously imitating Napoleon

Bonaparte, posing next to the same or a similar ornate chair visible in the earlier image and in front of a framed painting of the Arc de Triomphe.[24] But even in those somewhat later images from the 1860s that feature Agassiz in a more pensive pose, the refinement of his features (as indicated, for example, by the wrinkles around his eyes) and signs of exhaustion (the puffiness under his eyes) are balanced by the powerful facial features: the prominent nose, his expansive forehead, the large ears. If Agassiz is not looking at the viewer, it appears to be because his remarkable mind is focused somewhere else.

Undated autographed salt print, early 1850s. Photograph by John Adams Whipple.

Signed carte de visite, early 1860s. Photograph by John Adams Whipple.

Time had indeed been kind to Agassiz, where looks were concerned; he had aged gracefully. His hair might have become stringier, his sideburns whiter, and his entire body, thanks to decades of good living, rounder, but in the last image we have of him, taken by Antoine Sonrel, he looks more serene than ever. Though he is not overtly smiling here, his expression, as well as the faintly dimpled cheek, creates the sense that this man, despite his bouts with serious illness, constant financial struggles, and opposition even from close colleagues, has much to be happy about.

When he first came to the United States in 1846, at the age of thirty-nine, Agassiz quickly established a reputation as someone who knew how to live, and live well. Attuned to the pleasures of the body, the cigar-smoking, wine-quaffing Agassiz, who would seldom show up for breakfast before eleven o'clock,[25] had a talent for *savoir vivre* that his newly acquired American friends, stifled by two centuries of religious repression, could only envy. In a sense, the Puritans were still around. Their doctrine, to be sure, was fading away, but, as Longfellow's brother-in-law, the bon vivant Tom Appleton, testified, "Alas! Their kitchen remains."[26] The fun-loving Agassiz

Albumen print, 1860s. Photograph by George Kendall Warren.

Photograph by Antoine Sonrel, 1872.

quickly became the center of the Saturday Club, that loose association of prominent New England Brahmins who met for dinner at the Parker Hotel—so much so that some of the members began to refer to the group as "Agassiz's Club." Longfellow and his wife especially cherished the ease and European grace Agassiz had brought to chilly Boston, where many suffered from a lack of "regular, nourishing" relationships with others.[27]

Agassiz had begun his career with a dissertation on Brazilian fish. But he didn't just write about fish. He liked to eat them too—lots of them. In fact, Agassiz's Falstaffian rotundity became famous around

Boston and Cambridge. "I saw in the cars a broad featured unctuous man," Ralph Waldo Emerson wrote in his journal in November 1852, after coming back from an omnibus trip to the city, "fat & plenteous as some successful politician, & pretty soon divined it must be the foreign Professor."[28] Longfellow reported with delight that an evening of listening to Agassiz's interminable "fish stories" had a strange effect on him. He was inspired the next day to buy some halibut in town and picked up some mackerel as well on the way back when he heard a fishmonger advertise it, only to find more fish—sent by his good friend Agassiz!—waiting for him at home: "a beautiful turbot! A *splendid* turbot!"[29]

But virtually from the beginning of Agassiz's years in America, this ostentatious vitality was twinned with a curious vulnerability, which manifested itself in periods of appalling fatigue and poor health. While the perpetually ailing Charles Darwin used his persistent physical problems—vomiting, headaches, flatulence, eczema—to keep himself out of the limelight,[30] Agassiz exploited the dramatic, regularly recurring threats to his near-mythic vigor to bring himself even closer to his fans. Unlike Darwin's varied miseries, Agassiz's symptoms did not seem to be constitutional but caused by external factors, by the things he did against his better judgment. Or so he wanted people to think. Agassiz's health troubles weren't inconvenient interruptions of a life dedicated to science; they were part and parcel of his commitment to scientific truth, and he flaunted them whenever he could. Agassiz's sick, overworked body sent to the public a compelling message—sanctity comes with, and stems from, sacrifice. To maintain his vital presence in America, Agassiz needed to become ill periodically. This is not to say that Agassiz wasn't really unwell when he and others thought he was or that he didn't work much harder than most of his colleagues. He merely shuffled the cards he had been dealt in a way that enhanced his public image.

What laid the great Agassiz low was publicly defined as "nervous prostration," bouts of severe exhaustion. They began shortly after he had arrived in Boston, when he became overwhelmed with excitement over the opportunities before him. On April 10, 1847, Agassiz wrote to Spencer Fullerton Baird, then a professor of natural history at Dickinson College, "Conceive of the position of a naturalist entirely devoted to his studies without any other object before him, arriving in a world quite new to him, as so full of interesting objects as this is, and you will easily imagine how I have been carried away by the objects immediately around me." He was going to the market and the beach daily, grabbing "every species of animal I could obtain." The outcome was inevitable: "I was brought into such a state of excitement that I at last was taken sick so severely that I have not moved from my bed for these last three weeks." Yet in the same letter Agassiz also asked Baird for all sorts of specimens (a "great number" of all of the most common North American "*species in all their ages*") and added that though he was "not much of a botanist" himself, he also wanted to undertake, as soon as possible, "the most extensive collection of all the trees and shrubs of the United States." He planned to compare those living species and their fossil predecessors. Having just asserted that he had too much on his hands, Agassiz was asking for additional material. I've had enough; give me more![31]

In his letters, Agassiz deployed references to his medical state with strategic precision, feeding his worried fans with tantalizing reminders that he might not always be there for them. Even when he was not ill, he would complain to his correspondents about his tiredness, about his "inability to work" and the many ways in which he was "frittering away" his strength; how he needed "more rest" and had "mountains before" him "to level to the ground"; how he was now "greatly changed in physical energy" and had only a few hours left each day during which he would feel "capable of real exertion."[32] These laments were often combined with the gloomy prediction that he would never get better. He was spending the summer by the seaside in Nahant, he told Baird at the end of July 1854, "in the hope of restoring my health, which of late has seemed to grow worse and worse." (Nahant, a rocky resort town on a peninsula jutting into the Massachusetts Bay, was becoming increasingly popular with wealthy Bostonians.) Agassiz's eyes were giving him trouble. "I have to husband with such parsimony, the little amount of time, during which I can daily look at anything," he apologized a few years later, responding to Baird's request that Agassiz provide short descriptions of some turtles he had sent him. Writing was becoming burdensome too: "It is not every week I can stand even so trifling a tax of my eyes as is required to write a few lines," he said at the beginning of another letter to Baird, in which he apologized for his "laconism" (the letter then went on for at least another page).[33] But Agassiz's correspondents wouldn't have to wait for his letters to get the news about his health; they could read about it on the front page of their newspapers. When Agassiz had to interrupt one of his lectures because he didn't feel well, Baird read a report about the incident in the paper and dashed off a note to his friend, asking for reassurance that everything was all right. "It is unfortunately true," confirmed Agassiz on April 13, 1873. He had felt "the blood rushing" to his head and couldn't continue. No lasting harm was done, and he hastened to add, "I have already given two more lectures since."[34]

In Agassiz's personal letters and those written by friends and family, and also in the eyes of an adoring American public, Agassiz's complex body, alternately well and ailing, became inseparable from the science he practiced. It enabled, validated, and, during periods of illness, also endangered his work. "How sad for a naturalist to grow old," he sighed in a conversation with his publisher, James Fields, in 1866. "I see so much to be done which I can never complete."[35] Ironically, it almost seemed that Americans preferred to think of their great naturalist as on the brink of a breakdown. Here, as in many other areas of his life and work, it is remarkable to see how Agassiz and his friends, colleagues, and fans collaborated: Agassiz's public persona became a joint invention, a creation in which many parties had a stake. When the *New York Times*, on August 19, 1853, reported on the fever Agassiz had caught in the swamps of South Carolina, it also quoted a friend who, presumably speaking for all concerned readers, had said to Agassiz, "I am sorry to hear, Professor, that you have been dangerously ill." Agassiz answered, "Ah yes . . . I have been very sick, but no matter, I have found a fish without ventrals" (hind fins). And this is how the American public learned to view Agassiz too: as someone who would, for the sake of scientific discovery, heroically take on more than he should, at home as well as abroad, in the field as well as in his museum, where friends would always find him at work, his hands reeking of alcohol and dead fish. One of his Harvard students, the young Addison Verrill from Greenwood, Maine, once came across the Professor at home, where he had fallen asleep on his sofa "from pure exhaustion."[36] Verrill was impressed. Even Agassiz's wife, Elizabeth Cary

Agassiz, decided early on that a healthy husband was, in fact, boring. Agassiz's medical problems gave her something to do. Often she would write on Agassiz's behalf, telling impatient correspondents that the Professor, beset by a "crowd of engagements," was "quite unwell" and "ill from fatigue" and therefore couldn't reply himself.[37] When Agassiz came down with his swamp fever, she quickly saw the silver lining. At first, of course, she was duly terrified. "When I look back to his illness," she wrote to her mother when it was all was over, "and those terrible hours of a fear that I would not acknowledge in all its extent even to myself, it all seems to me like some hideous dream." But by then Agassiz's self-mythologizing had had an impact even on his wife. There *was* a purpose behind the suffering, and to help her mother and herself understand what she meant, she offered a literary analogy: "Don't you remember a story of Dickens, of a man who longs to give up the recollection of pain and sorrow; to have all that part of his recovery stricken out; the request is granted and how much of association with what is holiest and best in him and others goes with it, and the rest of his life, without that, seems meager and shallow and poor?"[38]

As Elizabeth understood, Agassiz's troubles were inseparable from his triumphs. Everyone in the United States knew about the daring athletic feats Agassiz had performed when he was young: his ascension of the Jungfrau summit in Switzerland, for example, or his courageous descents, dangling from a flimsy rope, into the cracks and fissures of alpine glaciers. Agassiz represented the union of brawn and brain, but one so precarious and fragile that disaster and dissolution always seemed imminent. It is oddly appropriate that most of Agassiz's health woes were neurological ones that caused distress in both mind and body.

Agassiz's self-mythologizing reflects a paradigm usually associated with the artist: the notion that suffering is a pathway to creative genius and that the limitations of the body also restrict, in unacceptable ways, what an individual may be able to accomplish. In the 1860s, Longfellow, Agassiz's closest friend, was working intermittently on a verse play about Michelangelo. Longfellow's Michelangelo has a hard time accepting the fact that he is mortal because there is so much he still needs to finish. Some of Michelangelo's most memorable lines — those about the "malaria of the mind," for example, the "fever to accomplish some great work / That will not let us sleep"—seem to be written with his friend in mind.[39]

But if Agassiz himself felt he was aging too fast, it is also true that in the mind of his American admirers he remained the eternal child, excited about every new discovery and always in need of being taken care of. In an ecstatic letter to his mother, written right after the Boston businessman Nathaniel Thayer offered him money to take a group of students and specimen collectors to Brazil, which was the realization of a lifelong dream, Agassiz, now almost sixty years old, said he felt like a child spoiled by an entire country, and he promised, once again, that he would "sacrifice" himself for the sake of America's scientific institutions and intellectual progress.[40]

What turned out to be Louis Agassiz's last year was filled, characteristically, with frantic activity, all on behalf of the American people. First and foremost, he had worked to get his new summer school on Penikese Island under way. Named after its sponsor, the New York tobacco merchant John Anderson who owned the island, the Anderson School of Natural History was Agassiz's official venture into coeducation. The concept behind the school was to offer nature enthusiasts, from Mrs. Burns, a public school teacher from Pittsburgh, Pennsylvania, to Lydia W. Shattuck, a veteran botany instructor at Mount Holyoke College, the opportunity to study natural history with the experts, in the style of a scientific camp-meeting. Intended for teachers and future teachers, Agassiz's summer school focused on the basics; no advanced scientific work was done on the island. Chosen from several hundred applications, a group of forty-four students, sixteen of whom were women, had assembled at Penikese on July 8, "ringed about by sapphire seas," according to the lyrical description by the poet John Greenleaf Whittier.[41] The only problem was that the dormitories hadn't been completed by the time the school opened. But no matter—Agassiz had not conceived of Penikese as a place for relaxation or "summer resort," as he had emphasized in a circular advertising the school. He did not spare himself, lecturing every day, sometimes twice, and assisted by a team composed of former students as well as old associates, such as the Count de Pourtalès. When he left Penikese at the end of the summer, he was exhausted. On October 28, he apologized for his long silence to his friend the paleontologist Leo

Lesquereux. He didn't even have enough energy left, he said, to look after his museum, the one thing to which he had devoted "all that is left of my strength."[42] That said, in other ways things were looking up. For example, the Harvard botanist Asa Gray, Darwin's "man" in the United States, had finally retired from active duty as professor of botany, relinquishing also the presidency of the American Academy of Arts and Sciences, which he had held for ten years. Buoyed by Gray's departure and by the success of Penikese, Agassiz must have felt emboldened to explain again why Darwin's theory of evolution didn't make any sense to him. "My dear Longfellow," he wrote to his friend in early December 1873, shortly before he collapsed, "may I trouble you with this proof? I have undertaken to write out my views upon the great question of the day and would like the advise [*sic*] of judicious friends. Write freely on the margin, if you feel like it."[43]

The page proofs contained the last essay he ever wrote, "Evolution and Permanence of Type." The piece, published posthumously in the *Atlantic Monthly* in January 1874, became Agassiz's swan song, a compact restatement of ideas he had been repeating all his professional life, most prominently the conviction that nothing in nature travels and that the divisions of the animal kingdom, following sound classificatory principles, as they exist today correspond to God's plan for the world. What is new, though, is Agassiz's recognition that Darwin might have indeed changed the rules of the game: "Darwin has placed the subject on a different basis from that of all his predecessors, and has brought to the discussion a vast amount of well-arranged information, a convincing cogency of argument, and a captivating charm of presentation." Note Agassiz's surprising alliterative play ("convincing cogency . . . captivating"). Was this a way of dignifying Darwin's theory, after so many years of hostility, at least through his choice of words? Or did he want to imply that Darwin's theory, at the end of the day, was merely a form of verbal pyrotechnics?

Agassiz went on to point out, with unexpected generosity, that science was a collective enterprise, a struggle for the right reading of nature, in which Darwin and Agassiz had, after all, been less opponents than partners, though with different ideas about what the final outcome might be: "It cannot be too soon understood that science is one, and that whether we investigate language, philosophy, theology, history, or physics, we are dealing with the same problem, culminating in the knowledge of ourselves." At times Agassiz seemed almost envious of Darwin, though by the end of a sentence he would usually manage to turn things around again—in his own favor. For example, Darwin's "concise and effective phrases," he wrote, "have the weight of aphorisms and pass current for principles, when they may be only unfounded assertions." But regardless of how good Darwin's writing was, Agassiz could never accept the premises of his argument. Show me those transitional forms, he demanded, those specimens that illustrate the transformation of one species into another. Why, he asked, were there so many examples of weak parents having "fine" children and vice versa, a fact of nature that "points perhaps to some innate power of redress by which the caprices of choice are counterbalanced"? Agassiz wasn't prepared to give up what still remained the basis of all his work: if long, careful thought was required to understand the world (and about *that* there could be no doubt!), then long, careful thought had created it. "Have those who object to repeated acts of creation ever considered that no progress can be made in knowledge without repeated acts of thinking?" The world began a great long while ago, to paraphrase Shakespeare, but we still don't know how and why—though with Louis Agassiz as our guide the path to knowledge was clearly outlined. As for Darwin's theory, that famous promise in the first paragraph of his book, that some light might be thrown on "the origin of species—that mystery of mysteries,"[44] had remained unfulfilled. Darwin had offered only a "conjecture," and not even the best one. Agassiz hoped that "in future articles" he might show that "however broken the geological record may be," a true scientist could make sense of the history of nature.[45]

Those "future articles" were never written. One is never prepared for death; one never thinks, as Marcel Proust would later put it, that it will occur this very afternoon.[46] Irrelevance attends our final moments. Three years earlier, when Brown-Séquard had first been summoned to Agassiz's bedside, the neurologist had forbidden him any and all intellectual exertions: "Nobody can ever know the tortures I endure in trying to stop thinking," Agassiz had complained then in a letter to his assistant Theodore Lyman.[47] But now, in his final illness, he couldn't think coherently even if he had wanted to. Most of the time he slept, regaining consciousness only intermittently. Alarmed relatives in Switzerland sent telegrams. "The voices of his brother and sisters were not wholly silent," wrote his wife Elizabeth, his first biographer, "for the wires that thrill with so many human interests brought their message of greeting and farewell across the ocean to his bedside."[48] The world that had seemed so large, so unconquerable, and yet so full of promise when Agassiz was a student in Germany, dreaming about joining a great expedition that would take him abroad, had gotten significantly smaller.

On what became the last day of her father's life, Sunday, December 14, 1873, Agassiz's youngest child, Pauline Agassiz Shaw, sat down briefly to write a note to Longfellow, at her mother's request. Father was still showing "signs of recognition," she told Longfellow, and he would answer questions, "though not very distinctly." Today he had been mostly asleep, sound asleep even, disturbed only "by increased heat in his head & great flushing of the face." There was no doubt that the end was near: "Sometimes today the breathing has been so uneven & inaudible that each hour seemed likely to be the last—then he rallies again & after that goes off into a sound sleep, breathing strongly & regularly & looking peaceful & natural—with an expression of *great, strong* calm." Agassiz had lost the ability to swallow and was now keeping his eyes closed most of the time: "his mind seems quite dormant, only occasionally roused by questions to make short answers—both in French & English according to the language by which he is addressed." Agassiz, master of several languages, was not gone yet. Everyone was hoping now that his end, when it came, might be "the death of mind & body at once"—that, in other words, Agassiz's body wouldn't outlast the collapse of his powerful mind. Pauline ended her letter by asking Longfellow to pass this news on to the Massachusetts senator Charles Sumner, who had also inquired after Agassiz. "My letter may be confused—I am thinking so of father that I can hardly collect my thoughts."[49] At 10:15 P.M., Agassiz quietly slipped away. The *New York Times* described his passing on its front page: "The last hours of Prof. Agassiz were apparently passed in unconsciousness." Agassiz's breathing simply had become fainter and fainter until the end was there: "The patient lay upon his side, and beyond an occasional convulsive movement of the limbs, there were no signs that he suffered pain, and the finale was scarcely perceptible."[50] There were no final words.

Or were there? Longfellow certainly thought there were. Agassiz's death had devastated him, and when, on December 15, 1873, he dashed off another note to his friend Greene in Rhode Island (who had probably just received the postcard with news about Agassiz's illness) he took recourse to a language he loved more than all others, Italian. Embedded in the little improvised poem he sent Greene were the words that he believed were Agassiz's final ones: "Jernotte alle dieci mori il nostro caro Agassiz, o / 'quel che *morir* chiaman li sciocchi.' / *'C'est la fin!'* furono le ultime parole sue."[51] Or, in translation, "Last night at ten our dear Agassiz died, or / 'what fools call dying.' / 'This is the end!' were his last words." The first quotation was taken from a fourteenth-century Italian poem, Petrarch's "Triumphus Mortis"; the second was supposed to come from Agassiz himself. It appears that some people, at least, could not let their "Prof" go silently into that good night. His assistant Louis François de Pourtalès was one of the first to claim that Agassiz had spoken before he died. "It's all over," he was supposed to have mumbled a few times, in French, the language of his childhood and the one in which he had written most of his books before he came to the United States. And in his final moment, raising himself up one more time, speaking "with great distinctness," he exclaimed, "Le jeu est fini."[52]

C'est la fin, Tout est fini, Le jeu est fini — "This is the end," "It's all over," "The drama is ended." One would wish for something more profound, more original, and more revealing as the last words of the man who, at the time of his death, was still one of the world's most influential scientists. Something bold, defiant, or at least wise, comparable to those that would be whispered, nearly a decade later, by Agassiz's great antagonist Darwin, as he ended his journey, disappointing all those who had expected a last-minute conversion: "I am not the least afraid to die."[53] Was Agassiz, who had often been accused of appropriating other people's ideas or observations, a plagiarist even in his final moment? To be sure, his last words — especially in the version reported by Pourtalès — sounded much like the lines attributed to the dying Rabelais ("the farce is over"), a similarity emphasized by Agassiz's former student and biographer Jules Marcou.[54] Maybe they were also reminiscent of Beethoven, who was alleged to have said, shortly before he died, "Plaudite, amici, comedia finita est." Applaud, my friends, the comedy is finished.[55]

Charles Darwin. Carte de visite, c. 1881. Photograph by Herbert Rose Barraud.

Except that this is probably not at all how it happened. Elizabeth Agassiz, fuming over the misrepresentations circulated by Agassiz's friends, steadfastly maintained that there had been no last words. On February 10, 1896, more than two decades after his death, having read the second volume of a biography written by Marcou (a "painful" experience), she wrote to her son-in-law Henry Higginson that there was not "a Shadow of truth" in the "melodramatic" final scene as Marcou had represented it. Pourtalès had been "neither in the room nor in the house." "Agassiz," she said, calling her husband by his last name, as she always had when he was alive, "had not spoken for a long time and he died quite quietly—merely stopped breathing." Marcou had repeated the lie about Agassiz's Rabelaisian final words precisely because they fit in with his desire, evident throughout the entire book, to describe Agassiz as a poseur, a player of multiple roles: "it really seems as if the whole scene with its theatrical 'le jeu est fini' were composed in order to keep up this idea to the end—in the very

next line he says, 'Life had been for him a long & successful play.'"
She realized that Agassiz was a public figure, and, of course, everyone
was entitled to his or her own opinion of him. But "downright false-
hoods" were unacceptable.[56]

In frustration, Elizabeth Agassiz turned to Agassiz's old doctor.
The eighty-three-year-old Morrill Wyman responded immediately.
He hadn't seen Marcou's book, but he had been present when Agassiz
died and he would have noted any movements or an expression like
the one Marcou had reported. Not one to misplace anything, Wyman
readily produced the medical note he had penned at the time: "Sunday, 14 December 1873. Pulse rapid, feeble; not to be counted at the
wrist; skin cool, not moist. Occasionally drawing up his legs, but the
hands remaining quiet. The respiration grew gradually more frequent
and feeble until 10.15 P.M. when he ceased to breathe without any
struggle or groan."[57] At the end, Agassiz went wordlessly, like Melville's Captain Ahab, whom he resembled in many ways, especially in
his dogged determination to uncover the secret of Nature, that "great
hooded Phantom," to aspire to the knowledge only a god could have.[58]
And, like Ahab, he took others with him. The night he died, Agassiz's
daughter-in-law Anna caught a cold, which quickly developed into
pneumonia. Eight days later, she was dead too. Some creatures, Louis
Agassiz had written in his *Essay on Classification*, "grow, and reproduce
themselves, and die in a short summer, nay, in a day," while "others
seem to defy the influence of time."[59]

Alexander had now lost his father and his wife within a period of
less than two weeks. For a long time, he was beside himself with grief.
"Life seems unendurable," he wrote to a friend two years later, from
South America.[60]

As Dr. Wyman's records show, Agassiz's death, though it came too
early for a man with such a multitude of plans, had been a good death,
by nineteenth-century standards. There was no protracted suffering, no excessive pain, no ranting or raging, no final appeals to God's
mercy. True, Agassiz, the expatriate son of a Protestant minister, had
never been much of a churchgoer. Longfellow, himself bored to tears
by the mandatory services for Harvard faculty members at Appleton
Chapel, called Agassiz—with a touch of envy—"a sparse and infre-

quent worshipper of the Gods."[61] Agassiz routinely rebuffed any invitations to join others for Sunday worship and once informed Eben Horsford, the Rumford Professor and Lecturer on the Application of Science to the Useful Arts (and the inventor of modern baking powder), that, for as long as he had been able to remember, he had "performed my devotion in private and . . . without communion with any body."[62] Agassiz thought, as he told the Yale geologist James Dwight Dana, "that each and everyone must settle his religious affairs for himself, without any regard to others." Dana had just sent him his review of a book that attacked science for allegedly destroying the biblical record, and Agassiz thanked him for "fighting so earnestly the cause of our independence versus clerical arrogance." Religious bigotry of the kind Professor Tayler Lewis had perpetrated in his *Six Days of Creation* (1855) appalled Agassiz.[63] Pseudo-scholars like Lewis would presume to tell Agassiz what to believe, which was in the scientist's opinion an entirely personal matter: "we derive as little comfort from the interference of others with reference to our intercourse with our Maker, as we do in matters of affection." Belief was a matter of choice, not of institutional doctrine. One can imagine how successful this attitude would have been with the Boston Unitarians.[64]

If Agassiz had seemed almost Christ-like to the Harvard student who had seen him walking on Divinity Avenue, he was a thoroughly secular messiah. Appropriately, his funeral service, on December 18, 1873, in Harvard's Appleton Chapel (the only sandstone building in Harvard Yard, an eclectic mix of Romanesque and colonial styles) was an aesthetic rather than a religious event— an expression not of humility, but of worldly power. First, there were the people, crowds of them—an overflow audience, with mourners standing, as the *New York Times* reported, "out of the doorway into the open air."[65] Flags on all public buildings were at half mast, following an order from Acting Mayor Cutter, and the bells of Boston tolled during the entire service. Harvard College was closed for the afternoon. Vice President Henry Wilson had come from Washington, and the Swiss consul from New York. The state of Massachusetts was represented by the governor, William Barrett Washburn, and two members of his staff, General Palfrey and Colonel Storer, as well as the

Speaker of the House, John E. Sanford. There were representatives of other colleges (Yale and the Massachusetts Agricultural College) and a number of Agassiz's former students. Naturally, Agassiz's friends, neighbors, and Harvard colleagues—the writer and lawyer Richard Henry Dana, the mathematician Benjamin Peirce, Ralph Waldo Emerson, James Fields, Oliver Wendell Holmes, and Henry Wadsworth Longfellow—were among the mourners, as was Nathaniel Thayer, sponsor of Agassiz's Brazil expedition. Agassiz's doctors Wyman and Brown-Séquard were present, and the transcendentalist extraordinaire Bronson Alcott, now an old man himself, had come from Concord, accompanied by the town's physician, Dr. Josiah Bartlett.

The Reverend Andrew Preston Peabody, chaplain of Harvard College, presided over a service intended to be as extravagantly simple as the man to be buried. Newspaper accounts of Agassiz's obsequies followed the script: stressing the plainness of the event, they mentioned the unadorned rosewood casket, draped in black, which was carried the short distance from Agassiz's Quincy Street residence to Appleton Chapel, as well as the austere liturgy that was used, taken from the services held at King's Chapel, the oldest Unitarian church in Boston. There was no eulogy, but plenty of music: Bach, performed by the young Harvard organist John Knowles Paine; excerpts from a Cherubini mass; a final hymn, arranged by Paine himself. The hymn, originally written by the British poet James Montgomery, highlighted the untimeliness of Agassiz's death as well as what was widely perceived to be its cause, his incessant labors for the public: "Go to the grave in thy glorious prime, / In full activity of zeal and power . . . / . . . Go to the grave; at noon from labor cease." At the end, Agassiz's coffin was carried out of Appleton Chapel to the sounds of the magnificent, slow-moving "Dead March" from Handel's *Saul*, music fit for a king, its stateliness enhanced by the fact that it is written in a resplendent D-major, an unusual key for a dirge.

This was plainness taken to the level of high art. The flower arrangements in the chapel, described in great detail in the *New York Times* article, gave it away: this service too was part of the myth of Agassiz, the larger-than-life scientist-artist-poet. Appleton Chapel was entirely decked with black, but any gloominess was dispelled by the calla lilies and evergreens fastened to the gallery drapings, the beautiful cross made of delicate rosebuds and fine white flowers intertwined with vines that adorned the pulpit, the profusion of rosebuds in a large basket hung with vines of smilax on a table in front, the flowers heaped on the casket and bound into wreaths everywhere. The air in the chapel was, concluded the *New York Times* writer, touched by the poetry of the event, "heavy with the perfume of flowers." Interment in Mount Auburn took place afterward, in the fading light of the winter afternoon.

But this is not how the *New York Times* writer ended his article. A curious postscript discussed, in some detail, Agassiz's autopsy, carried out in the presence of no fewer than seven doctors (as a comparison, Lincoln's dissection was attended by nine). Brown-Séquard did not participate; he had been called away to New York.[66] Autopsies had become civilized events by then, not the ghoulish rites performed earlier in the century in seedy hospitals that offered good money for bodies in usable condition. An 1860 manual for medical students emphasized that one ought to be able "to conduct a post-mortem examination from beginning to end, including every cavity and organ of the body . . . in your best dress suit, with only the cuffs of your coat and shirt-sleeves turned up."[67] It is not clear where Agassiz's autopsy took place. Harvard did not have its own hospital facility, and there is no file on Agassiz in the archives of Massachusetts General Hospital, perhaps the most likely setting.[68] But from accounts published in the papers we do know who was present. Two younger doctors with impeccable credentials were in charge (not Dr. Wyman, as some of the newspapers reported). Each would go on to make a name for himself, albeit in very different fields: one as an advocate of the new science of the mind known as psychoanalysis, the other as an authority on internal diseases. Dr. James Jackson Putnam, twenty-seven years old, a lecturer in nervous diseases at Harvard, had recently returned from studying neurology in Vienna, Leipzig, and London, and at Massachusetts General Hospital had started one of the first neurological clinics in this country. He went on to help found the American Neurological Association, became friends with Sigmund Freud, and subsequently turned into one of the main proselytizers for psychoanalysis in the United States. He also served as the first president of the American Psychoanalytic Association.[69] The other doctor wielding the knife that day was Reginald Heber Fitz, thirty years old and a new assistant professor in pathological anatomy at Harvard. Dr. Fitz would pioneer the treatment of appendicitis (a term he coined) and definitively described different forms of pancreatitis.[70]

These two rising stars of American medicine, both trained in Europe, as Agassiz had been, were closely watched by five mostly older colleagues, the best in medicine that Boston had to offer: the brothers Morrill and Jeffries Wyman; John Barnard Swett Jackson, Harvard's first professor of pathological anatomy and about the same age as Agassiz; and Calvin Ellis, the dean of the Medical School from 1869 to 1883, a clinical practitioner with some expertise in lung disease. Also in attendance was Samuel G. Webber, a young doctor who had obtained his M.D. in 1865 but had three years of experience as a navy surgeon under his belt. In 1894, he would become the first professor of neurology at Tufts University.

Most of these doctors had known Agassiz quite well, but none better than Jeffries Wyman, Harvard's Hersey Professor of Anatomy. Just the year before, Wyman had expressed concern about Agassiz's stance on evolution. He regretted that Agassiz, with all his expertise in paleontology and embryology, had wasted a golden opportunity to embrace and guide into the right channels a theory that seemed so much more promising than the "preposterous" concept of the "immediate creation of each species."[71] Unpretentious, thorough, and in chronically bad health that required frequent stays in Florida, the twice-widowed Wyman was a tall, spare man who liked to come straight to the point. "You all know," wrote botanist Asa Gray after his death, "that Professor Wyman never spoke or wrote except to a direct purpose, and because there was something which it was worth while to communicate."[72] Wyman preferred to work by himself, sharpening his own tools on a grindstone at his house, which was directly across from Agassiz's residence. And he was apparently free of jealousy, even though Agassiz's tireless advertising of his Museum of Comparative Zoology was constantly threatening to eclipse the Harvard institution Wyman had been in charge of since 1868, the Peabody Museum of Archaeology and Ethnology.[73]

One wonders what went through Wyman's mind as he looked at his two young colleagues working on the large, heavy body spread out before them. As an anatomist, Wyman had seen worse, though from the beginning of his career he had been more interested in animals (the first skeleton he ever prepared for display was that of a large bull-frog). But surely he couldn't forget that this wasn't just anyone's body. This was Louis Agassiz, the man who had joined Harvard the same year Wyman had, the man who had been his neighbor in Cambridge, the man who had sat next to him at faculty meetings. Wyman himself had less than a year to live; on September 4, 1874, a pulmonary hemorrhage killed him in Bethlehem, New Hampshire, a resort town watched over by the mountain that had been named after Agassiz.

The doctors performing the autopsy had resolved to subject Agassiz's brain to further microscopic study, for which they would have to let it harden, the *Times* writer solemnly explained. Agassiz had spent a lifetime extolling the virtues of microscopy; now he himself—or parts of him—were about to end up under the lens. The slides, if any were made, are lost. But the authoritative language of the report Morrill Wyman released in January 1874, reprinted or excerpted in numerous daily newspapers and magazines, removed whatever doubt left by conflicting reports about his illness. Morrill's language defamiliarizes, renders distant, the humanly recognizable Louis Agassiz, reducing him to a heap of sinews, inner organs, a skull divested of its skin. Agassiz was, the men found, brachycephalic; in other words, he had a relatively short but broad skull—a fact that confirmed, some thought, his Frenchness.[74] The brain did show signs of disease, but what emerged as the more immediate cause of Agassiz's dying was the circulation *at the base* of the brain. Obstructions in the left vertebral artery had gradually destroyed the left basilar artery and thus affected the brain as well:

The left vertebral was larger than usual—larger even than the basilar . . . Commencing at an inch below the anterior edge of the pons Varolii and extending downward, the walls of the left vertebral artery were stiff, in part calcified, and its linings loose. At half an inch from the point just mentioned, immediately over the left olivary body, was a reddish-yellow, opaque, friable plug (thrombus), completely obstructing the vessel; still lower was another more recent, but probably *ante-mortem* plug. The first was one quarter of an inch long, the second four inches long. A third plug, an inch long, was above the first, and touching it.[75]

The doctors didn't need to be told how important the little plugs, or thrombi, were that would have interrupted the blood flow to Agassiz's brain (the "olivary body" resides in the lower portion of the brain stem). They did note the swelling of the right posterior lobe at the bottom of the brain, and, as they worked away, they also realized that the heart, or more precisely the heart's left ventricle, had been a contributing factor: attached to the "wall at the anterior portion near the septum" (the membrane separating the two ventricles of the heart) the doctors found another plug the size of a "peach-stone," around which yet another, softer granular clot had formed. The muscle layer in the wall adjacent to the clot was thin, which, along with other factors, pointed to a past myocardial infarction, an incident that would have severely weakened Agassiz's overall health. The lungs showed signs of old inflammation, but that was an almost peripheral finding. What really mattered were those clots that had formed in the diseased basilar artery or had been thrown up as emboli from the atherosclerotic left vertebral artery. They had destroyed Agassiz's brain stem. The doctors knew what had killed him. In modern terms, their diagnosis would have been atherosclerotic cerebrovascular disease culminating in a cerebrovascular accident—the great Agassiz had died of a stroke. A lifetime of hard work reduced to nothing by these friable little clots.[76]

Agassiz would have been the first to enjoy the mix of strenuously technical language and accessible imagery ("peach-stone") in this report. Inveterate publicity seeker and popularizer that he was, he would have appreciated even more that it had appeared in newspapers from Massachusetts to Maryland, from New York to Ohio, from Georgia to San Francisco. More effectively than Agassiz could have ever envisioned, his postmortem validated what his life had stood for: the power and authority of science and the right of the people to share in its findings. In quite a literal sense, it confirmed once more the myth that had surrounded Agassiz in his lifetime: that he was giving himself, with every fiber of his being, to science. The fact that the autopsy concentrated on the brain also muddled the usual distinction, characteristic of much writing about nineteenth-century anatomy, between the dissector—the embodiment of pure knowledge, or *mind*—and the dissected, who is, by necessity, pure *body*, helpless matter.[77] Here, brains were focused on brain.

And so Agassiz lived on, after a fashion: as a specimen. His brain, the surgeons reported, was "large and heavy," which wouldn't have surprised the naturalist's admirers. To be precise, it weighed a whopping 1,495 grams, or "53.4 avoirdupois ounces."[78] One would have to allow, of course, for the atrophy of age, the doctors were quick to add; Agassiz's brain would originally have been even heavier—a useful detail, since the brains of other famous people, notably that of Agassiz's mentor, Georges Cuvier, had weighed in even higher. The size and weight of Agassiz's brain became news itself; newspapers that didn't report on the other autopsy results communicated with delight the weight of 53.4 ounces to their readers.[79] Incidentally, participation in Agassiz's dissection promised to be an excellent career move for the two younger doctors. From Philadelphia, Morris Longstreth, M.D.—green with envy, we might imagine—sent a hasty note of congratulations to his friend Putnam. After pointing out some errors in the published report, he wrote, apparently through gritted teeth, "It is particularly gratifying to pick up a daily newspaper and find that a class-mate has been called upon to make an examination that is likely to come so prominently before the public's eye."[80]

This public interest in Agassiz's brain volume was not extraordinary in this era, when fingering the heads of people living or dead, calibrating their "bumps" during phrenological exams, and measuring the size of human skulls or filling them with seed or buckshot to determine cranial capacity were popular pastimes. They were hoping to figure out why no two people thought and felt alike and, often enough, they also sought to explain why some people's brains were superior to others. In Josiah Nott and George Gliddon's *Types of Mankind* (1854), to which Agassiz contributed an essay on the geographical distribution of animals, readers would have found a paper by the late Philadelphia doctor Samuel G. Morton, the dedicatee of the volume, titled "The Size of the Brain in Various Races and Families of Man," which quoted the pithy verdict made by a German anatomist, Friedrich Tiedemann: "The brains of men who have distinguished themselves by their great talents are often very large." The same passage also contained a reference to Cuvier's brain ("four pounds, eleven ounces, four drachms, thirty grains") and the observation that Tiedemann had never found a female brain weighing more than four pounds.[81] What Morton, one of the most important influences on Agassiz after he had come to America, didn't choose to mention was that the careful Tiedemann (who had been one of Louis Agassiz's professors in Heidelberg) believed that the smaller size of the female brain was entirely due to the smaller physical size of women. Perhaps even more important, he had found no significant differences between the craniums of blacks and those of whites, which Morton also failed to note. Instead, Morton made a name for himself by comparing the measurements (in fact, *mis*measurements) of African, Asian, and Caucasian skulls, with devastating results for the Africans, of course. He would later find a worthy successor in the anatomist Edward Spitzka, who, after tallying the brains of 130 dead white males, cheerfully reported that Americans and Canadians had the largest organs and Germans and Australians the smallest. He included Agassiz on his American list, noting the thickness of his skull.[82]

Agassiz's oversized brain, powerful even in disease, helped perpetuate the Agassiz mystique. The fact that the autopsy was made public—that ordinary people, reading the morning newspaper, were invited into the dissecting room—had a similar effect: a fitting tribute to the giant of American science, who remained larger than life even after he was dead.

The day after Agassiz's funeral, the Boston newspapers were printed with a black border. Tributes poured in, celebrating Agassiz's continuing spiritual impact on the nation. Beside narratives that focused on his body were those that contemplated his larger-than-life soul. Speaking, on December 21, 1873, to his congregation in Portland, Maine, the Reverend Thomas Hill, formerly a president of Harvard University, claimed that Agassiz's sudden death "had been felt as a personal loss by thousands on both sides of the Atlantic." According to Hill, Agassiz's work, from the studies of glaciers conducted in

Switzerland to the turtles he dissected in Cambridge, was one gigantic "offering upon the Altar of Religion," proof that all true science leads to true faith. Though Agassiz was now gone, Jesus' observation that life was more than meat (Luke 12:23) applied to Agassiz too: "that which in him was 'mortal' has 'put on immortality.'"[83]

The Reverend Henry Ward Beecher, writing in the *Christian Union*, was only slightly less fulsome in his praise. Known for his friendly disposition toward all manner of liberal creeds, including Darwinism, Beecher briefly raised the possibility that Agassiz might have been wrong to oppose the theory of evolution. But then the Professor had always been so busy that he had never had time to iron the creases out of his theories, to mend the inevitable holes in his system. In Beecher's obituary, Agassiz, "with his stalwart frame and massive head," became like the Whitmanesque poet who isn't afraid to contradict himself. A man of many passions, "he dealt with a hundred phases of inquiry, outgrew and corrected his own convictions, generalized with sweeping audacity, affirmed with the zeal of a devotee, and denied with the vigor of an iconoclast." Delighted by the "largeness" of American existence, he had transformed the entire country into a vast stage for his "fairy tales" about science. Agassiz's schoolroom encompassed not only Boston, where audiences were always to be found, but the entire nation: "when the master took his blackboard and his problems to the smaller cities, drawing his queer diagrams, and unfolding their vast meaning before lyceum associations, normal schools, colleges, high schools, those benches, too, were crowded with eager and intelligent listeners." For Beecher, Agassiz was ultimately less a teacher than a prophet, a "John Baptist of science," someone who, electing poverty for himself, lived and died for science: "No wandering preacher teaching the purified Gospel from town to town," wrote Beecher, "no enthusiast declaring his new faith, ever more openly and simply invited death than did this over-taxed, eager, impetuous missionary of science." This did not mean that Agassiz's science itself was religious; what mattered to Beecher was the manner in which Agassiz had practiced it. Note how this reading quietly undercuts the idea that science is all about (truthful) results. Rather, it is an ongoing activity, the ceaseless effort of a quasi-heroic, yes, industrious individual. Agassiz would have been pleased.[84]

Even Agassiz's detractors would have felt the power of these postmortem narratives about Saint Louis Agassiz: someone who had accumulated treasures not for himself and not in heaven, but in his Cambridge museum, for everyone to enjoy. The details of Agassiz's will, published in the newspapers, lent these stories credibility. Apparently, the most important asset Agassiz had owned was his library, which he left to the Museum of Comparative Zoology, allowing his son, Alexander, to pick the volumes he wanted to keep for himself but hoping that he too would eventually donate them to the museum when he had no further use for them. His residence on Quincy Street Agassiz left to his "beloved wife"—but the house was heavily mortgaged. "I make no provision for either of my daughters, Ida and Pauline, not from any want of affection, but for the reason that my house in Cambridge . . . is the only remaining property that I have to dispose of."[85]

A few years after Agassiz's death, a large boulder from the terminal moraine of the Lower Aar Glacier was placed on Agassiz's grave. His son, Alexander, had ordered it, and Agassiz's cousin Auguste Mayor had selected it from among the blocks of the moraine near the Hôtel des Neuchâtelois, the rough shelter where the young Swiss scientist Agassiz and his party had once spent their nights while investigating the glaciers of the Alps. He chose "at last a stone so monumental in form that not a touch of the hammer was needed to fit it for its purpose"—so big, in fact, that it is hard to imagine that several men could have carried it, "à force de bras," using the strength of their arms, over a distance of twenty-five miles to a village in the Bernese Oberland, from where it was then taken by wagon to the nearest train station.[86] Now in Mount Auburn Cemetery the 2,500-pound stone stood, "rough as it came from the Glacier, untouched by the hand of the Stone-Cutter," with the exception of the inscription.[87]

The monument Alexander Agassiz had chosen for his father was appropriate on more than one level. It represents, of course, the landscape of Agassiz's youth, to which he remained attached throughout his life. But the boulder also stands for what was eventually recognized as Agassiz's most significant scientific achievement, the only one that even Darwin would later acknowledge. Agassiz had not come up with the idea that large sheets of ice had at one time covered significant portions of the globe (credit for that, as we shall see, belongs

The grave of Louis Agassiz, Mount Auburn Cemetery, Cambridge, Massachusetts.

to others), but he fashioned it into an elegant scientific theory that accounted for the large, dotted chunks of rock far removed from their place of origin: they had been transported by vast moving masses of ice. In a long appendix to the 1839 edition of his *Journal of Researches into the Geology and Natural History of the Various Countries Visited by H.M.S.* Beagle (now better known under the title *Voyage of the* Beagle), Darwin had mocked Agassiz's theory as "not supported by a single fact." Prodded by letters the geologist Charles Lyell had sent him, Darwin had watched ice fragments, which had broken off glaciers on the South American coast, drifting in the water, a sight that persuaded him how utterly wrong Agassiz was about his "imagined period of excessive refrigeration" (the ice age). Darwin went on to create a deliberately absurd image of the Alps rising under the ice sheets, with fragments of rocks breaking off and skidding giddily across the glaciers until the ice melted and they came to lie where they are now. Darwin's theory (not his own either, but essentially the one Charles Lyell had published a few years earlier)[88] was, he believed, infinitely better. Where Agassiz imagined sheets of ice, Darwin saw icebergs drifting in water—in his view, they had fallen off when submerged mountains had slowly risen up, and they were now pushing rock fragments with them, grinding into them while moving along. When such a flood subsided, the rocks were left, covered with scratches from the icebergs that had rubbed against them: the marks that Agassiz attributed to the powerful influence of slowly moving glaciers.[89]

Agassiz was right in this instance, as Darwin later had to concede. Agassiz had a special affinity for these boulders, which the Germans called *Findlinge*, "homeless children." Standing in a landscape to which they didn't belong, these masses were regarded by the locals as "strangers to the soil." They were, Agassiz wrote, "the wandering Bohemians among rocks."[90] And so, in a sense, was he. On the one hand, Agassiz's boulder, "a rock cut from a mountain by no human hand" (Daniel 2:44–45), was a reminder that Agassiz had, to the end, remained a *Findling* in the United States, a transplanted foreigner on the drab East Coast (after he visited Brazil in 1865, Agassiz kept telling James Fields how wonderful that country was compared with New England).[91] On the other hand, since Agassiz's theory explained how the forces of nature moved such boulders, the one on his grave retroactively "naturalized" Agassiz's presence in America (except that it had been brought here not by God but by human hands).

Though lifeless itself, Agassiz's boulder, a rough 2,500-pound rock from Europe placed in an American burying ground modeled after a French cemetery (Père Lachaise), captures an irony that lies behind Agassiz's science itself: the assumption, presented as a certainty, that in nature all living things stay as they are had been developed by a scientist who had not stayed where he was.

THE ICE KING

J EAN LOUIS RODOLPHE AGASSIZ was born on May 28, 1807, in Môtier, a Swiss village of about five hundred inhabitants, facing the Bernese Alps and nestled among fields and vineyards at the foot of Mount Vully and on the banks of a small lake, the lac de Morat. A major lake, the lac de Neuchâtel, was a short hike away. Agassiz's father was Louis Rodolphe Benjamin Agassiz, the minister (*pasteur*) of the Protestant congregation of Môtier, the sixth in an unbroken line of Protestant ministers in his family. His mother was Rose Mayor, the daughter of a respected physician in Cudrefin, a village just a few miles to the west, on the shores of the lac de Neuchâtel, where a street is still named after a member of the family. His wife hadn't moved far from her family, and Pasteur Agassiz's entire life was spent within a few dozen miles of his own birthplace, the town of Orbe in the Vaudois. Louis, or "*mon ami*," as his father was fond of calling him, was the first of their children to survive infancy.

Despite these limitations, Pasteur Agassiz was a reasonably educated, shrewd man. Well-liked by his parishioners in Môtier, he was apparently more successful in the classroom than in the pulpit. His letters, marked by careful penmanship as well as the desire not to let any available space go to waste, show that Pasteur Agassiz was deeply involved in the lives of his two sons, Louis and Auguste, and two daughters, Olympe and Cécile. None of his children, though, caused him as much anxiety as his oldest, the most gifted and, as it seemed to him, most erratic of them all. Louis grew up with a distinct interest in outdoor activities. An avid hiker and swimmer, he delighted in the untrammeled access to lakes and the pristine mountain landscape his upbringing had given him. Water and rocks, the primary features of the landscape around him as he was growing up, inspired his early passion for natural history and determined the scope of his scientific pursuits for the rest of his life. As Louis matured and Pasteur Agassiz moved from rural Môtier to new parishes, first in his native Orbe and then Concise, on the shores of the lac de Neuchâtel, their relationship became more complicated. Agassiz's father, by turns stern and clingy, meddled in his son's life wherever he could. He had distinct plans for him, and those emphatically did not include a career in science, an area about which he knew absolutely nothing. Louis ignored him. When he turned seventeen, he was reading Lamarck and Cuvier, the most important systematic biologists of his time. Louis's books had rendered him unsuitable, as Rodolphe came to realize, for the life of a small-town merchant (the first of Rodolphe's goals for his son). When Louis's uncle, Mathias Mayor, a physician in Lausanne, stepped forward and offered his financial support, Rodolphe amended his master plan and reconciled himself to the idea that his son would study medicine and then settle down somewhere in the Swiss countryside, preferably not too far from Concise. It is fascinating to watch Rodolphe struggle to retain his hold over his son as Louis moves farther and farther away from him, leaving the University of Zurich behind for Heidelberg University and then Heidelberg for the University of Munich, where he concentrated, defying his father's wishes, mostly on natural history.

At the time of Louis's birth, Pasteur Agassiz had been a Protestant minister in a largely Catholic area of Switzerland, the canton Fribourg, a fact that had prepared him well for coping with resistance to his ideas. A Calvinist by descent and circumstance, he did not proselytize, keeping his religious views largely out of his letters, apart from brief entreaties to God to bless his wayward son. Calvinism is a faith not traditionally known for encouraging ambiguity of thought and expression, nor artistic play, but Rodolphe had become a master of innuendo, capable of mixing praise with subtle scolding, all within one paragraph. An excellent example is his report, in a letter to his son, about chatting with a professor of zoology during a trip to Lausanne, which, as Rodolphe said, had convinced him that this was certainly a "pleasant way of spending one's evenings." Louis, whose scientific ambitions were solidifying, would have picked up on the irony.[1]

Rodolphe leavened his lingering disapproval of Louis with tentative expressions of interest, without lowering the pressure. Why don't you write — to us, your sister, your uncles? This refrain recurs in Rodolphe's letters. However, the implication that Louis was neglecting his family seems unfounded, in view of the many detailed, often desperately self-congratulatory letters Louis sent home to justify what looked to his father like academic dilly-dallying. Pasteur Agassiz excelled at making his son feel guilty: Remember, he would tell him, although I'm ready to sacrifice everything for your happiness, our resources are limited.[2] Science is no more than a balloon that will take you higher than anyone should ever travel; you will need medicine to parachute yourself to fiscal safety.[3] Come home soon and come directly, to a father's open arms and open heart.[4]

While his father bombarded him with letters, in which he obsessed about the smallest details, Louis Agassiz had embarked on a search for a father figure more congenial to his expanding interests. If his father wanted to keep him confined to a radius of a few miles from home, Louis thought of his life unfolding in the grandest of terms: "Will it not seem strange," he wrote to his sister Cécile on October 29, 1828, "when the largest and finest book in papa's library is one written by his Louis?"[5] This would impress his father, he felt, despite the fact that Pasteur Agassiz wanted nothing more than to see in the pharmacy a prescription written by his doctor-son. If approval from "papa" was not forthcoming even after he handed him a big book, well then, he would turn to someone else.

Although Louis didn't share this with his father, life at the University of Munich, where he had transferred in 1827 to take classes in both natural history and medicine, was not all the twenty-one-year-old had expected it to be. In a frank letter to his sister Cécile, Agassiz described how frozen he was after his evening walks through the snow-covered streets and how all his days tended to follow the same tedious pattern. But a ray of light shone on him during evenings at the homes of his professors, particularly that of Carl Friedrich Philipp von Martius (1744–1868), a botanist whom Agassiz visited "with the greatest of joys."[6] Martius, only in his midthirties himself, was an inspiration. He loved talking about his Brazilian travels, the sixteen thousand or so miles he had traversed with his sidekick, the zoologist Johann Baptist von Spix, working their way up from Rio de Janeiro over São Paulo to the mouth of the great Amazonas at Belém, where they then went up the river by canoe. Martius was the real thing. He had lived with the Indians, spent days walking through the steppes of Brazil without water, and bagged thousands of animals and plants. Martius enjoyed showing his students his magnificent collection of Brazilian freshwater fish every time they went to his house, and he must have noticed the glint in Agassiz's eye, a flicker of the greed that drives the truly ambitious. Spix's death in 1826, probably from a tropical disease he had caught in Brazil, had added to the mystique of their Brazilian adventure. More important, it gave young Louis an opportunity to prove his mettle. Taking note of his enthusiasm Martius asked his most promising student to compile the volume about Amazonian fish that Spix hadn't been able to write. Martius himself was keeping busy with the plants and palm trees.

The result was Agassiz's first publication, the big book he had anticipated: *Selecta genera et species piscium*, published in two parts, with ninety-seven hand-colored plates, in Munich, in 1829 and 1831, an enormously handsome work that pleased Agassiz's skeptical father too. What particularly excited Agassiz was that he got to name or rename several of the species collected by Martius and Spix. Now, scientific naming, since Linnaeus's *Species plantarum (Species of Plants)* of 1753, has not been a casual affair. In the Linnaean tradition, each new species receives a two-part name, designating first the genus and then the species. Such binomials help avoid the confusion that often ensues when a common name is used to refer to a species. Naming or renaming a species, for a scientist, is an expression of professional confidence, competence (the indication that he or she understands not only the general order of nature but also the specific place that the creature to be named or renamed occupies within it), and creative power. The latter makes it an imaginative act perhaps not unlike giving the title to a poem. In *Selecta genera*, Agassiz's favorite new creation in that vein was *Doras humboldti*, a black catfish found in the São Francisco River in the interior of Brazil. *Doras humboldti*'s charms are not available to casual inspection. Most prominent are the two rows of scales on either side of the fish's otherwise naked body, each of them equipped with little hooks or spines. Thanks to its large, elongated, snouty head and thick, swollen lips, *Doras* manages to look a bit menacing. In the surprisingly subtle drawing, presumably provided by Agassiz's artist at the time, Joseph Dinkel, *Doras humboldti* floats in the empty space of the page and seems to stare directly at us, out of remarkably unfishlike eyes, greeting us from a world that's definitely not our own. It doesn't look black at all, as the names given to it by other naturalists would lead one to expect. The French naturalist Achille Valenciennes, for example, had called it, in 1821, *Oxydoras niger*, a name that has prevailed right up to the present.[7] Neither the dried specimens Agassiz had studied nor the pickled one in Spix's collection at the natural history museum in Munich had seemed black to him, so he went ahead and had the fish rendered as "olivaceous" in color.[8]

Spix had originally named the fish *Corydoras edentatus*, a reference to its lack of teeth. But it appears Agassiz had also read and found quite inspiring the description of a similar species, evocatively named *Doras crocodili*, which the celebrated explorer Alexander von Humboldt had included in his *Recueil d'observations de zoologie et d'anatomie* (1805–1809), a work that was part of Humboldt's proliferating *opus magnum* about the New World, the multivolume *Voyage aux régions équinoxiales du Nouveau Continent*. And though he eventually decided that Humboldt's memorable catfish had little to do with his own specimen, Agassiz apparently did want to acknowledge Humboldt's influence on his own taxonomic efforts; hence the name he awarded to his fish. Incidentally, he turned out to be right about assigning Humboldt's *Doras crocodili* to a genus of its own.

Humboldt had encountered *Doras crocodili* on a dry, long river beach in Colombia in 1801, on one of those hot, thirsty days that glues the tongue to the roof of the mouth. There it was, in the sand, a tough individual that had gotten stranded, who knows how. But it wasn't giving up just yet and was trying to propel itself forward, to safety, by resting on its pectoral fins. And Humboldt touched it,

Corydoras edentatus (Doras humboldti). Plate 5 from *Selecta genera et species piscium* by Louis Agassiz. Apparently the plate was labeled before the name was changed.

though he instantly regretted doing so. The fish hurt him, grievously, as he said later. Reading this story, Agassiz realized the extent of the gulf that separated his own fumbling efforts to describe museum specimens from those of Humboldt, who had seen—yes, even touched—the thing itself. What Agassiz needed was experience in the field. Here, more than anywhere else in Agassiz's life, is the origin of his later desire to leave Switzerland. At some point during the cold Munich winters, listening to his professors hold forth, peering at the decaying fish in their jars at the museum, it must have dawned on Louis Agassiz that substituting another man's words or specimens for experiencing the animal itself, in the flesh, would not make him a great naturalist. Humboldt's catfish was an individual, a creature with a story, whereas Agassiz's "olivaceous" *Doras* existed only in a jar and in the Latin phraseology of taxonomic data. There was, Agassiz knew, a difference, a crucial one, between holding a cool, antiseptic vessel, neatly labeled in someone else's handwriting, and feeling, as Humboldt did, the fishiness of the fish, its spiny, unpleasant, tough living presence, even when, and especially when, it breaks your skin.[9]

And there was a difference, a crucial one, between a pastor's son from rural Switzerland and the man who, more than anybody at the time, epitomized the public importance of natural science. Alexander von Humboldt was sixty in 1829 when Agassiz was completing his work on the fish of Brazil. Humboldt had sailed the oceans of the world; had hiked, with his companion, the botanist Aimé Bonpland, to the highest point on earth ever reached by anyone; had observed the transit of Mercury in Callao, Peru; and had traveled to the sources of the Amazon River. Humboldt's advice was sought by the governments of Europe. He had stayed at the White House in Washington. At home in Germany, he filled the lecture halls of Berlin above capacity, speaking about nature in a way that appealed to people from all walks of life, from a bricklayer to the king of Prussia, Friedrich Wilhelm III.[10] Agassiz, even before meeting Humboldt, had found his father figure.

Agassiz's Brazilian research helped him obtain, in May 1829, his doctorate in philosophy, the degree then awarded to the student of natural history. And on April 2, 1830, he received his second doctorate, in medicine and surgery, from the University of Munich. Even before his studies were done, though, he fired off a letter to his parents in which he reminded them that he had respected their wish that he obtain "le titre de Docteur." But medicine wasn't where his heart was. The soon-to-be Dr. Agassiz desired, he said, to be known "as the first naturalist of his time, a good citizen, and a good son, loved by all who knew him." Note the order of items in the list: the good son comes last. Burning inside him, said Agassiz, was the strength of an entire generation. He pointed out that if he was allowed to become a science professor, his family would, ironically enough, get to see him more than they would if he settled down as a country doctor nearby: professors have, he said, regular vacations of one month in the spring and six weeks in the fall, which he could spend with his family. And how much pleasanter would those weeks be when he was in a good mood because he had been allowed to be what he wanted to be — "to live in my element," as he put it. But how does one become a professor with such benefits? First, he would have to develop a reputation in Europe as a scientist, and he was already well on his way toward that aim with his new book on Brazilian fish. Second, he had to go on an expedition like the one now being put together by Monsieur Humboldt, of whose sterling reputation his parents were surely aware. Humboldt was preparing to go to the Urals and the Caucasus, and several of Agassiz's professors had already recommended him and his two college buddies, Alexander Braun and Karl Friedrich Schimper, for the trip. Agassiz's mouth was watering at the prospect of being a member of a party that had already been promised the support of the Russian emperor. He was hoping his parents would give their consent.[11]

And that his parents did, as disappointed as they might have been about Agassiz's continuing reluctance to be a doctor in the provinces. "I understand very well, my dear Louis, that as absorbed as you are in your projects, everything vanishes behind your one great interest," his father wrote, plaintively. But, he admonished Louis, "we need to do our part for those who love us." Rodolphe went on to show that, as always, he was ready to do *his* part for Louis: given that his son wanted to go on an expedition, did he need any new underwear?[12]

Much to Agassiz's dismay, Humboldt did not pick him. Even a recommendation by a family friend, the politician Frédéric-César de la Harpe of Lausanne, hadn't helped. Humboldt had already chosen his assistants for the Russian trip. Toward the end of his life, Agassiz, in a speech given in 1869 on the occasion of the Humboldt centenary in Boston, would still remember the "passionate desire" he had felt at the prospect of joining Humboldt and would wistfully celebrate the results of that wonderful Asian journey in which he hadn't taken part. But it became clear that what mattered most to him about Humboldt was not the great man's discoveries. It was his wonderful ability to synthesize everything he found into a comprehensive view of the world. Agassiz had grown up in a household where details—the state of one's underwear, the letter one owed to one's parents—held ascendancy. Agassiz wanted his science to be different. Touched by Humboldt's genius, even "the most insignificant facts" became something strange and wonderful, he said in 1869, looking back at his first encounters with Humboldt's science. Humboldt thought big—about the height of mountains and the depth of the sea, volcanoes, the rotation of the earth, and the tides. He was the total package indeed.[13]

Rodolphe Agassiz did not have much time to rejoice that his son was now a medical doctor. He realized that the mere fact that his Louis had acquired a medical degree did not mean that he wanted to practice the profession. One of the angriest letters Agassiz senior dispatched to Munich came after Louis, freshly equipped with two doctorates, announced that although he was coming home, he was also bringing his personal illustrator, Joseph Dinkel, with him to the vicarage in Concise. Where in God's name are we going to put him? his father wailed. Come home, but don't bring the painter.[14] Dinkel came anyway. Insistent that his rights as a father be respected, Rodolphe Agassiz was also hopelessly smitten with his son. We will see that Louis would later display a similar mixture of despotism and emotional vulnerability in his dealings with his associates and students. (Alexander Agassiz, Louis's only son, managed to stay off his father's radar, quietly developing his own separate identity as a scientist and businessman.)

Louis Agassiz had not come home to Concise to stay. He had learned to ignore his father's needs to ensure his own survival—and if he had to lie to his parents to achieve his goals, he would. In October 1831, Agassiz, now twenty-three, left Concise for Paris, ostensibly to acquire some firsthand knowledge of the cholera epidemic, an explanation that pleased his father. In reality, he had gone there to study with Georges Cuvier, whose works he had first read when he was seventeen. Cuvier, the founder of paleontology as a scientific discipline, was the next best thing to Humboldt, but more ruthless than any of his colleagues. A charismatic professor of comparative anatomy at the Jardin des Plantes, the premier research institution in the natural sciences in the world, Cuvier had used his considerable power to eradicate any theory that suggested things had not always been the way they were now. His efforts were focused specifically on one target: the evolutionary ideas of his older colleague, Jean-Baptiste Lamarck, whom Agassiz had also read in his youth. Lamarck taught zoology at the Jardin and believed in "transmutation," the idea that organisms developed toward greater complexity both as a result of an innate force and the pressures of their environment. Lamarck, who was one of the first to use the term *biology* in its modern sense,[15] was interested in living things; Cuvier focused on fossils, which in his view held clues to one of the most vexing questions of the age: how old the earth really was, and whether or not geology could be used to confirm the ideas of theology. Cuvier and Lamarck represented two different options for the career of the young naturalist from Switzerland. Would he embrace orthodoxy, as Cuvier, sitting comfortably atop mountains of facts he had gathered, had done so brilliantly? Or would he push for the new, the untried, the speculative, for the sake of its explanatory power, as Lamarck had done? For now, Agassiz regarded Cuvier's vast collection of fossil fish as simply a convenient means of expanding his knowledge of ichthyology. If he could not go on an expedition to see the world, he would have the world come to him and sit still as he took its portrait.

There was an added boon to Agassiz's stay in Paris. He finally got to meet Alexander von Humboldt, who had lived there, with some interruptions, since 1808, working on his colossal *Voyage aux régions équinoxiales du Nouveau Continent* and acting as the king of Prussia's unofficial ambassador to the French court. If Agassiz had expected Humboldt to join the chorus of Cuvier's admirers, he was sorely mistaken. While listening to Cuvier's lectures at the Collège de France, Humboldt was appalled at the way the great naturalist rejected Goethe's morphological ideas as a quasi-evolutionary heresy, and he kept whispering disparaging comments right into Agassiz's ear. Agassiz went to visit Humboldt at his office in the rue de la Harpe, and Humboldt in turn showed up at Agassiz's modest quarters in the Quartier Latin, where he scanned his personal library, noting, "with mingled interest and surprise," among some of the usual suspects (Aristotle's *Zoology*, Linnaeus's *Systema naturae*, Cuvier's *Règne animal*) his own *Ansichten der Natur* and several handwritten copies of other works Agassiz had been "too poor to buy, though they cost but a few francs a volume." It seems that Humboldt took exception to a twelve-volume encyclopedia Agassiz owned, the *Allgemeine deutsche Real-Enzyklopädie für die gebildeten Stände:* "Was machen Sie denn mit dieser Eselsbrücke?" Humboldt asked. What on earth are you doing with this bridge of asses? Agassiz answered that he hadn't had time to study the originals; hence his reliance on books that would provide him with some prompt and easy answers for questions he couldn't yet solve himself. Humboldt liked this poor young doctor's candor and took him out to dinner at a fancy restaurant at the Palais Royal. "And for three hours, which passed like a dream, I had him all to myself," Agassiz remembered later. "How much I learned in that short time! How to work, what to do, and what to avoid; how to live; how to distribute my time; what methods of study to pursue—these were the things of which he talked to me on that delightful evening."[16]

Agassiz did get to experience the cholera epidemic firsthand, but in ways he hadn't expected: on May 13, 1832, his mentor Cuvier fell victim to what many believed were the effects of the disease. Bereft but not beaten, Agassiz returned home to Switzerland. The man who had once felt a passionate desire to accompany Humboldt on his journey to the Caucasus and the Urals made up for the missed opportunity by becoming an explorer close to home, in territory he had known from childhood, the Swiss Alps. In the scratches on the boulders that dot the Jura mountains around Neuchâtel, the glaciers that cover their slopes, the moraines that travel down the valleys, he found pages from the Book of Nature that spoke to him in his own native language. At the same time, he also—perhaps paradoxically—prepared to settle down and create the life for himself that Humboldt had never had: Agassiz started a family. He accepted an appointment as the professor of natural history at a small academy in Neuchâtel, a preparatory school that didn't even own a lecture hall.[17] And he married a young woman he had known for some time, Cecilie Braun from Karlsruhe in Germany, the sister of his college friend Alexander Braun.

Cecilie, nicknamed "Silli," was beautiful, smart, and artistic. Agassiz's biographer Marcou describes her as a lady of "regular and fine features, slender, and of very dark complexion," a description supported by her melancholy self-portrait from 1829, created when she was about twenty.[18] Cecilie's father, Karl Braun, was a high-ranking official in the German postal service and an ardent amateur naturalist whose scientific passions were balanced by an equally strong commitment to the arts, especially music, an interest he passed on to his children. He hired a singing teacher for his daughters but also made sure that Cecilie received lessons from one of the few well-regarded female painters of her time, Marie Ellenrieder (1791–1863).

From the beginning, the family was supportive of Cecilie's painterly aspirations. A cache of beautiful drawings recently located at the Natural History Museum in London shows that they had ample reason to do so.[19] Cecilie's talent was not limited to portraits—take a look at her drawing of the island Mainau in Lake Constance, made, if the inked inscription on the left is correct (14 September 1833), shortly before her wedding. Mainau, later known for its beautiful gardens, was about halfway between Neuchâtel, Agassiz's residence, and Karlsruhe, Cecilie's hometown. The drawing radiates calm. The assembled cattle in the foreground—represented in different poses—show that Cecilie was no amateur when it came to wielding a pencil. The human observer resting on the ground, surrounded by cattle in various positions, replicates the artist's appreciation for the view. Ceci-

Cecilie Braun. Self-portrait, red and black crayon, chalk, pencil, c. 1829.

lie handles light and shade expertly, lavishing extra care on the trees and shrubs and delicately tracing the reflections of the landscape and houses on the surface of the lake. Her drawing has the precision of a finished engraving.

Cecilie was a good match for Agassiz. Just two years younger, twenty-four to his twenty-six, as well as intelligent and artistically gifted, she became his new in-house illustrator, a prospect that must have delighted him. She had also picked up at least some French from a young Swiss girl named Cécile Guyot, who had come to Karlsruhe in 1821 to learn German and was a frequent guest in the Braun household. Mademoiselle Guyot had such an influence on the young Cecilie that she began to sign some of her drawings as "Cécile," a name change that apparently became permanent after her marriage.[20]

Given such auspicious beginnings, it is poignant that Cecilie Braun's voice has been virtually erased from history, whether through her husband's efforts or those of her family, for whom she would come to be the cause of some embarrassment.[21] In the biographies written about her husband, she leads a shadowy existence although she bore Agassiz three children—Alexander (born December 17, 1835),

"Meinau [*sic*] im Bodensee." Pencil drawing by Cecilie Braun, 1833.

Ida (August 8, 1837), and Pauline (February 8, 1841); even her first name, with its various forms, is ambiguous. Apart from occasional postscripts to letters written by her husband, I have found only one letter entirely in her hand. The other letters, even those written to Silli's own family, were produced by Agassiz.

Agassiz loved his Cecilie, no doubt. A draft of an early letter to his bride-to-be reveals how deeply he had come to depend on her, emotionally and otherwise. At times sentimental, he waxes lyrical about how "consoling" thoughts of her love for him always are. Switching back to his professorial voice, he lectures his future wife about the intricacies of the Austro-Hungarian monarchy (he had just returned from a trip to Vienna).[22] In another undated letter, a rather messy autograph draft that also dates from their courtship, he thanks Silli for being the only one in the world capable of giving him the strength to carry on with his lofty goals. Only she knows about his main weakness, knows how much he always needs encouragement. Almost coquettishly Louis then dances around the fact that he had earlier sent her only a fragment of a letter, intending to follow it up with a fuller, more complete testimonial of his love, namely the one he was composing just now (ironically, it's only a fragment of that supposedly more complete letter that has survived). At the end of this entirely self-absorbed missive, he goes on to praise himself for having picked up a particularly fine present for his Silli, an illustrated edition of Goethe's poetry, which he had seen in the bookstore where he went every day to deliver his page proofs. The illustrations were the delicate drawings of the young German artist Eugen Neureuther (1806–1882). They had pleased him so much that he now wants to share them with her, his artistically gifted lover, in an attempt to give her back at least half as much as he has received from her. Louis takes an almost childish pride in the fact that he had beaten her brother Alexander, who apparently had also wanted to get that same book for Cecilie, to the finish line.[23] These are the only real love letters by Agassiz that have survived. The modern reader is struck by how staged they seem, how conscious Agassiz always was of his own future importance.

Note, by contrast, the deep devotion evident in the gift of two poems Cecilie made to her "geliebter Agassiz" (beloved Agassiz) on October 27, 1832, in her best handwriting. A note left in the margin explains that she copied these poems on the occasion of a game known as Vielliebchen (literally, "most darling"), in which a pair of lovers ate either twin fruits or from an almond with two kernels. Whoever surprised the other person the next morning with a greeting of "Guten Morgen, Vielliebchen" ("Good morning, most darling!") had the right to demand a favor, usually a kiss. Did the shy Silli offer him these two poems instead? One of them is the Romantic German poet Novalis's "An Adolph Selmnitz,"[24] whose title Cecilie truncated to "An—" ("To"), so that she could substitute "meinen Agassiz" in parentheses. "What fits together must be rounded," the poem begins, adding, in somewhat strained doggerel, that those who get along must come together, and those who love each other must be together, and so forth. The poem culminates in an unambiguous plea for the lovers' unconditional lifelong commitment to each other. The second poem is a wistful little ballad by Georg Philipp Schmidt von Lübeck, "Das Mädchen der Hoffnung" ("The Girl of Hope"), in which a mysterious creature points the speaker to distant realms, alternately seeming to lead him there and then vanishing again.[25] Remarkably, this poem grants authority and agency not to the speaker but to the angelic, mysterious female. Was Cecilie going to be such a "girl of hope" to Louis?

In a lecture written around that time and likely delivered the month he got married, Louis Agassiz, now at the height of his personal and professional happiness, restated the main principles of his science, as they appeared to him then, and connected them smoothly to his personal situation.[26] The rule of humans over brute nature was, he said, the product of historical forces, and, regardless of their superiority in the scale of creation, humans had remained subject to the laws of nature too: there would always be death, suffering, and social injustice. To understand how we got to where we are today, Agassiz asserted, we must study the debris of the earth's lost past, the fossils of extinct creatures written into the layers of the soil. The influence of Cuvier's comparative anatomy—"the most beautiful monument yet erected to science"—is visible on every page of this lecture, as is Agassiz's pride that he is now one of those scientists too. On the basis of a few bone fragments, comparative anatomists could give us, Agassiz explained, a sense not only of the proportions of an extinct animal but of its height, its shape, and its fur or skin. They were the heroes of the day, the true historians of the world, the only storytellers we need. Landscapes had changed profoundly across the centuries and millennia, the oceans had not always been as deep as they are now, and the mountains not always so high. Humans had only come lately to this world, unbidden but oh-so-powerful. They were both similar to and different from animals, and one of the areas where this is most evident is the relationship between men and women. And here Agassiz, newly in love, finally came into his own, leaving behind all that he had learned from Cuvier. The question as to who was superior—men to women or women to men—was not a purely academic one. Agassiz scoffed at the notion held by some self-declared "philosophers" that women, because allegedly equipped with inferior intellects, had remained on a level closer to the animal kingdom than men. History had taught us otherwise: the more civilized the society, the more elevated the position of women. Or, in other words, the more things changed, the less they remained the same. As far as he was concerned, women, in affairs of the heart ("la vie intime"), were if anything superior to men. Men were animals, deep down. Would they really lose much, wondered Agassiz, when somebody else pushed them off the top rungs of the developmental ladder? Some of their male pride would suffer, but that was a good thing. Agassiz, speaking like a feminist, said he knew that it would take a long time for all the injustices men had inflicted on women over time to be rectified. But the history of nature, in which all manner of living things went from simple beginnings to ever more complex embodiments, was on the side of the women, as was the Creator, without whose knowledge not a single hair ever falls off our heads and who presides over a world in which everything from the smallest microorganism to the tallest tree is subject to the same laws.

It seems relevant that the final version of Agassiz's speech—the very same one I have been paraphrasing here—was transcribed in a hand that looks very much like that of Cecilie Braun.[27] She would have felt both the honor and the considerable weight her husband was attaching to her role in his future personal and scientific life.

Soon after the wedding in October 1833, Louis took Silli back with him to Neuchâtel. Beautifully situated on the largest inland lake in

Switzerland, the town offers a direct view of the Alps as well as the mountains of the Jura range, which rise right behind it. Back then, Neuchâtel was inhabited predominantly by pious *petits-bourgeois* and craftspeople. Technically, it was still a Prussian principality, though the inhabitants spoke French, of course. Coming from the mostly flat, imperial-looking Karlsruhe, Cecilie was probably fairly shocked by what she saw. Her hometown, often regarded as a model for Washington, D.C., had been designed with a spectacular baroque palace at its center, from which as many as thirty-two streets radiated like the spokes of a gigantic wheel. One can only imagine what Cecilie thought of the often steep, windswept streets of her new home. For better or worse, though, she had now become Cécile, the wife of Monsieur le professeur Louis Agassiz, a schoolteacher.

A letter she wrote to her "dearly beloved, good father" on December 5, 1833, a mere two months after the wedding, suggests that disenchantment had already kicked in. Silli sounds more like a young girl away from home for the first time than the devoted wife of someone who was planning to become the greatest naturalist of his time. Much of Silli's letter is devoted to her excitement about a package she is expecting from home, apparently a Christmas offering, full of beautiful things. She is so impatient to receive it that she goes out on a walk to distract herself; when indeed, upon her return home, she finds the package waiting for her, she is ecstatic. She tells her father that she has been working actively on becoming a better wife. She chastises herself for her absent-mindedness, a flaw that she recalls caused her parents much distress when she was a girl, and she praises Agassiz (whom she continues to call by his last name) for his unwavering support: he always knows what's right. She reports that she has taken charge of house cleaning, a task she claims has given her much satisfaction. Was this her way of telling her parents not to worry about her marriage?

If it was, the next sentence might have caused them concern. For Silli's tone abruptly changes as she begins to talk about her apartment in Neuchâtel, a dark, dank basement. Out of her window she can see the feet of people walking by. She can barely make out the Alps from her window; what she *does* see are other houses, raising the possibility of constant surveillance by her neighbors. The name of her street is rue des Pommiers, but she's still looking for the apple trees. Had she known about all this earlier, she would have asked Agassiz to find a different place. Nonetheless, Silli is soldiering on. Bravely, she mentions a "beautiful" walk she took in the company of Agassiz and his college friend Karl Friedrich Schimper, and states that while she felt tired the next day, she wasn't sore at all.

It is obvious from the few French phrases she uses in her letter that Silli's knowledge of the language was still imperfect. She comes across as frail and—she mentions a toothache as well as a foot that keeps hurting her—somewhat high-maintenance. And why wouldn't she be? Her story is a familiar one, reflecting what happened to many well-bred, gifted young girls who, after being cocooned by well-meaning parents, were thrust into marriage with little or no preparation. "Fare you well, my dear good father," she ends her letter, as if things were just dandy. Agassiz and she were so thankful for his lovely letters, and he would write too. They were content and happy and thought of Karl Braun with love, hoping to see him in Neuchâtel soon. The words sound hollow; the abiding image in the letter is the feet parading by her window, as if Silli were being held captive by her ogre-husband in some underground cave.[28]

Subsequent letters to Braun senior were written mostly by Agassiz, perhaps because he was trying to control the message that went out to Karlsruhe as best he could, filling the page with boasts about his many successes. In a contradictory vein, though, he also kept asking for Karl Braun's support. Sometimes he sought favors. Could Karl find out for him what had happened to a shipment he was expecting from Cologne? More often he requested financial help. Did his father-in-law know the name of a person in Karlsruhe who would be able to extend loans to him at better conditions than his uncle, Mathias Mayor, who was charging him 5 percent interest? It seems that Agassiz was hoping that his father-in-law would come to his rescue. This letter, incidentally, is a good example of Agassiz's dignified begging, a technique he would perfect over the years, drawing attention to his pecuniary troubles in a way that dramatized the exigencies of his situation without ever casting a bad light on himself. In this instance, Agassiz upped the pressure on Karl Braun by making a planned family trip to Karlsruhe contingent on getting the loan his uncle had just refused: "It was our intention," he wrote, "to depart next Monday and to arrive at your house during the course of next week. But now my plans have been crossed in a particularly ugly way."[29]

Cecilie initially helped Agassiz professionally, supplying drawings for his multivolume work, *Recherches sur les poissons fossiles*, published between 1833 and 1835, though her contributions extended to other subjects as well.[30] Illustrations had always been of paramount importance to Agassiz, a natural extension of the observations he wanted to convey in his prose. An exceptional draftsman himself, he demanded the utmost from his artists. When Joseph Dinkel, the artist he had brought home with him from Munich, was working on Agassiz's plates, drawing dead fish for four or five hours a day, Agassiz was constantly at his side, writing out his descriptions, giving directions, perhaps even snatching the pencil out of his hand to finish a particularly difficult detail.[31] Given the likely influence he had on Cecilie, a rare, exquisite drawing from 1834 signed by her (now as "Cécile") and kept among Agassiz's papers in Neuchâtel seems doubly remarkable. It is fine natural history illustration, to be sure. But Cecilie is also able to retain much of her own style. Consider the delicate way she handles her pencil, creating subtle effects of light and shade that beautify her subject—a fossilized, extinct starfish imprinted into the rock—and almost make it come alive for the viewer. In Cecilie's artistic transformation, the animal's petrified tube feet resemble a series of pebbles a child has arranged on the beach.

Agassiz had discovered that starfish, a fact he celebrated in the note accompanying the illustration. He wanted to dedicate his new species to Pierre Coulon, president of the Natural History Society of Neuchâtel, which Agassiz had helped found in December 1832. Effusively thanking Coulon for letting him use his well-stocked library and helping him with his "literary work," Agassiz proudly announced that he had decided to name his starfish *Coelaster couloni* in his patron's honor. In an additional, no less emphatic note, Agassiz went on to explain why his fossil discoveries were so important. Casting doubt on current classifications, they seemed to call for a new science of "genetic classification": one that would allow him to relate the systematic place of an organism to the period of its appearance in the history of the earth, and vice versa. Agassiz's note thus provides a glimpse of

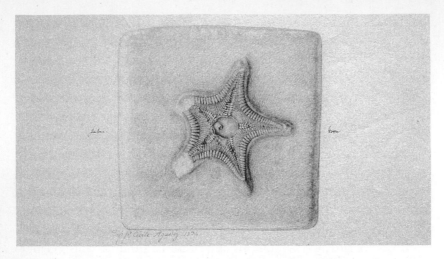

"Coelaster couloni Ag." Pencil drawing by Cecilie "Cécile" Braun Agassiz, 1834.

what would become the staple of his theory, the threefold parallelism between individual development, development of nature over time, and the place of an organism in the system of nature.[32] More specifically, *Coelaster couloni* had prompted Agassiz to demand that this starfish be placed in a genus of its own, an occasion for Agassiz to emphasize another important part of his emerging theory, one that would serve him well in his opposition to evolutionary notions of biology: there was, he said, no continuity between older and present forms of life. *Coelaster couloni* simply has no living equivalent today.

But note the two missing corners of the specimen in Cecilie's drawing, as if the petrified creature she portrayed had anticipated its own imminent destruction: the chronicle of a death foretold. On the one hand, the drawing appears to confirm Agassiz's contention that dead fossils are just that, dead fossils. On the other hand, Cecilie's subtle rendering seems to breathe new life into the specimen. It's tempting to read into this delicate tracing of an almost shattered creature some kind of personal significance.

Signs of trouble in the marriage of Louis and Cecilie first surfaced in one of Louis's letters to his father-in-law, written shortly after their son, Alexander, was born. He had had a difficult winter, Agassiz wrote to Karl Braun in the spring of 1836. There had been joyful events, to be sure, a reference to Alex's birth. However, Agassiz continued cryptically, some people were just incapable of being happy. They always

had to spoil the enjoyment of such precious moments with unimport-
ant and annoying trivialities. Agassiz was grateful, he said, that Alex
was developing extremely well, despite the obstacles he had darkly
hinted at. As far as Agassiz was concerned, his greatest source of happiness was watching his beautiful son grow. If the remark about the
annoying trivialities was a barb directed at his wife—quite an extraordinary thing, given that he was writing a letter to his father-in-
law that his wife presumably had read—she either didn't notice or
didn't let on that she did. In a postscript to the same letter, Silli spoke
of her plans for the future of her little family, promising her parents
that Alex would have a sibling soon; she mused about when to send
Alex to Karlsruhe so that he could spend time with his grandpar-
ents.[33] Obviously, she was not ready to give up yet.

A profile view Cecilie drew in pencil at the beginning of the year
1835 shows her husband, with sideburns and formally dressed in the
style of the time, holding a piece of writing in his hand. He is looking
intently at it, leaning slightly forward, his eyes partly closed, maybe in
an effort to see better. Leaving nothing to chance, Silli wrote in ink
the text that she wanted Agassiz to read, and she also retraced part of
the book's outline in ink, as if to reinforce her point. "Louis Ag[assiz]
loves his wife, and his wife loves Louis Agassiz," she had written, a
fond wish made true by artistic fiat. Study nature, not books, was the
mantra for which Agassiz would later become famous.[34] But in Silli's portrait-turned-fantasy, there was at least one book Dr. Agassiz
couldn't afford not to read—the book that told him of her love for
him.

As his marriage withered, Agassiz's relationship with his substitute
father, Alexander von Humboldt, continued to flourish. At the beginning of Agassiz's tenure in Neuchâtel, Humboldt had offered him a
generous loan with, in modern terms, no specific maturity date. Humboldt's letter announcing what probably amounted to a gift (there is
no evidence that Agassiz was ever able to pay him back) was full of
flattery. As he became more comfortable in the relationship, compliments to the young Agassiz were leavened by his donnish penchant
for them. Humboldt evidently enjoyed this familiar tone: "A man so
industrious, so talented, and so deserving of love as you are," wrote
Humboldt, "should not be left in a position where lack of good cheer

Louis Agassiz. Drawing, pencil and ink, by Cecilie "Cécile" Braun Agassiz, January 26, 1835.

disturbs his power of work." The "small credit" he was extending to Agassiz was merely a gesture exchanged between "friends of unequal age."[35] This, incidentally, was one of the few letters from Humboldt to Agassiz written entirely in German. Normally Humboldt preferred writing in French, his second language, whereas Agassiz more often than not wrote to him in *his* acquired language, namely German, a game of mutual ironic submission.[36]

Trained in the lecture halls and coffee shops of Heidelberg and Munich, Agassiz spoke and wrote German well indeed, though he had occasional trouble with capitalization, sometimes lowercasing his nouns as if he was in a hurry. But whereas Humboldt's letters, whether in German or French, shimmer with half-jokes, allusions, and innuendo, Agassiz's nearly always drip with worry about himself and the money he is or isn't making: Should he remain in Neuchâtel or take an offer from Heidelberg University? Should he print more than 150 copies of his *Poissons fossiles*? When Agassiz doesn't pity himself, he is foaming at the mouth with gratitude that he has been worthy of Humboldt's attention at all: "To know that I have occupied your thoughts a moment, especially in days of trial and sorrow such as you have had to bear, raises me in my own eyes, and redoubles my hope for the future," he writes revealingly from London, where he went in 1835 to study the fossil fish of England. The egomania so pronounced in Agassiz's later years, considered touchingly naïve by some and irritatingly off-putting by others, is beginning to rear its head. Having been apprised of the death of Humboldt's brother, Agassiz is mainly interested in the fact that Humboldt has written to him even under such trying circumstances, and what this means for their relationship. Apparently without a touch of irony, Agassiz tells Humboldt that he has risen in his own estimation. And he ends the letter by encouraging Humboldt always to keep a little place in his heart for him. He loved Humboldt tenderly, he said, indeed as if he were his son ("comme un fils"). Agassiz was playing out a fantasy here, one in which a son-in-control gives fatherly approval to his submissive dream parent. In Humboldt the young Agassiz had found the father he had always wanted: one who respected, without prompting, the importance of his scientific commitments and who didn't need to insist on his patriarchal rights.[37]

Agassiz's focused, goal-oriented assessments of his own growing importance are in stark contrast with Humboldt's florid delight in self-abasement. For Humboldt, it's never enough to say he is sorry not to have written in a while; he needs to begin his letter of apology to Agassiz thus:

I heartily wish, my dearly beloved friend, that these hastily scribbled lines will find you in a happy and therefore benevolent mood,
one in which you would be inclined to pardon a friend. And your
forgiveness for my indecent behavior I clearly am in need of, having left unanswered two most generous letters by you. I do not
know, in fact, how to express to you, vividly enough, the shame I
feel—to you who are so precious to my heart, whose talent, admirable works and beautiful, youthfully pure character are always
present to me. Be merciful, my dear Agassiz, rather than just—it
would be so futile of me to prattle about my fatal desire to tarry
till I could write to you letters that would be "scientifically interesting," futile to mention the inexorably growing burdens of business and other distractions weighing on my time, burdens due only
to my proximity to the king and life at court, futile to refer you to
the five octavo volumes of my geography of the Middle Ages . . .
which are nearly finished printing in Paris, futile, too, to mention
my health, which was less good this past winter—none of this ex-
onerates me in your eyes, my dear Agassiz. I throw myself on your
mercy . . . I have to control myself.[38]

In enumerating all the things that kept him from being a good correspondent, the sixty-seven-year-old Humboldt betrays a startling need
both to apologize for his behavior and to boast of his accomplishments. It is easy to forget that this world-famous scientist is writing
to a provincial schoolteacher nearly forty years his junior. Some "father" indeed.

Buoyed by such exuberant praise and chafing under the isolation his
teaching of Swiss children in Neuchâtel threatened to impose on him,
Agassiz became less and less enchanted with his domestic life. He
found more occasions to remove himself both mentally and bodily
from the "annoying trivialities" he had mentioned in the letter to his
father-in-law. His increasing involvement in the study of Swiss glaciers offered him a perfect reason to excuse himself from his spousal
and parental responsibilities—to become, as it were, the Humboldt
of his home region.

What became known as Agassiz's "ice age theory" wasn't Agassiz's own invention. Jean-Pierre Perraudin, a chamois hunter from

the southern Swiss Alps, had been one of the first to propose that the glaciers had not always been where they were now and that, in fact, entire valleys had once been covered with them. Not even the term *ice age*, or *Eiszeit*, was Agassiz's; the honor of having coined it belongs to his close friend from Munich, Karl Friedrich Schimper, who had concluded that ice had once covered large parts of the world during a period he called *Weltwinter* (world winter). In 1837, Schimper packed all his insights into a poem he titled "Die Eiszeit Ode" ("The Ice Age Ode"), which he then distributed, on February 15—his own as well as Galileo's birthday!—to the members of Agassiz's natural history society in Neuchâtel. Schimper's atrocious metaphors and halting meter might have obscured some of his more provocative scientific claims, but as a poet he still deserves credit for having managed to address, within a few stanzas, a polar bear, an *Alpenschneehuhn* (a ptarmigan), and what he called the *Ureis* (ur-ice) itself.[39]

Agassiz had originally been somewhat skeptical of the concept of an ice age, but Schimper's poetic intervention, more quaint than boldly competitive, made him spring into action. He staked out his own claim to the theory on July 24, 1837, in an opening address to the national natural history association, the Société Helvétique des Sciences Naturelles, which met in Neuchâtel that year. In this talk, which would later become known as the "Discours de Neuchâtel," Agassiz did acknowledge the work of other glacier enthusiasts and even credited Schimper for having shaped his ideas. Unfortunately, the reference to Schimper came in the context of one of the more speculative parts of Agassiz's argument, which was based (like much else in Agassiz's science) on a common-sense observation. Look at the human body, said Agassiz. It is more or less warm when alive and turns cold as ice when dead. Without a shred of positive proof, though he called his idea "a deduction," Agassiz simply asserted that the rhythms of human life and death were those of the earth too. In Agassiz's hands, casual analogy quickly turned into necessary connection. At the end of each geological period, he proposed, sudden temperature decreases accompanied the demise of all existing life. The earth would then warm up again at the beginning of the next period, when new life appeared too, though the temperature would not reach the same level as the mean temperature of the immediately preceding period. Agassiz's statement adds a new twist to the then generally accepted idea that the earth had been cooling off since the beginning of time. In his view this process was not continuous, but was instead interrupted by "oscillations" such as the last ice age. Agassiz no doubt thought he was gracious when he acknowledged Schimper's influence on his thinking: "This is the explanation of all these phenomena that I now think is the most plausible. It is the result of a mixture of my ideas on the subject with those of Monsieur Schimper."[40]

The concept of the ice age—or several ice ages—beautifully bolstered Agassiz's own solidifying scientific worldview, according to which God directly intervened in the natural history of the world, creating and re-creating all life on earth, rather than allowing for developmental continuity between extinct organisms and those now living. It was such a beautiful fit that Agassiz forgot that he hadn't proved many of his assumptions. Not everyone responded with enthusiasm. But Agassiz, never one to back down under pressure, repeated his claims at a meeting of the Société Géologique de France at Porrentruy a year later, in September 1838, after which he rushed on to the meeting of the Association of German Naturalists at Freiburg im Breisgau, in a publicity blitz that helped secure what by now he himself had become convinced was his own personal right to the ice age idea. To his credit, Agassiz at the time also began to back up his claims with fieldwork of his own, taking parties of devotees with him into the glaciers themselves, in the Bernese Oberland, the Haute Valais, and the Valley of Chamonix, cutting steps into the ice and scaling the summits of mountains (the Jungfrau, the Schreckhorn, the Finsteraarhorn, the Strahleck) that had been considered inaccessible, all in subzero temperatures and enveloped by punishing fog. On one of these excursions, Agassiz, forever curious about the composition of glaciers and how it affected their rate of movement, had himself lowered, on a rope, 125 feet deep into one of those crevasses that would later frighten his hapless American student Henry James Clark.

Soon Agassiz developed plans to take his show across the water. In 1838, at age thirty-one, he wrote what appears to be his first letter ever in (only slightly awkward) English to William Buckland, professor of geology at Oxford, a rather unconventional gentleman who claimed to have eaten his way through the entire animal kingdom and who had believed, before Agassiz convinced him otherwise, that a universal flood, though not necessarily of a recent date, had produced the current topography of the earth.[41] In his letter, Agassiz, tongue-in-cheek, celebrated his new insights: "Since I saw the glacier I am of a quite snowy humour, and will have the whole surface of the earth covered with ice and the whole prior creation dead by cold." There was no doubt in his mind now that ice "covered the whole place where the Alps now stand before they were up heeved and that the organic remains of the Diluvium were dead & enclosed in ice . . . from the north Pole to Italy and the South of France and that the ice melted after the elevation of the Alps and effect by drawing back and alternatively extending again the curious dispersion of erratic blocs." Others, such as the German-Swiss geologist Jean de Charpentier, had looked at the relation between these boulders and glaciers, but no one had connected such local evidence "with the whole process of cooling the earth undergo whilst after each soulevement a new elevation of temperature took place and with it a new encrease of organic life." Agassiz had met Buckland in 1834, during his first visit to England, which went so well that it must have given him an incentive to work on improving his English. By 1838, as this letter shows, he was remarkably fluent, though he still resorted to French terms (*soulèvement* means "upheaval") when matters got more technical, and struggled with the use of tenses and the third-person singular. But his command of the new language was flexible enough to allow him to state clearly his basic goal: to reconstruct as closely as possible, by imaginatively reversing the "progress of the earth," the exact conditions under which living beings had first appeared on earth. And he had learned how to be funny too, always a difficult accomplishment in a foreign language. Agassiz added that he was "very anxious" indeed to see what his English friends thought of his musings.[42]

He had a chance to find out about that when he addressed, in September 1840, his assembled colleagues at the annual meeting of the British Association for the Advancement of Science in Glasgow. It was his opinion, he explained pithily, "that at a certain epoch all of the north of Europe, and also the north of Asia and America, were covered by a mass of ice, in which the elephants and other mammalian found in the frozen mud and gravel of the arctic regions, were imbedded at the time of their destruction."[43] Buckland, who accompanied Agassiz on his hunt for glacial deposits through Scotland and

Wales, kept track of what his scientific colleagues were thinking of Agassiz. In October, he had important news for his friends. Agassiz had converted, wrote Buckland, England's most prominent geologist: "Charles Lyell has adopted your theory *in toto!!!*"[44] Left in the lurch were the original theorists of the ice age, notably poor bespectacled, round-faced Schimper, a man without a regular income or academic affiliation and with the unfortunate habit of writing down his discoveries on scattered leaves of paper, the backs of envelopes as it were, rather than fashioning them into full-fledged essays or books. When Agassiz published the book version of his ice-age theory, *Études sur les glaciers* (1840),[45] Schimper was strangely absent from its pages—the first prominent instance of the cavalier, unattributed use of other people's ideas that, in the eyes of Agassiz's critics, would become a hallmark of his career. For Agassiz, authorship did not have the romantic connotations we still associate with it today. It stood not for intellectual or spiritual ownership of ideas, insights, or discoveries but for a hard-won right. Whoever had spent the most energy or money on publicizing an issue could, in Agassiz's book, rightfully consider it his own. Industry was the prerequisite for success.

Agassiz's dealings with Jean de Charpentier, who had first suggested that the Swiss glaciers had once been more extensive than they were now, show a similar mix of ruthlessness and, for lack of a better word, naiveté. Charpentier, who had been studying glaciers since 1818, published his own *Essai sur les glaciers* just a few months after Agassiz's book. Ironically, Agassiz felt he'd been preempted. Writing to Charpentier, he expressed disappointment that Charpentier hadn't used *his* observations in the book in order to establish "synonymy" between "your theory and mine." Since he had just been given a taste of his own medicine, one would expect Agassiz to be embarrassed. But, never one to hang his head, Agassiz implied that his motives were purer than, apparently, Charpentier's: "You will not have to complain very much about me, because I am essentially concerned with the progress of science, regardless of personalities."[46]

Agassiz might not have cared about originality or priority of discovery, but he did care about the aesthetics of his books. If the idea behind your work isn't your own, make sure you at least present it well.

He had graduated from Cecilie's finely wrought pictures of dead fossils to vistas of alpine grandeur. His new draftsman was Joseph Bettannier; his printer Hercule Nicolet, whose workshop in Neuchâtel Agassiz had simply taken over. *Études sur les glaciers* was accompanied by an atlas with illustrations that are nothing short of magnificent. Collectively, they give us a view of what was on Agassiz's mind during the late 1830s, Agassiz's ice-age years. Consider, in Bettannier's rendering of the Lower Aar glacier, the startling effect the artist achieves by placing the medial moraine, a dramatic jumble of rocks, so that it cascades directly toward the viewer.

The plate, featuring one glacier on either side of a moraine, the Lauteraar and the Finsteraar, presents "before" and "after" in one image. That is, it shows both the glaciers *and* the results of their work, bits and pieces of matter piled up helter-skelter, in bizarre disorder. Moraines are, as Agassiz explains in *Études*, the accumulations of rounded rock fragments resting like ramparts against the margins of glaciers, which, "by rubbing themselves against the valley walls, drag

"Glacier de l'Aar." Plate 14, drawn and lithographed by Joseph Bettannier, from *Études sur les glaciers*, by Louis Agassiz, 1840.

along with them all the loose objects they encounter, which are therefore continuously ground against each other and against the rocky
walls forming their bed."[47] Bettannier's illustration also features the
curious ice tables that often occur close to such moraines—slabs of
rock of varying sizes elevated above the rest of the glacier, precari-
ously balanced on ever-thinning pillars of ice, always ready to break
loose and slide down farther.[48] Agassiz had seen one such table on the
Lower Aar glacier that was fifteen feet long, twelve feet wide, and six
feet high. Bettannier cleverly highlights the size of these tables by
including some diminutive observers standing or sitting on the left
edge of the moraine, gazing at the ice sheet below them as if it were
some kind of ancient river. Closer to the viewer but not much more
fully sketched are the two figures in the right foreground, cower-
ing in an improvised-looking shelter, under an inscription that reads
"Cabine de Mr. Hugi." Agassiz was interested in ice, not people.

Monsieur Hugi's cabin came to play a large part in Agassiz's quest
for proof that the great glaciers of the Alps had in fact moved and
were indeed moving still. In his *Études*, Agassiz reports how, in 1839,
he first came across the structure after having walked up the medial
moraine for about four hours, hoping to reach the juncture of the
Finsteraar and Lauteraar glaciers. He knew that in 1827, at the foot of
a rock called "Im Abschwung," the geologist Franz Joseph Hugi had
built a primitive shelter. To his great surprise, Agassiz came across
Hugi's hut much earlier than he had expected it, namely several thousand feet beneath its original location—an *Abschwung* (descent) indeed! Inside the structure, he found, preserved in a broken glass bottle, observations by Hugi himself, charting the movement of the hut,
first by just a few hundred feet, then, when he revisited it in 1836, to
a point twenty-two hundred feet away from its original location. The
bottle also contained, as Agassiz added in a footnote, notes by several
mutual friends from Neuchâtel who had visited the site.

Agassiz hurried to complete his own measurements and found that
by now the hut had traveled an impressive forty-four hundred feet.
In fact, it was still en route. Agassiz realized that by the time *Études*
would be published, the image featured in this plate would be no longer accurate: "This year," wrote Agassiz, "I found it, in very poor
condition 200 feet below last year's position, but the objects it con-

tained were still visible among the fallen blocks of the roof."[49] Agassiz added, again in a footnote, that he had left a written record of his observations in the visitors' book at the Grimsel Hospice, his supply base west of the glacier, in order that other visitors could add their own findings. And when he and his new partners in this new scientific enterprise—among them the German-born geologists Édouard Desor and Carl Vogt as well as Agassiz's young student, Louis François de Pourtalès—built another shelter, two thousand feet below Hugi's cabin, soon to be known under the witty moniker "Hôtel des Neuchâtelois," he scratched the parameters of the original location into the block that served as its roof. Even that wasn't enough: "I have, at the same time, carved reference points on both flanks of the valley."[50]

Agassiz predicted that soon Hugi's cabin would be gone entirely, joining other pieces of rock piled up on the moraine. Even now, the hut seemed out of place, and it looked funny to boot: consider the great boulder perched right behind it, topped by the improvised signpost, a ridiculously vertical human artifact in a world that was forever, if slowly, sliding downward. Ironically, the half-reclining position of the mountaineer in the foreground suggests calm acceptance of the glacially slow drama unfolding around him. The illustration, showing a moraine virtually rolling toward the reader, its force stemmed only by the frame of the image, thus stages the processes that Agassiz's book as a whole is about: nature is constantly on the move, with humans pushed to the margin (literally so, in Bettannier's plate), relegated to the role of observers and, we should add, writers and inscribers.

And the latter is indeed crucial. For what is so remarkable about the episode involving Hugi's and Agassiz's cabin is the sheer amount of writing that is going on there: as the ice sheet is inscribing its presence in the rock, leaving scratches, tracks, and striations to be deciphered by subsequent generations of naturalists, humans are trying to keep up, leaving their notes too inside the cabin, in visitors' logs, on the rocks themselves, or in a book like Agassiz's *Études*. Behold Agassiz's remedy against the sublime: while the awful might of the glacier threatens to nix all human attempts to understand it, the tracks that the moving ice sheets leave do ultimately confirm that they *can* be understood, measured, triangulated, mapped; Agassiz's "Hôtel des Neuchâtelois," filled with microscopes, thermometers, hygrometers, and so forth, is proof of that. Above all, though, as Agassiz sees it, the glacier is itself an enormous writing instrument. A world that to others seems stationary, cold, and lifeless is, to the scientist who knows how to read it, full of life, motion, change. "Just now," writes Agassiz, "most of the glaciers I have observed are advancing considerably, in particular those of the Bernese Oberland. The lower Aar glacier has grown more than a quarter of an hour in walking distance since 1811 . . . The Grindelwald glaciers and that of the Rosenlaui are also increasing appreciably. The great Zermatt glacier overlaps its left bank, while it appears to be stationary on the right one." Notice the reference to the Zermatt glacier's *rive*, or "bank": Agassiz writes about these glaciers as if they were rivers.[51]

In *Études*, Agassiz clearly had fun alluding to the conventions of traditional landscape representation. In "Glacier de Zermatt," for example, he had Bettannier include miniature portraits of the members of Agassiz's party having a picnic in the mountains, in full view of the glacier, whose crevasses, at least from a distance, make the glacier's surface look like waves. Here is a counterimage to the athleticism stressed elsewhere in Agassiz's book, the many references to the heights Agassiz scaled, the adverse weather he braved, the deprivations he endured. Any reader awed by the natural spectacle should just take a look at the bottles the travelers have consumed or are still consuming. One of them has fallen over, which perhaps suggests the picnickers have already emptied it.

Or, to further enliven the icy spectacle, turn to the outline drawing of the same view also included in the atlas—and voilà, the landscape is suddenly covered with writing: Petit Glacier du Breithorn; Glaciers du Petit-Cervin et de la Fürke-Flue; Partie du Glacier formée par la reunion des deux Glaciers du Breithorn et de ceux du Petit Cervin et de la Fürke-Flue (Part of a Glacier formed by the reunion of the two Glaciers of the Breithorn and those of the Petit-Cervin and Furke-Flue), and so forth. The words begin to undulate, attaching themselves to the sinuous forms of the landscape itself, suggesting movement and the possibility that there is no real conflict between image and word, natural reality and interpretation. Contemporary

Above: "Glacier de Zermatt." Plate 3, drawn and lithographed by Joseph Bettannier, from *Études sur les glaciers. Below:* "Glacier de Zermatt." Plate 3a, drawn and lithographed by Joseph Bettannier, from *Études sur les glaciers.*

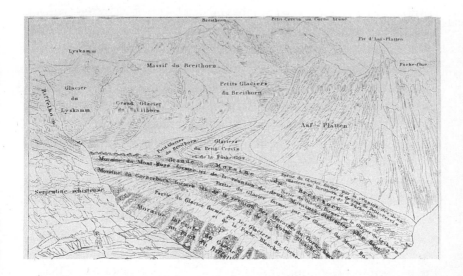

readers willing to take a closer look at the humans who are having such a good time in plate 3 would have recognized Agassiz as the one with the hat, lying down, an empty bottle next to him, his face turned toward the reader: See, here I am, taking it easy. Interestingly, Joseph Bettannier, the artist, has portrayed himself apart from the group, working on a piece of rock.

Agassiz's glacial exploits certainly highlighted his personal heroism. His readers would finish *Études* convinced that this author was not an armchair naturalist but a man unafraid of physical hardship. But *Études* paradoxically emphasizes the opposite quality too, namely, the extent to which teamwork—the shared efforts of mountaineering crews, the observations made by Agassiz's predecessors—had produced the results he was now able to share with yet another group of prospective participants in his work, his readers.

Pasteur Rodolphe Agassiz did not live to see the publication of *Études sur les glaciers*. He died on September 6, 1837, in his vicarage in Concise, killed by a fever. His father's death left no ripples in Agassiz's surviving letters, though those close to him could tell that he was deeply touched. Humboldt wrote him a sympathetic letter, expressing concern about the "congestion" of head and eyes Agassiz had mentioned. For mercy's sake, he chided Agassiz, take care of yourself. "I am afraid that you work too much, and (shall I say it frankly?) that you spread your intelligence out over too many subjects at once." Humboldt feared that Agassiz's glacial shenanigans were keeping him from completing his important work on fossil fish. If Agassiz didn't finish what he had begun, Humboldt joked, he would come back reincarnated as one of Agassiz's neglected fossils and haunt him, a menacing ghost ("une ombre menaçante"), carrying under his arm all the pages Agassiz had left unwritten, along with his own unfinished volume about "that eternal America." Humboldt was referring to his *Voyage aux régions équinoxiales*, which would indeed remain incomplete at his death.[52]

But Agassiz was far too busy to pay attention. High up in the mountains, he was building his own alternative family. No longer in need of traditional father figures, Agassiz had become a father figure himself, replacing, in the "Hôtel des Neuchâtelois," his biological family (a wife and, by spring 1841, three children) with a horde of assistants and devotees. Over a period of a few years, the core group engraved their names on a slab of rock in the makeshift shelter. Agassiz's name is, of course, the biggest and since it carries the date of 1840, was likely the first. Many of the names of the assistants and collaborators, who asserted membership in the "Hôtel des Neuchâtelois" would become familiar names themselves: Agassiz's assistants Carl Vogt and Édouard Desor; his student Louis François de Pourtalès; Charles Girard, the son of a peasant from Concise, whom Agassiz had just taken under his wing and whom he was grooming as his personal factotum; Jacques Burkhardt, another one of Agassiz's illustrators; the zoologist Jules Pictet from Geneva; the inevitable Karl Friedrich Schimper; the Scottish physicist James David Forbes, who would soon enter into a bitter dispute with Agassiz over who had first correctly described the internal structure of glaciers. Agassiz's guides left their names too, and so did several women: Elise Krantz, Mlle. Marie Chambeau, Madame Martins (the wife of the meteorologist Charles Martins, who had also signed his name), a certain Madame Martin from Strasbourg. From the beginning of his career, Agassiz wanted to make the study of natural history accessible to all.

In a way, the very name "Hôtel des Neuchâtelois" ironically alludes to the petit-bourgeois domesticity from which Agassiz increasingly wanted to escape. In his biography, Jules Marcou mentions that

"Hôtel des Neuchâtelois, August, 1842."

tourists were in fact sometimes confused by the name of the establishment, expecting a kind of hospitality that a ramshackle cabin composed of rock slabs couldn't provide. The roof soon began to show cracks, so that the structure wasn't particularly safe even for Agassiz and his men. When they were staying there, a member of the party had to walk around the cabin each night to make sure that nothing was about to come crashing down on them. Once Agassiz's family did come for a visit—an engraving from 1841 shows Cecilie and Alex trekking up the rocky path to the shelter's entrance—but as the circle of his followers grew, the original pile of rocks was replaced first by a tentlike structure known as "L'Arche" and then by an actual house, which they called "Le Pavillon."[53]

The (mostly) male camaraderie of the "Hôtel" soon also spilled over into what was left of Agassiz's private life in Neuchâtel. Agassiz's scientific buddies set up camp at his house, increasingly annoying Cecilie. Whether her husband was absent, on one of his frequent lecturing trips to France, Germany, or England, or present in the house (and in the latter case, entertaining his friends at home), Cecilie knew that the intimacy of their earlier relationship—touchingly invoked in the Novalis poem she had written out for him in 1832—was a thing of the past. It is difficult to tell what came first, Agassiz's disenchantment with Cecilie over the "trivialities" she placed in his way or Cecilie's irritation with his overflowing generosity toward strangers. But it seems clear that Agassiz did what he could to break up the domestic circle at home. He took in Desor and Vogt as regular boarders, along with Charles Girard, the "bootblack" of the group, in Marcou's description. Desor and Vogt's coarse, often antireligious remarks infuriated Cecilie, who, since Agassiz was now also subsidizing Nicolet's printing press, never had enough money at her disposal to feed all the people who were jostling for space around her dinner table. Her mother-in-law came for periods of time to interfere with her housekeeping. A toxic climate developed in which new hierarchies were formed, alpha males and underdogs assumed their respective roles, and Cecilie Agassiz found herself relegated to the margins. She couldn't have cared less about ice.

Humboldt couldn't either. From a distance, he watched with bemusement as his busy Swiss protégé trucked up glaciers, had himself lowered on ropes into crevasses, and shivered through dark alpine nights under rock piles in crumbling shelters. Extreme physical challenges Humboldt could understand. After all, he had modeled such manly courage for future generations of explorer-scientists in his own travels through South America. But extolling the wonders of ice fields instead of tropical volcanoes—Humboldt simply failed to see the benefit of that. Humboldt found Agassiz's primordial fields of ice, the glaciers on which great boulders rolled around, deeply unappealing: "Vos glaces me font peur" ("Your ice makes me shudder"). Berlin in the winter was all he could take.[54] In a letter to Agassiz written in late 1842, Humboldt, who called himself a "man of the equator," facetiously quoted Madame de Sévigné—"grace from on high . . . comes down slowly"—and added, tongue in cheek, that he absolutely wished the same would happen for Agassiz's ice age and "that deathly skullcap of ice" he wanted the world to wear.[55] Earlier the same year, he had informed Agassiz that he just couldn't understand how the world could have iced over so fast that the animals didn't even have a chance to decompose first.[56]

What Humboldt didn't realize was that Agassiz had, in a sense, already moved beyond the sphere of his influence. He might not have invented the theory of the ice age, but in bringing it "out of obscurity and into the public eye,"[57] and in assigning to ice sheets a much greater expansion than the available evidence supported, he had broken free of whatever boundaries his obscure position in Neuchâtel and his Swiss descent might have imposed on him. Now it was time to leave Humboldt behind too. Theorizing about global glaciers, Agassiz, the gifted provincial schoolteacher from Neuchâtel, had remade himself into a citizen of the world. He became like Humboldt by becoming unlike him. "You have made all the geologists glacier-mad here," wrote the Manx naturalist Edward Forbes to Agassiz in February 1841, "and they are turning Great Britain into an ice-house."[58] And in the United States, Edward Hitchcock, a professor of chemistry and natural history at Amherst College, who was just about then tutoring the young Emily Dickinson, became an early convert. "We learned to like the Fire," wrote Emily Dickinson later, "By playing Glaciers."[59]

This is not to say that everything was plain sailing. *Au contraire.* Leopold von Buch, the leading German geologist, who had been in the audience in 1837 in Neuchâtel when Agassiz gave his speculative address on glaciers, remained adamantly opposed. As late as 1866, Charles Darwin would use Forbes's joke about the "glacier-mad" geologists in an attempt to discredit Agassiz himself: "Many thanks for the pamphlet," wrote Darwin to Charles Lyell in 1866, after the latter had sent him one of Agassiz's articles on the geology of the Amazon in the *Atlantic Monthly*.[60] "I was very glad to read it, though chiefly as a psychological curiosity. I quite follow you in thinking Agassiz glacier-mad."[61] But Agassiz wasn't troubled by such opposition. His theory of the ice age, a global phenomenon, had turned out to be infinitely exportable, a universal scientific commodity that, in the eyes of the general populace if not in the minds of all of his scientific peers, made his science relevant wherever he went. It had made him, the natural history teacher from the Swiss provinces, personally indispensable too, as the discerning reader of glacial action in the rock.

Trekking through the glaciers of the Alps, Agassiz continued to ignore the signs of trouble at home. Remarkably, Humboldt, though he was far away and had nothing to go on but Agassiz's letters, did not. Be proud of your accomplishments and, for God's sake, be a father to your family rather than to others, he implored Agassiz in August 1840.[62] Agassiz paid no heed. The triumphalist public image of his science notwithstanding, his domestic life had come unraveled. While he was out scaling the mountaintops of Switzerland, his financial woes mounted. Cecilie turned to her brother Alexander, Agassiz's college friend: "You think too highly of the World and people," her brother responded to her on May 14, 1844. Peace was attainable only in heaven, he pontificated; the only true remedy for the evil that we experience in the here and now is to stand firm in our faith and to look at the sacrifices we need to make as God's way of purifying our souls. Alternatively, take your current troubles as deserved punishment for our sins. Personally, Alexander had denied himself all manner of extravagant things: foreign travel, for example, or other experiences that might have helped his research along. Would he have become a better researcher if he'd taken more risks like Agassiz, if he'd stepped boldly into the fray, his hands laden with specimens he'd collected himself, in the field? Suddenly there was more than a trace of self-pity in Alexander Braun's letter: "Agassiz," he wrote, "has in this regard always traveled a different route, one that I do not want to criticize."[63]

It is not clear if Cecilie Agassiz ever asked her brother for advice again. If she didn't, who would blame her? She had come to him for support, and look what she received in turn: a middle-aged brother's lament for the ways in which life had bypassed and cheated him. The message was clear: Agassiz might be a cad but, by God, look at what he has accomplished.

And yet by now Agassiz's scientific family was beginning to crumble too. It is possible that he himself didn't realize how deeply enmeshed he had become in a complex web of relationships that were beginning to threaten, rather than fortify, his authority as the new paterfamilias of glacial science. Two members of his inner circle, Karl Friedrich Schimper and Carl Vogt, opted out, seeking their luck elsewhere, while another valuable collaborator, the geologist Armand Gressly, succumbed to madness. Schimper became a bitter adversary. But not, it must be said, a very effective one. His attempt to wrest credit back from Agassiz came, as had his first announcement of his glacial theories, in a poem, at the end of which he attacked his contemporaries for subjecting him, "the singer of the Ice Age," to tortures worthy of a Galileo while applauding the "thieving magpie" who had pilfered his ideas (the French word *agasse* meant "magpie"; Schimper's pun would have been accessible only to rather erudite readers).[64] No wonder Schimper's attack missed its intended target. Vogt, who had worked hard on Agassiz's *Histoire naturelle des poissons d'eau douce*, a comprehensive natural history of freshwater fish, left for a similar reason: he felt Agassiz had not given him enough credit as the primary author of the only volume, on the embryology of the salmon, that had appeared thus far.[65]

But Agassiz swiftly rationalized those losses. The group's survival depended on the good fortunes of its leader. Agassiz was the brand name under which the products of his scientific factory were offered to the public. Insisting, against detractors like Vogt and later Desor, on his control over the means of production — to use the terms developed a bit later by Agassiz's near-contemporary Karl Marx — had become a way of maintaining order.[66] But now, inconveniently, the great

Agassiz was broke. Despite his international renown, he was still only a dignified schoolteacher, but one who had accumulated a fair number of devoted enemies.

Once again, Humboldt came to the rescue. Agassiz had long dreamed of spending some time in the United States, and in March 1845 he received word that Humboldt had managed to secure a small grant for him from the king of Prussia, which would allow him to spend two years in the New World. Thanks to the geologist Charles Lyell, Agassiz also received an invitation to give a series of Lowell Institute lectures in Boston, a distinguished honor that would involve explaining his science in a series of public talks. When Cecilie Agassiz wrote to share the news of Agassiz's upcoming American junket, Alexander Braun, torn between loyalty to his influential former buddy and some residual sympathy for his poor sister, breathed an audible sigh of relief. Let us hope, he wrote back, somewhat stiffly, that reports of the king's support for Agassiz's voyage will turn out to be true. The main part of Alexander Braun's letter was again devoted to useless advice: a lecture on how Cecilie should raise her children, in fear of God and in fervent expectation of the rewards of eternity. The best way to get there was absolute obedience. Make your children as dependent on you as you can; this is how they will learn to depend on God. One cannot help but feel sorry for Cecilie, who clearly must have thought she had nowhere to turn.[67] Thoroughly fed up with circumstances at home, she did what a modern woman would do: in early May 1845, she took her two daughters and left Agassiz and an environment in which she had been reduced to the role of a bit player. Alexander, who had just turned nine, initially stayed enrolled in a local boarding school. Agassiz's plans for a transatlantic journey had given her a perfect reason to do what she had wanted to do for quite some time.

She refused her brother's offer to live with him. Instead, she found her own apartment in Freiburg and attempted to create a new life for her truncated family, delegating more and more responsibility to her son, Alexander, when he eventually joined them. In one of his more affecting memories of that time, Alexander is skating over the frozen meadows of Freiburg, pushing his mother before him in her high-backed sled.[68] But in reality things were not going well. Alexander, longing for his father's more rigorous scientific pursuits, resisted

"Andromeda." Pencil drawing by Cecilie Braun, 1822.

his mother's efforts to nurture his artistic tendencies, resenting especially the violin lessons she made him take. And Cecilie began to show more symptoms of the tuberculosis that would finally kill her, on July 27, 1848.

Among the one hundred or so artworks in her portfolio—finely executed representations of muscular male bodies, copied from anatomy books; reproductions of Greek statuary; delicate sketches of flowering plants; complicated perspective views of architectural interiors, complete with columned courtyards and stately porticoes—one early composition stands out. The drawing shows Andromeda in chains, her gaze directed away from the ship in the distance that will bring, unbeknownst to her, her future husband. In Greek mythology, the Ethiopian princess Andromeda was to be sacrificed to a sea monster as punishment for her mother's boasting.

But Cecilie's drawing—perhaps appropriately, for a thirteen-year-old girl—avoids familiar representations of Andromeda as naked and chained to a rock, giving us instead only partial nudity, swelling drapery, and a pensive upward glance, a creative Victorian adaptation of a popular baroque iconographic formula associated with the Penitent Magdalene.[69] Through her art, young Cecilie—whose parents would, as she mentioned in her first letter from Neuchâtel, frequently lament her absent-mindedness—had apparently found a way of both confronting her fatal flaw and taking some pride in it, since this is what made her different from others. She completed this drawing in 1822, years before she would turn into Cécile Agassiz, and yet this portrait of a surprisingly strong yet clearly oppressed woman seems eerily prophetic. The name Andromeda means "she who is mindful of a man." If Cecilie Agassiz was still thinking of her man during the last lonely years of her life, her thoughts could not have been comforting ones. From her perspective, Agassiz had turned out to be more of a sea monster than a King Perseus.

While Cecilie's life was fading away, Agassiz, indefatigably optimistic, was thinking about the future—his own, that is. In a flurry of messages, Agassiz began to prepare his hosts for his impending arrival in the New World. He was indeed eager to arrive there, he informed the physician and conchologist Augustus Addison Gould in Boston, but there was so much to take care of: apprising himself of the latest scientific news in Germany, putting the finishing touches on his volumes about fossil fish, and so forth.[70] "Scientific labors cannot be hurried," he wrote to the trustee of the Lowell Lectures committee, John Amory Lowell, on July 6, 1846, from Paris, where he had relocated to get his work done. He didn't forget to mention that the Académie des Sciences had just awarded him the Prix Montyon de physiologie expérimentale in recognition of his work on fossil fish. The Montyon awards, endowed in perpetuity by the baron de Montyon in 1815 and given out in four different categories (one of them was, in fact, "virtue"), are now considered the forerunners of the Nobel prizes, and Agassiz was justifiably proud. In 1859, Louis Pasteur would receive the same award for his work on fermentation. Agassiz was so pleased with the honor that he had decided, as he told Lowell, to do "some ding" [*sic*] more in that vein (in fact, he was working on a sequel to his glacier book, the *Nouvelles études et expériences sur les glaciers actuels*). He realized that time was pressing and that the summer, as Agassiz put it, "was running away," so he'd sent ahead three large boxes with the illustrations, prepared by Joseph Dinkel, who would be coming with him later in the summer, "that I might never be at want of a man able to make concurrent illustrations of the interesting objects I may happen to observe."[71] Joining him, if a few months later, would be the remnants of his "other" family, the "Hôtel des Neuchâtelois," Édouard Desor, Louis François de Pourtalès, and the infinitely useful Charles Girard.

Agassiz left Europe for good, though he didn't yet know it, in September 1846. Humboldt said farewell to him in one of his most personal letters. On July 16, 1846, writing from Sanssouci, he assured Agassiz of his continued love and his admiration "for your magnificent travels." But he also warned him of the veritable avalanche of questions (my pun, not Humboldt's) that his glacial researches had kicked loose. Did he really want to address all these things the public now wanted to hear about—whether or not and when the whole world had frozen over, the ancient height of snow mountains across the world, the real causes for the striations and traces on the rocks, where glaciers occurred frequently and where not, what in fact happened during catastrophic climate changes? Humboldt, for one, would remain supportive. Not for him the dogmatic stubbornness, the "100,000 leagues of disdain" of Professor von Buch. Science, unlike theology, did not require one to believe whole cloth; it was possible here "de croire 1/8, 1/16, 1/32," in other words, to believe in fractions or increments rather than in the whole thing. Humboldt was hoping to live long enough to read the latest about Agassiz's "grand and ingenious conceptions." In Humboldt's eyes at least, Agassiz, over the years, had grown immeasurably as a scientist, and Humboldt added, with mock humility, that he was naive enough to believe that if his friends had acquired greatness, that meant he was quite something too. "Give me the first place in your heart in the category of friend, dear Agassiz." The almost-eighty-year-old Humboldt promised he would send him the second volume of his *Kosmos* hot off the press so that Agassiz could warm himself a bit on his eternal glaciers. Perceptively, Humboldt signed his letter as "Votre illisible, affectueux Humboldt": your illegible, affectionate Humboldt. Not exactly a passing of the torch, that letter.[72] But unlike Rodolphe, he was happy to let his scientific son go forth.

· 3 ·

HUMBOLDT'S GIFT

IN HIS GLACIER STUDIES, Agassiz had managed to combine commitment to local detail with an expansive, panoramic vision. By replacing Humboldt's obsession with the sun with his own preference for ice, Agassiz had, as it happened, positioned himself for popularity in the New World. It didn't even matter that he would shift his interests again, to new problems, new areas of research. He had hit on a perfect template for success that he maintained for the rest of his life: combine local fieldwork with pronouncements about the world in general and then talk about these investigations in terms that made sense to everyone, from a Cape Cod fisherman to the king of Brazil. For Agassiz, the local was the universal, and the universal was always local. His physical involvement in his glacial research—the fact that he would scale the summits of mountains after trudging through ice sheets—became the epitome of masculine derring-do, the frontier spirit that Americans were ready to appreciate. Herman Melville, in his book about the ultimate frontier of men's dreams, *Moby-Dick*, compared the white whale, the object of the sailors' fierce hunt, or rather the mottled and scarred surface of its skin, to the marks and scratches left by Agassiz's movable ice.[1]

As far as Agassiz was concerned, the match between his scientific theories and the reality of the New World was perfect. He liked to recall that when his steamer, the *Hibernia*, docked in Halifax en route to Boston, everything immediately corresponded to his expectations. "Eager to set foot on the new continent so full of promise for me," he said, "I sprang on shore and started at a brisk pace for the heights above the landing. On the first undisturbed ground, after leaving the town, I was met by the familiar signs, the polished surfaces, the furrows and scratches, the *line-engraving* of the glacier, so well known in the Old World; and I became convinced of what I had already anticipated as the logical sequence of my previous investigations, that here also this great agent had been at work."[2] For Agassiz, the global prophet of the ice age, nothing looked strange. Humboldt had given him to the New World so that he could explain America to the Americans.

The *Hibernia* arrived in Boston on Saturday, October 3, 1846, with 109 passengers. The voyage from Liverpool had taken thirteen and a quarter days.[3] Agassiz's American colleagues had prepared a full itinerary for him, taking him, over the next few months, by train to all centers of learning and power in the United States: New Haven, New York, Albany, Princeton, Philadelphia, and Washington. What he saw seemed like Italy to him, except colder, he reported to his mother, Rose, back home in Switzerland. "The trees now appear in magnificent colors, red, yellow and orange, against the background of the firs and junipers, and the brilliance of the sun only enhances the beauty of that contrast." Ever the scientist, Agassiz ventured a guess why the foliage should be so special here. The dry climate and the pure air make the leaves ripen as if they were fruit, he opined. Of course, the landscape as a whole impressed him too. He told his mother that he wished he could paint for her a panoramic view of the Hudson between New York and Albany, and he vividly evoked for her the beauty of the Long Island Sound.

The egalitarianism of American travel, however, appalled him not a little. On American trains one's personal belongings, he observed with a shudder, get thrown together in big piles, a democratic mess of hat boxes, purses, overnight bags, trunks, and so forth. In fact, the term *pêle mêle* crops up when Agassiz wanted to convey to his mother what was so different about the United States, whether it's the way Americans mingle in public or the food they devour, "en cinq minutes," for dinner: roast beef, fruit, potatoes, rice, all heaped indiscriminately on the *same* plate. Agassiz found the American cuisine "detestable," with the exception of the poultry and the many "excellent" dishes made with corn. The plate of snipe he once saw being served in a hotel was nothing but a pile of foul-smelling carrion. "Ah quel pays!" What a country. If the culture and habits of the Americans occasionally let him down, however, nature never did. And who knew what science could do to improve them!

Agassiz, recently arrived from a continent littered with artificial borders, did appreciate the lack of barriers and of currency exchange offices— of anything, really, that would put obstacles between a traveler and his destination. Hotels cost the same for everybody! For Agassiz it was clear that the astonishing mobility of Americans had something to do with the climate, the pure sky, the fresh air. The climate of the Old World had a downright soporific effect, but Americans, invigorated by their environment, were forever eager to learn. Before Agassiz's inner eye there arose generations of eager natural history students, a nation of potential scientists. Everyone, down to the humblest worker, he told his mother, will don a clean linen shirt just to attend a meeting in which the establishment of a new library is discussed. Self-improvement and education were goods Americans held sacred. He hadn't seen any beggars, except, of course, in New York. There were some drawbacks to this democratic leveling of differences. American women, for example, were almost frighteningly entitled. The demeanor especially of the young girls reminded him of French *grisettes*. But he remained deeply impressed by the mixture of tolerance and religious zeal he encountered wherever he traveled, which contrasted favorably with European indifference toward vice. The American Constitution, as Agassiz saw it, offered a basis for the reconciliation of religious and philosophical differences. Here, finally, was a society that had room for his own unorthodox religious views. In the United States, the spirit still had a chance.[4]

Agassiz's Lowell Institute lectures on "The Plan of the Creation, Especially in the Animal Kingdom," given during the winter of 1846– 1847, have not survived; nor do we know much about the more academic lecture in French, "The Glaciers and the Glacial Period," that he delivered on the same occasion.[5] But we have a complete transcript of Agassiz's lectures in New York, presented in the hall of the College of Physicians and Surgeons in the fall of 1847, and they were substantially the same as the ones he had delivered in Boston. The transcript of the New York lectures was produced collaboratively by Dr. Houston, an Irish physician-turned-stenographer who also worked for the U.S. Senate, and one Mr. Brydges, who "rapidly" copied Agassiz's improvised sketches from the blackboard. Dr. Houston recorded everything, even noting the copious applause Agassiz received.[6]

An unsigned biographical notice preceding the transcript characterized Agassiz as "a man of very striking and prepossessing appearance." Tall and "formed with as much strength as elegance" and with a "rather florid complexion" (an indication of his penchant for the good life?) as well as dark hair, Agassiz seemed appealingly foreign to his American audience, an impression enhanced by his distinct accent. Agassiz himself apologized for his clumsiness in English, though he immediately added that the study of natural history didn't need the "aid of rhetoric to invest it with attractive charms," a disingenuous statement if ever there was one. Agassiz's lectures as a whole were clearly calculated to be as attractive as he could make them.[7] He certainly knew how to render his subject accessible to listeners with no prior knowledge of natural history.

Take his initial comparison, in these lectures, between the study of nature and the study of Homer. For a true understanding of the *Odyssey* or the *Iliad*, argued Agassiz, simple translation was not enough. "Would it by any means follow because we have thus spelled over the pages of Homer, that we understand him?" As far as Agassiz was concerned, another, and higher, sort of mental process was required to understand such a sublime writer. And that mental process involved putting things in their proper historical context: "It is only when we have become acquainted with the condition of human society in that age — the rivalry which existed between the nations of Asia and Greece — and the mythology of that remote time, that our sympathies approach the level of the poet's work and our hearts own the influence of the poet's spirit." Agassiz's Homeric comparison might strike us as a bit facile today, but at a time when the historical study of literature was not established practice in the college classroom (though Longfellow's Harvard classes on Dante and Goethe, taught in the 1830s and 40s, had blazed the trail), Agassiz's call for contextual interpretation must have seemed cutting-edge. At the same time, the distinctly literary basis of his science — understanding God was like understanding a great poet—would have rendered his lectures more broadly appealing, even to people less inclined to nature study. Agassiz had made literal the age-old metaphor of the Book of Nature. God's plots were as multilayered and as context-filled as Dante's *Divine Comedy*. "Understand, then," he told his listeners, "that the study and knowledge of Nature consist in something more than acquaintance with the isolated beings which exist upon the surface of our globe. We must understand the connections existing between these beings, and the relations which they sustain to the Creator of them all."[8]

In his textbook *Principles of Zoölogy* (1848), a collaborative effort involving his Boston colleague Dr. Augustus Addison Gould and his assistant Édouard Desor, Agassiz would later offer an even more extensive version of this analogy: "The spirit and preparation we bring to the study of Nature, is a matter of no little consequence," he claimed. And he went on to offer a lively defense of what, in literary criticism, we would now call the "biographical method": "When we would study with profit a work of literature, we first endeavor to make ourselves acquainted with the genius of the author; and in order to know what end he had in view, we must have regard to his previous labors, and to the circumstances under which the work was executed." Taking the long view meant appreciating the literary work of art as a part of a larger, intricately structured whole. "Without this, although we may perhaps enjoy its perfection as a whole, and admire the beauty of its details, yet the spirit which pervades it will escape us, and many passages may even remain unintelligible." What Agassiz was proposing was a more scientific version of the aesthetic method recommended by Humboldt, who had asked his readers to contemplate the whole of nature as if it were a well-executed painting.[9]

Paradoxically, Agassiz's insistence that his science was literary in *method* allowed him to emphasize that the *objects* of scientific work were not literary themselves. "Study nature, not books." Reading nature as if it were a book meant that one didn't need any other books in order to study it. And the natural things Agassiz brought to his lectures were so unusual that few of his listeners—or should one say, spectators—would ever forget them. Much of what he had to offer was provocative enough to grab people's attention, such as his passion for animals that were the lowest of the low: the polyps that form coral reefs or the jellyfish that many of his listeners knew from their own walks on the beach. How wonderfully organized were even those beings "which occupy the most inferior condition of existence," he exclaimed during his first lecture in New York. Polyps, for example, only had one organ, the stomach, and yet we find in them almost all the functions of animal life. And as far as the jellyfish were concerned, a single leaf of paper would contain as much solid matter as a full cartload of these animals when dried. In effect, Agassiz was asking his audience to admire creatures so substanceless that they seemed hardly present at all, organisms whose sole purpose in life seemed to consist of digesting their food.[10]

Agassiz wasn't content with merely theorizing about his marine animals. He pulled one out of his pocket, so that everyone could appreciate its symmetrical structure: "I have here before me," he said, "one of those animals which show this radiated appearance most distinctly. It is a star fish, of the common species, found living on the American shores of the Atlantic." Nothing, not even the most accurate drawing, could show an animal as it really is. "Things are not so easily seen in Nature," Agassiz warned his audience, in a typical attempt to validate and elevate his own research. And lest anyone misunderstand his interest in invertebrate creatures living at the edge of the sea as a covert attempt to topple humankind from its central position in God's universe, Agassiz went on to mount a vigorous defense of anthropocentrism. Here was the combination that became Agassiz's recipe for success during his American career: conservative values (humankind's leading position in the order of creation; a belief in the innate differences between human races; the confidence that God leaves nothing to chance) reaffirmed by apparently innovative methods (science as a democratic activity to be carried out in the field by people who have been suitably instructed).[11]

For Agassiz, it never was doubtful that humans were, structurally at least, animals. They inhabit the world within boundaries "similar to those occupied by natural groups of animals." That said, humans, unlike all other animals, were equipped with the ability to know not only themselves but everything else, even what happened before they came to exist. Paleontology held the key to the future: "Since the ripple-marks of the ebbing tide, and the slightest impressions of the feet of animals can be recognized, we have evidence that the time will come when we shall know all that has transpired on the surface of the earth, at a period when Man did not exist, and we can reconstruct the form of the whole Animal Creation only by these slight evidences." Agassiz's audience clapped appreciatively. Humans were central both to nature *and* to the understanding of nature, since nature itself cannot understand what it means: "We feel in ourselves that we are not mere matter. We have a soul. We have an intelligence. We have feelings by which we are in connection with each other. These feelings—that intelligence—carry us beyond the limits of our globe." While the structure of their bodies identified them as animals, humans were divine by virtue of their intellect: "We thus rise to the notion of a God." Since the human and the divine are analogous, if not identical, there was no reason at all to assume that humans weren't in a position to fully grasp nature's plan. Because of their intellectual nature, humans, even as their animal bodies rooted them firmly in the soil, enjoyed a privileged relationship with the Author of all things.[12]

In Agassiz's view, nothing in nature ever moved or shifted laterally, a point he would frequently make to counter Darwin's theory. Instead, the history of nature is one gradual rise—metaphorically as well as quite literally—from the ground, culminating in humankind. Thus we leave behind the snake in Paradise, in the dust to which it has been condemned. "As we ascend in the scale of animated beings we behold them raising their heads a little. Snakes have no feet, but they are able to elevate the head; and if we proceed farther we find successive types in which the position becomes an oblique one, until the head is raised more perpendicularly." To man alone is given the "vertical position, which allows him to make use of his hand and fingers and raise his eye directly toward the heavens." As we shall see, Agassiz's own flamboyant lecturing, in which the naturalist's hand and fingers, holding a specimen or a piece of chalk, becomes so important, itself becomes an illustration of his theory—and of the human privilege to handle God's creatures as we see fit.[13]

Agassiz's lectures were, literally, a sight to behold. Newspaper reporters marveled at the sheer athleticism of his performances—for them, the fact that he was ambidextrous and therefore capable of working on two diagrams at the same time was just icing on the cake. Transcripts of Agassiz's public lectures in American newspapers were sprinkled with phrases such as "illustrates from board" or, more extreme, "illustrates from diagrams which cover the whole wall of the hall." Some transcribers felt ready to throw in the towel: "It is difficult to convey a correct idea without these illustrations," interjected the reporter for the *New York Evening Post*. "Hence the pre-eminent value of Prof. Agassiz's lectures above any idea of them conveyed on paper."[14]

Agassiz didn't just *use* copious illustrations; he made them the *topic* of his lectures. One of his favorite party tricks was the reconstruction of a fossil fish from the most limited evidence, namely a single scale, or rather, a chalkboard outline of it. In real life, he had actually once been forced to do such a thing. Some time ago, he told his listeners in New York, someone in England had sent him the scale of a fossil fish, "and from it [I] drew the fish to which I considered it to belong." The imagined illustration appeared in the first installment of his work *Poissons fossiles*. A year later, the entire fish was found, and he included a drawing of it in another installment of his work. Now here was the surprise: "I have the satisfaction of saying that the two delineations do not differ in any essential way, even in the details." His imagined sketch and the illustrations taken from the real thing looked alike! Feigning humility, Agassiz lavished praise upon himself: "That all that can be done with precision I had the good fortune to be able to demonstrate in a rather striking manner." Loud applause from the audience.[15]

Enjoying the moment, Agassiz announced that now, in this room, today, he was repeating the experiment again, for the benefit of his distinguished listeners. After sketching out some typical modifications of the structure of the fins of fossil fish and a few examples of scales that he had found in his paleontological work, he paused for effect and said dramatically, "I will not try your patience by going into details, but I will only show you how easy it was, from the knowledge of these relations of the scales to other portions of the animal, to give the probable and approximative outline of a fish when you have had only a single scale as a starting point." More applause. "Let me draw a scale," said Agassiz. He began to sketch. "I will," he added, "make the scale of a size which will enable me to give the whole thing on the board." The following words we may imagine as being spoken while Agassiz had his back turned to his audience, his hands gliding rapidly over the board: "You see then what an easy task it is to draw scales of about the same form, perhaps forty in that line, and you will have to make a fish that is about as high as it is long. You at once draw your outline and when placing your scales you will find that they fit easily, and you draw them with as much precision as if you had the living model before you." But scales alone don't make a fish: "You have now got a fish without fins!" said Agassiz, mockingly. "The question is where are you to put the fins? And, again, what sort of a head are you to put to such a body?" Laughter from the audience. And Agassiz, hovering before his board, a little God of his creation, albeit with a French accent and a crumbling piece of chalk in his hand, explained, step by step, all the decisions he was making as he rapidly completed his imaginary fossil fish: "A fish which has a flat, ovate form like that will be a fish of not very rapid motion; and we know that all fishes not possessed of powers of rapid motion have rather elongated dorsal and anal fins, and that the caudal [i.e., tail] fin is not forked." Now Agassiz added the fins. Still, the fish lacked a head. No problem. Fossil fish with such a broad, flat body were usually not voracious and therefore wouldn't have long snouts, said Agassiz, turning to the blackboard again to give his fish a suitable, short-snouted, roundish head. Voilà! The fish was done, and so was Agassiz, who bowed graciously, again to the applause of his audience.[16]

Agassiz's show-and-tell was nothing new. When he was studying with him in Paris, Agassiz would have seen the great Cuvier perform similar feats, using a single bone of a fossil mammal found near Paris in order to restore several genera. Mindful that the more conservative among his new American admirers might indeed suspect him of showmanship, Agassiz hastened to point out that there was nothing miraculous about such reconstructions, as long as one knew there were limits. Some of Cuvier's disciples, he said, had gone further than they should, "giving even hair to these animals and dots to their colors! They accomplished all that, but there were as many lies as additions to the figures." The audience chuckled. Clearly, Agassiz wasn't one of those guys.[17] Spellbound, they watched him as he effortlessly transitioned from his chalk drawings to real specimens, drawing out one "leetle indiveedual" after another.[18] "I have here the vertebra of the alligator!" he would exclaim, or "I have here the lung of the snapping-turtle!" Sometimes he even performed mini-dissections for the benefit of his audience: "If, as I have done here, you remove the mantle," he said, holding up an oyster, "you see similar flat membranes, which are the gills." And if such minuscule procedures were a bit hard to visualize, Agassiz wasn't reluctant to use even his own body for display purposes. Holding up his hand, he demonstrated what really separated man and monkey: "The difference is here: We can open and close the thumb with each successive finger, which we cannot do with our toes." Applause.[19]

For Agassiz, the stubborn reality of the natural thing itself—an oyster, the hand of a man, a turtle's lung—proved the absurdity of the notion that a species could change, that animals could turn into something other than what their immediate ancestors had looked like. Evolutionary ideas were in reality "old-fashioned," he announced confidently during his New York lectures, remembering Cuvier's favorite target, Jean-Baptiste Lamarck. The latter's theory of transmutation—the view that species were not unalterable and that organisms, guided by new needs and changes in the environment, developed toward ever greater complexity—was vigorously rejected by Agassiz, as it had been by his former teacher.[20] We know now, of course, that it was Agassiz's own theory that was "old-fashioned" even then. But it is worth pointing out that his *methods* weren't old-fashioned at all. Agassiz's reliance on illustrations and, better still, on actual specimens changed the course of American instruction, ushering in progressive school curricula that centered on "object lessons." Beginning in the 1860s, the New York Public Schools superintendent Norman Allison Calkins, working with Agassiz's assistant Joel Asaph Allen, would develop teaching units, as we would say today, "on the shape, color, and qualities of . . . animals and plants and various other objects" that were intended to "precede and supplement" the conventional techniques used in elementary education.[21]

As Agassiz worked his magic in the lecture halls, a coalition of interested Bostonians was busily plotting to keep him in the States for good. In June 1847, Edward Everett, the president of Harvard, had successfully convinced the cotton manufacturer Abbott Lawrence to donate a substantial sum toward the creation of a new scientific school at Harvard that was to be named after him. It was to make use of the excellent resources already in place at Harvard (and the presence of scientists such as the botanist Asa Gray and the mathematician Benjamin Peirce) but also provide the funds for a new professorship. Abandoning his initial stipulation that the new school would focus on the applied sciences, Lawrence began to endorse Agassiz as a candidate for the new position. In September 1847, less than a year after arriving in the United States, Agassiz accepted. A few months later, the Harvard Overseers confirmed the appointment.[22]

Agassiz spent his first summer as a Harvard professor enjoying life to the fullest. Rallying newly acquired friends and students around him, he embarked on a specimen-collecting trip to Lake Superior, an excellent opportunity to solidify his reputation for fieldwork. The party, consisting of students from the Lawrence Scientific School at Harvard and the Dane Law School, seniors from Harvard College, the amateur enthusiasts Joseph P. Gardner and J. Elliot Cabot, and the naturalists Joseph Le Conte, Jules Marcou, and William Keller, left Boston on June 15, 1848, and returned— soaked, mosquito-bitten, and just plain tired—ten weeks later, on August 25.

The book that came out of the trip, *Lake Superior,* co-written by J. Elliot Cabot and Louis Agassiz, offered a blueprint for Agassiz's future literary ventures. For example, in the first part of the volume, called "Narrative," the voice of the scientist is framed by the more mundane observations of a nonscientist writer, J. Elliot Cabot, while the second part of the book consists of more formal papers about the natural history of the region. This is a move that Agassiz would repeat again and again: relinquishing authorship at least partially to someone else, he reemerges as a character within a narrative of his own making, a character with definable, quaint traits and inevitable props, in this case especially his portable blackboard, "consisting of a piece of painted linen on a roller." Instead of writing about himself, he has others write about him, elevating himself to a position that is both mythical and appealingly mundane. Cabot shows Agassiz, dissecting knife in hand, "with fishes little and big before him," engaged in reading the American landscape to amateurs and cognoscenti alike. His science appears in the form of quotations within Cabot's text. It has been said that we quote to taste greatness—and it is indeed such greatness that Cabot's text attaches throughout to the copious quotations from Agassiz.[23] "It is a remarkable fact," we hear Agassiz explain, authoritatively, to the men in his boat and to us at home, the readers of his book, "that the leading changes in the geological features of North America take place in a north and south direction. Thus the fissures forming the beds of the rivers, as those of the Connecticut, the Hudson, the Mississippi, and the rivers of Maine. In the Old World, on the contrary, most formations are parallel to the Equator, as the Alps, the Atlas, and the Himalayas."[24]

Agassiz's appealing oddness remains a topic of chief delight throughout Cabot's narrative: while the other members of his fishing expedition are clad in waterproof garments, insulated against the punishing weather, the Professor himself would lecture unprotected, "soaking in the canoe, enraptured by the variety of the scaly tribe, described and undescribed." Agassiz was funny but fearless. And so were, by virtue of their association with him, the members of his expedition. Cabot applied the mock-heroic mode also to the party as a whole, as in the description of the canoe they used, which was "distinguished by a frying-pan rising erect over the prow as figure-head, an importance very justly conferred on the culinary art in this wilderness, where nature provides nothing that can be eaten raw except blueberries."[25]

In truth, the trip had been more rigorous than any of these New Englanders had expected. The sun blistered their hands and faces, they had to take their baths in the icy water of the lake, and there was little relief from the no-see-'ems, mosquitoes, and black flies wherever they went—powerful obstacles to scientific curiosity: "One, whom scientific ardor tempted a little way up the river in a canoe, after water-plants, came back a frightful spectacle, with blood-red rings round his eyes, his face bloody, and covered with punctures." At night, though, they saw the northern lights, three bows arching across the sky, surrounded by flickering flashes of light, a sight that even the normally restrained, self-mocking Mr. Cabot found "beautiful." Crossing the lake in their canoes and hiking along the shore, they found few animals apart from loons, arctic woodpeckers, and occasionally a silent, solitary pigeon.[26]

Empty as this part of the country seemed, it allowed Agassiz to highlight an argument that would prove popular with American audiences: America was, he kept saying, really the Old World. Coming to Lake Superior was, wrote Cabot, "like being transported to the early ages of the earth, when the mosses and pines had just begun to cover the primeval rock." When the members of Agassiz's party de-

"Pic Island, from Camp Porphyry." Lithograph by Antoine Sonrel, based on a drawing by J. Elliot Cabot, from *Lake Superior: Its Physical Character, Vegetation, and Animals*, by Louis Agassiz, 1850.

cided to live it up one night near Fort Williams and dance the night away, no members "of the fair sex" showed up. This was a world intended for men only—real men, that is. The stark images accompanying the book, like the one shown here, add to the primitive effect Cabot wants to convey: uprooted trees, with roots still attached, in the foreground; blocky glacial erratics littering the shallow water in the middle distance; and mountainous ridges in the background. The scene looks like a recent transcript of geological action. As if resting after cataclysmic activity, nature seemed caught, as Cabot put it, in "a dead, dreamless sleep."[27]

In his role as the expedition's scribe, Cabot himself doesn't try particularly hard to establish himself as an informed observer. For example, he compares the Ojibway language to Plattdeutsch (Low German) and describes the Indians—who are on the brink of starvation wherever Agassiz's men go—as speaking, well, "Indian." But that naiveté made him a particularly receptive audience for Agassiz's blustery demonstrations in the field. "The Professor before starting showed us a rock at the south entrance of the bay, which he considered a proof positive of the correctness of the glacial theory." What Cabot saw was a granite plateau ground to an even surface that extended a few hundred yards down to the edge of the water, polished and scratched, with the scratches closer to the lake pointing more toward the west than the others. They could be, as the Professor pointed out, traced right into the water, which ruled out the possibility that some "floating body" had produced them. Water action, Agassiz remarked later the same day when he took the party to a beach, leaves the harder parts of a surface prominent, while glacial action grinds down the surface uniformly, scratching it in straight lines. What Agassiz's party understood, and what became increasingly clear to the reader, was that none of these features had been formed in "one creative act," like a bell forged in a furnace, but instead over a long, long time. Hence the need for the kind of science Agassiz propagated, one that relied on rigorously trained observers to keep track of the movements of God's mind throughout nature.[28]

On July 27, 1848, as Agassiz was enjoying himself on Victoria Island in Lake Superior, giving an extended lecture on the genesis of mineral veins in rock, Cecilie died in Freiburg, Germany. When he had made the decision to remain in Boston for good, Agassiz must have known that he would be severing permanently the fragile ties that connected him with his ailing wife. He never spoke about his reaction to her death. However, while he was busily perfecting his new American public persona, happily producing science talks for the use and profit of the masses, his other family, the transplanted "Hôtel des Neuchâtelois," was causing him trouble. A family friend from Switzerland, the Reverend Charles Louis Philippe Christinat, had joined the group in September 1847 in the three-story brick house on Webster Street in East Boston that Agassiz had rented as a combined home, laboratory, and studio.[29] Christinat took over the management of an increasingly chaotic ménage. An army of expatriates had assembled here, some useful (such as the painter Jacques Burkhardt and the lithographer Antoine Sonrel, who brought his printing equipment with him), others not so much. In April 1848, Agassiz moved his fractious household from Boston to a house he had rented on Oxford Street in Cambridge, which brought him closer to the university where he was now teaching but also drastically reduced the available space, with disastrous consequences. Soon as many as twenty-three people were staying with him, sleeping on mattresses all over the house.[30] Not surprisingly, the same annoying trivialities that had spoiled Agassiz's happiness in his traditional family would surface in this chaotic scientific family. Much of this had to do with Édouard Desor, who had gradually transformed his position, before Agassiz fully realized it, from assistant to master of the palace, assuming more and more responsibility even for Agassiz's scientific work and alienating others in Agassiz's orbit.[31] Desor's attempt to pass off some of Agassiz's research as his own—at least this is what Agassiz believed he wanted to do—led to a public falling out. Desor then launched unpleasant charges against Agassiz, including improper behavior with his Irish servant girl, Jane, and neglect of his "real" family back home.

When Agassiz sat down to list his charges against Desor, the most important ones concerned authorship. Even back in Switzerland, Desor had tried to get in on Agassiz's ice-age business with his own rather presumptuous (in Agassiz's eyes) narrative accounts, during which glaciers were traversed and mountains ascended. But what led to the decisive rupture between the two, and to Agassiz's impression that Desor was a scheming good-for-nothing rather than a devoted friend, were two publications: a catalog of echinoderms that Desor had published, adding himself as a co-author, in *Annales des sciences naturelles*, as well as a brief article on the embryology of starfish that he had managed to place in the *Proceedings of the Boston Society of Natural History*. Desor had—fraudulently, claimed Agassiz—renamed species that Agassiz had discovered (Agassiz invoked Professor Valenciennes of the Jardin des Plantes to certify that Desor had barely dropped in to examine the specimens kept there), and he had stolen the results of Agassiz's embryological work. Concluded Agassiz, "He probably thought that the time had come when I could not dispense with his services in the way of writing."[32] Of course, there is a great deal of disingenuousness in Agassiz's holier-than-thou attempt to accuse Desor of appropriating his ideas. Obviously, Desor had observed the master appropriator himself, and he had learned his lesson well. But no matter—Agassiz kicked Desor out of his house, beginning an ugly public battle during which each side tried to discredit the other.

The Harvard classicist Cornelius Felton and the young architect Edward Clarke Cabot tried to arbitrate between the two men, and failed. Agassiz, desperate for a way to resolve an intolerable situation and to end the rumors that were swirling around Boston and Cambridge, agreed to subject himself to what we would probably now call a mediation process. He and Desor each nominated a trusted person to serve on the committee (Desor picked D. Humphreys Storer, a Boston physician and ichthyologist, while Agassiz opted for his benefactor, John Amory Lowell), and the two nominees then chose a third member, the physician Thomas B. Curtis. The inquiry addressed all the matters in dispute between the two: that Desor had appropriated money as well as some of Agassiz's research, that he had mistreated Agassiz's assistant Charles Girard, that Agassiz had had improper relations with his Irish servant girl, and so forth. Both parties agreed to abide by the decisions of the committee.[33]

Some of the committee's investigative activity bordered on the ridiculous — the question as to whether Agassiz had tried on some new shirts in the presence of his maid Jane, for example — while other charges were summarily dismissed, as errors due to the Professor's imperfect familiarity with the English language. Agassiz's contention that Desor had stolen some of his work and simply renamed a genus that Agassiz had discovered in order to disguise his theft was easy to substantiate. The committee had seen one of the original specimens, still bearing Agassiz's tag, which they thought once and for all proved his right to claim the discovery. One particularly embarrassing item on the list was Agassiz's claim that Desor had been responsible for the breakdown of his marriage to Cecilie Agassiz or, in Agassiz's own uncharacteristically straightforward version, that he had been "previously the cause of Mr. Agassiz's domestic troubles and especially of Mrs. Agassiz's leaving her husband." In turn, Desor, who adamantly rejected the allegation, had threatened to divulge "what he knew of the past life of Prof. Agassiz in Europe" in order to "ruin him in America."

The question of Desor's involvement in Agassiz's marriage loomed large in the discreetly prying minds of the three gentlemen from Boston. Much of the evidence came from Agassiz's relatives or friends, and the logic the members of the makeshift tribunal employed was often patently absurd, dictated more by an underlying desire to please the illustrious naturalist than by a disinterested search for the truth.[34] Among the evidence introduced into the proceedings was a letter from Cecilie Agassiz's old childhood friend Cécile Guyot, who confirmed that Madame Agassiz was elated when she heard, during her final illness, that her husband had sent Desor packing, "stating that she attributed to his pernicious influence a great part of her domestic misfortunes." An even more damning document was a letter from Agassiz's mother, Rose Mayor Agassiz, dated November 1846, a month after Agassiz's arrival in the States, in which Rose expressed her concern that both Desor and Vogt had been living "profusely" at her son's expense: "You have shut your eyes but mine have remained open." Desor had become his master, she said, intent on sharing Agassiz's glory while also taking advantage of him financially and morally: "He has cared nothing for expense, since you paid all; abusing your confidence, he has possessed himself of all your most intimate secrets; if they are known, & have reached me, it is through *him*." Not to worry; she had burned his letters. Desor had not only pushed Agassiz's wife aside, but he had rendered his mother superfluous too. Wrote Rose Agassiz, "It would have been too hard a task for me to break the chain that binds you to this man." Now that Agassiz had left for America, though, a golden opportunity had arisen to get rid of Desor. Agassiz could now find himself a better and happier home "than your former one." Apparently Rose wasn't deterred by the fact that Cecilie was still alive as she wrote, "I have always hoped that an amiable wife would one day be your portion—to this end M. Desor must no longer partake of your labors . . . No woman will submit to his domination." Desor was presented throughout these documents as an almost mythical force, a one-man movement intended to wreck not only Agassiz's professional life but his home life too: he was Agassiz's new quasi wife, replacing Cecilie in his affections. And, ruling and dominating Agassiz, he was a quasi husband too. The committee was unfavorably impressed.

After collecting testimony from people as far away as Switzerland, Drs. Curtis and Storer and Mr. Lowell, on February 5, 1849, voted unanimously in favor of Agassiz on all points, though they also decided, as Felton and Cabot had before them, that Agassiz owed Desor the sum of $100 (more than $3,000 today) for work he had performed on *Principles of Zoölogy*, the textbook Agassiz claimed to have co-authored with Augustus Gould. Agassiz sent a check. He had been vindicated. A hollow victory, perhaps, given how his private life had suddenly been dragged into the limelight.[35] But there's no evidence that Agassiz minded too much.[36] Perhaps he felt that the committee's verdict had placed the seal of approval on his presence in America. The path seemed clear now.

Freshly widowed, Agassiz was eager to move on and embrace his new life. He sent for his son, Alexander, who marked his departure for the New World by jumping on the violin his mother had made him learn to play.[37] And Agassiz was actively courting the woman he would marry, on April 25, 1850, in Boston's Tremont Street Temple, Elizabeth Cary, from one of Boston's most respected families. His scientific family hadn't worked out, so why not try a new one, a real one this time? But just as things were beginning to go well, another member of the "Hôtel des Neuchâtelois," rather than quietly accepting his own inferior status, began to act up too.

Having suffered silently for many years, Charles Girard, the son of Swiss peasants, had become increasingly obsessed with the things he thought both Agassiz and Desor had done to hurt him. Eventually he left, compiling a voluminous package in which he addressed his treatment at the hands of Agassiz, recapping, in excruciating detail, the sad milestones in their failed relationship and interspersing English summaries with copies of the original letters he had written, in French, to Agassiz.[38] Girard retroactively cursed his harebrained decision to follow his flawed master to the States "in hope of receiving that long delayed reward," that is, payment for his services. Like a rejected son, Girard, in halting English, listed all the deprivations he had suffered in order to please someone who, as he now realized, had barely even noticed him: "For him I had withheld the circle of a family, for him I had sacrificed my personnel [sic] comfort, all the advantages of Society in order that all my time should be spent for him, belong to him." This dossier was Girard's "J'accuse." By turns naive, self-pitying, angry, and sanctimonious, Girard delivered an impassioned performance that lent a voice to all the things we may assume Cecilie Agassiz never dared to say out loud.

At the same time, Girard was adamant that he wasn't seeking publicity. No outsider—and especially no American—would be able to understand his close relationship with his teacher, which was, after all, a European thing, and something special, and wonderful too:

"The matter I have always thought that it should remain private, because it would hardly be understood by any of those that have not seen European society. Moreover, the position which I had at Prof. Agassiz, has no analogues in this country." Obviously, Girard was still deeply attached to Agassiz. In his dossier, he included a copy of a letter he had written to Agassiz in January 1850, a letter both gut-wrenchingly honest and theatrical. For ten long years, Girard said, had he done Agassiz's bidding, on bad days and on good days, in sickness and in health. During that period, he hadn't had time to think a single thought of his own—everything he had done for *him*, everything had reported to *him*—and this Agassiz, in their last furious conversation, had dared to call *égoïsme*. That fiend Desor had once told him that the only thing he was good for was "being fired"—well, look, now he was leaving on his own. Without any mentorship Girard had worked on his difficult tasks, which included describing the fish of Lake Superior for Agassiz's new book. And what thanks had he gotten for his efforts? "I have served you body and soul; my attachment to your person increased, but the more you grew in stature, the more I was subjected to jealous skirmishes. I wanted your absolution. What I gained was your condemnation. The sacrifice was complete."[39] Now he only wanted to be free.

In one of his interspersed comments written in English, Girard recalled how Agassiz had tried to keep him. "Prof. Agassiz, in an excited—but I thought—kind outbreak said that I was ungrateful towards him, that for a long time he had been thinking of making me an independent position and that just as the moment had come to bestow it upon me I was going to abandon this opportunity of his to do something for me." Agassiz even shed tears, whereupon Girard took his hands, held them and told him that "I would try to go along with him and do all what was in my power in order that he should never have to regret of having ever known me." Once again Agassiz offered to pay him; once again, nothing happened.

On November 20, 1850, Girard finally left Cambridge for good. But he wasn't done complaining. From the steamer *Bay State*, bound for New York, he wrote yet another letter, "the last, the very last." "Je suis parti—adieu" ("I am gone—good-bye"), the letter begins dramatically, only to launch on another round of settling scores. As if he were a son disinherited by a cruel father, Girard obviously still wanted Agassiz to fix things: "A promise made to a poor person is, for that person, a sacred thing; he believes in it as if it were a reality. To break one's word with him means wresting a fact away from him and not an idea; it means tearing his heart apart. A poor person's heart is simple and good; it distinguishes him from the person that deceives him." He took issue with Agassiz's claims that he had pulled him up from the gutter and fed him for ten years: "*Eh! Mon Dieu,*" he exclaimed, "my work was what has nourished me, work that you haven't done the half of; therefore, there's no merit at all to your claim that you have in such a manner raised and mentored me." If he had gotten anywhere in his scientific career, it was entirely because of his own efforts, not because Agassiz had ever given him special consideration. And here was Girard's parting shot, intended to hurt: although he had shared his life, in sickness and in health, and been close to him for such a long time, Agassiz had not told him that Cecilie Agassiz had died, an event about which, he added darkly, many sad pages were still to be written.[40] And it seemed that everyone but him, Girard, had known that Agassiz was about to marry again!

Girard eventually ended up in Washington, where he embarked on a fruitful partnership with the Smithsonian's Spencer Fullerton Baird. While Agassiz no longer wanted Girard around, he wasn't ready to allow him to become part of anyone else's scientific family. In fact, Agassiz went to the trouble of warning Baird never to entrust Girard with responsible research. Girard had no judgment, he told Baird, was "as obstinate as a mule," and needed to be led "with a high hand and kept in an entirely subordinate position."[41] Rodolphe Agassiz's larger-than-life shadow was hovering right behind Louis. But what became evident too was that this American Humboldt-to-be did not have the grace or generosity in his dealings with his adopted sons that the European Humboldt had once lavished on him.

As the keeper of Agassiz's collections, Girard knew only too well that Agassiz's success as a popular lecturer was tied to the nature of the evidence he had at his disposal. While he was losing people, he hoarded specimens. And as he was hoarding specimens, he hoped to gain people again — not so much fellow scientists as members of the general American public, the so-called amateurs, who became the largest and most grateful family he had ever commanded. If Alexander von Humboldt was loved by the bricklayers of Berlin, Agassiz was confident he could win the trust of the farmers, merchants, and ministers of New England by the sheer force of personal example and by showing everyone that he was serious about natural history. When he first came to Boston, Agassiz quickly developed a reputation not only for raiding the fish markets of Boston for specimens (sometimes fifty a day) but also for carrying live animals around with him. Jules Marcou remembered that he would beg for a specimen he coveted "like a spoiled child who wanted a long-desired toy."[42]

Word got around quickly in Boston about Agassiz's mania for collecting. The Unitarian minister Thomas Hill, for example, liked to talk about an excursion by rail to Littleton, New Hampshire, led by Agassiz himself in the summer of 1849, the year after his Lake Superior trip. Hill, who was to become president of Harvard in 1862 after the death in office of President Cornelius Felton, noted with pleasure how well-rounded the Swiss professor was: "I was surprised, during the journey, to find that Agassiz knew the plants along the road as well as I did. I never knew him to make any mistake in naming a wild plant, but once; and then it was a mere slip of the tongue, calling a Lespedeza a Hedysarum." The trip started as a typical pleasure jaunt, with a local train picking up the various members of the party (among them Professor Felton) in Charlestown, Cambridge, and Waltham. As they were waiting in South Acton for the train that would take them to New Hampshire, Agassiz's son, Alexander, fresh off the boat, began to hunt butterflies with a gauze net stuck to a pole, and that's when Agassiz let go, excitedly jumping and skipping around in search of butterflies too. "Agassiz seeing a fine specimen on the wing called to the boy to come and catch it. 'Alexe! Vite! Beau Papillon.'" Apparently, Agassiz's exhortations were often premature: "The boy ran up and seeing that his fine butterfly was a black beetle, burst into such a merry laugh, that none of us, not even Mr. Felton himself, could resist joining; and 'Beau Papillon' became the watch-word of our party."

From Littleton to Franconia they took a coach, but they spent more time outside the conveyance, running alongside it, than sitting inside it. And what a spectacle that must have been: a half-grown boy and a bunch of adults jumping around and "turning over stones and sticks, for hidden reptiles or insects; looking on the underside of leaves to discover butterflies, or snails; rapping the bushes, to start lit-

tle moths, and occasionally shouting one to another 'Beau Papillon.'"
The driver finally couldn't stand it anymore and asked Professor Felton, who had remained on the seat next to him, who these men were.
Felton replied, "They are a set of naturalists, from an institution near
Boston," meaning Harvard, of course. Their enthusiasm was conta-
gious: a solemn-looking man, who had so far silently traveled with
them, also got out and, seeing a remarkably beautiful butterfly, made
a dash for it, screaming, at the top of his voice, "Beau Papillon."

When the stage traveling in the opposite direction met theirs and
the driver of that one wanted to know too who in God's name these
strange men were, Agassiz's driver responded, "in a confidential whis-
per, 'They are a set of naturals from that insane asylum near Boston.
Their keeper just told me so.'" (He was probably thinking of McLean
Hospital, then known as the McLean Asylum for the Insane.) Hill's
appreciative vignette is an eloquent testimony to how Agassiz's widely
publicized craziness—his enthusiastic, no-holds-barred desire to
stockpile specimens, his excitement to be in a country with sheer un-
limited natural resources—had become an indication of his value to
American society.[43]

And while the Americans thus learned to appreciate Agassiz, they
would have been pleased that the Swiss professor's commitment to
his new American home had firmed up too. Agassiz was not going
back to Europe. "I have identified myself with American life as much
as one can, when two cultures are as different as ours and the American are," Agassiz wrote to his friend Achille Valenciennes, the former collaborator of Cuvier's at the Jardin des Plantes, in 1856. His
beneficial influence on "la vie Américaine" was growing every day,
and it was a distinct pleasure to see new scientific societies spring up
"like mushrooms" in towns founded just yesterday. Agassiz had found
his mission: to turn the raging passion for action that was one of the
hallmarks of the American character into disinterested science. Valenciennes had just told him about the appointment of a new chair
of comparative anatomy in the Jardin des Plantes, Antoine Étienne
Serres. Agassiz responded that such things seemed remote to him
now that he was in America. Besides, Serres had merely been re-
hashing ideas that he, Agassiz, had first formulated. The tables had
turned. With the deeply unoriginal Serres in a place formerly occu-

pied by Cuvier and the mediocre Jean Pierre Flourens, an expert on the nervous systems of rabbits and pigeons, appointed to the Collège de France, French science had been thrown back by half a century, joked Agassiz. America, thanks to him, had the upper hand now.[44] And in a draft letter to Sir Philip de Malpas Grey Egerton, a British paleontologist whom he had met in Switzerland years earlier, Agassiz bragged about how well located he was in the United States, especially when working in his seaside laboratory on Nahant, the peninsula east of Boston where his new wife's family owned a summer house overlooking Nahant Bay. On one side of him there were, a mere five days away, the reefs of Florida, while on the other side Europe and the Jardin des Plantes beckoned. All the vessels of the Coast Survey were, Agassiz claimed, at his command, "from the borders of Nova Scotia to Mexico and if I choose all along the American coast of the Pacific." Why leave?[45]

Agassiz's popularity in America transcended class as well as regional boundaries. The critic Edwin Percy Whipple compared Agassiz's success to that of the "Swedish nightingale," the celebrity soprano Jenny Lind, and, for good measure, also threw the Pied Piper of Hamelin into the mix: "His fame was so diffused that no queer living thing was caught in wood or river, no strange rock unearthed in opening the track for a new railroad, that was not sent to him as the one man in the country that could explain it."[46] Visitors to Agassiz's Oxford Street house could testify to the ubiquity of "queer" things. Turtles, for example, were everywhere, drifting glassy-eyed in jars, piled up as dried specimens on the shelves, or, if they were lucky enough not to have been dissected yet, hiding under the stairs and floating in the bathtubs.[47] And yet there was always room for more. When the word was out that Dr. Agassiz wanted turtles, the citizens delivered. Henry David Thoreau sent a Blanding's turtle from Walden Pond. And a school principal named John Whipple Potter Jenks from Middleboro, Massachusetts, one early Sunday morning harvested some fresh turtle eggs for Agassiz and, using his horse to intercept a freight train, delivered the precious cargo within three hours to Agassiz's doorstep.[48]

Agassiz's undaunted turtle-deliverer, braving the odds as if he were the Paul Revere of natural history carrying a message to the rebel troops, wasn't an isolated phenomenon. Agassiz's Barnum-esque acquisitiveness reached out to the entire country. When, in the summer of 1853, he announced his intention to publish a "Natural History of the Fishes of the United States of America," thousands of circulars were distributed, instructing citizens in the proper mode of collecting and then properly shipping dead fish to Cambridge. And lo and behold, amateur collectors from all over the nation rose to the challenge, proud to be recognized as members of the national family of science Agassiz was assembling. Many of the original recipients of Agassiz's circular would in turn recruit others—local guides, farmers, soldiers—to help them collect for Agassiz, and Agassiz's extended family grew even larger. Take William Chauvenet, a mathematics professor at the Naval Academy in Annapolis, Maryland, who wrote to tell Agassiz that "his" fisherman Joe Parkinson, who doubled as a watchman at the academy, was all aflutter about Agassiz's call for specimens: "He is going to work at once to get barrel and jars and whiskey and alcohol and is studying your circular with all his mental powers."[49]

Not all the correspondents immediately grasped the extent to which they were getting involved in serious *scientific* work. A physician from Memphis, Tennessee, Milton Sanders, honestly told Agassiz that he had always preferred fish on his dinner table rather than in a specimen jar. "The subject of fishes has claimed but little of my attention," he admitted. There were, he joked, several varieties of fish caught locally, which were "not unpleasant to discuss immediately after taken from the skillet," but his knowledge of ichthyology really went no further. Now, however, the seeds of curiosity had been sown. In the creeks and bayous around Memphis were large numbers of what Dr. Sanders had always cavalierly referred to as "minnows." Now he was beginning to suspect that these might in fact be different varieties of fish. One could always hope: "Even if a single specimen of a new variety should be found among them, I shall consider myself amply rewarded for the little trouble I may put myself to in procuring them."[50]

Silvanus Thayer Abert, a civil engineer from Pennsylvania who was currently on assignment in South Carolina, also offered to do all he could. He would love to collect, he said, without exception, "such specimens of the zoology of the region as come within my reach." And he apologized profusely that when it came to "Science" (which he spelled with a capital *S*) he was merely an "Amateur" (that word, for good measure, he capitalized as well), though he was hopeful that "at some future period" he would become "more intimately acquainted with its facts and the great ideas to which they lead." He promised that he would extend his collecting efforts also to marine specimens (he'd even travel to Beaufort, for Agassiz's sake) and would distribute Agassiz's circular widely. He did have a question, though, about the toad he had recently obtained, a horned toad, he thought, "altho' its motion is rather that of running than loafing." It had come to him all the way from Vera Cruz in the Gulf of Mexico, and it wasn't pretty: a grayish colored reptile, its head was covered with hard points that tapered into horns. "It is still alive," he informed Agassiz. "I am in doubt whether to include in my collection, as they are far from being rare." It is not clear what he expected Agassiz to do in the matter and whether the toad survived.[51]

Some of the correspondents were intimately familiar with Agassiz's work. E. R. Andrews from Ohio, for example, had read Agassiz's *Lake Superior* from cover to cover and let himself be inspired by it in his own survey of the Youghiogheny River in West Virginia: "I explored the Youghy & its tributaries in that vicinity quite thoroughly & have brought home all varieties I found." Some species he hadn't been able to collect and that annoyed him: "I could find nothing of Rafinesque's 'Black Trout' which he assigns to the Youghy—nor could I learn from the oldest and most intelligent fishermen that such had ever been seen." Agassiz marked that passage in red. He also underlined a promise Andrews made in the next paragraph regarding the Ohio River: "My collections from this region are increasing slowly. I have engaged a good Ohio River fisherman to save for you a full sorte [*sic*] of all he catches this fall & winter." Andrews, who apparently didn't shy away from spending his own money, was a man after Agassiz's heart. And he even thanked him for his support: "Your approval of such an undertaking affords me the highest pleasure." What more could a naturalist ask for? Agassiz was probably so absorbed in the promise of even more specimens that he skipped the next passage, where Andrews expressed the fear that without proper "Books" to aid him (he capitalized the word), he wouldn't be able accomplish much that was worthy of Agassiz's high standards.[52]

More than 150 years later, these men live on in their eager notes, in their desire to know more about their own local environment, and, above all, in the seriousness with which they approached their self-imposed tasks. Agassiz's circular brought excitement into their lives, the chance not only to collect a few fish but also to collect themselves, the possibility to think of themselves as belonging to something larger than an engineering detail in South Carolina, as being engaged in something more broadly significant than teaching mathematics to naval recruits in Maryland or setting someone's broken bone in Memphis, Tennessee.

Even the U.S. senator Charles Sumner proved not to be immune to the lure of Agassiz's personality. Buying fish in the market was never the same for him after he had read Agassiz's circular. Now he'd become a collector too. "This forenoon,—walking though the market—I stopped, as is my custom, at the fish-stalls, particularly to take a look at the eels, which our Izaak Walton calls 'the Helena of fishes,' & also to enjoy the various stripes on the back of the mackerel, when my attention was arrested by a small fish, which at first I took for a flounder, but which then I saw differed from any thing fishy within my experience." Sumner casts himself as an expert and connoisseur (someone who goes to the market every day, not only to buy fish but to admire them from an aesthetic point of view) as well as the ordinary man on the street with an interest in "any thing fishy." This is the Sumner lost to history—playful, comical, subtly allusive, not the ponderous egomaniac glued to his lectern in Congress: "On inquiry, I was told that it was caught yesterday, by a net, in the Mystic River, & that, though a large number of persons, amounting, it was said, even to a 'thousand' had seen it, nobody knew what it was, and had ever seen any thing like it before." Sumner had a keen ear for the way fishmongers talk, their easy hyperbole and grandiloquent assurance. But his letter is also an indirect tribute to his native city, both gritty and magical enough that one of the rivers surrounding it (and an aptly named one) would yield this mystery find.[53] Within a few lines, the unidentifiable fish had been elevated from something fishy to The

Unknown Fish or "*l'innominato*," as the multilingual Sumner announced: "For your sake & the sake of science I secured *l'innominato*, & now send him to you in a strawberry box. And I have promised the dealer in the market to let him know your report of the monster. What is it?" Sumner's "*l'innominato*" was a reference to a dark, mysterious character, a robber baron who undergoes a surprising conversion, in the Italian writer Alessandro Manzoni's novel *I promessi sposi* (*The Betrothed*, published in 1827). Sumner could obviously assume that Agassiz would get this "high culture" joke the same way he would understand the more popular allusion to P. T. Barnum's displays of a "connecting link" between humankind and the animal world, the "What-is-It," a "thing," as Barnum wrote, "not to be called *anything* by the exhibitor."[54] And now the Unknown Fish was traveling in a strawberry box to Cambridge, in pursuit of the one man who, unlike the "thousands" of self-declared fishmongering experts in Boston's Haymarket, would surely recognize it straightaway and would bestow upon it its rightful name: "On inquiry at Mr. Cary's, I was led to believe that you are now at Cambridge," wrote Sumner in a postscript. "Accordingly, I send the fish there, trusting that he may surely find you."[55] Whether or not Sumner received the desired information, later exchanges showed that he stayed on friendly terms with Agassiz, sending potential donors as well as cases of excellent wine his way.[56]

As the fish from South Carolina, Tennessee, and Boston were piling up in Cambridge, Agassiz was ready to take his plans to the next level. From the beginning, he had envisioned a museum at Harvard: "Without collections lectures will remain deficient," he informed Harvard president Edward Everett in February 1848.[57] With support among his peers and ordinary Americans steadily rising, Agassiz waited for the right moment to address the topic publicly. He did so for the first time in May 1854, in a letter to Abbott Lawrence, the man who had made his American appointment possible in the first place. Conveniently, Agassiz had just been offered a professorship at a new scientific school in Zurich, later known as the Eidgenössische Technische Hochschule. Immediately, he embarked on a game still played by academics today, using outside offers as a bargaining chip. "I will not say I have not been tempted by the offer," he told Abbott Lawrence. But he would never take such an opportunity to ask anything for himself. "I would not consider it right." But then, the folks in Zurich had promised him a museum. "You can certainly not find it impertinent if under these circumstances I take the liberty of recalling to your mind a vague plan of another building connected with the Sc. [Scientific] School respecting which you once asked my opinion." Remember the museum I asked you for? "I am ready to devote all my energies to it."

He couldn't simply continue to solicit specimens the way he had been doing so far, using up all his spare time to forge contacts with amateur collectors all over the country and putting up his own money to store their collections in an old bathhouse in Cambridge. "While I work in that way the years pass & I am unable to publish the results of my investigations, which might otherwise contribute to the advancement of science & not remain sealed up in my portfolios." So far, he had paid the enormous sum of over $3,800 in cash (about $102,000 in today's money) for the arrangement and preservation of the collections he had personally assembled, collections that had de facto become the property of Harvard.[58] "Yet you know my salary is only $1,500," Agassiz pointed out acidly. "As I have nothing but what I earn; I must spend half my time away from Cambridge to make more & thus constantly interrupt my studies & fritter away my strength merely to enlarge & keep in order a collection which is after all no longer my own." This was the supreme irony of his situation. He knew he could be everything to America that he had promised to be, and yet he lacked the resources. He really didn't want to move again: "All my sympathies are now with this country, my best affections are here; I have strength enough to fight my way through, but I am saddened by the thought that the means at my command do not allow me to make the best use of my opportunities & abilities." He also reminded Lawrence of his incredible popularity: "I have for instance established the most extensive correspondence over the whole continent. I have written more than 2000 letters & distributed over 4000 circulars in behalf of the Museum during the past year which now brings in more specimens than I can personally take care of."[59] Unfortunately, Lawrence died a year later, before he could help Agassiz with his museum (though he did leave money in his will for Agassiz's future salary needs).

Unlike Humboldt, Agassiz did not enjoy the continued patronage of a king. But he was planning his still nonexistent museum around Humboldtian principles: he wanted it to be vast, cosmic, brimming with displays showing Nature at a glance, unlike the Jardin des Plantes, with its countless drawers and closed cases. Driven by the conviction—not one that Humboldt would have shared—that science could solve the puzzle of life, Agassiz envisioned a completely transparent collection, one in which natural things might reveal themselves to us all at the same time, without the crutch of explanatory narratives.[60] To use one of his favorite metaphors, he wanted his museum to be an ever-expanding library of all the volumes of natural history ever written, while at the same time he also wanted it to be only one Book, a fully accessible record of God's fully transparent message to man, one the visitor could read without really having to read it, the way Harriet Beecher Stowe's Uncle Tom approached the Bible: "There it lay, just what he needed, so evidently true and divine that the possibility of a question never entered his simple head."[61] Agassiz's museum was to be the institutional equivalent of Humboldt's *Naturgemälde*, a cosmos in miniature, in which the whole, the "great magical picture of nature," would be more than the sum of its parts: unity in diversity.[62]

However, Agassiz's two goals—compiling an inexorably growing library of specialized books and painting, in bold strokes, the grand picture of Nature itself—would soon turn out to be well-nigh incompatible. What Agassiz first and foremost needed was space. His makeshift shelter for specimens on the Charles River, a former bathhouse thirty feet long and fifteen feet wide, was bursting at the seams. Specimens were also piling up in the basement of Harvard Hall. Help finally came when Francis Calley Gray, a fellow of Harvard College, left $50,000 for the museum (more than $1.2 million in today's money), to which the Massachusetts legislature and Agassiz's subscribers added their share. By November 1859, the first floor of the new building on Oxford Street was already done. When young Addison Emery Verrill from Maine joined Agassiz's staff in 1859, his new boss was exuberant: all existing museums, especially the European ones, in which things were purposely kept away from the visitors, were terrible. His new future museum, by contrast, was going to be great, "the *best* and *most useful* of any in the world but also the *best looking*." He told Verrill that ordinary visitors would be guided into the purpose of the museum immediately upon entering, namely, when they found themselves in the so-called synoptic room, the "epitome of the whole animal kingdom."[63]

This room, where the range of animal life could be understood "at one view" and "at a glance," assumed iconic importance in Agassiz's public statements about his projected museum. In 1868, almost ten years after he had founded the museum, Agassiz would still tell the Massachusetts legislature about it, in terms that suggested that this room was just about to be finished.[64] One wall would be devoted to the Mammalia, he said, the type "to which we ourselves belong." He would show animals in stuffed form, as skeletons, as fossils, and as embryos, so that their colors, their structure, their history in past ages, and their growth as individuals would be immediately evident. The same part of the wall would also feature lower vertebrates like birds, fish, and reptiles. Amphibian animals, such as frogs, toads, and salamanders, would be located on the wall's other half. The insects and worms would be placed on the short western wall, adjacent to the higher mammals and facing the mollusks on the opposite side. On the large wall opposite the vertebrates, the wall with the windows, were, Agassiz fantasized, the Radiata, that is, the starfish, corals, and sea urchins. For Agassiz, it mattered a great deal where each specimen was placed and what precisely it was next to.[65] As Agassiz saw it, his synoptic room was not an artifact; rather, it was a direct echo of the relationships in nature itself. Nature, rightly understood, didn't need human interpreters.

In addition to his synoptic room, Agassiz also envisioned rooms devoted to each part of the animal kingdom, with each of them impressing on the visitor its "fullness, richness, diversity, endless variety, and complications of form." Those additional rooms would represent different faunal areas, the succession of animals in geological time, and embryological series. In this museum, visitors would not view specimens in isolation but would look at them as parts of sets, to be compared and contextualized within the continually unfolding whole that was infinitely bigger than each set, though at least in theory fully comprehensible to all those who'd dare to look. "This museum was to be unlike any other museum ever formed," he bragged to Verrill and his fellow students, promising that it would be "the greatest institution of the kind in the world," an oasis of liberalism in a sea of illiberal approaches to museum-making—provided, of course, that Verrill and his mates would work for Agassiz with a "will unceasing and serious" and without expecting to get paid much.[66]

On November 13, 1860, the new museum on Oxford Street opened its doors to the public. And yet it was far from finished. In fact, Agassiz's great museum, the place where exploration and teaching were supposed to go hand in hand and amateurs would mingle with professionals and professionals with amateurs,[67] never came to fruition, or at least not in the way he had seen it in his dreams. It seems necessary to fast-forward this book's narrative by a few years to get a sense of what became of Agassiz's grand plan. Over the next ten years or so, a nightmarish scenario unfolded behind these brick walls, with specimens from all sides, wanted and unwanted, crowding in on Agassiz and his staff, a kind of return of the repressed, the rebellion of sheer stuff against order, economy, predictability, the revenge of the broom against apprentices *and* the sorcerer.[68] Responsible for his collecting disaster was not only Agassiz's greediness (though that played a role), but also an unresolved conflict at the heart of his museum concept. Agassiz believed that showing must supersede telling; he thought that the more he showed, the more self-evident the realms of the animal world would become. This meant too that Agassiz just couldn't stop collecting. "Imagine yourself unpacking and arranging one hundred thousand specimens acquired for the museum within the last six months," he wrote to his brother-in-law Tom Cary in 1860,[69] and all this "in addition to all the contributions I have received from friends of the institution in San Francisco & elsewhere." Could Tom imagine the weight that was upon him every day? Although he had a dozen young men, and sometimes women too, "hard at work" in the building, he couldn't process the incoming packages fast enough to prevent huge pile-ups of unopened boxes. It was gratifying to see how now even the European museums, "informed of our rapid additions" especially from the Pacific, were all begging for a share.

The consequences of such no-holds-barred collecting became only too evident to a committee that visited his museum in 1864. They found specimens everywhere: in casks, jars, and in boxes, some arranged and labeled, some not. They were all crowded together, "waiting for room in which to be displayed for the purposes of instruction." Even the roof was taken up.[70] Under such circumstances, the promised important insights into the geographical distribution of species—a question that Agassiz believed had to be settled satisfactorily before anyone could pretend to know anything about the origins of biological diversity—weren't forthcoming, not any time soon.

Agassiz's assistants knew that things weren't headed in a good direction. In 1865, Alexander Agassiz, who had taken over the directorship temporarily while his father was amassing even more specimens in Brazil, complained that the number of exhibition rooms was "not large enough to enable us to follow the plan originally laid out for the arrangement of the specimens." The museum was losing its instructiveness, if it had ever had any, and Alexander predicted that this defect would become more glaringly evident each year. With boxes pouring in from abroad, working conditions in the museum had become precarious: "I would call the attention of the trustees to the unsafe condition of the cellar for storing the alcoholic collections."[71]

Things quickly went from bad to worse. In 1866, even Louis Agassiz conceded that something was wrong. His beloved museum had become, he wrote in his annual report for the Massachusetts legislature, "rather a store-house, than a well-arranged scientific collection." But boxes, barrels, and bones continued to accumulate, crowding basements, temporary shelves, and passageways. Sighed Agassiz, "The museum overflows from garret to cellar."[72] In 1870, Agassiz lamented the want of room that had prevented him from making his museum accessible to the public in a meaningful way. But a year later, "rapid growth" was still the buzzword. Agassiz never connected the dots.[73] Humboldt's warning that Agassiz was spreading himself too thin had come true. A Humboldtian *Naturgemälde* depended on a balance between the whole and its parts. In Agassiz's museum, the parts had crowded out the whole.

It was in the midst of this situation that Agassiz received an invitation to be the keynote speaker at a celebration the Boston Society of Natural History was hosting on September 14, 1869, Alexander von Humboldt's hundredth birthday. All over the United States, Humboldt, for whom cities, mountain peaks, and bays had been named, was being fêted. In Pittsburgh, where Ulysses S. Grant was in attendance, the festivities included a procession, the laying of a cornerstone for a monument, and the transmission of "electric greetings"

in the form of a telegram to Humboldt's German protégé, the chemistry professor Justus von Liebig. In New York's Central Park, the
Humboldt Monument Association unveiled a bronze bust, recently
imported from Germany; and the citizens of Milwaukee had piled
tropical flowers and astronomical instruments on the stage they had
set up for the occasion.[74] But only Boston had Agassiz to offer.

Agassiz instantly accepted the invitation. And instantly he panicked. He reserved a room at the Boston Public Library exclusively for
his use and worked there three or four days a week, from nine o'clock
in the morning to three o'clock in the afternoon. More than two hundred volumes in different languages were delivered to his desk, and
he skimmed everything that Humboldt had ever written, minus one
pamphlet, which could not be found anywhere in the States, according to the Reverend Robert C. Waterston, the chair of the committee
in charge of the Humboldt festivities, to whom Agassiz sent anxious
little notes describing his progress: "My friends will never know what
anxieties I have to go through on this occasion." He wrote out a draft,
"not exactly as I would like to deliver it but such as I may be compelled
to read should the occurrences of the day unfit me for an extemporized discourse." This was truly out of character for a lecturer who
prided himself on his ability to speak without notes. Worrying that he

Ticket for Louis Agassiz's Centennial Lecture on Humboldt, Boston Society of Natural History, September 14, 1869.

might lose his train of thought, Agassiz went even a step further and had his notes typeset, just in case.[75]

As his museum was slipping away from him, Agassiz once again needed his former spiritual father to prop him up. In his speech, given in Boston's Music Hall, Agassiz held forth about Humboldt's mind-boggling productivity, his versatility, his many-sidedness: Humboldt was "ever active, ever inventive, ever suggestive, ever fertile in re-source." Getting caught up in the passion of the moment, it seemed at times as if Agassiz, in speaking about Humboldt, was really speaking about himself: "His life was associated with the political growth and independence of the New World, as it was intimately allied with the literary, scientific, and artistic interests of the Old."[76] Note the differ-ence in the size of the typeface on the tickets distributed to the pub-lic: after so many years, Humboldt's name still dominates that of his former disciple, here identified by his academic credentials. But Agas-siz knew what he had going for him: unlike Humboldt, as everyone in the audience would have realized, Agassiz had not just visited the New World; he had stayed. Wasn't he speaking to them now in one of the largest public halls in the world?

Later that day, during a celebration in Boston's Horticultural Hall, a new scholarship in Humboldt's honor was announced, "to be for-ever devoted to the aid of students of Natural History in the Museum of Comparative Zoology at Cambridge." Honoring Humboldt meant honoring Agassiz after all—so much so that when rumors circulated in the papers that Agassiz had in fact founded the scholarship him-self, he hastened to assure everyone that this hadn't been the case: "It would have been very ungracious in me," he wrote to Waterston, "and would have shown, to say the least, a great want of delicacy, had I sug-gested an endowment for the Museum in which I am personally inter-ested. It was, as you know, a proposition made spontaneously, without any reference to me."[77] If honoring Humboldt, in late 1860s America, meant honoring Agassiz, honoring Agassiz meant honoring his mu-seum.

But what museum? In a sense, Louis Agassiz's Museum of Compara-tive Zoology became the first *virtual* natural history museum ever—a vision rather than reality, a figment of the imagination, an impossible dream endlessly deferred. The citizens of Boston and Cambridge, when they did get a chance to visit Agassiz's crowded rooms, never felt that they saw anything other than the "Agassiz Museum" (the name under which it was widely known), anything other than one man's insightful version of nature: an artifact, an abstraction, drawn or rather *with*drawn from nature itself. The critic Edwin Percy Whipple, one of Agassiz's most tireless cheerleaders, portrayed the museum director as a kind of latter-day Saint Francis, so appealing and kind that even the "most evil members of the animal kingdom" were virtually begging their master to be included in his museum. There, under "the literal 'Speakership' of Agassiz," guided by a man "who was alone capable of being the interpreter of their language, so that its signs could be clearly understood by the human race," they would begin their new existence as museum displays. At least, and Whipple couldn't resist the tasteless pun, they were in "excellent spirits."[78]

Whipple's fantasy of a grateful parliament of stuffed or pickled predators with Agassiz as their faithful translator is not an outlandish one. As any visitor to the "Sue" store at the Field Museum in Chicago can attest, there are countless books, games, and toys featuring the dinosaur reawakened, from skeletal desiccation, to vibrant life and activity. Confronted with death, decay, and immobility, we like to think of life, color, movement. During one of his visits to the Agassiz Museum, the publisher James T. Fields took a shine to one of Agassiz's turtles and immediately went home to write a poem about it, "The Turtle and Flamingo: A Song for My Little Friends," inspired perhaps by the recent publication of *Alice in Wonderland*.[79] In Fields's poem, Agassiz's gutted, petrified turtle becomes young again, a lively young Lothario who lives on the river Jingo and falls in love with—the rhyme requires it, though science forbids it—a beautiful flamingo! Wheezing with desire, the turtle asks the "perfectly modelled flamingo" for her hand: "You blazingly beauteous flamingo! / You turtle-absorbing flamingo! You inflammably gorgeous flamingo!" It turns out that the flamingo is up on her zoology. Mercilessly she rejects the blundering reptile: "I'm an ornithological wonder of grace, / And you're an illogical turtle,—/ A waddling, impossible turtle! / . . . / A highly improbable turtle!" Depressed, the turtle departs and falls asleep, only to be "gobbled up" by the greedy naturalist, the "turtle-dissecting Agassiz." The speaker ends the poem by inviting his young readers—for Fields had intended this poem for children—to join him on a visit to Agassiz's museum:

> Go with me to Cambridge some cool pleasant day,
>   And the skeleton-lover I'll show you;
> He's in a hard case, but he'll look in your face
>   Pretending (the rogue!) he don't know you!
>   Oh, the deeply deceptive young turtle!
>   The double-faced, glassy-cased turtle!
>   The *green*, but a very *mock* turtle!

What the visitors found at the Agassiz Museum, Fields's poem implies, was not nature itself, waddling turtles and graceful flamingoes, but skeletons under glass. Agassiz himself liked to say that his massive collecting served a practical purpose, the creation of capital for his museum, a perfectly reasonable explanation if one ignores the fact that often even Agassiz himself couldn't locate the specimens among the piles of boxes that he wanted to swap with other institutions. In fact, Agassiz's messy museum didn't often look like the one described in Fields's poem. And so here's another hypothesis: could it be that Agassiz, Humboldt's ambiguous gift to America, with his nonstop, feverish hoarding of all kinds of material, wanted to stave off indefinitely that moment of glassy-cased finality mocked in Fields's text? Agassiz's science depended on the idea that there is an end to all science, a moment of clarity when all specimens and natural facts have assumed their rightful places and we see the world as God sees it. And yet it also depended, crucially, on there not being an end, ever—because this moment of clarity would also mean the end of science as we know it, an end to the traveling, collecting, writing, drawing, sifting, weighing, cutting, comparing, stuffing, and displaying of which Agassiz was so fond. In this respect, Agassiz did finally most fully resemble his old mentor Humboldt. His museum had become the equivalent of the latter's monumental, forever unfinished *Voyage aux régions équinoxiales*, a specter evoked by Humboldt himself in his letter to Agassiz of December 2, 1837. From a distance, the ghostly German scientist beckoned, carrying under his arm all those still-unwritten pages.

4

DARWIN'S BARNACLES, AGASSIZ'S JELLYFISH

L OUIS AGASSIZ'S WORLD, in which each living thing occupies its assigned place in a taxonomic system and each scale tells us all we need to know about the fish to which it belongs, may seem static to some, frozen in predictability. But as we have seen in the last two chapters, *e pur si muove,* it moves nevertheless. In his mind, glaciers shifted and descended, fossils floated, jellyfish undulated, and fish frolicked in rivers too deep ever to be exhausted by fishermen. If rocks defined one pole of his imagination, water was the other one. Louis Agassiz was a marine biologist long before he had beheld an ocean.

And now, for the first time, settling down in his house on Webster Street in East Boston in the spring of 1847, he was living next to one. Agassiz was barely able to contain his excitement over being able to see, for the first time and in the flesh, some of the creatures he had studied for so long only as fossils or preserved under glass in a museum. The sea and its manifold inhabitants held powerful sway over his imagination, as they did over many of his Victorian contemporaries. Now that the surface of the earth had been mostly mapped and the animals inhabiting it had been described and classified, exploring the depths of the sea became the next great challenge. Fueled by accessibly written handbooks such as British naturalist Philip Henry Gosse's *The Aquarium* (1854), Charles Kingsley's *Glaucus* (1855), or

George Henry Lewes' *Sea-Side Studies* (1858), keeping those fantastical underwater creatures in one's parlor turned into a popular pastime. Americans went crazy for aquariums, which could be endlessly and easily restocked after each rock-pooling excursion: sea anemones were less troublesome to keep around the house than a hippopotamus, George Henry Lewes joked.[1] For those who shied away from the effort, public museums offered lavish displays of live marine animals. In 1858, the Boston Aquarial Gardens opened its doors.

Agassiz, never one to stimulate the public's interest without trying to take charge of it, had focused on animals that no one would be able to keep in an aquarium. From the fossil fish that had preoccupied him during his years in Neuchâtel, creatures cast in stone, Agassiz moved on to organisms that seemed to consist of nothing but water—jellyfish or medusae (as free-swimming jellyfish are also called), extremely fragile marine organisms that did not survive in captivity. On May 8 and 29, 1849, almost three years after his arrival in Boston, Agassiz, his English now less halting than it had been when he first set foot on the American shore, addressed the American Academy of Arts and Sciences about several new species of naked-eyed medusa—hydromedusae, in modern parlance—he had discovered. The written form of his remarks was published in 1850 in *Memoirs of the American Academy of Arts and Sciences*.[2] Asserting with a flourish, on the very first page of the article that there was "a deep scientific interest connected with the study of Medusae," Agassiz admitted that, since his arrival in Boston, his eyes had "hardly yet fully opened." *Seeing, observing, watching*: for Agassiz, the New World was one giant invitation to take a closer look. And with jellyfish, perhaps more so than with other creatures, the right kind of seeing makes all the difference. The members of the genus *Sarsia*, for example, don't exactly make things easy for the human observer. Fragile, transparent, unpredictable wisps of twitching, perishable matter, they refuse to sit still for their portraits. Transferring captured *Sarsia* swimming in a spoonful of seawater into a larger tumbler filled with more seawater will kill it instantly, as much as one tries to preserve the creature's original environment. All the more remarkable, then, that Agassiz had used, as he reminded his readers, *living* animals for his descriptions whenever possible.

Throughout his article, Agassiz insists that when it came to choosing his specimens, he never cut corners. Never once did he simply place his objects of study instantly under the microscope where they would dry out. Instead, he looked at them while they were still alive, in narrow glass jars, surrounded by plenty of water. To him these jellyfish resembled beautiful flowers, and he gave them the care beautiful flowers deserved. Describing them was an education of the mind as well as the senses: the naked eye of the human observer adapts itself to the motions of the naked-eyed medusae. Here, indeed, we "learn . . . to look."[3]

Agassiz held that scientific observers share a fatal propensity to "force their views upon nature." Not so Agassiz, who would wait for darkness to settle and then place a candle behind his jellyfish jar, gazing at his specimen with rapt attention because now "nothing about them can escape the attention of the observer," especially one of Agassiz's caliber. Amid a profusion of detail—a medusa's epithelium, chymiferous tubes, pennate muscular bundles, and nerve plexuses—Agassiz, the questioning, puzzled, exhilarated investigator, remains always present, hungry for more. He makes no attempt to hide his excitement when he describes himself watching little *Sarsia*, freed from its earlier existence as polyp on a stem at the bottom of Boston Harbor, move forward by alternately contracting and extending its tiny body, its tentacles five times longer than the animal's diameter: "Of course, the changes of form which it assumes in these different movements are almost endless; and though several are represented in Plate IV., they hardly give a complete idea of the beautiful diversity of aspect which this animal exhibits in its movements." He reminds his readers that the evidence he has gathered is not always conclusive, that there is always a frustrating need for more work: "I must confess that I never met with more perplexing difficulties than those I experienced in satisfying myself of the real nature of what so clearly seemed a structure, which always vanished under certain influences of light, while it was so plain under others." But Agassiz also takes care to communicate to his readers that what might seem discouraging at times is really quite exciting as well as aesthetically satisfying:

It is indeed a wonderful sight, to see a little animal not larger than a hazel-nut, as transparent as crystal, as soft as jelly, as perishable as an air-bubble, run actively through as dense a medium as water, pause at times and stretch its tentacles, and now dart suddenly in one direction or another, turn round upon itself, and move suddenly in the opposite direction, describe spirals like a bird of prey rising in the air, or shoot in a straight line like an arrow, and perform all these movements with as much grace and precision, and elongate and contract its tentacles, throw them at its prey, and secure, in that way, its food, with as much certainty, as could a larger animal provided with flesh and bones, teeth and claws, and all the different soft and hard parts which we consider generally as indispensable requisites for energetic action; though these little creatures are, strictly speaking, nothing more than a little mass of cellular gelatinous tissue.[4]

Agassiz's long sentence is constructed for rhetorical effect. He begins with the attributes of the jellyfish (transparency, softness, smallness, perishability, transparency) and ends with those of the kind of animal a jellyfish is *not*. But the clear implication is, at least for now, that a mass of gelatin, a heap of cells (as Agassiz says elsewhere), can, if in different ways, do all that we take for granted in a much larger, firm-bodied animal. So much energy, so much activity, so much evidence of volition, such powerful movements, such a voracious appetite! Wouldn't that lead us to expect a far more complicated structure than the "primitive simplicity" that characterizes the jellyfish? Or is it not so primitive after all? All the comparisons Agassiz offers (jellyfish are like a hazelnut, an air bubble, a bird of prey, an arrow, and finally a "larger animal," which, significantly, remains unnamed) follow from the simple attempt to take a closer look at this little creature and to understand it on its own terms.

Appropriately, in an essay that is so much about the best ways of looking at a jellyfish, the question soon arises how it is that jellyfish themselves look at the world around them, perhaps even at Agassiz himself, the scientist hunkering down, candle in hand, next to the small glass container in which they float. Some readers might remember Melville's meditation, written about the same time, on the powers of vision of a very different, and of course larger, animal. In the chapter "The Sperm-Whale's Head" from *Moby-Dick*, Ishmael, Melville's excitable narrator, contemplates whether the whale's double vision is fundamentally different from the way humans view the world. But

Agassiz is not content with speculation: in his article, the medusa's naked eye yields readily to the lens of the microscope (he chloroforms the living specimens so that he can get a better look) and, eventually, to the hand that wields the knife. Agassiz even provides the settings for his instrument, made by the firm of Georges Oberhäuser and imported from France: "I may say, that I have been successful in investigating all parts in their natural relations in the living animal," Agassiz writes about *Hippocrene*, another genus of naked-eyed medusa, "with powers as high as Ocular 1, Objective 6, of Oberhäuser's microscope, and that I could apply any higher powers after cutting the body into halves . . . Some details . . . were examined from fragments cut entirely free."[5]

The eye of *Sarsia*, finds Agassiz as he is slicing away at the tissues he has gathered, is connected with the creature's tentacles. This shortcut from brain to hand, explains Agassiz, "is another curious adaptation in nature, where the organ of sight is combined with one which is destined to catch the prey." An odd and not at all scientific analogy threatens to emerge here: the scientist's eye and hand might seem almost as connected as the eye speck of the jellyfish and the tentacle on which it sits. But no, this little hemispherical body sitting atop a mass of other cells—a "speck" if ever there was one—is really quite different from the corresponding organ in higher animals: there is no transparent lens to refract the rays of light, so all it will be able to do is give rise to vague "sensations in the dark," a subterranean life not comparable to that of humans. The "life of the parts" surrounding *Hippocrene*'s central digestive cavity is "more active and intense than that of any other part of the body," writes Agassiz. So is the jellyfish then nothing but a sort of weird colon with tentacles? Not so fast, warns Agassiz. Writing about *Tiaropsis*, a "pretty little Medusa," he first notes how this animal performs its "movements in a very gentle and quiet way, full of grace and elegance," unlike *Sarsia*, whose movements are brisk and violent. There is a difference of temperament here between the genera, "indicating milder habits, and a less rapacious or voracious disposition." And when Agassiz proceeds to describe the eyes of *Tiaropsis*—in addition to the eye specks it sports eight large eye bulbs that remind him of the compound eyes of insects—he admits how deeply impressed he is with "the diversity of structure which exists among these lower animals, which is so great that the necessity of extensive comparisons" between them "seems to me almost of greater importance than among the higher animals." When dealing with jellyfish, in other words, don't use yourself as a basis for comparison. If you want complexity, just look at other jellyfish.[6]

If Agassiz was obsessed with jellyfish—small ones, big ones, slithery ones with long tangled tentacles that propel themselves through the water, and others that barely move—Charles Darwin in England dreamed about barnacles: fantastical-looking creatures with feathery, curly feet (hence their wonderfully evocative name, *Cirripedia*) that spend their lives tucked away in their shells or burrowed into the bodies of other marine animals such as clams or snails. If Agassiz's quivering jellyfish were hard to obtain, as he so often complained, Darwin's little barnacles, ubiquitous residents of the shoreline, attaching themselves to rocks, trees, or the crumbling hulls of old boats, virtually offered themselves to the collector and were portable enough to be sent by mail. While Agassiz and his associates waded after jellyfish off the New England coast, Darwin, in the security and comfort of Down House, unwrapped packages of barnacles sent to him from all over the world. Unlike Agassiz, he worked entirely from preserved specimens. Charles Darwin was in the audience when Agassiz, soon to board his steamer in Liverpool, bound for the United States, gave a speech at the meeting of the Ray Society in Southampton on September 15, 1846. On this occasion he said that someone should write a book about barnacles or, in Darwin's words, that "a monograph on the Cirripedia was a pressing desideratum in Zoology."[7] Darwin took his advice. And so it was that Agassiz, poised to conquer the United States, would soon hear about Darwin's passion for barnacles. He did what he could to facilitate Darwin's work by sending him some of the barnacles he had collected in Boston.

On October 22, 1848, Darwin sent Agassiz a progress report on his barnacle work. His letter walks a fine line between humility (after all, who was Darwin, compared with this scientist of now global renown?) and self-assertion. On the one hand, Darwin admonished Agassiz not to share what he was telling him here. The barnacle might be small, but in Darwin's world his discoveries about its anatomy were Big News: "I shd be glad if you would not mention my present results, partly because I shd like to have the satisfaction of publishing myself what few new points I have found out, & partly because one is more free to alter ones [*sic*] own views, when they are confined to one's own breast." On the other hand, Darwin also said, almost sheepishly, that he would be "proud if anything I could say, would interest you." To that effect, he filled his letter to Agassiz with new information about his little crustaceans, about what they look like as larvae, how they molt into adults with "black spots" for eyes, how they glue themselves to everything from driftwood to the flank of a whale, how the substance they use to do this is like cement, "one of the most remarkable parts of their Natural History." And then Darwin switched gears. Cirripedes were hermaphrodites, he informed Agassiz. Strangely, though, they were also able to fertilize each other. One specimen, whose penis had been cut off (Darwin had performed this mini-castration himself, peering anxiously through the microscope, his hands resting on the pieces of wood he had fashioned himself to keep himself steady), was undeniably pregnant. But then there was also that genus he had found wherein the sexes were distinct, or at least sort of: the male here permanently attached himself to the female. Weirder still, in one genus whose males all have smallish sex organs, supplementary penises would suddenly arise: some of the embryos never made it to full barnaclehood but instead transformed themselves into tiny sperm-filled replacement males, detachable penises as it were, genitals on call, slated to die once they'd discharged their load.

And then Darwin stopped himself, as if all this talk about penises big and small, ovaries pregnant or not, and sperm, lots of sperm, in a letter to another man, a scientist far away whom he hardly knew, had gotten out of hand. "You will laugh at this account," Darwin declared, "but I assure you I would not presume to tell you anything, of which I was not *sure*." And the last line of the letter inadvertently brought the conversation back into territory that would have been instantly familiar to Agassiz: "I do not suppose I shall finish my Monograph for two or three years—my health allows me to work very little."[8] Bad health was something Louis Agassiz knew about too.

And so they stayed in touch, Agassiz and Darwin, if only intermittently. When his account of the Lake Superior expedition came out, Agassiz sent Darwin an autographed copy, which Darwin acknowledged on June 25, 1850 ("I have seldom been more gratified"), sending him thanks too for some *Cirripedia* Agassiz and his associate Gould had mailed him, which had proved to be of "great service." His letter was addressed to Agassiz "at Cambridge University."[9] In 1850, evolution was nothing more than a blip on Agassiz's horizon, and he had no indication that Darwin would ever cause him as much personal and professional trouble as he ultimately did. But Darwin, who had begun his first notebook on the "transmutation of species" in July 1837, fully realized that if he wanted to continue on his quest for the common origin of all living things, on a path that led him deep into areas that required him to theorize rather than compile evidence gained through personal observation, he would have to grapple with Louis Agassiz, fieldworker extraordinaire. Darwin knew that Agassiz, especially when he felt that his ideas were under siege, would be the first to point out any lack of proof, the first to fling real evidence in a detractor's face. No one knew more than Agassiz, and that fact hadn't changed with his move to the United States. Darwin's barnacle letter of 1848 beautifully epitomizes the dilemma in which Darwin found himself. On the one hand, he was certainly out to impress Agassiz with his empirical credentials: "I assure you I would not presume to tell you anything, of which I was not *sure*." On the other hand, the bewildering variety of his barnacles' sexual mores helped him formulate a theme that would dominate the great "abstract" of his theory that Darwin was to publish eleven years later—namely, that all that had been preserved of the grand Book of Nature were a few short chapters "and of each page, only here and there a few lines."[10] Agassiz couldn't have disagreed more. He still felt that he could decipher the entire book—if not now, then soon enough.

Given the battle in which the two men were to be embroiled, it is hard not to find something symbolically important about the difference between Darwin's scrappy, promiscuous, libidinous barnacles and Agassiz's pulsating, exceedingly fragile jellyfish, yielding their precarious beauty to the observer ready to appreciate it for what it is, token of God's love for the world. While Darwin returned from his barnacle research to the theorizing on evolution that had kept him busy since the late 1830s, Agassiz, after his immigration to the United States, couldn't move beyond his turtles and jellyfish. Watching Agassiz's meteoric rise to fame and importance, Darwin must have noticed, with some satisfaction, that the man who had once lorded it over him seemed to dry up as a scientist. Darwin constantly worried about his scientific competitors —just recall the breathless allusion, at the beginning of *On the Origin of Species*, to Alfred Russel Wallace, who had almost beaten him to the finish line. Darwin would have taken note of the fact that of Agassiz's projected ten-volume masterpiece, *Contributions to the Natural History of the United States of America*, financed by public subscription and intended to describe, with the help of lavish illustrations, the animal life of the entire American nation, only four volumes ever appeared, two of which were, again, about jellyfish. But Darwin also knew that Agassiz still was capable of doing damage to him. Even if his interpretations were wrong, Agassiz certainly knew his facts, even about barnacles. And he was not a simple-minded taxonomist for whom nature stayed the way it had always been; in fact, Agassiz never tired of pointing out how the tiniest turtle contained in itself the mystery not only of the form it would take as an adult but the history of its own turtle tribe as well as the entire history of life on earth.[11]

Darwin was a sharp observer of other people's foibles. He knew that Agassiz's Achilles' heel was his irrepressible desire to be appreciated by as many people as possible. As he was working to get his theory into a form he could share with others, Darwin used that fact to his advantage. He found an unexpected ally in the botanist Asa Gray, one of Agassiz's own colleagues. Gray had come to share Darwin's view that Agassiz's work was "impracticable rubbish";[12] like Darwin, he loathed Agassiz's need to talk to "the rabble."[13] To Darwin and Gray, Agassiz was like one of his jellyfish: weird, infinitely interesting, capable of inflicting a certain amount of harm, but ultimately destined to fade into insubstantiality.

Asa Gray had not always disliked Agassiz. Just three years younger than his foreign colleague, he had been his chaperone on that first triumphant tour of the United States in the fall of 1846. Like Agassiz, Gray had been trained as a physician, but whereas his Swiss colleague had attended prestigious universities in Heidelberg and Munich, Gray, from the Mohawk Valley region of New York, had studied at the new Fairfield Medical College on the edge of the Adirondacks. At the time he met Agassiz, he was working furiously on his *Manual of the Botany of the Northern United States*, a comprehensive textbook intended for a wide readership. Gray thought that Agassiz was "an excellent fellow" and told a friend, the New York botanist John Torrey, "I know you will be glad to make his personal acquaintance."[14]

In fact, the two men could hardly be more different. Gray was everything Agassiz was not. While Agassiz was of more than average height and squarely built, Gray was short and thin (in his forties, he still weighed only 135 pounds). If Agassiz reminded the poet James Russell Lowell of a "mountain oak," Asa Gray made him think of fragrant and "gaily innocent" flowers.[15] While Agassiz was given to taking leisurely walks in public, letting himself be fêted by those who recognized the great man, Gray always was running somewhere, perennially late for class or an appointment. A staunch Presbyterian, he had been "a constant church-goer, everywhere," recalled his wife, Jane Loring Gray. "When traveling he always made Sunday a resting-day if possible, and would go off quietly in the morning to find some place of service."[16] During his years in New York and when he first came to Cambridge, he taught Sunday school. It seems amazing even today that an outsider like Gray, without amassing wealth or formally converting to Congregationalism, managed to find his place at Harvard and in Boston Brahmin society.

Gray was of Scotch-Irish origin, which was not an incidental factor in his future dealings with the French-speaking Agassiz.[17] He was emphatically not a cosmopolite. True, he had spent a year in Europe, from November 1838 to November 1839, to do some sightseeing and also to buy books for the University of Michigan, where he was teaching then. But that was a mixed experience, as he frankly admitted in a series of letters home, marked by the kind of dry, self-deprecating humor that Agassiz would have been incapable of. American to the bone, Gray discovered that he was not much given to "parlez-vous-ing," as he told Eliza Torrey, the wife of his botanist friend John Torrey. The featherbeds of Austria made him feel uncomfortable, and he came to the conclusion that Paris, "as a general thing," wasn't in fact "very beautiful," and that the Rhone valley was "scarcely as fine" as the "Hudson between New York and the Highlands." Venice he found "queer," though the many Jews he saw there did remind him of New York.[18]

Whereas Louis Agassiz took to the lectern like a fish to water, Gray disliked public appearances. In 1844, two years before Agassiz,

Asa Gray. Carte de visite, c. 1864–1866.

Gray was asked to give the Lowell Lectures in Boston, a task he approached with great anxiety. He delivered the lectures freely; though he had prepared some sketchy notes to refer to, in "a desperate lunge" he decided to abandon them in order to connect better with his audience. Using a long pole to point at the large pictures and diagrams he had brought, he extemporized and therefore found himself unable to finish on time; he was forced to "break off in the midst of the best of it." His hope was that his audience liked him the better for it.[19]

In his science writing, however, Gray left nothing to chance. He prominently began his botany textbook, *How Plants Grow* (1858), with a quotation from Matthew 4:28–29: "Consider the Lilies of the Field, how they grow: they toil not, neither do they spin: and yet I say unto you, that even Solomon in all his glory was not arrayed like one of these."[20] While this epigraph seems to set a religious tone, it actually does something that is more important to Gray: it reminds readers that nature study is not a means to an end. *How Plants Grow* is a textbook, to be sure, as reflected in its proudly plodding structure, the neatly numbered paragraphs, and pithy summaries that end each section.

But Gray had a more provocative pedagogical goal. Between the lines of sometimes arid botanical description, he was mounting a quiet assault on the humanist values that were and still are the bedrock of American education. Dr. Gray believed that learning "*how to observe* and *how to distinguish things* correctly" was more important than all other subjects, even than the study of language: "For to distinguish *things* scientifically (that is carefully and accurately) is simpler than to distinguish *ideas*."[21] Science, to Gray, was just that: *science*, and an aid to personal growth only insofar as science in general is an aid to personal growth. Which Gray of course emphatically believed it was. Yet for Gray, science was not a pathway to spiritual self-improvement, as Agassiz would have claimed. Neither was it Gray's aim to minister to a new generation of budding botanists. Throughout *How Plants Grow*, we never forget that there is a distinction between the botanical observations schoolchildren are encouraged to pursue and the painstaking work of the professional, well-trained botanist. Gray's books emphasize discipline and distance. He makes no attempt to diminish the gulf that separates him, the botanist, from his nonspecialist young readers: "Remember that every one has to creep before he can walk, and to walk before he can run. Only begin at the beginning; take pains to understand things as you go on, and cultivate the habits of accuracy and nice discrimination . . . Then each step will render the next one easy; you will soon make more rapid progress." There is development, movement, then, in the study of natural history, but not necessarily of a kind that would push students beyond the framework of recitation and rote learning. As Dr. Gray's students grew in their knowledge of nature, they would also advance in the catalog of Gray's books. When you have mastered "this little book," Gray told his students, you "will be well prepared to continue the study in the *Lessons in Botany and Vegetable Physiology*, and in the *Manual of the Botany of the Northern United States*, by the same author." Obviously, Gray wanted them to study not just nature but also the books, specifically *his* books.[22]

Not that *How Plans Grow* and *Lessons in Botany* are particularly memorable as books. Gray did not aim to write great literature: where Agassiz liked to indulge in rhetorical flourishes, Gray's prose

was workmanlike, focused on the issues at hand, free of any straining after superficial eloquence. Dr. Gray dwelled in the world of facts,
where fancy words are not needed. "The object of the Flower," he in-
structs us with complete blandness, "is to form the fruit." Throughout his textbook, Asa Gray strives to remain anonymous, even at the
risk of grammatical fuzziness: "Cutting the apple lengthwise, these
dots come to view." When he does appear in his narrative, it is to
express disappointment over unnecessarily difficult botanical terms
that obstruct his pedagogical purpose ("It is a pity these three words
are so long . . .") or to commend his plants for a quality he well understood, the hard work they display in the manner of their growing: "No great result is attained without effort, and long preceding
labor." Shortly after the last statement, the reader comes across one
of the few moments of true emotional intensity in the book, namely,
when Gray explains that in the world of plants, preparedness is all: the
blossoms we admire in our gardens in June or July come from material gathered long before, "in the dark earth, where the flower-buds
lie slumbering in the protecting bulb through the cold winter, and in
summer promptly unfold in beauty for our delight." But those areas
of metaphorical intensity were not where the good Dr. Gray had really meant to travel. Thoreau would read such statements in Gray's
books as an indication that all clear ideas, "Antaeus-like . . . readily
ally themselves to the earth, the primal womb of things," but to paraphrase Gray's biographer Hunter Dupree, Gray meant nothing more
than what he said: that moisture and darkness are a necessary part of
the process of a plant's florescence.[23]

Gray was a herbarium man. His preference for pressed plants, a
stationary contrast to Agassiz's twitching medusae, was just one index
of the differences between the two men. Unlike Agassiz, Gray was
content to let the world come to him rather than making an effort to
go out and find it. And come it did.

It has become customary to blame the reactionary Agassiz for the delayed acceptance of Darwinian theory in the United States. But Darwin's correspondence with Asa Gray shows that in fact the opposite
was true: rather than slowing the triumph of evolution in the United
States, Agassiz's surprisingly emotional, scattershot opposition to any
theory that smacked of developmentalism helped focus Gray's pro-

motional efforts on Darwin's behalf. While Agassiz was entranced with the beauty of his soft jellyfish, watching their captivating motions, and drunk with the spectacle of a nature willing to open itself to him, Darwin and Gray engaged in another kind of spectator sport: watching Agassiz. The Swiss scientist served as the convenient "other" against which Darwin and Gray and their American followers could define themselves, regardless of the differences they might have had with one another.

Agassiz was what brought Darwin and Gray together: "I am particularly obliged to you for sending me Asa Gray's letter," Darwin wrote to his friend, the botanist Joseph Hooker, director of the Royal Botanical Gardens at Kew, on March 26, 1854. "How very pleasantly he writes." He had talked to Gray before, at Hooker's house in Kew Gardens, and he knew that neither Gray nor Hooker were entirely convinced yet by his theory. "To see his & your cautions on the species-question ought to overwhelm me in confusion & shame; it does make me feel deuced uncomfortable." But never mind—there was always Agassiz. It was delightful to hear all that Gray had to say about Agassiz, Darwin added. "How very singular it is that so *eminently* clever a man, with such *immense* knowledge on many branches of Natural History, should write such wonderful stuff & bosh as he does." And he passed on a story the geologist Charles Lyell had told him—how Lyell had gone up to Agassiz after a lecture and joked that what he had heard "was so delightful, that he could not help all the time wishing it was true." Good stuff. Agassiz was a force to be reckoned with, to be sure. Darwin admitted to Hooker that he seldom saw a paper from North America that didn't bear the imprint of his doctrine. But with men like Gray and Lyell at his side, Darwin felt he wouldn't have to worry.[24]

Darwin and Gray began writing to each other regularly in 1855. At that time, as we have seen, Agassiz was fully absorbed in creating the grand summation of his science, the Museum of Comparative Zoology in Cambridge, daily congratulating himself as new specimens kept pouring it. Riding the crest of his fame as the new leader of American science, he was emotionally and intellectually unprepared for a debate that would fundamentally challenge his authority as a scientist. Darwin, by contrast, was in the trenches of scientific discovery, still patiently accumulating all the data he could lay his hands on.

In April 1855, he sent Gray a list of alpine plants he had copied from the latter's *Manual*, hoping that Gray would tell him, "from memory," if any of those occurred anywhere in the United States other than the locations given, or, for that matter, anywhere else in the world. Clearly he was concerned about the migration of species. He also asked about the distance between the White Mountains and the "Mts. of New York," since maps had yielded no reliable information on the low land between them in which such plants wouldn't be able to grow. Gray's answer followed suit ("I do not believe there is a plant there which is not in Labrador . . ."), and a correspondence unfolded that became crucial to the reception of Darwin's theory in the United States.[25]

It wasn't long before Agassiz's name, associated with the very concept of the fixity of species that Darwin and Gray, in their different ways, were working to unsettle, came up: "I should like to write an essay on *species*, some day," Gray announced blithely, apparently still unaware of Darwin's own plans in that direction, "but before I should have time to do it, in my plodding way, I hope you, or Hooker, will do it, and much better far." Gray was particularly intrigued by a series of experiments Darwin had conducted recently, which proved that seeds could germinate after having been immersed in saltwater for a number of days, thus adding another important piece to the puzzle of the global migration of species that they both had been trying to solve. According to Agassiz, of course, nature didn't travel—all of God's creatures stayed in their assigned places. Delightedly, Gray imagined how Darwin's new findings, if published in the foremost American science journal of the day, would confuse Agassiz: "I shall have it nearly all reprinted in Silliman's Journal, as a *nut* for Agassiz to crack."[26]

As Darwin was casting his net wider and wider ("It would be a very curious point . . . to compare the list of European plants in Tierra del Fuego . . . with those in N. America"),[27] Gray's role expanded too. Botany as a discipline was more "philosophical" than zoology, asserted Darwin, and it had the added advantage that Agassiz knew even less about it than he did, despite the extended botanical excursion on which Gray had recently taken him.[28] And so Darwin and Gray bonded against a man they agreed was an embarrassment to the true cause of science. They chose as their rallying cry a casual remark

Agassiz once made to Charles Lyell: "Nature never lies." Darwin first mentioned that phrase in a letter he sent to Gray on January 1, 1857. The context was not a favorable one for Darwin himself: he was disappointed with Gray's assertion that the interchange of alpine plant species must have happened via Greenland and not, as Darwin had hoped, in a northern or southern direction originating from the polar caps. (What was at issue between Darwin and Gray was not the assumption that species had migrated—only the precise manner in which this might have taken place.) Gray's observation "riled" him mightily, wrote Darwin. "Lyell told me, that Agassiz having a theory about when Saurians were first created, on hearing some careful observations opposed to this, said he did not believe it, 'for Nature never lied'—I am just in this predicament & repeat to you that 'Nature never lies'; ergo, theorisers are always right."[29] Writing to the confirmed empiricist Gray, whose conclusions he knew were always based on "careful observations," Darwin used Agassiz's misplaced confidence to make fun of limitations of his own, which Gray had exposed. But was he really as bad as Agassiz?

Gray's answer came a few weeks later, on February 16, 1857. The letter was written in typical Gray style, with some attempts at humor but otherwise seething with anger: "Your anecdote of Agassiz, 'Nature never lies' is most characteristic. Instead of learning caution from experience A. goes on *faster* than ever, in drawing positive conclusions from imperfect or conjectural data, confident that he reads Nature through and through, and without the least apparent misgiving that anything will turn up that he cannot explain away."[30] Gray had just begun working on the Japanese plant specimens that he had received from Charles Wright, a member of the North Pacific Exploring and Surveying Expedition from 1853 to 1856, and he felt he was about to make his most important botanical discovery—one that would deal the death blow to Agassiz's pet idea of "separate creations."[31] Wright's specimens would help him prove that similar plant species, or even the same one, could grow in geographically distinct locations on the North American continent or in areas as different as the eastern United States and eastern Japan. While Agassiz was jumping to conclusions, Gray was taking his time, making sure that his science remained solid.

Gray's answer must have come as a relief to Darwin, though he somewhat sheepishly admitted that, seen from Gray's perspective, much of his own current work looked hypothetical too, gained by "induction from too few facts."[32] But Agassiz's absurd mantra, "Nature never lies," at least helped him keep his own missteps in perspective. Later the same year, on June 18, 1857, he used it once again to make fun of his own theory regarding the geographic extension of so-called disjoined species, that is, the same species occurring in locations far distant from each other. He had originally suggested, in a letter to Gray of May 9, 1857, that such plants ought to belong to smallish genera (ones more likely affected by extinction), a hypothesis Gray quickly refuted in his answer, pointing to the evidence he had collected. Darwin conceded without really conceding anything: "I look at Extinction as common cause of *small* genera & *disjoined* ranges & therefore they ought, *if they behaved properly* & as nature does not lie to go together!"[33]

While Darwin and Gray both believed in evolution of species, they had radically diverging opinions about the larger implications of the processes they had uncovered. Darwin was convinced that a God who would watch the sparrow's fall with perfect indifference also had no real interest in the lives of people. The Presbyterian Gray, however, felt that the very complexity of Darwin's theory proved, rather than dismissed, the existence of a benevolent God who had designed the natural world for our benefit. In one of his *Atlantic Monthly* essays, "Darwin and His Reviewers," he offered a simple analogy for the process Darwin had called natural selection. Streams of water "flowing over a sloping plain by gravitation," he wrote, may have worn their actual channels into the ground as they flowed, following the course nature dictates. But so many times we see them flowing where they actually sustain life, in unanticipated, glorious ways, by "forming definite and useful lines of irrigation, after a manner unaccountable on the laws of gravitation and dynamics." Such developments cannot be accidental: these rivers flow not only where they must, but where they ought to. "We should believe that the distribution was designed."[34] After reading Gray's essay Darwin felt the need to explain himself once again to his devout friend. Gray had argued playfully that no reasonable person would take the fact that "multitudes of raindrops fall back into the ocean" as a good enough reason to conclude that, therefore, also "the rains which are bestowed upon the soil with such rule and average regularity were *not* designed to support vegetable and animal life." The exception proves the rule, in other words. The raindrops metaphor intrigued Darwin, and in his response to his friend he declared that it all came down to one's point of view: Gray preferred to think about the raindrops that fall on the land, nourishing the infinite varieties of life, whereas Darwin was always looking at those that fall into the ocean and vanish without a trace.[35]

For all their differences, though, there was one thing Darwin and Gray could always agree on: Agassiz was wrong, terribly wrong. Thus Agassiz served to unite Darwin and Gray in the common quest for the truth.

Gray was Darwin's, and Darwinism's, most effective spokesman in America. But what informed Gray's advocacy was really a tangle of personal as well as professional motives. He had, in fact, started out in a place not so different from where Agassiz still stood. In 1846, he had written a scornful review of *Explanations,* a sequel to *The Vestiges of Creation* (1844), the widely read pop version of evolutionary thought. Like its predecessor volume, this book had come from the pen of the Scottish publisher Robert Chambers. Gray's main argument in that review—now perhaps an embarrassing misstep he wanted to forget—had been that species were originally created "as perfect as they now are."[36] If Gray more than a decade later was helping Darwin find acceptance in American scientific circles, Darwin in turn helped Gray solidify his own beliefs. When Gray went into full attack mode at the beginning of 1859, Agassiz had just received word of the bequest from Francis Calley Gray that would allow him to launch his Museum of Comparative Zoology. Preoccupied with completing the transition from practicing scientist to institution-building administrator, he did not anticipate the debates into which Gray's zeal would hurl him head first. Despite his undeniable power, Agassiz had become, as the astute Gray must have realized, a soft, exceedingly vulnerable target. Gray was ready; Agassiz was not.

On January 11, 1859, the American Academy of Arts and Sciences met in the Boston home of Charles Greely Loring, Gray's father-in-law, as good a place as any to begin the anti-Agassiz campaign. After talking about his Japanese plants and their astounding similarity to their North American counterparts, Gray announced, in Agassiz's presence, that to attribute the distribution and origin of species to Divine Will would put an end to empirical science as such. A few months later, Gray moved in for the kill. During a meeting at his own house on May 12, he sprang Darwin's evolutionary views on the unsuspecting members of the Cambridge Scientific Club. His reasons for doing so were not entirely pure. He enjoyed rattling his colleagues a bit, but most of all he had wanted to "maliciously vex the soul of Agassiz with views so diametrically opposed to all his pet notions."[37]

The appearance of the American edition of *On the Origin of Species* a year later only confirmed what Agassiz's and Gray's friends in Cambridge now already knew: that the falling out between the two most eminent members of the faculty of the Lawrence Scientific School was about to become permanent. Gray by then was delightedly providing Darwin and Hooker with juicy details about Agassiz's well-deserved descent into insignificance and permanent humiliation. Now that he had read at least part of Darwin's abominable book, Agassiz was growling like a "well cudgelled dog," Gray told Hooker.[38]

One could actually feel sorry for Agassiz. Darwin had not done him the favor of presenting a direct, all-out attack. Consider a long passage from the chapter "Geographical Distribution," in which Darwin explains his theory of the common origin of all living beings. Darwin's real target here was Agassiz, specifically the latter's attempt—harebrained, if you asked Darwin—to attribute the diversity of living beings (including the diversity of human races) to different ancestors, created separately by divine fiat. But Darwin didn't put his cards on the table right away. Instead, he began his argument by rehearsing the central facts of his friend Gray's discoveries. At least Agassiz was forewarned: "It is indeed a remarkable fact to see so many of the same plants living on the snowy regions of the Alps or Pyrenees, and in the extreme northern parts of Europe but it is far more remarkable, that the plants on the White Mountains, in the United States of America, are all the same with those of Labrador, and nearly all the same, as we hear from Asa Gray, with those on the loftiest mountains of Europe." Darwin then continued to make fun of those naturalists who, faced with such coincidences, would still believe in the idea of separate creation. But instead of naming Agassiz, instead of taking him seriously as an opponent, he reached far into the past:

"Even as long ago as 1747, such facts led Gmelin to conclude that the same species must have been independently created at several distinct points." And whom did one have to thank for exorcising such old wives' tales? Now Darwin had a surprise up his sleeve: "We might have remained in this same belief, had not Agassiz and others called our attention to the Glacial period, which, as we shall immediately see, affords a simple explanation of these facts."[39]

The indignity of it. Unintentionally, Agassiz, with his work on the moving glaciers of the world (work that Darwin himself had once doubted), had himself dealt the fatal blow to the idea that species had been separately created. Or so Darwin claimed. A once-pervasive glacial climate could explain easily why arctic species were found in different parts of the world: they had migrated across tracts of land that had since become too warm to sustain them. It's hard to think of a more effective way of dismantling Agassiz's "ideal science," as Gray liked to call it. In one single paragraph, throwing in Gray's name for some additional fun, Darwin had completely eviscerated the powerful Agassiz. And, for Darwin's money, the parallelism Agassiz had postulated between the embryological development of living beings and the geological succession of seemingly extinct species (which, in a way, assumed that the embryos of current species were "quoting" and then rejecting the past) was an elegant and useful confirmation of the principle of natural selection anyway, of the continuity of the struggle for life Darwin had attempted to document. Or potentially useful at least, because, as Darwin added with a smirk, Agassiz's parallelism was as yet but a dream, "incapable of demonstration."[40]

Agassiz had suffered the ultimate irony: seeing some of his own theory adduced in support of Darwin's theory, but summarized in such a manner that his work would strike the reader as even more hypothetical than Darwin's.

It was left to Gray to deal Agassiz the coup de grâce. Writing in the *Atlantic Monthly*, usually an outlet for Agassiz's ideas, the year after Darwin's *On the Origin of Species* had been published, Gray discussed what he said were Agassiz's "synthetic types" (Agassiz actually preferred the term "prophetic types"): extinct creatures, such as reptile-like fish, that combine characteristics of classes that are now separate.

With pleasure he noted that the very fact of their extinction in the struggle for life in fact proved Darwin right. He saved his most stinging barb for the last sentence of this paragraph, delighting in the twist he had put on Agassiz's cherished "prophetic types": "If these are true prophecies, we need not wonder that some who read them in Agassiz's book will read their fulfillment in Darwin's." The supreme anti-evolutionist as evolution's unwitting prophet—Gray must have been proud of his cunning.

In "Darwin and His Reviewers," Gray had similar fun with Agassiz's contention that species are "categories of thought" (*divine* thought, Agassiz would have insisted), "whatever it may mean in the Aristotelian metaphysics." Exactly true, adds Gray, which is why—natural selection, here I come!—the actual individuals, as "material things," may change over the course of time so that now we have "almost innumerable categories of thought."[41]

What Darwin and Gray's opposition did to Agassiz was more far-reaching than the specific challenges they mounted against his science. They were threatening to wrest away from him the role he had worked so hard to achieve: America's chief scientist, the authorized teacher of an entire nation. As Gray saw it, and as he attempted to show his colleagues in Cambridge and elsewhere in the United States, Agassiz's science, based as it was on the idea "that all species were directly, instead of indirectly, created after their respective kinds, as we now behold them," had become the "customary," orthodox, and therefore boring view. The likes of Darwin and Gray represented the spirit of true scientific inquiry.[42] Buoyed by Gray's unwavering support, Darwin, from the safe distance of Down House, felt smug about Agassiz's increasingly unsuccessful attempts to salvage his position: "I was rather surprised that the latter did not attack me with more skill," he wrote to Jeffries Wyman on December 3, 1860.[43] And in America, Gray, liberated by Darwin's support, leaned back in his front-row seat and gleefully watched Agassiz self-destruct. He savored every moment and circumstance, sharing with Darwin the "absurd lengths" to which Agassiz went in his rejection of evolution. Agassiz, "foolish man," he wrote to Darwin in late 1860 or early 1861, had come close to denying that we are "genetically descended from our grt-grt grandfather" and was insisting that "evidently affiliated languages e.g. Latin Greek Sanscrit owe none of their similarities to a community of origin." The seemingly uncultured Gray, who took Sir Walter Scott to be the pinnacle of literary accomplishment and admired Hawthorne's *Wonder-Book for Girls and Boys*, had driven the multilingual Agassiz into a corner: "Agassiz . . . admits that the derivation of language, & that of Species or forms stand on the same foundation, & that he must allow the latter if he allows the former,—which I tell him is perfectly logical."[44]

Gray's condescension must have driven Agassiz crazy. In August 1864, a verbal altercation took place on a train that carried both men back from a meeting of National Academy of the Sciences in New Haven to Boston. Agassiz had worked so hard to deserve his preeminent place in American science, but now Gray the upstart from the Adirondacks was showing him up. Just last year, Gray had won the presidency of the American Academy of Arts and Sciences despite the objections raised by Agassiz and his friends. Now, instead of cultivating his botanical garden in Cambridge, Gray had gone to New Haven to celebrate another victory: Spencer Fullerton Baird of the Smithsonian and George Bond of the Harvard Observatory—people Agassiz had come to dislike and didn't want to see as members—had been elected to the academy, partly because of a backhanded move by Agassiz's opponents that had allowed the Yale geologist James Dwight Dana to shift allegiances and vote with the zoologists.

We don't have Agassiz's account of this crucial confrontation, another instance of the problem that a biographer of Agassiz constantly comes up against: he wasn't one to run home and confide his innermost feelings to his journal. But one is tempted to picture what happened on the train from New Haven, a scene rich with possibilities. We have already seen that American trains had appalled Agassiz from the moment of his arrival in the States: the rampant egalitarianism of it all, the piles of luggage thrown together in a parody of democratic ideals, the never-ending chatter of the passengers. Going back over what had happened at the meeting, his thoughts keeping time with the landscape rushing by—houses, lanes, and fields emerging from, then disappearing into thick clouds of smoke—Agassiz must have felt anger welling up. He rose, red-faced, to confront his colleague. Was Gray sitting close by? Did Agassiz have to walk a distance, his body swaying with the unaccustomed movement of the train, in order to find Gray? Trembling with rage, Agassiz ended up face to face with him, wanting nothing more than to slap that puny little man, to yell at him, to stop the nonsense once and for all. This wasn't how things were supposed to happen. His voice breaking, Agassiz blurted out that Gray was "no gentleman." A rather tame insult, by most standards, but apparently not for Mrs. Gray, who later scribbled on the flyleaf of her copy of Marcou's biography of Agassiz that the man had used "some violent language to Dr. Gray."[45] The rift had become irreparable.

The official version of the controversy posits an impeccably behaved Gray against an apoplectic Agassiz, who loses the biggest battle of his life scientifically, politically, and morally. This certainly reflects Gray's assessment, which biographers and historians have largely chosen to follow.[46] Yet Gray's correspondence with Charles Darwin shows that there are problems with this narrative. High moral principles did not rule the exchanges between the Garden House in Cambridge and Down House in Kent. Gray himself said that he felt largely unrestrained when he wrote to Darwin: "It never wearies nor bores me to write to you—in the off hand way I do. I enjoy our correspondence too much to consent to curtail or interrupt it."[47] And a considerable part of this enjoyment consisted in a "delightful" activity Gray pithily described, on February 9, 1863, as "torment[ing] Agassiz."[48] Largely irrelevant as a scientist, Agassiz had become useful as a joke.

For there was no hope for him at all. On May 26, 1863, Gray informed Darwin that "Agassiz is writing very maundering geology & zoology, and worse botany (fossil) in the Atlantic Magazine. He tells his readers that the *embryology* of the trilobites (about which not a fact is existant [*sic*]) is better known than that of Crabs!!" Agassiz was, said the avid Bible reader Gray (quoting Hosea 4:17), "'joined to his idols,' and I have no expectation that he will ever be of any more direct use in nat. history."[49] Interestingly, at least in this instance Gray was wrong: the development of the trilobites had in fact been comprehensively (and surprisingly accurately) described and illustrated by the French naturalist Joachim Barrande, whom Agassiz explicitly mentioned in his essay. But it appears that such facts didn't matter much anymore; something larger was at stake. The debate had taken on a life of its own. The indignation of the late 1850s had given way to unrestrained merriment. Take Gray's letter of November 23, 1863, in which Gray recommended that he should take a look at Agassiz's new essay on glaciers in the *Atlantic Monthly*. "It will not strain your brain, tho' it may your diaphragm to read how the hairy elephants and the *bears* & c. were luxuriating in a tropical climate, with their thick coats on to keep them comfortable, when, all of a sudden it changed to bitter winter,—so suddenly that they could not run away, nor even rot, but were *frozen up* before there was time for either."[50] Gray is referring to a passage at the beginning of Agassiz's essay, which he takes to be representative of the fantastical nature of Agassiz's science as a whole: "A sudden intense winter . . . fell upon our globe; it spread over the very countries where these tropical animals had their homes, and so suddenly did it come upon them that they were embalmed beneath masses of snow and ice, without time even for the decay which follows death."[51] Modern geologists have basically confirmed that the last ice age happened relatively fast, though not literally overnight; if Agassiz can be faulted on this point, it would be for getting caught up in the momentum of a text he had conceived, from its very first sentence ("The long summer was over"), as a gripping narrative rather than a scientific explanation. But in his letter to Darwin, Gray seizes upon those narrative features and seeks to cast Agassiz as a storyteller alone, the pied piper of American science, rather than a serious investigator.

For Darwin's further amusement, Gray also described how Agassiz was running around Cambridge waving a note from the eminent physicist Michael Faraday, who had declared that Darwinism had "had its day" in England. Come on, said Gray, who had seen the document in question: "When, at length, A. showed me Faraday's note, I could not see that it said or implied anything of the sort. It is amusing to see how *worried* Agassiz is." Gray is right, though Faraday's letter is certainly not a rousing endorsement of Darwin either: the seventy-two-year-old experimentalist, a devout follower of the evangelical Sandemanian faith, only said that while he had "little or no right to judge" Darwin's theory from a "philosophical" point of view, the evidence cited by its adherents was so "weak & feeble that I feel as if they had no more right than I have."[52]

The story of Darwin's journey toward the publication of *On the Origin of Species* and its aftermath has been told many times, often in the heroic mode, occasionally with a few elements of the mock heroic sprinkled in (Darwin's taste for popular fiction; Darwin playing music for his worms): the story of a humble, publicity-shy gentleman naturalist and failed medical student who, his body racked by intestinal troubles and splitting headaches, defied conventional wisdom and singlehandedly changed the face of science as we know it. But the correspondence between Darwin and Gray reveals another side of Darwin's influence, one that Joseph Hooker succinctly captured in his letter of March 16, 1860, to Gray, in which he wrote regarding *On the Origin of Species:* "To me one of the most interesting studies the book opens, is that of the kinds & qualities of minds that ignore, or sneer, or read, or mark, or learn, or inwardly object."[53] Gray excitedly embraced that aspect of evolution, dividing his colleagues into those who had seen the light and those who were stumbling over their own furniture in the dark. When Darwin's prominent London colleague Richard Owen publicly declared his support for some kind of evolutionary process, if not for Darwin's theory of natural selection, all Gray (who adroitly described Owen's theory as a version of "Hamlet, with the part of Hamlet left out") could think of was how he would now be able to "tease" Agassiz even more. "Rare fun," he called it. Agassiz's supporters were defecting to Darwin's camp on both sides of the Atlantic now. And Agassiz couldn't even defend himself anymore, he was "so cross and sore."[54]

The funnier a figure Agassiz cast in public, the better the news for Darwinism in America. By 1867, if we believe William Winwood Reade, a traveler and frequent Darwin correspondent, evolution by natural selection was "a *fait accompli* in the States: everyone when I was there . . . accepted your hypothesis."[55] Darwin's own eleven-year-old son Horace succinctly captured his father's attitude toward the dark ages of the life sciences when, on November 23, 1862, a mere three years after the appearance of *On the Origin of Species*, he asked Darwin if "people *formerly* really believe[d] that animals & plants never changed." According to Darwin, Horace went on to shrug "his shoulders with pity for the poor people who *formerly* believed in such conclusions." Added Darwin, "I believe Horace is a prophetic type, as Agassiz would say, of future naturalists."[56]

Oddly, it was Agassiz who took the first step in bringing about some kind of reconciliation. Late in 1866, he apologized to Gray for his conduct on the train two years earlier. Gray conveyed the good news to Darwin: after "a mere outbreak of spoiled temper," Agassiz and he were now again on "amicable terms." Note how Agassiz, despite having taken the initiative for this "handsome apology," is relegated to the role of an unruly child.[57] Gray was so excited about the news that he spread it among his friends. "I am . . . much pleased," wrote Joseph Henry, the secretary of the Smithsonian Institution, "that Professor A. and yourself have again come together."[58]

The path was now clear again for what Darwin the armchair naturalist really needed—Agassiz's expertise as an observer. A question Darwin sent to Gray regarding the sexual coloration and head crests of Amazonian fish Gray passed on to Agassiz, and Agassiz answered it directly and honestly. Darwin pretended to be surprised: "I certainly thought that you had formed so low an opinion of my scientific work that it might have appeared indelicate in me to have asked for information from you, but it never occurred to me that my letter wd have been shewn to you." As if he and Gray had never joked about Agassiz's "rubbish," Darwin now felt compelled to assure Agassiz that "I have never for a moment doubted your kindness & generosity, & I hope you will not think it presumptuous in me to say that when we met many years ago at the Brit. Assoc. at Southampton I felt for you the warmest admiration." Agassiz's letter had provided him with precisely the information he needed: "I was aware . . . that many fishes differed sexually in colour & other characters, but I was particularly anxious to learn how far this was the case with those fishes, in which the male, differently from what occurs with most birds, takes the largest share in the care of the ova & young."[59]

If Agassiz had felt gratified by Darwin's apparent readiness to play the student, his satisfaction couldn't have lasted long. Agassiz's letter to him appears in Darwin's *The Descent of Man*, published in 1871. And there Darwin makes clear, triumphantly so, that what Agassiz and even the Amazonian tribes couldn't figure out ("I never could ascertain that it subserves any special function, and the Indians of the Amazon know nothing about its use"), Darwin had been able to explain fully: "There can be little doubt that this crest serves as a temporary sexual ornament, for the female does not exhibit a trace of it."[60] With the right theory, observations suddenly make sense.

An emboldened Darwin occasionally continued his raids on Agassiz's vast knowledge bank, again with the help of intermediaries. "I will hand the slip with question to Agassiz," promised Gray to Darwin at the end of October 1869. [61] Asa and Jane Gray were in England then, back from a European sojourn that had included a cruise on the Nile. They had just visited Darwin at Down House. Three months later, on February 14, 1870, Gray informed Darwin that he wasn't hopeful that Agassiz would ever respond. Agassiz had suffered his first stroke the year before. "A. had a serious and peculiar attack of trouble in the brain, which we fear betokens serious mischief, and has laid him up wholly." But this wasn't the time for sentimentality. Ask Agassiz's son, advised Gray: "He can either inform you or find out."[62] But rumors of Agassiz's impending demise turned out to be somewhat exaggerated, and Agassiz even made an attempt to answer Darwin's question, which concerned certain species of fish sitting upon their eggs. Unfortunately, Agassiz didn't know anything useful. Through Gray, Elizabeth Agassiz sent her husband's reply: "Tell Darwin that I cannot answer his question, for I have never succeeded in securing one of the fishes sitting upon the eggs separately from others. They never bite at the hook at that time and as their nests are generally crowded it is impossible [to] catch a single fish with a net. I'll try next summer by shooting at them."[63]

Sick and apparently no longer in possession of much of the information Darwin needed, Agassiz *père* had outlived his usefulness for Darwin. But why still worry about losing the old man when his son Alexander, a successful businessman as well as a shrewd scientist, stood ready to take over? Alexander would have his own disagreements with Darwin, regarding the formation of coral reefs, but meanwhile he was available and amenable: "Very many thanks for your kind letter and curious facts about the fishes," wrote Darwin to Agassiz junior on June 1, 1871. "I am also particularly glad to hear about the pedicellariae of the Echinodermata, the homologies of which I did not in the least know."[64]

Asa Gray regarded Louis Agassiz's response to Darwin as exhilaratingly ineffective, and subsequent historians have largely shared this assessment. Instead of truly engaging with Darwin's arguments, Agassiz had apparently resigned himself to a listless recitation of his most dearly held beliefs. And yet, if the sometimes shrill, sometimes hilarious exchanges between Darwin and Gray have shown one thing, it's that the division between the good guys, concerned only with the truth, and the scientific bogeymen, concerned only with their reputation, is difficult to uphold. The reader who returns from Darwin and Gray's correspondence to Agassiz and his jellyfish is in for a bit of surprise. While Darwin and Gray were trying to make a clown out of him, Agassiz was working on the two jellyfish volumes in *Contributions to the Natural History of the United States of America* (1860; 1862). Read carefully, they reveal that Agassiz's anti-Darwinism was, from a scientific as well as from an aesthetic point of view, more sophisticated than is usually assumed. Both books document the deep interest Agassiz had in the living individual—not as a taxonomic fact, but as a source of wonder. "Individuals alone have a definite material existence," he wrote in the third volume of *Contributions*. "They are for the time being the bearer, not only of specific characteristics, but of all the natural features in which animal life is displayed in all its diversity; individuality being, in fact, the great mystery of organic life"—a view directly contrary to the famous ending of *On the Origin of Species*, where "grandeur" is assigned to the great inscrutable laws that produce "endless forms most beautiful and most wonderful." For Agassiz, Darwin habitually "overleaps" the facts, thinking on a large scale while neglecting what Thoreau called the "insect view" of the world.[65] One long footnote in *Contributions* is devoted to a recitation of all of Darwin's errors. As Agassiz enumerates them, his prose turns into a kind of Whitmanesque chant, though driven by frustration, not exuberance:

> He would thus have us believe that there have been periods during which all that had taken place during other periods was destroyed; and this solely to explain the absence of intermediate forms . . . He would have us believe that entire faunae have disappeared before those were preserved, the remains of which are found in the lowest fossiliferous strata . . . He would have us believe that the oldest organisms that existed were simple cells . . . He would have us believe that these lowest first born became extinct, in consequence of the gradual advantage some of their more favored descendants gained over the majority of their predecessors . . . He would have us believe that each new species originated in consequence of some

slight change in those that preceded . . . He would have us believe that animals and plants became gradually more and more numerous . . . He would have us believe that animals disappear gradually; when they are as common in the uppermost bed in which they occur, as in the lowest, or any intermediate bed . . . He would also have us believe that the most perfect organs of the body of animals are the product of gradual improvement; when eyes as perfect as those of the Trilobites are preserved with the remains of these oldest animals . . . He would have us believe that it required millions of years to effect any one of these changes; when far more extraordinary transformations are daily going on, under our eyes, in the shortest periods of time . . . He would have us believe that the geographical distribution of animals is the result of accidental transfers; when most species are so narrowly confined within the limits of their natural range, that even slight changes in their external relations may cause their death.

The summary of the charges makes Darwin seem guilty not merely of recklessly fabricating his evidence and offending his readers, whom he treats as if they were gullible morons. Agassiz also accuses Darwin of slighting those who, unlike Darwin, have worked hard in the field to gather the facts rather than soliciting them from far-flung correspondents. "And all these, and many other calls upon our credulity, are coolly made in the face of an amount of precise information, readily accessible, which would overwhelm anyone who does not place his opinions above the records of an age eminently characterized for its industry; and during which, that information was laboriously accumulated by crowds of faithful laborers."[66]

Agassiz's own position rests firmly on the idea once also shared by Gray, namely, that everything in this world has been created and therefore material facts correspond to immaterial causes. Ralph Waldo Emerson had put a different spin on the same concept when, in his manifesto *Nature*, he asserted that the facts of natural history were "symbols" of spiritual facts. Later, in "The Poet," Emerson would draw a direct parallel between natural objects—say, the parallel nodes of a shell—and human artifacts—say, the rhymed lines of a sonnet.[67] Agassiz, in his refutation of Darwin, insisted that there was no fundamental difference between the workings of the divine intelligence (his preferred way of referring to God) and human creativity: "There are naturalists who seem to look upon the idea of creation—that is, a manifestation of an intellectual power by material means—as a kind of bigotry; forgetting, no doubt, that whenever they carry out a thought of their own, they do something akin to creating; unless they look upon their own elucubrations as something in which their individuality is not concerned, but arising without an intervention of their mind, in consequence of the working of some 'bundles of forces,' about which they know nothing themselves."[68] When God creates, in other words, he does nothing that is categorically different from what we do when we have a new thought and act upon it. By the same token, what we do when we have a new thought is not so different from what God does when he creates. This is how individuals are made—jellyfish, poems, scientific essays.

Agassiz believed that Darwin shunned this joyful embrace of the intellectual and material worlds. Natural selection is not a creative power. Rather, it is an abstract agency that prevents us from viewing the whole of nature as a work of art whose individual components refer to and cite each other and yet remain defiantly individual. As any embryologist knows, "A young snake resembles a young turtle or a young bird much more than any two species of snakes resemble one another; and yet they go on reproducing their kinds, and nothing but their kinds."[69] Or take the jellyfish, that strange watery creature we find when walking on the beach, washed ashore by the receding tide. We pick it up, we look at it, we touch and destroy it, yet we still haven't learned a thing. As the jellyfish "melts away" on our naked, clumsily interfering hand, so does our knowledge of its "slight" existence, unless we take our looking seriously:

> When we first observe a jelly-fish, it appears like a moving fleshy mass, seemingly destitute of organization; next, we may observe its motions, contracting and expanding, while it floats near the surface of the water. Upon touching it, we may feel the burning sensation it produces upon the naked hand, and perhaps perceive also that it has a central opening, a sort of mouth, through which it introduces its food into the interior. Again, we cannot but be struck with their slight consistency, and the rapidity with which they melt away when taken out of the water.

As we move from our first impressions to a more informed sense of how each perceived detail will assume its place within a larger context, the microscopic becomes the macroscopic. Seeing is believing. Where there was a jellyfish we see the whole world:

> But it is not until our methods of investigation are improved; and when, after repeated failures, we have learned how to handle and treat them, that we begin to perceive how remarkable and complicated their internal structure is;—it is not until we have become acquainted with a large number of their different kinds, that we perceive how greatly diversified they are;—it is not until we have had an opportunity of tracing their development, that we perceive how wide the range of their class really is;—it is not until we have extended our comparisons to almost every type of the animal kingdom, that we can be prepared to determine their general affinity, the natural limits of the type to which they belong, the distinctive characteristics of their class, the gradation of their orders, and the peculiarities that may distinguish their families, their genera, and their species.[70]

This extraordinarily well-crafted passage accomplishes several purposes. First, though it is part of a learned work of natural history, it suggests that the scientist's perspective is not much different from that of an ordinary observer. Seeing an animal for the first time, "we" all begin in a state of comparative ignorance. The sting of the jellyfish comes as a surprise to us, and we do not yet know what to make of the "central opening" in the middle of its bell-shaped body. All we see is a shapeless gelatinous mass. Descartes famously argued against relying too much on our senses in our dealings with nature: a sensation of tickling caused by a feather does not resemble anything *in* the feather.[71] But far from excluding such evidence, Agassiz's approach to nature, in fact, depends on it—on what the naked, incautious hand, burning from the unexpected encounter, feels, or what the eye, straining to give shape and meaning to what appears to have no definite outline, has perceived. Slowly, step by step, our familiarity with this creature increases. *Really* understanding it, however, involves much more than repeated observations. It means looking at what's inside that transparent mass, looking at other animals unlike it, and watching its development from the egg to adulthood. The repetition of "how" ("how remarkable and complicated"; "how greatly diversified"; "how wide") in this passage indicates the vastness of conclusions that can be drawn from our experience of this one blubbery mass, so soft that it quickly dissolves when taken out of its element. For Agassiz, all living creatures are both individuals and parts of a whole. It is no coincidence that Agassiz's long sentence ends with "species," a word that had become a cornerstone of his attacks on Darwin, who regarded species as transient and ephemeral.

The relentless focus on seeing an individual both for what is it and how it fits into God's plan for the world underwrites Agassiz's efforts to establish his jellyfish, starfish, and sea urchins as belonging to a larger whole: "But while the Radiates are thus shown to differ in every respect from the Mollusks, Articulates, and Vertebrates, they at the same time become more and more intimately linked together, in proportion as we are better acquainted with the typical features of their organization." So individuality, the unique features of the specimen pointing to the features of the species it represents, once it has been sufficiently asserted, collapses again when seen with the eyes of the taxonomist, someone who knows the whole as well as its individual parts. For him or her, even the most obvious physical differences are really differences in "construction only." But when Agassiz deals in such generalities, individual distinctions inevitably emerge again. The whole of nature, for Agassiz, is a play of correspondences and differences, of allusions that identify, as they would in any literary text, both the uniqueness of a creature and the role it plays within a larger whole. The bodies of Radiates are arranged around a central main axis, the center of radiation, as it were. This makes them different from other branches of the animal kingdom, the Insects, Worms, and Vertebrates, with one intriguing exception: "The significance of this upright position of the lowest type of animals with a radiating structure is most striking in view of the upright position of man, at the head of the animal creation." By pointing out that a whole "branch" of animals is organized around the principle of verticality, while this is true of only one species of vertebrates, Agassiz both challenges and upholds the uniqueness of "man."[72]

To return to Agassiz's riff about touching a jellyfish (deliberately left unnamed). While it makes the scientist think about the whole of nature and how this creature fits into it, the passage also re-creates, in a nutshell, how one comes by such knowledge, how one learns to understand and appreciate such individuality, from Aristotle's first, sketchy account ("They have the mouth in the middle, and live from the rocks as from a shell") to Michael Sars's papers on the developmental stages of medusae, published in Norway in the 1830s and 1840s, to the present moment, distinguished by Agassiz's efforts. Agassiz's summary conveys the extraordinary complexity of the subject: weighty tomes have been devoted to animals that dissolve into nothing as we try to hold them in our hands. Ironically, though the entire passage about the jellyfish is cast in terms of a religious revelation (first we see through a glass darkly, but then we shall see all), the process itself—our looking, touching, feeling—is much more important than the result. For Agassiz, the "primary consideration in . . . education" was, as he explained in one of his annual reports to the members of the Massachusetts legislature, to teach his students "how to observe." From the beginning, he placed specimens rather than books in their hands, watching them constantly as they were dealing with them, until he had ascertained "what are their ability of seeing for themselves, and their aptitude for this kind of studies."[73] Seeing, not reading, was Agassiz's educational mantra. The only genuine textbook he accepted was, he liked to point out, the Book of Nature itself. That didn't mean Agassiz never read books himself. He did own a large library, but he was notorious for treating his books cavalierly. He would pile them up, in shabby bindings, in common wooden bookcases, as his shocked sister-in-law, Emma Forbes Cary, remembered later. Books, for Agassiz, were *tools*, to be used and, frequently, argued with—good examples are his profusely and passionately annotated copies of Darwin's *On the Origin of Species* and Haeckel's *Natürliche Schöpfungsgeschichte*, now kept in the archives of the Ernst Mayr Library at the Museum of Comparative Zoology.[74]

As Agassiz never tired of pointing out, the observation of nature was serious business. In *Methods of Study in Natural History*, Agassiz recommended that under certain circumstances the student pursuing microscopic research adhere to "a special diet before undertaking his investigation, in order that even the beating of his arteries may not disturb the steadiness of his gaze."[75] The inconvenient fact that jellyfish are notoriously hard to watch, far from being a deterrent, is actually further grist for Agassiz's mill: yet more proof that natural history is hard, to be pursued only by those who don't give up easily and who learn to see properly.

For all his obvious love of words, his fondness for rhetorical flourishes, Agassiz was entranced with nonverbal, visual ways of understanding and representing nature. So was Darwin, as recent studies have shown.[76] But as the one and only illustration included in *On the Origin of Species* underlines, Darwin's mind naturally gravitated to the diagram. For Agassiz, illustrations weren't just *of* individual species; they were individuals in their own right, to be pursued with all the passion one brings to the relationship with a loved one. His beautiful claim that the draftsman's pencil was "one of the best of eyes" comes to mind,[77] as do the blackboard sketches that the ambidextrous Agassiz himself produced, to the delight of his audiences. While Darwin's artistic talents were modest, Agassiz, as a draftsman, could compete with the best of natural history illustrators. No wonder, then, that he was, as his longtime assistant Theodore Lyman remembered, a "pitiless critic of a zoological drawing" and rarely satisfied even with the "finest work."[78] Agassiz's natural history illustrators—Joseph Dinkel, Joseph Bettannier, his wife Cecilie Braun—worked for him only as long as they were useful to him; only one of them, Jacques Burkhardt, the best, stayed with him virtually throughout his career.

And then there was "the man who never failed to please him," according to Lyman—the lithographer Antoine Sonrel, unmatched master of the jellyfish drawing.[79] We know very little about Sonrel's life, except that he was born in Nancy and that he died in 1879 in Woburn, Massachusetts, where a street bears his surname. His first name remains a mystery, to some extent. In French documents, he shows up as Auguste, but his death notice lists him as Antoine.[80] In 1848 he traveled across the Atlantic to join Agassiz in Boston and found employment as a lithographer with the firm of Tappan and Bradford. But he had brought his own lithographic press with him, and in 1850, he was able to open his own shop in Boston, establishing a reputation as one of the finest scientific illustrators of his time. When Agassiz published his essay on the naked-eyed medusae in 1850, the illustrations were Sonrel's, as were the lithographs in *Lake Superior*. Without Sonrel's help, Agassiz declared, without his "quickness in seizing the characteristic features of organized beings, and in reproducing them with a delicate touch," he would not have been able to conjure up anything for his audience.[81]

Sonrel became one of Agassiz's most essential collaborators on *Contributions to the Natural History of the United States of America*, and it was Sonrel's representations of jellyfish that acquired particular importance to Agassiz, precisely because of the challenges that were involved in simply seeing these creatures for what they are. "I have never felt more deeply the imperfection of our knowledge of some of the most remarkable types of the animal kingdom, than in attempting to describe the beautiful representative of the genus Cyanea," Agassiz wrote about *Cyanea arctica*, the largest known jellyfish, now considered a subspecies of *Cyanea capillata*, better known as "lion's mane." He went on to explain why:

> I can truly say that I have fully shared the surprise of casual observers, in noticing this gigantic Radiate stranded upon our beaches, and wondered what may be the meaning of all the different parts hanging from the lower surface of the large gelatinous disk. It is true that naturalists have long ago given particular names to all of them,—they have distinguished a mouth, a stomach, ovaries, tentacles, and even applied the name of eyes to some prominent specks on the margin . . . [But] is that which is called mouth, in Jellyfishes, truly a mouth? is the so-called stomach truly a stomach? are the so-called ovaries really ovaries? . . . have the parts designated as arms any resemblance to the upper limbs of the Vertebrates?[82]

In the next paragraph, Agassiz gives us an extended description of *Cyanea arctica* that again flirts with images taken from the world of human experience. The medusa's long, toxic tentacles are, Agassiz writes, like "floating tresses of hair," while the thicker lobes behind them seem like "rich curtains, loosely waving to and fro." Linnaeus, the father of modern biological taxonomy, had been the first to note a resemblance between the stinging tentacles of jellyfish and the snaky locks of the Medusa, and Agassiz is clearly alluding to this mythological image. But he also realizes pretty quickly that such standard comparisons won't do anymore. "The most active imagination," Agassiz admits, "is truly at a loss to discover, in such a creature, any thing that recalls the animals with which we ourselves are most closely allied. There is no head, no body, there are no limbs."[83]

Words fail us when we try to describe this animal. All the questions we ask of nature have to be formulated in language, as do the answers we find. But language inevitably returns us to a world shaped by our own notions and expectations, and that is, Agassiz realizes, *not* the world of the medusa. Evidently, even the term *medusa* itself isn't appropriate. And if the jellyfish is not really a medusa, it is certainly not a fish either. Nor is it really made of jelly. Agassiz's prose brilliantly confronts this problem, dancing around its own insufficiency.

Consider now Sonrel's illustration of *Cyanea arctica*, which Agassiz included in *Contributions*. Spilling down the page, *Cyanea arctica* seems otherworldly, a spectacle of fragile and mysterious beauty, a phantasm more than a natural history specimen. Sonrel takes evident pleasure in the contrast he has developed between the medusa's thin, wispy appendages occupying the lower two-thirds of the page and the bulging shapes that loom behind them in the upper third. More persistent viewers who still want to think of this creature in terms of the human face and human hair will be sobered by the explanation, offered in Agassiz's text, that the "mouth" we're looking at is actually the creature's digestive cavity and that the two sacs we see precisely where the eyes should be are, in fact, the genital pouches. But we don't really need Agassiz's commentary to understand the picture. Sonrel's illustration radically confronts us and in fact revels in the reality of a life utterly different from ours, infinitely more complex than can be captured in language limited by the narrow horizon of human self-experience. This medusa really exists; it is not, as Darwin said about species, merely an artificial combination made for the convenience of the naturalist.[84]

Anthropomorphic thinking, often taken to be a direct expression and consequence of the unexamined notion that humans are primary among the diversity of beings, had come under fire at just about the same time that Agassiz got involved in his research on medusae, and Agassiz's discussion of the jellyfish shows that he had thought about the issue too. For example, in his *Sea-Side Studies*, George Henry Lewes cautioned against attributing "irritation" or "alarm" to sea anemones, an approach that he felt was detrimental to "scientific seriousness." To claim that mollusks "see," he said, does justice neither to the mollusk nor its human observer: "Molluscan vision is not human vision; nor in accurate language is it vision at all."[85] Sonrel's illustrations did their share in exploding the boundaries conventionally imposed by a human observer intent on relegating a living creature to the status of a scientific specimen.

To Agassiz, who had spent years studying the marks and scratches left by glaciers on the rocks and mountains of the world, "stone drawing" (the literal translation of *lithography*) must have seemed an eminently suitable medium for natural history illustration. Agassiz would never forget a moment in his earlier life as a European savant when, during a visit to a museum in Germany, he saw a perfect impression of a fossilized medusa on two slabs of slate, the pliable, watery creature immortalized in the rock: "The impression made upon my mind by the preservation, through countless ages, of an animal so soft as a jelly-fish, was so vivid, that, though I have never seen those fossils since, I well remember their general appearance." What else did nature itself do but draw in stone?[86] And now here was this artist, Sonrel, who had made a career out of doing deliberately and with great perfection what nature did so casually, so effortlessly. Since jellyfish consist of 98 percent water and lose their shape immediately when taken out of their element, Sonrel would draw their likenesses directly on the stone, using specimens he had freshly netted or watched swimming in the water off the coast of Massachusetts. Sonrel's art, like Agassiz's science, was a way of bridging the difference—if only up to a point—between the world of humans and the world of jellyfish, which was otherwise so unrecoverably different. No human observer, Sonrel included, would come across a medusa exactly like this representation of *Cyanea arctica*, drifting lazily against a calm white paper background.

But there was a remedy, and Sonrel knew just what to do. In order to behold the medusa in its full glory, Agassiz's reader had to fold out the plate, only to be told in the notes accompanying it that the actual specimen depicted, "an adult of ordinary size," had in fact been four times larger. In Sonrel's drawing, the lower ends of the tentacles are rather unceremoniously cut off, a reminder that this image is not the real thing, but just that: an image, a representation. "When perfectly undisturbed," writes Agassiz, "the tentacles may be extended to an extraordinary length."[87] But now look at the left margin of the picture: by refusing to cut the tentacles off there, by letting them undulate beyond the lithograph's inked border, Sonrel seems to be telling us that this plate is not just an image. Somewhere out there was, indeed, a real animal, touched, caressed, disturbed by the artist's hand so that he could make its portrait. The medusa as we see it in Sonrel's drawing is at the same time found and constructed, its representation a self-conscious act of both discovery and invention, a celebration of the kind of individuality that is, in Agassiz's opinion, the cornerstone of natural history.

Agassiz knew how much he owed to Sonrel's skill. Normally, he regarded research that had been performed for him, either at his museum in Cambridge or his lab in Nahant, as *his* property: its authors had to be acknowledged, but only as part of the institutional framework within which they had produced their results. But these rules didn't apply to Sonrel's work. His artistic vision put him in a class of his own; he was no mere laborer in Agassiz's scientific vineyard. In the course of a long passage comparing *Cyanea arctica* with another genus of medusa, *Aurelia*, Agassiz's praise for Sonrel's extraordinary skill quickly turns into praise for the complexity of the living, moving thing that his artist has captured so well in a medium so little suited for the representation of life:

> I cannot suppress my admiration for the skill with which Mr. Sonrel has reproduced all these tentacles in their wonderful entanglement, and yet with such distinctness, that every one may be traced in unbroken continuity, from its point of attachment to the furthest distance to which it stretches. He has succeeded in giving them all the variety of aspect which they present in active motion, when in the same bunch some of the tentacles may be entirely drawn in to within a fraction of an inch of their point of attachment, and others stretched to their utmost length, while others, again, wave from one bunch across the other bunches, or flow in undulating lines, or bend upon themselves, or are twisted in a spiral, and still others appear like heavy leads sinking among the rest.[88]

Agassiz deliberately emphasizes the difference between visual and verbal representation, making his words strain to capture, for the

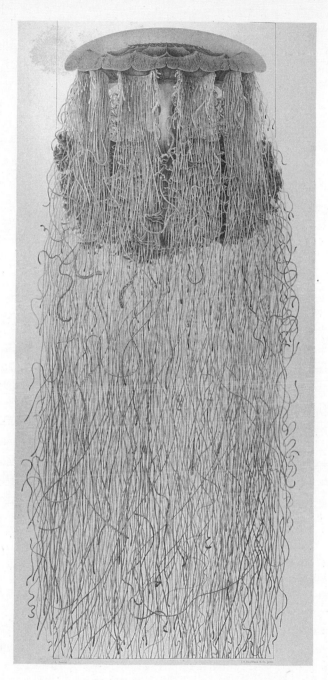

Cyanea arctica. Drawn and lithographed by Antoine Sonrel. From *Contributions to the Natural History of the United States of America,* by Louis Agassiz, volume 3, plate 4, 1860.

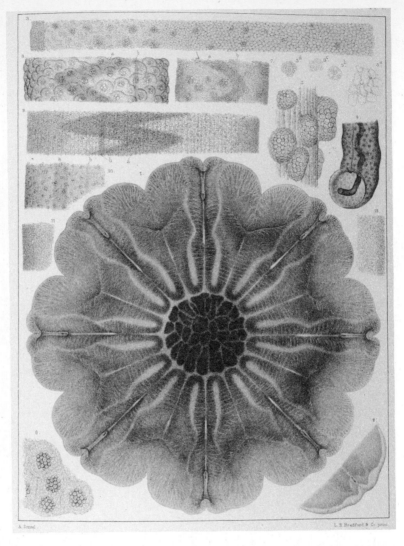

Cyanea arctica, showing the surface of the disk. Drawn and lithographed by Antoine Sonrel. From *Contributions to the Natural History of the United States of America*, by Louis Agassiz, volume 3, plate 5, 1860.

reader's ear, the very same impression Sonrel's drawing produces instantaneously for the viewer, namely, that of a multifaceted organism in constant flux. Note how syntax ("when . . . and others . . . while others, again . . . or . . . or . . . or . . . and still others") and sound ("*ten-tacles . . . en*tanglement"; "wi*th*in a *f*raction *o*f an *in*ch"; "undu*l*ating *l*ines") work together to "entangle" the reader in an experience that, as Agassiz realizes, defies conventional methods of representation.

Another lithograph Agassiz includes in this volume of *Contributions* gives us a view of the surface of *Cyanea arctica*'s disk. Agassiz's accompanying text reveals that here Sonrel's skill was put to the test even more than before: "it must be borne in mind . . . that what might be taken for lines upon the surface of the disk, are, in reality, the optical effects of parts occupying the thickness of the disk, and its lower surface." Agassiz reaches for a metaphor to describe what words cannot convey and what Sonrel's drawing catches so effortlessly: the unequal transparency of the disk, thick in some places, thinner in others. "It is as if a mass of transparent jelly of a flat, hemispheric form, was resting upon a surface adorned with various structural details, which could all readily be seen through the jelly."[89] Unlike Sonrel's first lithograph of this creature, this image is more of a scientific illustration, complete with letters and numbers keyed to the explanations Agassiz provides elsewhere in this section. Sonrel gives us a plethora of structural details; *Cyanea arctica* appears not as an organic whole but as the sum of its many parts. The straight edges of the segments of lobes, appendages, and tentacles show the effects of the naturalist's relentless knife. Surrounded by severed limbs and magnified cells, the tessellated disk of *Cyanea*, spared by the naturalist, has remained intact. Intricately patterned and luminous, it sends the viewer, once again, groping for analogies.

An interesting difference emerges between Agassiz and Sonrel's treatment of *Cyanea arctica* and the representation of jellyfish in the works of Agassiz's hotheaded German contemporary, the Darwinist Ernst Haeckel. If Huxley was "Darwin's bulldog" in England, Haeckel was his "German shepherd" on the Continent,[90] a prolific and aggressive polemicist but also a consummate artist. Entranced, like Agassiz, with the sinuous curves of marine animals, Haeckel attacked Darwin's American opponent wherever and whenever he could, finding fault with his theories, classifications, and morphological descriptions. When we turn to Haeckel's own prose, however, in *Das System der Medusen* (1880) as well as in the later *Kunstformen der Natur* (1899–1904), we discover, to our surprise, that the proud harbinger of evolutionary progress still thinks about jellyfish in unabashedly anthropomorphic terms, to the extent that he names two of them, the small *Mitrocoma annae* and the large *Desmonema annasethe*, after his deceased first wife, Anna Sethe, of whose beauty and blond hair he had been powerfully reminded when contemplating these elusive creatures.[91] Haeckel's decorous language prettifies even the medusa's sexual organs, such as the "enticingly ruffled" gonad, which hangs suspended from a "delicate light yellow apron" or "*Geschlechtsgardine*" (literally, "genital drape").[92]

Haeckel's own drawings regularly "improve on" the specimens he is depicting, creating swirling tableaus of flowing lines and perfect symmetry that have more in common with the conventions of art nouveau than the organisms he had observed.[93] In plate 8 of his *Kunstformen*, for example, Haeckel arranges three specimens, all of them known as Discomedusae, as if they were performing a kind of ballet. His main purpose seems to be to create the impression of weightlessness. The two smaller medusae in, respectively, the lower-right and the upper-left corners of the composition mark an invisible diagonal that intersects with the visible and much stronger diagonal connecting the upper right with the lower left, embodied by Haeckel's favorite medusa with its sinuous tentacles, *Desmonema annasethe*. So strong is that diagonal, striving against the gravitational pull, that it overrules the more conventional diagramlike view of the medusa's disk seen from below, which Haeckel gives us in the center of the lower third of the picture. Scientific seeing is pushed aside by the artist's conception of nature. By contrast, Sonrel's vertical *Cyanea arctica* occupies its own separate space. Haeckel's superficially more dynamic composition self-consciously advertises the fact that it was *made*, created for a purpose, guided by the artist's need to produce a beautiful pattern or, rather, several patterns, of the kind that Haeckel also used in his home in Jena, the Villa Medusa, where his "jellyfish love" manifested itself in the sinuous forms of the medusae covering his ceilings, his furniture, his porcelain, and his velvet cushions.[94]

It is evident that Sonrel's love of visual detail had served as an inspiration for *Kunstformen*. Though Haeckel had nothing good to say about Agassiz, he praised Sonrel's "prachtvolle Figuren" (splendid illustrations) to the skies.[95] But the ideology underlying Haeckel's rep-

Discomedusae. From *Kunstformen der Natur,* by Ernst Haeckel, plate 8.

resentations of nature couldn't be more different from Sonrel's. In the preface to *Kunstformen,* Haeckel said, in Darwinian fashion, that he wanted to represent "the laws" underlying the formation and development of his marine organisms, as well as penetrate, in his capacity of draftsman and painter, the secret of their beauty. If Haeckel wanted to *know,* penetrate the secret, Sonrel—and through him Agassiz—wanted to *be* the secret, to enter, via the knowledge of nature's details, into the mystery of God's creative power. Haeckel's medusae bring, in the language of the preface to *Kunstformen,* "hidden treasures to light"; Sonrel's plates of *Cyanea arctica* point to a reality the illustrator is able to capture only by reminding the viewer that he cannot ever hope to capture it.[96] Featuring a world alien to the human observer, the plates Sonrel produced for Agassiz's book aren't just visual aids. They are certainly precise enough to convey accurate scientific information. Interestingly, a key to marine invertebrates published by the Marine Biological Laboratory in Woods Hole still uses, without attribution to Sonrel, a modified version of the first image of *Cyanea arctica* shown in this chapter.[97] But Sonrel's images also gesture beyond their frames, at a world no human imagination can, at least currently, grasp fully.

A medusa is an infinitely complex *living* being; it is therefore not, to use the anti-evolutionist Michael Behe's now infamous image, a mousetrap.[98] And to Agassiz it was not (as Darwin and Gray would have said) an ephemeral, temporary manifestation of jellyfishness in a long history of random changes leading to who knows what. Agassiz's son, Alexander, for all his growing interest in Darwinism, captured well what this natural thing meant to his father. In 1865, he published an extraordinarily evocative piece in the *Atlantic Monthly*, a poetic meditation on the catching of jellyfish during the day ("The Idyia glitters and sparkles with ever-changing hues") and at night, when the jellyfish illuminate the sea and the water looks like "rills of molten metal." Choose a particularly dark night, "when the motion of your boat sets the sea on fire around you, and a long undulating wave of light rolls off from your oar as you lift it from the water." Alexander emphasizes how "wild and weird" the experience is, how transformative for the human observer. It is no coincidence that he employs the language of the sublime here: it "at once fascinates and appalls the imagination."[99]

Agassiz's dream of complete transparency, of nature shining a light upon itself in a manner that can be easily communicated, via text and images, to the masses, drew scorn even from his more conservative contemporaries who shared his opposition to evolution. The painter Ernest Wadsworth Longfellow, for example, though he admired Agassiz's fugitive blackboard drawings, had only disdain for the hope the "poor dear man" harbored that science and art could be made one: "A slavish copying of nature is not art, and . . . art does not concern itself with fauna and geological periods, but with the im-

"Louis Agassiz (speaking with himself)." Albumen print, carte de visite, by Antoine Sonrel, c. 1871.

pression a particular scene or effect has on the spectator and can be made to have on the imagination of others."[100] Ernest Longfellow's characterization of Agassiz's alleged category mistake (confusing illustration, as a slavish copying of nature, and true art liberated from such constraints) is typical even of modern approaches to the genre of scientific illustration, which has often been shunned by art historians.[101] Lithographs, by their very existence, challenge traditional conceptions of art: instead of one "original" they give us many copies. At the same time, since there is no original (many lithographers reused or destroyed the stone on which they drew the "original" image), each of the copies could well be considered original. Out of the one, many.

Photography was the next logical step, and this is precisely where Sonrel was headed. Far swifter than the hand that draws, to paraphrase Walter Benjamin, is the eye looking through a lens.[102] One of Sonrel's later photographs shows not a jellyfish but a human or, perhaps, two humans. In a staged studio setting, we see none other than Louis Agassiz facing, well, Louis Agassiz, across a small table. On the right, Agassiz number 1 is engaged in writing, his head bent in concentration over a small notebook, with a stack of other books behind him. His doppelganger on the left, however, Agassiz number 2, is apparently already finished with his task. Before him, an open book or notebook; his left hand, now relaxed, is still holding the pen, while the right hand is resting comfortably on his thigh. Is he waiting for the ink to dry? Or is he about to begin again? Both scientists look pleased.

By providing different views of the same person in *one* portrait, Sonrel intentionally confuses the beholder, substituting two images where we would expect to see only one. Late-nineteenth-century photographers developed such double portraits in part because they were a neat trick (after the first exposure, the subject of the photograph quickly had to move into a different position so that the second half of the picture could be made).[103] We can't know if Agassiz had a hand in the creation of this image, but I submit to the reader that Agassiz's double portrait is more than mere gimmickry. Duplicated by the lens of Sonrel's camera, Agassiz the scientist acquires a status not unlike that of his jellyfish—an individual, yet not. Note that the two figures are not identical — they are copies of each other, yet each is unique. In this image at least, Agassiz was not one of Darwin's multiple dissectible barnacles, not the "well cudgelled dog" of the Gray-Darwin correspondence, but a creature as fluid and outrageous as any of his jellyfish, knowable and unknowable at the same time.

5

MR. CLARK'S HEADACHE

IF ANTOINE SONREL, Agassiz's favorite illustrator, provided
Agassiz with the images that made *Contributions to the Natural History of the United States of America* so unique, much of
the fieldwork for the volumes was done by Agassiz's favorite student,
the extraordinarily gifted Henry James Clark, an expert on jellyfish.
Right in the preface to the first volume of *Contributions* (1857), Agassiz thanked Clark fulsomely: "I owe it to Mr. Clark to say, that he has
identified himself so thoroughly with my studies since he took his degree in the Lawrence Scientific School, that it would be difficult for
me to say when I ceased to guide him in his work. But this I know
very well, — that he is now a most trustworthy observer, fully capable
of tracing for himself the minutest microscopic investigation, and the
accuracy of his illustrations challenges comparison."[1] It would have
mattered a great deal to Agassiz that Clark had originally been Asa
Gray's favorite student too.

"He has identified himself so thoroughly with my studies . . ." To
understand Agassiz, we need to understand the people who worked
for him, who saw him daily, who were subjected to his influence.
Among all the people in Agassiz's pull, we most need to understand
Henry James Clark. For one thing, it is Clark who will help us better understand Agassiz at the height of his influence in America. For
the longest time, Clark was closer to Agassiz than anyone else, with

the exception perhaps of Agassiz's wife, Elizabeth. Clark was fundamentally different from Édouard Desor and Charles Girard, the two most memorable members of the "Hôtel des Neuchâtelois," long defunct by the time Clark arrived at the Lawrence School. Clark was not a more or less private assistant to a famous public naturalist. A father himself, he had no interest in becoming anyone's son. He was no Desor, eager to bask in the master's reflected glory and to scoop up what Agassiz didn't want or had forgotten—crumbs from his table. And he had none of Girard's endless capacity for masochistic suffering. Clark wanted more. He was, in modern terms, Agassiz's first important graduate student. American to the core, his main goal wasn't to please Agassiz or to take advantage of him, but rather to learn from him what he could in order to create a career for himself. Put succinctly, this chapter tells the story of Clark's failure to do so. It also inevitably tells the story of Agassiz's failure to make his American dream—of being a great professor at a university and a natural history museum rivaling the best institutions of Europe and teaching great students to carry on his legacy—come true. Agassiz does not tell that story himself, except in a few scattered sentences, and so this chapter will make room for the voice of Henry James Clark. As we will see, Clark carries on, in somewhat different fashion, the debate about individuality that Agassiz was having with Darwin and Gray.

Like his boss, Clark was a careful investigator, a dedicated microscopist, and a gifted draftsman. Unlike his boss, he was not a great communicator—not in public, that is. His best writing Clark did for himself, in his journals and not in his few published articles, which are, for the most part, workmanlike, although occasionally lightened by the kind of rhetorical flourishes or flights of metaphorical fancy for which his teacher was known. Not that his writing was ineffective. It is true that after reading *Mind in Nature*, the only book Clark published during his short life, Darwin caustically remarked to Benjamin Walsh, a correspondent in Illinois, that he was interested in it mainly "on psychological principles as shewing how differently two men viz. the writer and the reader can view the same subject."[2] In other words, what poor Mr. Clark regarded as incontrovertible evidence, Darwin regarded as a bunch of bull. But Darwin was less than candid. His copy of Clark's *Mind in Nature* has survived in the library at Down

House, and Darwin's marginalia and a note on a separate piece of paper he inserted between pages 94 and 95 show that he didn't just skim Clark's book. Nor did he disagree with everything Clark said. In fact, he was rather fascinated by Clark's observations on the reduced form of individuality one encounters in underwater creatures like the sea anemone, which will create new life through self-division. And he did pay attention to the remarks on "projecting" with which Clark ended the second part of his book. There Clark, in rather tentative terms ("What, then, shall we say . . ."?), discussed what happens when the differences between individuals born to the same parents multiply over the course of subsequent generations. The distant offspring of a "long past progenitor" will be, he said, so different from each other that they "would hardly be recognized as of the same race." Obviously, to Darwin, that passage sounded like a variation of his own idea of natural selection.[3] As he would have realized, Clark's narrative was a far cry from the predictable, statically unfolding history of nature, punctuated by separate acts of divine creation, that Agassiz had imagined in his work. Clark was no fool, and in spite of the tone he took in his letter to Walsh, Darwin knew that he wasn't Agassiz's stooge either.

If Clark didn't reveal too much about himself in his scientific work, he gave us more than a glimpse of his inner life in his comprehensive journals, now kept at Agassiz's Museum of Comparative Zoology at Harvard: six octavo-sized books with torn, smudged covers and page after page filled with Clark's neat, smallish handwriting, which leaves no margins and has a tendency to start leaning to the right when the author is excited.[4] Other than Clark himself, Agassiz is the main character in these entries.

In what might be the only close-up portrait of Clark that has survived, his face is unforgettable, even haunting. The unkempt, scraggly beard contrasts oddly with the soft, sensitive eyes and the neatly parted hair. Averting his eyes from the camera, Clark seems insecure and shy. This was a man who defied easy categorization. It is easy to guess why Agassiz became interested in him—and easy to guess too why their relationship was destined for disaster.

Henry James Clark was born on June 22, 1826, in Easton, Massachusetts. The son of a Swedenborgian minister, the Reverend Henry Potter Clark, and the former Abigail Orton, Clark grew up mostly in

Henry James Clark. Undated carte de visite.

Brooklyn.⁵ Throughout his life, he felt strongly connected to his family, especially to his brother Thomas Edward Clark, whose nickname "Ned" appears on almost every other page of his journal, often with double underlining and almost always written in letters larger than the rest.

In 1848, Clark graduated from the University of the City of New York, as New York University was then known, with a bachelor's degree in the arts. He went on to teach school in White Plains, New York, where he became interested in local natural history. When one of his friends memorialized him later, he said Clark's love for science had grown out of his "fondness for flowers."⁶ During one of his rambles through the neighborhood, Clark found a flower that he thought was new, and immediately brought this fact to the attention of Asa Gray in Cambridge: "This," wrote Clark's wife, "I call the date of his *Scientific* birth."⁷ Gray was impressed and encouraged Clark to come work for him. He said he could offer him no money (a song that Clark would hear again in the years to come) but plenty of other benefits, including "tickets for you for any courses of scientific lectures you may desire to attend.—so that you would pass your time advantageously in a scientific respect."[8] That was enough for Clark to pack his things and move to Cambridge, where he joined Gray. To supplement what Gray offered him, Clark taught for a while at Westfield Academy, a large coeducational school about a hundred miles west of Boston.

Gray was a good mentor, precise, impeccably logical in his thinking, but also kind and understanding. Nevertheless, it seems that Clark, his mind on fire with the possibilities that both nature study and the city of Boston offered him, quickly became bored with Gray's understated personality, his careful handling of scientific evidence. Soon he found himself in the orbit of Agassiz. While Gray stayed in his herbarium, Agassiz took his students to the beaches of Massachusetts or the mountains of New Hampshire.

Clark eagerly soaked up what Agassiz had to offer. His brother Ned joined him. In 1854, both brothers graduated from the Lawrence Scientific School, each with the newly established bachelor's degree in science (Clark's second degree). Intrigued by his raw talent for nature observation, Agassiz asked Clark to work for him. Things were going swimmingly. The same year, Clark married Mary Young Holbrook of Boston, with whom he would have eight children, four sons and four daughters, seven of whom survived infancy. Ned, made of lighter metal than his brother, fled Agassiz's commanding influence and went to Germany, where he studied chemistry. Later he worked as a physician, apparently first in California and, by 1872, in New York.[9] Henry stayed. A photograph taken sometime in 1856, when Clark would have been in his second year of working for Agassiz, is said to show him among a group of people on the steps of Agassiz's Quincy Street house.[10] The image, long thought to be extant only in later reproductions, is a stereoview by Frederick Langenheim of Philadelphia. Agassiz, wearing a stovepipe hat, is presiding over a motley assembly that includes his Swiss illustrator, the white-bearded Jacques Burkhardt, as well as someone who looks much like Agassiz's lanky neighbor, the anatomist Jeffries Wyman. Sitting across from Agassiz, Wyman (or the man resembling him) is listening in on a conversation Agassiz is enjoying with two unidentified men, one of whom is holding, or reading from, a book. But that conversation definitively does

On the steps of the home of Louis Agassiz, Quincy Street, Cambridge, Massachusetts. Stereoview on glass by Frederick Langenheim, 1856.

not include the young man with the dark mustache, who might or might not be Clark. Standing all the way to the back, he looks straight ahead, thinking who knows what.[11]

Clark's diaries begin on March 11, 1857, and end on March 16, 1873, the year both Clark and his former teacher Agassiz died. The entries, one every day for almost the entire period, reveal a man in near-constant agony, worried about his failing health, his inexorably growing family, and his mounting financial responsibilities—worried too that he might not be good enough at what he was doing. Who but a deeply anguished person would name his firstborn son Xenos, "stranger"? In the spring of 1857, on Xenos's second birthday, Clark happened to be reading a book about the Humboldt brothers and immediately fretted about his suitability both as a scientist and as a father: "When I reflect upon the training the brothers Humboldt received and the eminence these young minds attained to I cannot but feel the profoundest anxiety for the intellectual development of my own dear boy . . . Would that I could command more patience amid all my cares!"[12] Though he was working with the man who wanted to be considered the American Humboldt, Clark feared that he himself wasn't fit to mentor even his own son.

But the diaries also show another side of his personality. Clark was an avid reader. Some books he borrowed from the library of the College (Shakespeare, Tennyson, a biography of Goethe); others he purchased, and then he didn't skimp, gravitating to Humboldt as his leisure reading. On April 2, 1857, he bought a four-volume edition of *Cosmos* ($3.50), along with a half-length photograph of the German explorer. More than anything, Clark adored opera, and he was hopelessly star-struck when it came to the theater, recording in his journal every move the actors made, what their faces looked like in a moment of extreme tension, how their voices sounded when they were angry or sad. In the first few months of 1857 alone, he attended Fanny Kemble's public readings of Shakespeare, a performance of Beethoven's *Fidelio*, a concert given by the Italian contralto Elena d'Angri, and a play now forgotten, called *Lazio; or, The Italian Wife*, presented at the Boston Theatre. Watching the latter from the closest seat to the stage he had been able to find, he fell helplessly in love with Matilda Heron, the actress who played the role of Bianca: "I would see every shade of expression on her countenance. Her eyes are *beautiful*, but have a tremendous power of expression . . . Without hesitation she is the greatest American actress that ever lived, and bids fair to *rival* any that ever lived *anywhere*." As happened whenever Clark was seized by a powerful emotion, his diary entry ended anticlimactically: "Eve Headache. to bed early."[13]

Agassiz, for all the lip service he paid to culture, for all his friendships with poets and philosophers, apparently did not share Clark's love of the stage. He preferred a good dinner to an evening spent listening to Beethoven. Sometimes, though, Clark would run into other students of Agassiz at such events—Theodore Lyman, for example.

But Ted Lyman, the son of a former mayor of Boston and the grandson of a successful shipping magnate, was to the manor born. It seems amazing that, given his workload as Agassiz's assistant, Clark was still able to make time for these outings—and even more amazing that he found the money somewhere to buy theater tickets. For Clark's taste in theater, music, and *savoir vivre* ("*In Boston*, trying to get some extra good tea & Mocha coffee")[14] as well as his generosity toward others was desperately at odds with his financial situation. A poignant leitmotif throughout Clark's diaries is the money he owes to various people.

At first, at least, Clark's decision to work for Agassiz paid off. Under his excitable new mentor's guidance, Clark transformed himself, in just a couple of years, into an excellent practitioner of science, equally adept at peering through a microscope and wielding his drawing pencil, often doing both at the same time. He also became an expert on a rather spectacular-looking species of little jellyfish with bell-shaped bodies, known as *Lucernaria*. Like Agassiz, Clark turned to live specimens whenever he could. In May 1857, for example, he brought home fifteen pairs of copulating toads, some of which he believed to belong to different species. Using his India rubber net, he had scooped dozens of these animals—"faster than Agassiz could pick them up," he pointed out—from a pond near the Botanic Gardens on Linnaean Street. At home he kept a few of these strange couples in separate vessels to see if the females would lay their eggs. It is not clear what Clark's wife thought of the arrangement.[15]

Clark's correspondence reveals how much of his time was eaten up by work on the *Contributions to the Natural History of the United States of America*, the monumental volumes that were supposed to solidify Agassiz's status as the founder of American natural history. A thorough, tireless, detail-oriented worker, Clark felt confident enough to challenge his mentor, citing observations he had made himself in the field. A beautiful example is this letter sent from Cape Cod, where Clark had just discovered what he thought was a new species of jellyfish: "The border tentacles, *thirty in each bunch*, are the same in nature as figured in your monograph; but there I believe they numbered but *twenty two* in each parcel. I do not recollect that you have noticed the double eye spots upon the two middle ones." Clark added a quick sketch and continued. "The larger ones are on a level with those on the other tentacles & the smaller nearer the base." Clark loved fieldwork: wading in shallow water, listening to the buzz of insects in the summer air (some of them whirred as loudly as hummingbirds), reaching for the fish whizzing past his naked feet.[16] When he was in Cambridge, his mysterious headaches became often unbearable, to be relieved only by the frequent walks he took to Fresh Pond or Mount Auburn Cemetery. Even the birth, on April 5, 1857, of a daughter—a "stout & hearty" child, with a thick head of dark hair and a powerful voice, a picture of health the way Clark was not—hardly made a difference in how he felt: "My headache & biliousness continued all day." The next day Clark bought a ticket for Fanny Kemble. Now *there* was something to look forward to.

During the days, however, he was mostly at Agassiz's museum or at home, writing up paragraphs on embryo turtles and preparing countless drawings of specimens he had dissected and then inspected under the microscope. It fell to him to supervise the brilliant Antoine Sonrel, whose designs he reviewed, marking the spots where the draft could be improved or measurements struck him as incorrect ("darker," "lighter," or "reduce to one half its diameter"). Clark's own drawings, now also held in the archives of the Museum of Comparative Zoology, combine absolute photographic precision with artistic grace. He handles his pencil, pen, and brush lightly, creating three-dimensional, lifelike images of the minutest organisms just as we would see them if we were looking over his shoulder or through his microscope. He knows how to make tissues interesting. One of the most remarkable features of Clark's style is the suggestion of spatial depth and plasticity even when, for the second volume of *Contributions*, on the turtles, published in 1857, he is drawing eggs that are less than an inch in diameter.

Consider the image Clark drew of a turtle embryo, which in its haunting, otherworldly oddness is hard to forget. The sketch, ultimately incorporated into plate 14 of the second volume of *Contributions*, shows a six-week-old embryo of a snapping turtle. Clark made the drawing on July 31, 1855, the day he opened the egg. With its ghostlike eyes, large head, and paddle-shaped limbs, the turtle-in-the-making looks both like and unlike a human embryo. The turtle is, Agassiz would write, perhaps after seeing that drawing, "an individual, free from its parent, before it even shows to what branch of

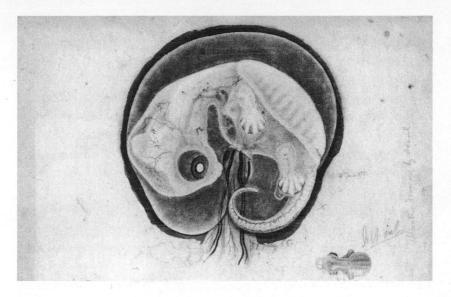

Chelonura serpentina. Draft sketch by Henry James Clark, July 31, 1855.

the animal kingdom it belongs . . . Thus Nature herself teaches us the true value and dignity of individuality."[17]

If only Agassiz himself had heeded what his natural history investigations taught him about the need to let individuals grow. But he would not leave Clark alone. Many entries in the first volume of Clark's journals record the long evenings spent, after long days in the lab, at Agassiz's Quincy Street house. Often Agassiz, still not tired, would ask Clark to take a midnight walk with him around the Cambridge Common. During these walks, Agassiz would engage in his favorite activity: making grand plans for the future. Sometimes he even began to accompany Clark home, stopping halfway to run back to his study for more reading, more writing, more plotting. Clark was beginning to feel a little unnerved by Agassiz's bragging: "Agassiz told me that he had spent an hour or more before his students in a lecture upon the subject of Analogy, in which he broached some new ideas that had been upon his mind for a long time. He said that he dictated his memoir upon the Naked Eyed Medusa in thirteen days and that upon the Beroïd Medusa in ten days and then had to rest for a month." Apparently Agassiz was oblivious to the effect that some of his confidential disclosures had on Clark: "Another thing he told me of enjoining me that I was 'not to mention it till after his death' is that he *never* wrote out the description of animals whether of species, genera, families &c. with the specimens before him; it was always done from memory."[18] Agassiz, the great proponent of *looking*, apparently wanted to remind Clark that he had a powerful brain too. But it is likely that Clark, who spent countless hours each day peering through a lens, his eyes burning from the effort, the only sound in the room the scratching of the pencil on the coarse sheet of paper spread out beside him, wasn't too impressed. One can imagine what he was thinking: Agassiz was a liar and his much-vaunted empiricism an elaborate ruse.

During the spring of 1857, Clark's journal entries also showed an obsessive concern with trees that had been "girdled" (meaning the bark had been stripped away around the circumference of the trunk) and had still somehow managed to stay alive. Girdled or "ringbarked" trees do not need to be chopped down: since the flow of sugars from the leaves to the roots is interrupted, they are dying a slow death. Yet on May 10, 1857, Clark found several such white birch trees on Somerville Hill—trees so damaged that they shouldn't be alive anymore—in full blossom "and the leaves coming out," though some of them had been deprived of bark *"for the length of the foot."* A week later he was back, driving his own knife into the bark to make "two long cuts on the north side" and taking tissue samples home with him to study them under the microscope. Those resilient trees interested him beyond measure.

On May 27, 1857, in an uncharacteristically long entry, Clark recorded his participation in the surprise serenade Cambridge students had organized in honor of Agassiz's fiftieth birthday. Clark and a fellow student met with a group of German musicians at the omnibus depot in Boston at 11:30 P.M. The party reached Cambridge around midnight and went straight to Agassiz's house on Quincy Street, surprising him and his family with a "magnificent" Bach chorale. All of Agassiz's students at the time—Theodore Lyman, Frederic Ward Putnam, and Sanborn Tenney among them[19]—were there, and after the first two pieces were finished and a beaming Agassiz had appeared in the door, they all went up the steps and "a great shaking of hands" with the master and his wife commenced. More "enchanting" music by Mendelssohn and Schubert followed inside. Everybody was, noted Clark, overcome by "kindly feeling," most of all the great Agassiz himself. Champagne and claret were flowing freely, toasts were given. "Agassiz," wrote Clark, "overran with joy—saying that the greatest work he wished to publish was to send forth a body of young men well trained in science, to whom students from Europe erc many years would flock as they do now from here to the continent." At last they all parted "in high glee, leaving Agassiz and the family in a most happy state." Life didn't get much better than that, both Agassiz and Clark must have thought—and indeed, it wouldn't. The only jarring note in Clark's report about the evening is the little postscript scribbled at the end: "My share in this serenade was $5.00." In today's money, Clark paid around $129, not a small sum for a lowly museum assistant who was not on anyone's payroll but depended on the occasional checks Agassiz wrote.

The next day, May 28, Agassiz's actual birthday, the wellsprings of love and goodwill hadn't dried up yet. When Clark reported for duty at the Quincy Street house, the library was decorated with flowers. Agassiz finally came down, well-rested and still happy, at 11 A.M., and Clark "received another shower of compliments and exhibition of good will." Agassiz informed Clark that "he was very glad to *know* me." Clark pragmatically responded that he hoped Agassiz could always say so. "I know I shall," a smiling Agassiz replied. "I can trust you *Clark*, for I know you." And, as if to assert his parental rights to Clark's life and career, Agassiz now combined praise with gentle admonishment. Never focus on too narrow a topic in your work, he lectured Clark: "There is one thing you must beware of, and that is *specialties*, it is a mean selfish mode of investigation. You are *able* and *talented* and for this I say seek higher themes, generalizations, let your field of research be a wide one . . ." In other words, try to become like me.

It was three o'clock in the afternoon when Clark finally returned home, to his crowded house on Wendell Street, a mere stone's throw from Agassiz's museum. As so often, he was tired. His headache had come back. After napping for a while and eating his dinner, he went outside, planted a dozen tomato vines ("which I bought yesterday for 50 cts"), and dug a hole for flowers under his front parlor window. To Agassiz's grand predictions for his future and his encouragement to branch out, Clark responded by tending, like Voltaire's Candide, his garden. Despite Agassiz's encouragement, Clark remained skeptical about his professional prospects: "*What next!* An appointment to some Western professorship to teach Hoosiers how to breed boys or girls at pleasure?"[20] Clark was no Charles Girard, looking for love in all the wrong places. What he wanted was a career in science.

When he was done with Agassiz's turtles, Clark moved on to the jellyfish. In September 1858, we find him working on *Cyanea arctica*, which he drew in its hydroid form (the stage in which the medusa exists as part of an underwater colony). Almost in passing, he discovered the "horny sheath" (now known as the perisarc sheath) at the creature's base, a finding Agassiz happily incorporated into his *Contributions*. At the same time, Clark was constantly trying to make adjustments to his microscope, to match the precision of European-made instruments and save on the high cost of imports. He exchanged multiple letters with the microscope maker Charles A. Spencer in Canastota in upstate New York and visited him twice, during the summer in 1858 and 1859.

In January 1859, Clark told an audience at the American Academy of Arts and Sciences about the days he spent with Spencer, "testing his objectives with the tissues of every creature which we could find." Forgetting entirely the format and venue of his presentation, Clark recalled his "astonishment and delight with which I occupied day after day, plunged into the hitherto unknown depths of organic life." Spencer's lenses combined high power with wide angles, and they helped Clark immensely as he turned his attention to some of the smallest and yet most abundant of organisms: protozoa. He was able to see "an isolated cell, in a manner totally unexpected to me" and gain a view of its inner surface, "as if it were actually cut across." With Spencer's microscope, every cell could be treated as if it were a separate body. An almost "transcendental" view, Clark called it. What he now needed was, above all, time: "Now we know that every second of the life of a cell, or series of cells, may be traced most minutely, minute by minute, hour by hour, and day by day." Clark spoke dismissively of investigators who based their observations on anything other than a living body (probably the majority of the scientists in the audience that day). Not realizing what damage the slightest pressure did to a fragile specimen, they would "monomaniacally" smother the thin-walled yolk cells of a turtle or a bird with a piece of glass for better viewing under the microscope because that was the thing to do. "I feel that I cannot urge too strongly the utmost necessity of studying living beings as nearly in a state of nature as is possible; to attempt this by all available means and contrivances, and, above all, patiently, not begrudging the time, because more numerous observations might be obtained by making a piecemeal and hurried show of dismembered Nature." And, a sign of troubles to come, Clark referred to his master's forthcoming volume on the jellyfish, wherein the outer wall of a hydroid jellyfish had been described as "a structureless membrane"; now, with his new microscope, Clark had found it to be in fact composed of multiple polygonal cells, "as distinct as any in other parts of the animal."[21]

Agassiz, in the audience, didn't flinch. Ever the publicity hound, he was so proud of his promising assistant that he cared little what precisely Clark's own investigations were about, as long as the process he was using was spectacular. After Clark had spoken about his modifications of the microscope and its uses in the study of minute organisms, Agassiz loudly praised his "*first American* pupil" and announced that Clark's "new use of the Microscope was to Histology and Zoology in general what Herschel's resolving the nebulae was to Astronomy." Now even the normally despondent Clark felt impressed with himself. "Very good!" he wrote in his diary. He was distracted enough to forget to pick up his wife, who had gone to visit her father in downtown Boston, and "so she staid in town all night."[22]

Later the same year, on April 12, 1859, Clark was back at the academy, this time presenting what he called "my little paper," titled "On the Origin of Vibrio," which are bacteria that he thought he had observed emerging from the fibers of the muscles of the arrow worm. Agassiz was riding another emotional high, announcing once again to the assembled gentlemen that Clark had proved himself a "*Microscopic Observer without equal.*" This time, however, the careful Clark thought that Agassiz's praise sounded hollow. Agassiz's accolades notwithstanding, he knew that there was much in the field that he hadn't yet seen or understood. Later that night his doubts found their way into his diary, where he noted drily, "So much for my adopted *principle* of the *utmost rigidity* and *thoroughness* in my researches without regard to time consumed or the value of the results."[23]

Did Clark realize how far and fast he was moving away from his master? Agassiz was a firm believer in the ordering hand of a divine intelligence, and "spontaneous generation"—which is what Clark had now become interested in—had no place in his theoretical repertoire (it didn't in Darwin's either, of course). In his *Principles of Zoölogy*, Agassiz was unambiguous about the subject: "That all animals are produced from eggs," he wrote, "is an old adage in Zoölogy, which modern researches have fully confirmed."[24] *Omne vivum ex ovo.* But Clark's own research was on a roll now, and he felt he no longer needed Agassiz's blessing to continue. A few weeks after the April 1859 meeting, he was talking to the members of the academy again, reporting on the apparent spontaneous generation of "pseudo-animate bodies" from inside the decomposing proboscis (the sucking and feeding organ) of a jellyfish. The cells were dancing, he said, using a simile that would have pleased the flamboyant Agassiz, as if they were buckshot shaken around in a flat pan. Clark was using Agassiz's language to prove something that would have appalled his teacher.[25]

In early 1860, Clark purchased the London edition of *On the Origin of Species*, for the extraordinarily high sum of $4 (around $108 in today's money). Despite this considerable investment, there is no evidence that Darwin had any immediate effect on Clark. But perhaps he did feel that, in his own way, he too was getting closer to what Darwin had called that "mystery of mysteries," the origin of life—a problem that Darwin had mentioned on the first page of his book and then apparently forgot. However, in March 1860, a bored Clark walked out of a meeting hosted by the American Academy of Arts and Sciences in which the amateur botanist John Amory Lowell and the Harvard philosopher Francis Bowen denounced Darwin's argument as "weak." Interestingly, Clark didn't mention who got up and made the case *for* Darwin that night: Asa Gray. Clark was, finally, on his own.

By then, the signs of trouble in his relationship with Agassiz had become too visible even for his onetime mentor to ignore. In an effort to repair what was already broken, Agassiz came up with a consolation prize for his valued worker, one that didn't cost him a dime: "Today I received the announcement," wrote Clark on June 22, 1860, "that I had been yesterday confirmed by the Overseers as *Adjunct Professor of Zoology* in the *Lawrence Scientific School of Harvard University* Cambridge Mass." If Clark realized that this was an unpaid position, he didn't mention it in the entry, though his use of the term *adjunct professor* instead of his official title, *assistant professor*, might indicate that he *did* know.[26] As elsewhere in his diary, Clark's elation manifests itself in vigorous underlining, as well as in the need to write out the full name of the august institution of which he is now a faculty member. The next day, he proudly informed his family—"Ned, Father & Mother"—about the "professorship."

Buoyed by this recent development, Clark left for an extended trip to Europe, from August to November 1860. Such grand tours were not uncommon for nineteenth-century academics on the brink of a major appointment. Henry Wadsworth Longfellow, poised to become the Smith Professor of Modern Languages at Harvard, immediately departed for Europe, spending time in Denmark, Sweden, and Germany, where he studied at Heidelberg University. Eben Horsford, before he began his appointment as the Rumsford Professor for the Application of Science at Harvard in 1847, likewise left for Germany, where he visited Justus von Liebig; although he never obtained a degree, he stayed two years.

There was one crucial difference: Clark did not have a major appointment waiting for him and he had no money. If his mentor had come to the New World to expand his horizons, Clark would go to the Old World to do the same. But Clark's time and contacts were limited; moving restlessly through half of central Europe, he visited Switzerland, Germany, France, and England. If the purpose of this trip had been to allow Clark to find himself, it was a colossal failure. Wherever he went, Clark saw traces of his mentor's all-encompassing activities. Running away from the master had only brought him closer to him. As he was hiking with his brother Ned in the Swiss Alps, Clark found ample confirmation that he was no Agassiz. While dutifully commenting on the "magnificent views" around them as they were making their way up, partly on foot, partly by stagecoach, through the Alps from Geneva to the Bodensee, Clark inwardly cursed himself for undertaking such a dangerous trip. Crossing the famous Mer de Glace on the northern side of Mont Blanc, for example, a glum Clark stared down into the deep crevasses (*"frightful chasms"*) and, remembering the famous story of how Agassiz once had himself lowered into one of those holes, he shuddered: the whole thing, to him, was "the most tiresome and in some places dangerous, adventure I have ever undertaken." Clark's bowels troubled him, his hip hurt, the headaches were back with a vengeance; he felt dizzy and weak.[27]

When the publisher James Fields hiked through the same area a few years later, he too saw Agassiz's name everywhere, but for him this produced a pleasant feeling of familiarity: "I walked beneath no alien skies," Fields intoned. "The glacier shone to gild his name, / And every image in the lake / Reflected back his fame."[28] No such blissful moments of recognition for Clark. When he spent the night near the Jungfrau massif, he woke at five o'clock in the morning to the sound of avalanches, a low rumbling interrupted by jarring sounds like "the fall of sod on a coffin"—his personal memento mori, it seemed. All around him were the "glacial grooves" that had featured so prominently in his master's ice-age theory—Agassiz writ large, as it were. It was only fitting that among all these ancient scratches and striations he should finally discover, on the aptly named Höllenplatte (the dev-

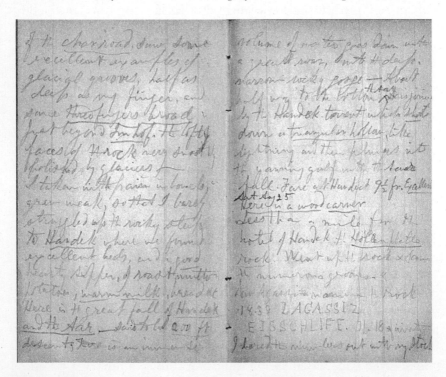

Entry for August 25, 1860. From Henry James Clark's "Journal in Europe."

il's plateau) near Handeck, his master's name engraved in the rock.[29] Driven by devotion or despair, Clark used his bergstock to retrace some of it: "1838 L AGASSIZ EISSCHLIFE." He copied the words into his journal, inadvertently misspelling the German word for glacial slope (*Eisschleife*), and noted how faint the "18" in "1838" had already become.

There were flashes of happiness, moments when Agassiz wasn't hovering right behind him. In Martigny, Clark enjoyed the white wine, "the first I ever tasted," and he loved the "Semmels" (soft white rolls) he was served in Munich.[30] His sense of constraint seemed to leave Clark when he visited the art galleries of Europe, especially the Old Pinakothek in Munich, where he gushed over the Van Dycks and Raphaels, busily making notes in the French-language catalog he had bought. Friedrich Kaulbach's *Die Zerstörung Jerusalems durch Titus* at the New Pinakothek, a monumental painting commissioned by the Bavarian king Ludwig I, had a powerful effect on him: "the most magnificent design I ever saw." In Dresden, he admired Raphael's *Sistine Madonna* ("the face of the mother is *perfect*") and wandered around the city the next morning, waiting impatiently for the gallery to open again so that he could take another look. Although Clark did not have a knack for languages, the names of the Italian painters rolled effortlessly off his pen. One can almost hear him mouthing along as he is writing them in his journal: Titian, Correggio, Andrea del Sarto, Carlo Dolci, Paolo Veronese, Annibale Carracci.[31]

Clark diligently worked his way through a list of must-see scientists, meeting with the botanist Alexander Braun, Agassiz's former brother-in-law, in Berlin and the anatomist Carl Gegenbaur in Jena. Ever the underdog, he noticed in Weimar how much smaller Friedrich Schiller's house seemed (though it was on a fine "plaz") in comparison to that of his more famous colleague Goethe.[32] In Giessen, the zoologist Rudolf Leuckart handed him some specimens, a rare fish and a sea snail from the Mediterranean—they were intended, alas, for Agassiz.[33] Königsberg was more fun: Clark sat in on a convention of German scientists and had the opportunity to hear Ernst Haeckel ("Dr. Häkel") lecture on "new Radiolaria," the amoeboid protozoa he had studied during his recent trip to the Mediterranean. Clark understood little, since his German was poor, but he was pleased to see that these Europeans accepted him as their peer. Both Gegenbaur and

Haeckel were among the earliest supporters of Darwin in Germany, and it is conceivable that they might have let slip an occasional remark against the great Agassiz, of the kind that would have lightened Clark's mood.[34] One of the purchases he made in Königsberg was a medallion featuring Leopold von Buch, the same Buch who had vigorously opposed Agassiz's ice-age theory.[35] When Clark was in Berlin, Alexander Braun warmly encouraged him to come back and "visit him whenever I have time." And Agassiz's old teacher, the world-famous Carl Friedrich Philipp von Martius, invited him to his home in Schlehdorf, south of Munich, where they played billiards and talked about Darwin (if they discussed Agassiz at all, Clark doesn't mention it—he *did* write a letter, on Martius's behalf, but it was addressed to Asa Gray). Martius and Clark parted affectionately: "we kissed each other on the cheek, three times."[36]

Elsewhere in Europe, Agassiz's spectral presence caught up with Clark again. When Clark visited the Jardin des Plantes in October, the labels on the fossil fish were in Agassiz's handwriting, a discovery that had the predictable effect on him: a "sharp headache." Clark ran back to his hotel, where he drank hot chocolate "and then strolled on the Boulevards and in the arcades." That helped. "No headache," he ended his entry. The next day, Clark walked all the way to Père Lachaise to pay his respects to the man who had been Agassiz's mentor, the great comparative anatomist Georges Cuvier. After silently contemplating the monument, Clark, in a gesture touching in its simplicity, broke off a twig of arbor vitae and planted it within the enclosure around the grave, "hoping"—certainly something that Clark was also hoping for himself—that "perchance it may live."[37]

Paris had its delights, though, and for Clark they again were theatrical ones. On the evening of his visit to Cuvier's grave, he soaked up Meyerbeer's *Le prophète*, a tremendously successful opera at the time, considered one of the finest examples of a new musical style that focused on the conflicts between an individual and society. This was an oversized production—no problem for Clark. The man who was, in his work, happiest when peering through a microscope liked his grand opera large and loud. "Orchestre"—note how French spellings creep into Clark's prose—"over a hundred in number, and a still larger Chorus. The scenery was the finest and grandest I have ever seen." One can picture Clark leaning forward with excitement in his seat when Jean van der Leyden, the false Anabaptist prophet brought to his senses, blows up his palace, with "hundreds of feasters" inside—tabula rasa, a violent ending beyond the mild-mannered Clark's wildest dreams. He also treated himself, on his last evening in Paris, to a show at the Comédie Française, where he saw Molière's *Tartuffe:* "such spirit, such expression, so natural and life like!" Tartuffe, the pious con man who doesn't practice what he preaches, would have reminded him of someone he knew only too well.[38]

Clark left Paris for good on October 19, 1860. His final purchases he recorded in his little diary, laboriously converting French francs and cents into more familiar American money: two dozen stereoscopic views, mostly of Paris, for six cents each; some views of flowers and statuary for ten cents a piece; and a pair of thick wool socks for thirty. For his new India rubber high-top shoes he had paid eleven francs, and his bill at the hotel, for a stay of eight days, had come to nineteen francs twenty cents—two amounts Clark left unconverted, perhaps because they seemed so exorbitant. That same night, he took a train to Calais, where, while he waited for the boat that would take him to England, he strolled on the beach, collecting shells for his little ones back home. He arrived in London at 4 P.M. the next day.

The next two weeks were filled with yet more visits. He got along well with "big-jawed" Professor Richard Owen, superintendent of the natural history collections at the British Museum, whom he met at his house, Sheen Lodge, in Richmond Park and found quite strange but not unpleasant.[39] Like Clark, Owen believed that invertebrates held the key to creation, but if they discussed their mutual interest in jellyfish, Clark didn't record it. He used a note from Agassiz to gain access also to Darwin's friend Huxley, who shared with him his microscopic preparations of plankton. He also made an attempt to see Darwin himself, but he had gone to Eastbourne for his daughter Henrietta's health and wasn't available to see "Agassiz's man," as he called Clark in a letter to Asa Gray.[40] One would like to think that Gray, Clark's erstwhile mentor, cringed when he read that phrase.

The handwriting on the last pages of Clark's European diary is different, unsteady, squiggly, the letters awkwardly plastered onto the page. Clark was falling apart. When his wife's letter with the long-awaited forty dollars for the return ticket finally came, he booked a second-class passage on the steamer *Canada*. All the way over from

Liverpool (the *Canada* was one of the faster ships of the Cunard line and made the passage in twelve days) he was "more or less sick." On November 15, 1860, at one o'clock in the morning, Henry James Clark arrived in Boston. He slept on board the ship till daylight. We can picture him taking the omnibus and then running home to Wendell Street, the shells for his children clattering in his knapsack. By 9:00 A.M. he was there. Mary was waiting—and so was Louis Agassiz.

Back in Cambridge, Clark seemed less compliant, less willing to take orders from Agassiz. If his European trip had shown him that no matter how far away he removed himself from Cambridge, Agassiz was already there, why not stay put and take him on here? He would have known that Edward S. Morse, another one of Agassiz's students, had left the museum in high dudgeon in December 1861, asserting his indignation over the Prof's expectation that he continue to work for him but "live on nothing."[41] But as other students were forming a secret group they called the Society for the Protection of American Students Against Foreign Professors (whose existence Agassiz soon discovered),[42] Clark was still hoping to forge a career for himself at Harvard. The collections of the Museum of Comparative Zoology contain a note written to the "Honorable Committee for visiting the Lawrence Scientific School," signed on January 2, 1862, in which Clark describes the ambitious course he taught in the spring of 1861: a series of lectures "upon the cellular structure and development of the Animal Kingdom; including a comparative view of the histology of the vegetable kingdom; especially, showing the parallelism in the modes of origin and growth of the cellular constituents of the two divisions of organic beings." In his vision for the future at least, he was emphatically *not* an adjunct professor but a fully vested faculty member, supplying an essential part of the Harvard curriculum: "These lectures were given as a promise of what might be done in future, provided that increased and sufficient means were furnished to carry out a full course, which in reality would require two years for its completion."[43]

But Clark's great plans for the teaching of histology at Mr. Agassiz's Museum did not bear fruit. The inevitable showdown between Agassiz and Clark came on March 20, 1863, when, driven to despair by his lack of money, Clark finally lashed out: "I denounced [Agassiz] for keeping my family in distress and want for the last six months. I think it is time I had put a check on his overbearing way of speaking to me. No honorable man ought to allow his assumption of superiority, especially when it is aired in such an insolent manner as he exhibited today." Deeply hurt by this unexpected and, from his point of view, unnecessary insurrection, Agassiz terminated his relationship with Clark, ordering him, in a note written a few days later, to return all his books and lenses, as well as the keys to the museum. He liked individuality—but in animals, not in assistants. "I now close irrevocably," he announced, "a personal intercourse which I could no longer base upon confidence." He added that he felt no anger and wished Clark the best for an "independent career," in which he would win "the best honors that could ever have been wished for you by your old teacher."[44]

Clark didn't go down without a fight. Agassiz had made him the assistant curator of the museum, and in this capacity he felt he should be allowed to retain access to it. He also demanded that he be recognized as the co-author of Agassiz's *Contributions*. But none of Agassiz's colleagues—not Jeffries Wyman, not Oliver Wendell Holmes, and certainly not Harvard's President, the Reverend Thomas Hill, who had been in office less than a year—were willing to confront the powerful man in public, though they privately professed to be appalled by what had happened. No one, that is, except Asa Gray. Clark ran into him on Garden Street and accompanied him all the way to his house: "He at once said that in case of a quarrel I, having behaved so well and worked so faithfully for Ag. the latter must be in the wrong. He also said that he had dreaded the quarrel for some time. He said 'if the affair came out to an investigation it would hurt Agassiz very much' . . . He also told me that Agassiz went about Boston decrying *Harvard*, and abusing certain professors."[45]

Reassured by Gray's support, Clark later the same afternoon showed up at the office of President Hill. Even if Hill had been inclined to help Clark, he would not have been a powerful ally. The author of books with titles such as *First Lessons in Geometry*, Hill nevertheless had a healthy respect for serious science and, in remarks made to the Harvard Natural History Society in 1853, had argued against endeavoring to "force the language of Genesis and the facts of Geology into temporary agreement."[46] Yet, as we saw earlier, Hill's personal ties with Agassiz dated back to his time as a minister in Waltham, eager to accompany the foreign professor on his collecting jaunts. Although he introduced a number of important changes at Harvard (he allowed students choice in selecting courses and established an academic council consisting of the faculties of the college and professional schools, as well as new professorships in geology and mining), he had trouble dealing closely with frustrated faculty members. As president of Harvard, he served for only six years (Charles W. Eliot, who became his successor, stayed on for forty); since then, only the scandal-ridden Lawrence Summers has had a shorter tenure. When Clark came to see him, Hill had been in office for barely over a year. He wasn't one to take on Agassiz, who, as Hill very well knew, had friends in high places, notably among the "Lazzaroni" (the name was a mocking tribute to the beggars of Naples), an informal group of power brokers in the scientific community, which included luminaries such as the mathematician Benjamin Peirce at Harvard and the Coast Survey superintendent Alexander Dallas Bache.

Whether Clark was aware of Hill's limitations is not entirely clear. In any case, he was not particularly careful in his choice of words and came straight to the point: "I told the President that I had had a quarrel with Agassiz, and asked him if the fact of a quarrel between Agassiz and me, could, in any way, deprive me of my rights on the Museum—as far as a professor in the Zoöl department of the Scientific School had any rights there." Hill didn't think so. The conversation that ensued, as far as we can reconstruct it from Clark's journal, is fascinating, especially since it shows that Clark, who had a much more nimble intellect than Gray had assumed, was always a few steps ahead of Hill. After Hill tentatively confirmed that the rights that came with his faculty position, unpaid as it was, should not be affected by Clark's falling out with Agassiz, Clark showed him Agassiz's letter that disputed precisely those rights. Mortified, Hill responded that he couldn't imagine Agassiz wouldn't let him continue his lectures at the museum. Clark answered that doing so would also involve having access to the specimens, the laboratory, and the books in the library. Clearly Hill had only a vague idea of what a natural history lecture was really about.

As far as Clark was concerned, the conclusion was clear: lecturing without access to the museum facilities was impossible. "Unless

Agassiz acceded to all my demands for my rights, I could not take it upon myself to go to the Museum and lecture as I would by this act appear to confess that I was in the wrong and glad to accept any compromise." Then Clark became threatening. He told Hill that "if I do not get an affirmative answer to my demands by the time our lecture day comes I would then proceed to make a written memorial to the *Corporation*, as he himself had said would have to be done." Hill said he would find a way to prevent this and offered "to take it upon himself to say that I had a right to use the lecture room of the Museum, as that was an understood arrangement with the board of overseers." Clark was surprised to hear him say "overseers," since even he, a lowly adjunct professor, knew that the day-to-day business of the college was dealt with by the smaller Harvard Corporation ("no doubt he meant corporation").

Evasive, fuzzy on the details, and apparently confused about larger issues, such as Harvard's structure of governance, Hill began to look suspect to Clark. "I reiterated that the right to use the lecture room, I had always thought, and did now think, also included the right to use the laboratory, and specimens and library of the Museum." Attempting to salvage what was left of his authority, Hill objected that Agassiz had always told him that he had himself paid for the library. Clark immediately gave him chapter and verse of the passage in the past year's museum report, in which Agassiz had stated "that the library was purchased by *private subscription*." Hill interjected weakly and somewhat inconsequentially that Agassiz had allowed his students to have their own keys to the museum cases. Was this intended to serve as an example of Agassiz's generosity? Clark responded quickly that the benefit had been entirely in Agassiz's favor: a large proportion of these "students" were Agassiz's assistants. In fact, as it later occurred to Clark, he could have told Hill that *all* these young men, not just the ones officially regarded as assistants, were working for Agassiz: everything they did, every box of specimens they moved, every fish scale they drew or classified, was listed as "Museum work" in Agassiz's publications and annual reports. Not much generosity there. It is easy to picture Hill wiping his balding forehead after Clark left his office.[47]

Asa Gray's predictions of imminent harm to Agassiz notwithstanding, things didn't go well for Clark. A report submitted by Judge Ebenezer Hoar and President Hill on May 30, 1863, concluded that the Harvard Corporation was in no position to extend museum privileges to Clark "until the duties and rights of the Director & Curator have been distinguished and defined by the joint action of the Board of Trustees and the President & Fellows." Their recommendation, in the interim, was that Clark "apply himself to the Director and Curator" to obtain whatever it was that he desired.[48]

Agassiz was deeply affected by the controversy. "I have been feeling unwell," he wrote to Joseph Henry of the Smithsonian, "and somehow I am so prostrate I am unable to do anything serious." If only he had more "good workers" at the museum![49] When Clark did approach Agassiz, not about the museum but about his share in the published volumes of the *Contributions to the Natural History of the United States of America*, Agassiz adamantly refused to allow a panel of judges to review Clark's charge that Agassiz had stolen the fruits of his labors at the microscope.[50] He had nothing but contempt now for the man he had once praised to the skies: "I have done more than justice to whatever assistance I have received from you in the preparation of my Contributions to the Natural History of the United States," Agassiz snapped back in a letter mailed from Nahant. "On many occasions," he claimed, he had acknowledged Clark's "cooperation" (note the carefully chosen word) "in a way which often verges on exageration [*sic*] as to your real share in the work." Agassiz's much praised bonhomie yielded to undisguised anger in the last lines of the note: "I can therefore be perfectly indifferent as to your own estimate of the matter. As to your pecuniary claims upon the Museum they are as imaginary as your complaints of my treatment of your merits."[51] One can easily imagine Agassiz's side of the controversy. Years of selfless work had created the conditions that allowed men like Clark to thrive scientifically, and this is how they thanked him for his efforts!

Clark now decided to do what Agassiz would have done in his situation. He went public with his grievances and published, at his own expense, a leaflet, which was distributed in Cambridge and elsewhere. In "A Claim for Scientific Property," he accused his former mentor of having published his observations and ideas without proper attribution: "All scientific men . . . did they know the truth of the matter, would regard it as their duty to acknowledge that I should be held as a responsible authority in scientific history, for what is there written." The three-page pamphlet was a rhetorical masterwork. For the first two pages or so, Clark barely mentioned Agassiz as the target of his attacks. Instead, Clark referred to him as "another person" or as the one "whose name is on the title page." Gradually he built up his claim to a fair share of Agassiz's insights, beginning with the second volume of *Contributions,* the one about the turtles, wherein most of the embryological observations, from the self-division and physiology of the yolk cells ("only to be understood after many days of constant watching and experimenting") to the lining of the shell, are identified as the result of Clark's work. For anyone willing to read between the lines, a strange but compelling parallel emerges between the development of Clark's ideas ("my own independent thought") and the formation of the turtle's embryo ("an independent, freely developed cell"), between the observer and the thing he claims he has spent so much time observing.

Clark was careful, at first, not to slam Agassiz completely, praising him for providing the material basis for Clark's experiments: "Professor Agassiz spared neither pains nor expenses in bringing together materials, turtles and their eggs by hundreds, from all parts of the United States." And Clark also made sure that he wouldn't come across as exaggerating his own share: "In the third volume I had only to do with the genus Pleurobrachia," he admitted, listing individual pages on which he corrected Agassiz's findings. Having thus established himself as the embodiment of modesty and reason, Clark felt free to save his most powerful attack for the end: "In regard to the fourth volume," the one devoted to the anatomy of the jellyfish, "I would say that so large a proportion of it sprung from my hands that I have no room, nor time at present, to point out more than a few things." Now the gloves were off. "The paragraph on page 199," which dealt with the nervous system of the small *Coryne mirabilis,* "was expressly elaborated by me to prove in the most positive terms, that, what Professor Agassiz had, several years before, described as a nervous system, and upon which he has based some of his grandest generalizations in regard to the sensorial functions of these animals, is, according to my own investigations, nothing more than a membrane folded upon itself." Not a nerve, not a muscle, just a thin layer of cells. And suddenly there were no more convoluted sentences, no torturous qualifications. Clark's conclusion is so powerful that the reader almost imagines him shouting it from the rooftops. No longer was he going to hesitate when his friends asked him, as they had done so many times before, if he "was doing anything for science." Here, finally, was his answer, loud enough for everyone to hear: "Yes! I tell them; I have done hard work, I have thought much and written much, but what I did was appropriated by another, and was published as his own." No wonder that after this salvo on behalf of scientific originality, any prospect of reconciliation between Clark and his former teacher and employer evaporated.[52]

A slim majority of the faculty still supported Clark. In early September, Agassiz declared at a faculty meeting that "he had been grossly insulted in his laboratory by 'his Assistant Professor'"—so much so that it would be painful for him to sit in the same room with him. Therefore he would move, said Agassiz, according to Clark's indignant retelling of the incident in his journal, "that Prof. Clark be requested to withdraw from the Faculty sessions until the difficulty was settled between him and *me*."[53] Seething over Agassiz's treatment of Clark, Asa Gray also enjoyed (as he told Darwin in a letter cited earlier) tormenting his scientific opponent; quietly but with great deliberation he then inquired if Agassiz wanted a formal discussion and vote on the issue. Agassiz, flabbergasted that a matter he considered self-evident was to be the subject of a debate, hesitated; his motion to eject Clark was defeated by a vote of four to three. James Mills Peirce, a newly minted assistant professor of mathematics, apparently voted along with the physicist Joseph Lovering, Asa Gray, and Jeffries Wyman in support of Clark. Angrily, Agassiz stormed out. Agassiz's ally on the faculty, the mathematician Benjamin Peirce, who also happened to be James Mills Peirce's father, then proposed that the action of the faculty be reported to the corporation, a measure Gray supported because it struck him that Clark's case might benefit if the higher-ups knew that the majority of the faculty supported him. The sly Gray surely understood that Peirce had actually intended to embarrass and censure those of his colleagues acting against Agassiz.

Agassiz, however, had the final word in the matter. In November 1863, the Harvard Corporation, at the recommendation of Judge Hoar and Thomas Hill, voted that it was no longer Clark's "duty" to attend faculty meetings, which meant that he was no longer welcome. Thus, the corporation nixed the documented opinion of the faculty. Clark was informed about the vote in December and merely recorded it in his journal.[54] A month later, his fifth child, "a stout, healthy boy," was born.[55] Barred from the museum that he helped create and therefore lacking the specimens he needed for teaching, with no money other than handouts or loans, Clark now threw all his energy into the preparation of a series of public lectures, which he had been invited to deliver before all hell broke loose at the museum. Once, way back in 1846, the Lowell Lectures had helped launch Agassiz's career in America. Now they sounded the death knell for Clark's grand professional aspirations.

As a mentor, Agassiz was grandiose, narcissistic, exploitative, and manifestly unfair. He was also inspiring, passionate, often caring, and wonderfully adept at convincing people to open their pockets and pay for his dreams. Not all students went the way Clark did, from enchantment to deep disappointment and despair. Consider the example of Addison Emery Verrill, an aspiring young scientist from Maine. He had left Norway, Maine, where he had attended preparatory school, in early May 1859 to study under Agassiz when he was barely twenty years old. The fact that Verrill emerged relatively unscathed from his dealings with Agassiz, whereas Clark did not, tells us something important not only about Clark but about the always ambivalent nature of Louis Agassiz.[56]

Within a few months after his arrival, Verrill graduated from birds and mammals to one of Agassiz's favorite areas of study, marine invertebrates and, more specifically, corals. He thought Agassiz was "first rate," a kind, tolerant, and not at all narrow-minded teacher. Adamant that he not confine himself "to one channel of thought," Agassiz advised Verrill to study not just Henri Milne-Edwards's handbook on the natural history of corals but also Shakespeare and the "English classics."[57] Impressed by Agassiz's work ethic, Verrill began to spend every available minute in Agassiz's laboratory. At the end of the year, he was quite satisfied with the progress he had made. The final entry in Verrill's private journal for the year 1859 is touching in its earnestness:

> Thus closes the year of 1859, a year which will mark an important era in my life . . . During this year I have entered upon my course of study which I hope, with the advantages bestowed upon me by the

great leader of the scientific world and by whom I am instructed and supported and through whose kindness and liberality I have become connected with the museum of Comparative Zoology, will finally make me a man of science in reality as well as in reputation, and one worthy of great advantages.[58]

By all accounts, Verrill and his friends also knew how to have a good—or as Verrill would put it, "jolly"—time. Even their ineptitude was a source of amusement to them. Verrill's diary contains, for example, a distinctly macabre account of a sick cow that they tried to "make into a skeleton" for the museum, but which, despite the joint efforts of Agassiz's students, just wouldn't die ("she continued to live for a long time in spite of large doses of chloroform").[59] Once, a rather aggressive woodchuck Verrill kept in his own room at Zoological Hall gnawed through his cage and escaped into the garden of Henry W. Torrey, the McLean Professor of Ancient and Modern History, where Verrill recaptured him, not without being bitten first.[60] When Verrill received some caribou from his native Maine to add to Agassiz's museum, he skinned them but also cooked the meat, which tasted, he reported, "excellent."[61] During the day he studied the Prof's corals, but at night he absconded to Somerville, where he went to visit some ladies at the "Highland Avenue Seminary."[62] He was particularly taken with a Somerville girl named Paulina, "a good, simple-hearted, pretty, plump and fresh young lady" who did not have "much education," as Verrill noted cheerfully. His evenings with her he enjoyed "very much," though he was also careful not to sever his ties with a girl back home in Norway, Maine, named Flora. As it turned out, Paulina had her own agenda. When the eager Verrill asked her for her ambrotype,[63] she announced she wanted him to "join the Sons of Temperance" and start attending church. Verrill panicked: "I find that I'm getting too hard-hearted to be coaxed even by a pretty girl!"[64]

A less complicated source of amusement was the Aquarial Gardens in Boston, where he went to inspect the "Happy Family," an exhibit made famous by P. T. Barnum, which Verrill was able to admire without worrying too much about its implications for the study of natural history: "One old Monkey had taken a fancy for the rat and carried it about in her arms as if it were her own young and took the greatest possible care of it." Clark went to the opera to relax; Verrill got the seals at the Aquarial Gardens to play a tune for him on their hand-organ.[65]

Verrill's diary during these first two years is carried by a general sense of excitement about being in the right place at the right time. Agassiz wasted no opportunity to remind him how lucky he was: "We took a long walk," Verrill wrote on January 7, 1860, "and he told me that he almost envied us our chance and that for years he was obliged to study natural history only through the glass of the cases in European museums. He also told me in what poor circumstances the European naturalists are situated and how they are obliged to sell their collections very cheap in order to get money to continue their studies, and said that he should have been glad to have done the same thing ten years ago." Even Cuvier, when he visited the British Museum, had to look at specimens under glass. Agassiz's students, however, could handle what they pleased. This was, in short, going to be a collection ordered according to principles befitting a democracy, and he, little Addison Verrill from Greenwood, Maine, was going to help him create it: "He said that a specimen worth one cent is as important in the museum as one worth a thousand dollars and that we must treat it in the same manner."[66]

Verrill was so taken with Agassiz that he apparently didn't notice how what he thought of as conversations were in fact mini-lectures, self-absorbed monologues, which Agassiz was able to deliver at a moment's notice. Here is one salient example. At the Boston Athenaeum, Frederic Edwin Church's *Heart of the Andes* (1859) had sent Verrill into fits of ecstasy: "the most magnificent painting that I have ever seen. It seemed as if I was really beholding the beautiful landscape among real Andes and from a window in some rustic mansion." Then his scientific instincts had taken over and he had examined the surface of the painting with an opera glass, which, however, "revealed only new beauties instead of imperfections." He wanted to share his fascination with his master, who immediately began to hold forth. "He said that the practice of some artists of substituting their own fancies for real nature was the result of mere *laziness*." Agassiz apparently then went on to compare such artists to "those naturalists who adopt some pleasing but false theory like that of Darwin instead of investigating the difficult points of Science." Asa Gray, Agassiz had recently learned, much to his surprise, "inclined to that theory." (Though Verrill wouldn't have realized it, Agassiz was being more than a tad disingenuous now.) Did Verrill know that botanists, in general, were "far behind Zoologists in regard to true classification"? Church's painting was forgotten.[67]

By now, trouble was brewing in Agassiz's kingdom. On September 11, 1860, Verrill was still working on Agassiz's corals when Agassiz told him that his job was to "describe all of the *new species* but that he would define the *genera*." Verrill disliked the suggestion: "I think the last part much the best, and would rather have the privilege of defining the *genera* myself and then I dont [*sic*] care who describes the species." He was angry. As he was walking home, late for dinner because Agassiz had kept him, a mad dog made a move to attack him, "but one kick in the breast sent him tumbling and over end against the opposite fence with howls and yells, that were more amusing than terrific." Verrill added a mini-triptych of ink drawings, signed by "our own artist," which records the three stages of the dog attack, from the initial act of aggression, to the dog's climactic somersault, to the crazed animal's departure for, presumably, the next victim (drawn in outline only). In the last image, Verrill, who has represented himself wearing a stylish hat at a rakish angle, can be seen walking off—what the dog might be doing to others is no concern of his. In the howling dog, Verrill attacked not only his own frustration but, vicariously, his teacher's aggressive behavior toward his assistants. Every day at the museum, Agassiz's other side—his "foreign temper," as Verrill's fellow student Edward Sylvester Morse called it—was now more frequently in evidence. "He is the most genial man alive," declared Morse, "but take him out of his sphere and he is not only ungrateful, but actually impolite, rude, and unjust."[68] But where Clark would despair or seek respite in the theater, Verrill drew funny cartoons.

Driven by a mixture of Maine grit and irrepressible scientific curiosity, Verrill began to pursue his own work on the side, as Clark had done. Accompanied by his fellow students Nathaniel Shaler and Alpheus Hyatt, he went on field trips to the Maine coast, the island of Anticosti in the Gulf of St. Lawrence, and Labrador. Like his friends, he began to write his own accounts of what he had found. In 1862 and 1863, while officially working as Agassiz's assistant, he wrote and published twenty-two (if mostly short) papers, on minerals, plants,

Detail from the entry for September 11, 1860. From the journal of Addison Emery Verrill.

reptiles, shrews, and other subjects. His most ambitious effort was a proposal for a new system of classification for polyps (colonial corals) of the eastern coast.[69] He also started experimenting with a new medium of scientific representation, photography, purchasing plates and chemicals whenever he got the chance: "In afternoon printed eight photographs and finished them in the evening, toning with a new Phosphate bath. Had very satisfactory results."[70]

When Agassiz found out what his student had been up to, he was livid and demanded an explanation: "I remarked that I had told him about it some time ago and I had made it a private affair and so considered it and did not suppose it would much interest him. He continued to talk and became more and more excited and closed by threatening to abandon the museum altogether the first of Jan. unless he could have more confidence from the students!" Later the same day Verrill walked home "with Prof" and made another attempt to explain the situation. He had, he said, not told him about his extracurricular activities because this would have also meant reminding Agassiz that he hadn't paid him in quite a while. Agassiz countered with the argument that abusive bosses often make: they (Agassiz, his wife, and the assistants) were all one big family. He said that he wanted to know everything about his students' lives and that "he had felt the students were not confidential enough with him.—he wanted to know all about our private affairs, our difficulties, hopes, fears and anxieties." Verrill explained that if the students hadn't shared much with him, this was only because they all felt that "he had already enough cares of his own."[71]

Shades of Rodolphe Agassiz: in dealing with his assistants, Louis Agassiz was repeating the mistake his father, Pasteur Agassiz, had once made in his dealings with his wayward son. By *demanding* that the students confide in him, he had pushed them away. When Agassiz, a few days after his conversation with Verrill and in the presence of President Hill and Professor Benjamin Peirce, gave a lecture on loyalty at the museum, it became clear that he was trying to regain what he had already lost:

> He alluded to the low financial condition of the museum and expressed his intention of resigning unless presently relieved. He then spoke of the students and stated that he could not be responsible for their hopes and aspirations. He spoke about some of us comencing [sic] publishing and gave a rather personal and, as it seemed to me and others, uncalled for account of cases of plagiarism towards him from some of his former students, and stated that there was a paper in preparation which he had not seen, but was sure was full of improprieties and he would like to have the chance of taking it up and criticizing it!

For Agassiz, things had become personal. He demanded that all papers produced by his staff be shown to and approved by him first. To Verrill, he now seemed a bit like Saturn devouring his own children: "The drift of all these remarks appearing to be that he was jealous lest some of his students should rob him of some of his honor and glory by not giving him credit for everything that he *had ever done*, (published or not) and a little besides! I wonder if there may not be some chance, judging from my own experience, of the students having reasons for making the same complaint of him!" President Hill, spineless as ever, seconded Agassiz's remarks, and Peirce launched a diatribe on plagiarism, "seeming to take it for granted that we had all or part been guilty of it and bringing up before us the awful tribunal of European usage and judgment!!!!" Still more amused than disgusted, Verrill added, "I wanted to propose a psalm in longmetre [sic] to close with."[72]

Verrill's reverence had thus yielded to sarcasm. He himself wasn't about to quit; Agassiz's collections were too useful to him. The entries over the following year show that he kept "exceedingly busy" or "very busy" and worked "too late" at night. Agassiz even came around to the idea of using photography. Professing to be "highly pleased" with Verrill's work, he borrowed some plates to show them to his wife.[73] When James Henry Clark publicly quarreled with Agassiz, Verrill merely recorded the incident in his journal. Even when Agassiz formally passed new rules for his assistants, announcing that no one was to publish anything without his consent, Verrill, though clearly disgusted, did not immediately leave. What he did mind, as his diary indicates, was not getting paid. Agassiz demanded obeisance though his wallet was empty. He had given out some checks in February, but when Verrill took them to the bank they turned out to be unsigned. By December 1863, Verrill had had enough. "Since I was dependent on my salary for a living a discontinuance of that must oblige me to leave," he told Agassiz. His fellow students Frederic Ward Putnam and Alpheus Spring Packard were leaving too. "He flew into a great passion and accused us of all manner of ill usage and wickedness of which the principal consisted in criticising and finding fault with him."[74] When Agassiz wouldn't listen to any "business propositions," Verrill's mind was made up. At home he was raptly reading Josiah Gilbert Holland's *Bitter-sweet* (1858), a vastly popular, long-winded, saccharine dramatic poem chiefly memorable for its re-creation of the old Bluebeard story. Verrill was greatly impressed, perhaps not surprisingly, by the story of the cruel old man "whose castle was built upon a splendid plan" and the "curiously inclined" Fatima who discovered her "lord and master's" secret, "the mystery forbidden," and then had to run for her life.[75]

Like Bluebeard with his wives, Agassiz had piled up the corpses of his students around him, "side by side." Three days after his run-in with Agassiz, Verrill went where Clark had gone, to Dr. Jeffries Wyman, who supported him in his wish to transfer to medicine and asked what the trouble was with Agassiz. Verrill gave him some notes. "I had a long and pleasant talk with him and he assented to the justice of nearly all my remarks." In reality, though, things weren't nearly as dramatic as they seemed. Like Holland's Fatima, Verrill got out of Agassiz's castle unharmed. And he had learned more from Agassiz than he would have been ready to admit in those bleak December days of 1863.[76] Just a few months later, Yale University offered him its first professorship in zoology, an office he held until his retirement in 1907. In 1873, in a grand gesture of reconciliation, Agassiz invited Verrill, along with Putnam, Packard, and Morse, to teach in his newly created Anderson School of Natural History on Penikese Island. Putnam was then the director of the Peabody Academy of Science in Salem, Massachusetts, where Packard worked as a curator, and Morse, who would become one of the nation's foremost experts on Japanese paleontology and culture, held the chair of zoology at Bowdoin College. Agassiz's students, in modern terms, had placed well.

Verrill took more than a page from his master's book: he went on to publish more than 350 papers and monographs during a career that lasted for just over six decades and ended in 1926 with his death, at age eighty-seven, in Santa Barbara, California. Verrill is credited with having described more than a thousand species of animals in almost every major taxon. Like his former teacher, Verrill apparently abused his body in the service of science: "Sleep to him . . . seemed to be in large measure a casual indulgence," wrote Verrill's biographer, "taken, quite frequently, while fully dressed and reclining in his desk chair."[77] He would work until daybreak, taking a brief nap on his couch before breakfast, and then he was off to his laboratory again. Like Agassiz, Verrill was in love with science as an activity in and of itself; when his teacher disappointed him, he sought his own direction. And fortunately, Verrill, a man of large stature with piercing blue eyes, was, unlike Agassiz, physically equipped to withstand the pressures of the life he had chosen. He undertook his last collecting expedition, to Kauai Island on Hawaii, when he was eighty-five.

Clark was not made of the same sturdy material. He was not a doer, but a thinker, and his independence from Agassiz came at a heavy price. His 1864 Lowell Lectures reveal his intellectual stance after he had severed the cord: still beholden to Agassiz's creationism, he seemed ready to embark for new shores. Clark reworked the lectures into the volume he called *Mind in Nature*, his only book to appear in his lifetime. It is a remarkable text, no matter what Darwin, in his letter to Benjamin Walsh (quoted earlier), thought of it. On one level, it does offer a fairly conventional narrative. He hasn't, Clark assures his audience at the outset, lost his belief in an "intelligent being, designing, ordaining, and controlling" the "succession of beings from a lower to a higher type," a chain of being ending gloriously with man, the pinnacle of complexity. In language Agassiz would have approved, Clark was appropriately dismissive of the "insidious form in which

Materialism has attempted to make its first approaches to the citadel of our belief in a ruling Providence."[78] American reviewers of Clark's book, still enthralled by the great Agassiz's ideas, liked this kind of reasoning: "No matter into how many links the chain of secondary causes is broken," no matter how many factors had influenced and modified the development of life on earth, "the chain itself must be attached to Jupiter's chair," declared the *New Englander and Yale Review*.[79] Like Clark's initial statement of faith, the reviewer's response was intended as a swipe at Darwin's ideas on evolution.

Clark's garden-variety anthropocentric view rears its head in other passages of *Mind in Nature* too; for example, he calls the human brain creation's "crowning effort," "the throne of thought, before which all the other faculties stand in inferior ranks." At the same time, however, Clark subtly undermines all this talk about human superiority by showing, throughout his book, an abiding, irrepressible interest in tiny organisms, amoebae, difflugiae, and so forth, "*living beings* so exceedingly simple in structure that they may be compared to a drop of gum or mucus, but from which they are distinguished by being held together and *animated* by the affinity which is called the *principle of life*." Almost slime, but not quite.[80]

Clark's book, despite occasional ponderousness, is thus not without touches of humor and drama. Here's Clark on the squid: "With these arms, and a pair of large, staring eyes, (*e*) the Squid may be truly said to have a formidable aspect. And such it proves itself to be to one who may incautiously take hold of it; quick as a cat it throws its head around to the hand which seizes it, fastens its slimy arms to the skin, and buries its sharp, hooked jaws (*m*) in the flesh." Fortunately, the American species (now there's some unexpected proof for the count de Buffon's famous hypothesis that nothing in the New World grows to be larger than its Old World equivalent!)[81] was much smaller than the foreign ones, which sometimes sport "arms as thick as a man's thigh, and jaws as large as those of a snapping-turtle." The letters inserted into Clark's text refer to features of a truly complicated schematic drawing, showing a squid with its back upward: a web of thin white lines and circles on a black background. Dotted lines extend to the explanatory letters above and below (from *a* to *t'*) like so many needles in a pincushion. Was he making fun of his own science—the arrogance of the scientist's brain, which pretends to dominate something that, in one ill-fated moment, will sling its tentacles around this human expert, in a parody of an affectionate hug?[82] What a relief that all the American species can do is draw a little blood.

Clark does worry about his more traditionally inclined readers. Quoting Psalm 139, he imagines them wondering "how we creatures, who are so 'fearfully and wonderfully made,' who embrace in ourselves such a variety of forms, relations, proportions, and properties," should be in any way subject to the laws that govern nonhuman nature. But could it be that our imagined worth rests on a rather crumbling foundation, namely a false, uninformed view of simplicity? *Mind in Nature* is full of moments when Clark finds digestive, circulatory, and, yes, nervous systems (*complexity*, that is) where you wouldn't expect them, namely, in the lowest of the low animals. Take the *Rotalia veneta*—unicellular organisms with limblike prolongations called pseudopods—found, for example, crawling in the slimy mud of the lagoons of Venice. Clark lavishes some of his best prose on a description of the tasks performed by these amoebas, how they project through the fine pores of their shell, how they seize their prey and envelope it in a "glairy" (slimy) "mass" by fusing their sides together, thus forming a kind of temporary stomach, which begins processing nourishment from the helpless victim before the food ever enters the pseudopod's body. "I think this will suffice to show you," says Clark, "what is the extent of the duties which these simple creatures perform. It is true that their functions are not very complicated, but yet they are far more so than any one, knowing their simplicity, would suspect them to be capable of." All animals, in their development from simplest forms to maturity, resemble at one time those basic organisms that, like the pseudopods of Venice, seem to come out of nothing and whose individuality researchers have yet to learn to recognize. Seen from the vantage point of such loosely defined individuality, the boundaries between the animal and the vegetable world, between animate and inanimate matter, become fuzzier. From instances of life found where it ought not to be found, Clark effortlessly moved to his pet theory: spontaneous generation, the idea that organisms might arise *"altogether independent of a parent!"*[83]

It is difficult not to perceive a personal subtext behind Clark's reasoning. In *Mind in Nature*, he does limit his attacks on Agassiz to a few asides and footnotes. Clark's "fusillade," observed the *Atlantic Monthly*, taking for granted that all its readers were aware of the controversy, "occurs at two or three points" in the book only. Reading the rest of it, the reviewer said, with the Civil War fresh in his mind, was "like a peaceful voyage down the Mississippi after the few guerilla-haunted spots are passed." But the same reviewer also admitted that the views afforded from on board the ship were sometimes anything but familiar. To switch metaphors, the iconoclastic keynote of the book—living things will come out of nowhere and change into what one would never expect—had come through loud and clear.[84] Like one of his Venetian pseudopods, Clark was his own creature—beholden to no one, en route to who knows where. By the time his readers had reached the end of the book, they would also know that Clark was no adherent of Darwinism either. His book ended with a powerful evocation of the cycles of creation and destruction all life undergoes, which sounds much like the final pages of Edgar Allan Poe's cosmic prose poem *Eurcka* (1848). "Every day reveals to us new channels in the courses of nature," declares Clark. But these channels are all part of a great current and will all end up in the "universal ocean," to which everything will return in due course, "in one eternal circle of changes, from the elaborate composition of the body of the growing man to his going down again into the disintegrating, fluttering atoms, and their final diffusion into the primitive vapors." And it is from that same ocean that new life, when the time is ripe, will emerge again.[85]

But in Clark's case, life refused to imitate science. The theme of Clark's final years was disintegration and diffusion, not re-creation. He left Cambridge for the State Agricultural College of Pennsylvania, later known as Penn State, where he taught botany, zoology, and geology from December 1866 to April 1869, when he became a professor of natural history at the Agricultural and Mechanical College in Lexington, later the University of Kentucky. Somehow he managed to hold on to his research interests, although his main effort at both institutions went into teaching. His public fight with a man of Agassiz's power had no doubt isolated him among his peers. Expelled from Agassiz's museum for insisting on his rights as an individual, he became completely entranced with precisely those species in nature that seemed to redefine any conventional sense of individuality.[86]

For Clark was now into sponges, simple creatures whose place in nature was not at all certain in the minds of nineteenth-century naturalists. Sponges have no nervous system and a simple internal structure; though they are multicellular, any of their cells can assume any function in a sponge's repertoire of cell types. Were they plants or animals?[87] In his research, Clark noticed the similarity between the "choanocytes" of sponges (the collar cells whose flagella generate a current that draws water and food particles through the body of the sponge) and unicellular organisms now called choanoflagellates. Essentially, he was arguing that the sponge (his most extensive paper on the subject focused on the American genus *Spongilla*) was an aggregation of unicellular organisms close to the unicellular Infusoria.[88] Soon a transatlantic controversy over the nature of sponges unfolded. For example, Ernst Haeckel—Agassiz's main antagonist, Darwin aside—was convinced that sponges were highly organized animals, not just a bunch of protozoa and that what to Clark had seemed like Infusoria were simply the cells lining the sponge's stomach wall. (Did Haeckel remember the shy American assistant professor who had listened to his paper in Königsberg in the fall of 1860?) The controversy is still unresolved today; in fact, answering the question of how multicellular organisms evolved from single-celled ancestors is one of the primary tasks the National Human Genome Research Institute has set for itself.[89]

For all the serious effort that Clark put into his sponge research, autobiographical concerns surfaced here as well. Having almost reached the end of his article on sponges, Clark could no longer control his disappointment over the fact that he was now in Kentucky: "Our specimens were gathered, and studied on the spot where they lived, in the western part of Massachusetts," he sighed, as if he wanted to pretend that he was part of a multi-person task force, "several hundred miles away from our present residence." He had wanted to feed the sponges with colored matter to track the progress of the food through their inner cavities, but "circumstances" had prevented him "from carrying out our designs." Despite such obstacles, Clark did successfully make his point that the flagella-bearing objects (or "monads") inside the sponge were not merely parts of the sponge's membrane or "cell-components of a tissue" but enjoyed a kind of individuality. On the basis of his own microscopic research, with a good dose of speculation added to the mix, Clark suggested that each of them could be regarded as an "independent body, although closely connected with others in a common bond."[90] It is not difficult to see the latter description as a rebuttal of the situation in Agassiz's museum and the constraints placed on assistants like Clark, young men who were expected to give up their independence to be mere components of a larger body. Clark's "quasi-individuality," a term I have borrowed from a review by the British microscopist Henry Slack of Clark's sponge research, is a far cry from the standard metaphysical conceptions of what it means to be an individual.[91] Yet it asserts the right of even the most dependent-seeming part of a composite organism not to be completely identified with it. Perhaps ironically, finding such individuality had also been Agassiz's main concern—we need only remember his description of the *Cyanea*. Clark had learned his lesson well.

One can only surmise what life in Kentucky must have been like for someone so attuned to the pleasures of urban culture. Clark's teaching responsibilities left him little time for research, but what really bothered him was loneliness. In a letter he sent to his parents, Clark pleaded with them to write back to him, underlining his address so they couldn't ignore it. He complained that the cottage he had been given was too small for the family (Clark had seven children by now) and that his health wasn't improving. Plagued by neuralgia and swelling of the ankles, he had barely been able to walk: "The doctor said it was over-work, which exhausting the nervous system, rendered me liable to such attacks in this climate."[92]

He did manage to get out of Kentucky a few years later, but his new position had even less to do with research. In 1872, after the intervention of Asa Gray, he became professor of veterinary science at the Massachusetts Agricultural College in Amherst. "Dear Clark," Gray wrote, "Welcome to *Mass.* once more."[93] By then, however, Clark was a broken man.

Among the few Clark papers in Amherst Special Collections is a draft of a contract for a house Clark wanted to have built on Mount

Pleasant Street in Amherst, for a total price of $5,000, to be paid in three equal installments, "as the work advances," with a three-year mortgage for $1,500, to cover the rest of the money he owed. Clark was providing the contractor with "special drawings and specifications," adding requirements as to when the cellar walls should be built ("before the freezing weather"), what lumber should be used ("good, and thoroughly seasoned"), and how to absorb moisture and prevent staining: "The *first and second floors* to be *protected* by a coating of *sawdust* during the operation of plastering." The contractor, a Mr. Grainger, couldn't have had an easy time of it. "No *scars or dents* will be left in wood or plaster finish," Clark informed him in the draft of the contract that is now in Amherst Special Collections. "Every precaution [will] be taken to avoid damage from the carelessness of workmen." He also stipulated that "all *broken glass*" (more underlining) would have to be "replaced by perfect lights of the same quality as that specified." Clark expected the keys to be handed over on May 1, 1873. After his years in exile, he was trying to shore up the fragments of his life by building the perfect house—on Mount Pleasant, no less.[94]

He didn't have time to enjoy his new residence. Barely a year after his move to Amherst, the forty-seven-year-old Clark was on his deathbed. "Don't ask me to think," he told his wife when she brought him the well wishes of a former student and wondered if he remembered her name. The final, saddest entry in Clark's last diary, written on July 1, 1873, was in his son's hand: "Consumption of the bowels," a reference to his father's final, fatal illness. Clark's last words, as noted by Xenos Clark, were "My father," which Xenos then realized were addressed to "My father in Heaven." Clark added "Farewell," and died. Ned Clark, in a note scribbled right after his brother's death, left no doubt as to what or in fact who had killed him: "His health broke down entirely from hard work while with Agassiz, and he never recovered from the severe blow."[95]

The patient, self-effacing Mary Holbrook Clark also found it hard to forgive and forget. She recalled that whenever she had asked her husband, "after some new discovery," what this would "bring your family," Clark would stereotypically reply, "a name that will live when I am gone." She was hoping that her husband's "good name" would indeed prove to be "better than riches." Of course, Mary was writing this to Clark's former colleague Alpheus Packard, but the general tone of her letter indicates that as far as she was concerned, some more tangible riches would have come in handy too. In the meantime, at least, she had the house on Mount Pleasant, presumably with all the glass intact: a "Mrs. H. J. Clark" appears in the Amherst town directories until 1895.[96]

At the time of his death, Clark was just about to complete his monograph on the *Lucernaria*, the very project that Agassiz had resented so much, since it was his museum and his specimens that Clark had used for his personal research. Clark had not lived long enough to proof the plates for the volume, which therefore contained several mistakes in the lettering when it was finally published in 1878, as installment 242 of the series *Smithsonian Contributions to Knowledge* His former classmate Addison Verrill had edited it, noting the errors, and Joseph Henry, the secretary of the Smithsonian, added an unctuous preface, in which he kept mum about the Agassiz disaster and noted that Clark had passed away "in the flower of his age."[97]

Accompanied by Clark's own wonderfully filigreed drawings, *Lucernariae and Their Allies* is, once again, centrally concerned with quasi individuality. The jellyfish he deals with here, *Haliclystus auricula*, are curious animals, only a few centimeters in size, pale green and pinkish, and therefore quite different from the more spectacular jellyfish Agassiz admired, such as *Cyanea arctica*.

Behaviorally, this species, which is also known as the "stalked jellyfish," is fairly simple. It is primarily sessile, or sedentary, in its habits and spends most of its life attached by pedal secretion to seaweed and eel grass: "Although we have waded time and again for hours among the eel-grass where they were so numerous as to almost swarm," writes Clark, "we have never once witnessed anything that could be compared to the pulsating movement . . . of a genuine oceanic Acaleph."[98] Its purpose in life is the processing of food, survival for the sake of survival. Using its tentacles around the mouth, *Haliclystus* captures and then devours small prey: small bivalves, snails, brittle stars, and crustaceans. Once these organisms have been consumed, it spits out the shells.

Haliclystus auricula. Engraving after a drawing by Henry James Clark.

As immobile as these jellyfish seem in nature, confinement by humans does not suit them: "It will appear, to the inexperienced eye, to be perfectly well and fully expanded for three, four, or five days after capture, but during all this time it is quietly exfoliating its epidermis, both externally and internally, and finally indicates its illness, in its extreme, by falling from its attachment, and lying inactive at the bottom of the aquarium, contracted and rolled up into an almost shape-less mass."[99] This is a beautiful sentence, evoking as it does Clark's privileged understanding of animals that won't reveal themselves to the uninitiated until it is too late and they are dead. If you think *Hal-iclystus,* seemingly held prisoner by the blade of grass to which it is attached, can be easily transferred to the aquarium, that Victorian epitome of nature held captive and made entertaining, well, think again. The jellyfish might deceive you for as many as five days, look-ing healthy and well on the outside (Clark adds drama by gradually increasing the number of days it might survive), during which only the naturalist's "experienced" eye—an eye like Clark's—will know what's really going on. In Clark's description, the carefully chosen adverb *quietly* skirts the limits of scientific observation, as does the startling description of the condition of *Haliclystus* as "illness." Clark stops just short of anthropomorphizing the animal but implies that there is purpose behind its covert disintegration, a determined re-fusal to enter into communion with the ordinary observer. Every line of this description reflects Agassiz's influence, no wonder he had once been so proud of his student.

Haliclystus is life in the raw, nature *in statu nascendi.* It is so unlike us that we scramble for analogies to describe it, until we remember reading about a time in our own individual history (our "ontogeny," as Haeckel would call it) when the embryo's nervous system was "just dawning into existence" and when there were "no vessels to carry ma-terial to the newly forming tissue, and no allantois to spread out these vessels over its surface, in closest proximity to the air."[100] Perhaps this "Lucernarian" isn't so different from us, then, and we not so different from it.

If Clark's flamboyant style identifies him as Agassiz's student, his choice in personal pronouns indicates that, as a researcher, he wants to be perceived differently. Where Agassiz would have automatically introduced the more subjective *I,* Clark prefers the authorial *we,* at pains to suggest that proper methods of investigation were used. The man Agassiz had deemed the best microscopist of his time is still proud of his abilities, limited as they are by the insufficient state of the available technology at the institution where he is now teaching. When he reports on what he saw through his microscope, Clark's prose, interrupted by adverbial phrases and qualifying clauses, suddenly begins to stutter, becoming awkward and hesitant, thus mirroring the difficult process of observation. Although he doesn't understand everything he sees, he (and the reader with him) knows at least one thing, that the science involved here is good:

> It was difficult to persuade ourselves, at first, that the egg of so lowly an animal could be so highly organized; we suspected some mistake; yet repeated observations only led to the same result; and we therefore present it here as an isolated fact, but with the remark that, as far as it goes, *i.e.*, as a representation of the consummation of one stage in the life of the animal, it is as full in detail and physiognomy as the best lenses of the time enabled us to make out.[101]

Clark's fight with Louis Agassiz wasn't over. But rather than repeat the accusations leveled against his former master in *Mind and Nature*, Clark now resigns himself to implicit critique (he is slow where his master was fast) or shifts the focus of his attack to the son, the crown prince ascended to royal power. A crushing footnote finds a crucial mistake in Alexander Agassiz's catalog *North American Acalephae*, where the description of a young *Haliclystus auricula* doesn't match the image provided: "There is here such a marked discrepancy between the figure and the ostensible description that we are driven to suspect that the latter was intended for a totally different animal." All this helps to establish Clark as a rigorous researcher, an impression reinforced by a strongly worded passage in which he attacks other scientists who do their work "piecemeal," writing "a few notes made here, and a few there, with no particular reference to anything except the novelty of the subject," and who squirrel away the results of their investigations as if harboring their own personal secrets: "One cannot sometimes help fancying that a large part of the so-called *facts* of science are the results of the labors, or we might say the struggles, of innumerable incompetents, who, like some of the inmates of an insane asylum, delight in secreting valuables in out of the way places."[102]

If Clark sounds a bit cranky, it might be because he has returned to an area where he is particularly comfortable, histological research. Page after page he devotes to the fibers dispersed throughout the creature's gelatinous body mass, which cross each other "just as the bristles of two brushes do when forced together face to face," and to the cilia, the minuscule projections extending from the cells forming the interior walls of *Haliclystus*. Again, Clark's hidden theme is individuality, and he makes a strong case against the arrogant human assumption that these minute appendages are not subject to the animal's control: "Cilia are commonly treated like masses of men in an army, all moving to one determined end; as if the recorder of their movements did not think that the animal possessing them had the discriminating power of controlling the actions of any one separately." Aren't the legs of a centipede masterminded by the centipede itself? Clark adds a drawing that shows the cilia of the genital sac of *Haliclystus* in different attitudes: "Some of them project in rigid, straight lines from their bases; some again are straight at the base and undulating rapidly near the tip; others are in long curves from end to end, while here and there one vibrates in short, sharp curves throughout its length." We are not aware of their movements, but cilia also extend from the surface of almost all cell types of the human body. Contrary to conventional wisdom, Clark suggests that an analogy between the cilia of the cells of the jellyfish and those of human cells is flawed. Instead, he invites his readers to think of the cilia of the jellyfish as the equivalent of a man's arms and legs: "We do not believe that it has been observed," writes Clark, "to what extent vibratile cilia are individualistic in their movements, at times, just as an arm or a leg is individualized."[103]

Like Clark, Agassiz never quite recovered from the final confrontation he had with his "first American student," which overshadowed the last decade of his life. Right after his 1863 confrontation with Clark, he included a rant in his annual report for the museum trustees. Complaining about the rampant ingratitude of the students who had been privileged to work under him and were now striking out on their own, he said they were obviously thinking "themselves more learned than men who have stood at the head of their respective departments." Of course he was referring to Clark. None too delicately, Agassiz approached the burning question of his American career — the question of who was the real owner of the knowledge that students had garnered from studying the specimens in the museum he had worked so hard to establish. Agassiz talked about such knowledge in terms of a financial transaction, as a loan extended that became due once the students wanted to be scientists in their own right and therefore had to be made to understand "to what extent they have been working with borrowed means, which honesty requires they should pay back."[104]

Even if we grant that Agassiz's anxieties were exacerbated by the contemporary lack of satisfactory copyright and patent laws, the story of his relationship with Clark will sound only too familiar to modern graduate students. It touches on well-known subjects: academic rivalry, personal jealousy, and mentorship gone awry, about a brilliant teacher's unwillingness to let go and a student's irrepressible desire to leave. In a more general sense, though, it raises the question as to who owns the rights to the findings of scientific research. Agassiz might have been instrumental in founding the American graduate school as we know it today, but he also stands at the beginning of the current rush of universities and scholars to defend their knowledge exclusively in terms of ownership. Once regarded as a kind of gift or privilege, academic work (and academic freedom too) is now complicated by issues of intellectual property rights.[105] In a letter to his student Frederic Ward Putnam, who had taken with him some papers when he quit Agassiz's service, Agassiz bluntly distinguished between authorship and property, the latter of which seemed to be the more important of the two: "I would remind you of the relations of an author to a publisher furnishing the means and materials for a book to be brought out by him. The one has the rights of authorship, the other of ownership."[106]

The foreign-born Agassiz, trained in Heidelberg and Munich, certainly appealed to those hordes of American scholars who, in the words of Josiah Royce, felt as if Germany were their "mother-country."[107] However, this was not the only reason for Agassiz's unprecedented success and power in mid-nineteenth-century America. If he had been merely the model of the imperious European professor, which is how Stephen Jay Gould has described him,[108] the story of his treatment of Henry James Clark would be just a footnote in the history of American higher education. The way Agassiz ran his museum had, in fact, far-reaching consequences for American research universities: he combined the hierarchical German regimen of academic knowledge, dependent as it was on the star power of the charismatic professor, with a canny sense of academe as business. The consequences would become clear later. Consider the response of the German theologian Adolf von Harnack after a visit to the United States in 1905. He returned home with a shuddering sense of the possible pitfalls of the corporatization of knowledge: "mechanization of the work, overemphasis on collecting and processing materials as opposed to spiritually penetrating them, and not to mention a sort of stupefaction of the [academic] workers." But he also thought that this way of "mastering the world"—despite the obvious dangers—was inevitable.[109]

Agassiz realized that his mingling of teaching and research was a tightrope act; hence his desire, in his annual report, to reintroduce an ethical component into his argument. He was, he said, aware of "the subtlety of all intellectual property," a source, to be sure, of "great perplexity." But as far as he was concerned, the case was clear. His unprecedented generosity in extending his intellectual "loans" to his students, allowing them to "borrow" his expertise, had added a moral duty to the purely financial obligation his students had incurred: "I may add . . . that I have made my students participants of all my investigations to an extent which I have never found any other teacher to allow them." One of his colleagues had cautioned him not to be too generous with his time and materials and not to "speak freely" in front of his students about his "scientific plans and aims." But, Agassiz said, the purity of his intentions made him disregard such carping from the sidelines: "I have only one object in life, which is the advancement of science, and I shall not change my course for the sake of self-protection merely."[110]

Agassiz the selfless promoter of scientific truth? His former disciple didn't think so. Clark, who was happiest when the waters of the Atlantic lapped around his feet as he looked for new jellyfish, found himself as a student caught between two personalities and two worldviews: Agassiz, the omnivorous Captain Ahab of American natural history, entranced less with the results of scientific investigations than with the idea of science as a heroic activity in which everyone could participate as long as the captain himself remained in charge,

and the benign Dr. Asa Gray, who believed that only patient accu-
mulation of facts would, in due course, yield knowledge—specialized
knowledge, that is—that would not interfere with, or contradict, established religious belief. Agassiz's master student, the son of a Swedenborgian minister, eventually pursued what he perhaps never himself realized was a fantasy: that he had been present when life, as he
conceived of it in the passages on spontaneous generation in *Mind in
Nature*, first came into being. In this fantasy, Henry James Clark was
in a sense the world's first scientist, one who had incurred no debts,
financial or otherwise, and who didn't need anyone to teach him or
tell him what to do. Someone, in short, who was the product of his
own spontaneous generation.

But that is not quite where the story of Henry James Clark and Louis
Agassiz ends. Every bit as brilliant and troubled as his father, his son
Xenos—the same "dear boy" whose future had worried his father
in 1857—picked up where the elder Clark had left off. In a letter
to his friend, the eccentric philosopher Benjamin Paul Blood, Xenos
Clark complained that his father's early death (he was only eighteen
when he added those final lines to his father's diary) had left him "a
waif," without a "philosophical bent" of his own.[111] But in fact, Xenos
had inherited his father's aptitude for science, his melancholy, and his
penchant for art—along with his poor health. A photograph taken
during his student days at Amherst shows a serious face with a mere
hint of a chin; the dark eyes and full lips suggest that Henry James
Clark was perhaps right to be concerned about his boy's prospects in
life.

Under Blood's quirky influence, Xenos Clark became hooked on
"anaesthetic philosophy," a form of meditation induced by the inhala-
tion of ether or nitrous oxide, otherwise known as "laughing gas."[112]
The drugs helped Xenos understand the degree zero of metaphysics
(in his letters to Blood, Clark junior invariably uses the symbol ø) and
to conclude that life was a "journey that was accomplished before we
set out."[113] If Clark senior, while realizing full well the complexity of
superficially simple organisms like his sponges, had still desperately
wanted to drive life into a corner in order to determine its origin and
purpose, Clark junior had given up trying: "The competent intelligence does not think of origin," he told Blood. "Men say 'Why?' to

Xenos Clark. Phi Sigma Kappa photograph.

the Universe—as beavers build dams in parlors."[114] The only thing to do was to open the self to the "thunder of existence" in your ears and accept it for what it is.[115] Drug-befuddled Xenos Clark, enemy of purpose and design, was, in a sense, Agassiz's last victim.

Xenos Clark's correspondent William James, who had, like Xenos's father, studied with Agassiz, tried out the drugs too and found himself powerfully moved to acknowledge that all around the boundaries of our normal waking consciousness lay other forms "entirely different." In one of the long footnotes appended to his *Varieties of Religious Experience*, James quoted Xenos with the sobering insight that we "are forever half a second too late," along with a question that makes us think of his father's little jellyfish: "What is it that keeps existence exfoliating?" Xenos Clark's answer: There is no propulsion in life, only momentum. "It goes because it is a-going." We run through life trying to catch up with our heels, like a hound hunting his own tail.[116]

Death, Xenos Clark had written cryptically after one of his intense anaesthetic experiences, belonged to that momentum. It was a mere "slipping past," a gentle "disadjustment" spreading "the ø out into a panorama" and reminding us of where we all are from, a place where "nature resembles Nothing."[117] It was into that great, seductive, all-encompassing, panoramic Nothing that Xenos Young Clark, age thirty-four, crossed over, on June 4, 1889, in Amherst, Massachusetts, in the same house on Mount Pleasant Street where his father, Louis Agassiz's most favorite and then least favorite student, had died too.[118]

· 6 ·

A PINT OF INK

A FTER HENRY JAMES CLARK had moved to Kentucky in the late spring of 1869, he complained that it was hard to find servants to assist him with his large family. One girl, who was "half white," turned out to be "lazy and stupid." He replaced her quickly with one who was "black as night" and a "good breadmaker." But he wasn't confident that she would stay long in his employ: "Negroes are very unsteady here," he told his parents, "and need watching without exception." When it came to racial politics, Clark had internalized his master's lessons to the hilt.[1]

Like a bad odor, Agassiz's views about race have attached themselves to his damaged reputation, as if his stubborn resistance to evolution wasn't enough to condemn him. One of the greatest puzzles about Agassiz's racism, however, is that he came to hold and broadcast these views at all. Ethnography had interested him only marginally before he came to the United States. His first publication on Brazilian fossil fish had ended with a series of plates showing mostly naked native people engaged in fishing and related activities, but the only comment on them to be found in the book came in the preface provided by his teacher, Martius.[2] In 1833, he would still write about how humans, come lately to the planet, lived in different places of greater or lesser physical elevation, but were otherwise the same.[3] A bit later, Agassiz would permit himself—as he did in an article published in the *Revue suisse* in August 1845 — to speculate on the extent to which the distribution of human races around the globe matched that of the animals.[4] But there was no evidence yet of the extreme views that would seem to isolate him from some of the leading figures in his field.

His mentor Alexander von Humboldt, for one, firmly believed in the basic unity of humankind. In the first volume of *Kosmos* (1845), Humboldt said as clearly as he could that there were no inherent differences between the various races of human beings. He didn't care whether there were *five* races, as the German physician Johann Friedrich Blumenbach had argued, or *seven*, as the English ethnologist James Cowles Prichard had found: "We fail to recognize any typical sharpness of definition, or any general or well-established principle in the division of these groups." More particularly, Humboldt said he firmly believed in racial equality: "While we maintain the unity of the human species, we at the same time repel the depressing assumption of superior and inferior races of men." Quoting his brother Wilhelm, he insisted that the only goal worth striving for was "our common humanity," a world in which the "barriers which prejudice and limited views of every kind have erected" among humans have vanished, and all humankind, "without reference to religion, nation, or color" had become "one great community."[5]

As we have seen, Agassiz admired Humboldt, but he must have skipped that section when he read *Kosmos*, or he wasn't thinking about it when he came to the United States in 1846. Emerging from the white world of Swiss glaciers, the multicolored landscape of the United States disconcerted him. Scholars have assumed that his racial prejudices were purely visceral, beyond his conscious control, the result of one shocking encounter with black servants ("domestiques") in a Philadelphia hotel in the fall of 1846.[6] Agassiz does evoke that experience in a long letter discussed in chapter 3: "I hardly dare describe to you the painful impression that this has left me with," he told his mother.[7] The feelings these servants had triggered in him directly contradicted "all our ideas of the brotherhood of humans and their common origin." But the truth, he declared, takes precedence over noble egalitarian fantasies: "la vérité avant tout." As much as he pitied that degraded and degenerate race, given that they were undeniably human beings, he couldn't help but feel that the blood flowing through their veins was different from his own. And then Agassiz allowed himself to experience a kind of Jeffersonian moment, conjuring up more luridly than Jefferson ever did the specter of physical otherness: looking at the faces of the black servants, "their thick lips, their grimacing teeth, the wool on their heads, their bent knees, their elongated hands, their large, crooked fingernails and, above all, the livid color of the palms of their hands," he became so absorbed that, as he put it, he couldn't even cry out and tell them not to come any closer. Agassiz's expression of disgust, even if uttered in a private letter, seems remarkably unpleasant. No wonder that Elizabeth Agassiz omitted the passage in her biography, as her successor Edward Lurie would do too, when he published his biography half a century later.[8]

When he saw a black waiter's "hideous" black hand coming toward him, about to serve him his plate, Agassiz wished that he was somewhere else, chewing on a piece of dry bread, instead of eating a good dinner in his hotel, the unwilling beneficiary of such unwelcome service. What unhappiness was the lot of those whites whose lives were too closely tied to those of the blacks! Agassiz was now thinking of America's "peculiar institution," of course. "I cannot shake the suspicion," he wrote, perhaps forgetting that he was writing a letter to his mother rather than a newspaper editorial, "that the current state of things in the American South will not one day spell ruin to the entire United States of America." As bad as things were in the South, blacks in the North didn't fare much better, because even there the "white man" would be inclined to keep them at arm's length, driven by instincts he himself might not be aware of.

In this pseudo-rational vein, Agassiz held forth about the current racial situation in America, a subject that, in 1846, was still largely unfamiliar to him. But lack of knowledge or experience never dampened Louis Agassiz's desire to weigh in on an issue. As far as he was concerned, both the abolitionists and the slaveholders had it wrong. The latter, holding on to the past and their property, ignored the fact that the blacks, despite their skin color, had a natural right to enjoy their freedom like all other human beings. And the former, while preaching equal rights for whites and blacks, would never admit that they personally would never marry a black woman or consent to seeing their daughters marry a black man. Agassiz's conclusion would seem merely hypocritical, were it not for the complete earnestness with which he presented it. Maintaining the (dismal) status quo, abolitionists and slaveholders alike were, he claimed, cheating the blacks out of their rights. They wouldn't let them return home (Africa, where they would all thrive in the warm sun). Nor would they allow them to create a life for themselves here. Through the back door, as it were, Agassiz established a kind of white pseudo-consensus on blacks that makes the question as to the evils of slavery almost secondary. White people, whether for or against slavery, didn't want to be around black people. Why not just let black people go, to live among themselves? For Agassiz, ending slavery thus became a matter that would, above all, benefit whites, allowing them to carry on with their lives in peace. Conveniently, physical separation of the races would also do away with miscegenation, which would become the main concern of Agassiz's theorizing about race. It posed a threat to his view of the natural world, wherein every living thing kept to its divinely assigned place.

Agassiz was sharing all these thoughts with his mother back in the Swiss countryside. Poor Rose Agassiz. In reality, though, he was now talking mostly to himself, rehearsing a script to which he will return again and again. And—lo and behold—suddenly he imagined himself addressing his new countrymen. Agassiz was rehearsing his future role as the teacher of an entire nation: "Go ahead and create negro communities in the tropical regions if you don't have an interest in their future here, but don't let yourselves be seduced by misguided philanthropists into believing that the future of the white race is with that of the black race." The inevitable result of espousing the latter idea would be a repetition of the horrors of the slave uprising in Santo Domingo.[9]

Modern readers will find Agassiz's letter deeply offensive, all the more so because its setting is Philadelphia, the City of Brotherly Love. It seems particularly strange coming from someone of Agassiz's education, savvy, and scientific sophistication. His words are marked by "visceral revulsion," according to the biologist and essayist Stephen Jay Gould. Agassiz did attempt to pass off his knee-jerk reaction as "the truth," and he mingled it with a rational-sounding, half-baked explanation as to why racial integration was, at least in practice, a bad idea. He must have realized, on some level, how problematic his reasoning was. Let us not forget, though, that Agassiz's early experience did not extend far beyond the boundaries of his family's canton in Switzerland. When Agassiz saw a black person in the flesh for the first time, some of that old parochial peasant mentality asserted itself under the thin veneer of cosmopolitanism he had acquired during his student days in Heidelberg and Munich and his subsequent stay in Paris. His mother would have understood.

Fast-forward to the experiences that the writer James Baldwin recorded about a hundred years later, when he, the only African American ever to have ventured there, spent time in a village high up in the Swiss Alps and encountered what he called, rather sarcastically, "European innocence . . . a state in which black men do not exist." The interest of the Swiss villagers, who had "never seen a Negro before," is directed exclusively toward Baldwin's physical appearance, especially his hair, which they think has the color of tar and the texture of wire. In the white, icy landscape of Leukerbad (Loèche-les-Bains), living among unthinking racists, Baldwin looks to them like the devil himself. The mountain people do not realize, of course, that Baldwin, owner of the only typewriter in the village, is intellectually ahead of them. He inhabits the future; they are creatures of a benighted past, unable to understand and accept that "this world is white no longer, and it will never be white again."[10]

Unlike the peasants in Baldwin's essay, Agassiz, newly arrived in America, realized that the connection between "whiteness" and power had become precarious. In Switzerland, he probably never expected that his own white European identity would be challenged in any way. But confronted with the reality of the New World, the fact of his own whiteness—that "dumb blankness" we so desperately wish to fill with definite meaning, as Melville would demonstrate in *Moby-Dick*[11]—began to haunt him, as did the nonwhiteness of others. Insistence on racial difference, for Agassiz, became a way of asserting the continuity of his identity as a European after he had left his native country.

While he was in Philadelphia, Agassiz visited the "craniological collection" of Dr. Samuel Morton, which boasted nine hundred skulls, many of them from Native American tribes: "This collection alone had been worth the visit to America," Agassiz declared in his letter to his mother.[12] Morton (whose influence on Agassiz was discussed in chapter 1) presented his American visitor with a copy of his *Crania Americana*. Interestingly, as Morton used it, the adjective *American* referred to the native inhabitants of the North American continent only. As he was touring the United States, fêted by his American peers, Agassiz came to view his New World counterparts as "better Europeans" rather than "Americans," people less encumbered by tradition and precedent than the Europeans he had known, but still *more* like him than the non-European races who also inhabited the cities he visited. Morton's typology of races directly appealed to Agassiz. The "Caucasian Race," according to Morton, was "characterized by a naturally fair skin," fine hair "of various colors," and well-proportioned features. While their faces might seem small "in proportion to the head," this drew even more attention to their skulls, which are oval and large. From this study of anatomy Morton easily shifted to cultural analysis, maintaining, without proof, that the Caucasian race "is distinguished for the facility with which it attains the highest intellectual endowments." Members of the "American" race, by contrast, have brown skin; long, black, and "lank" hair; "deficient" beards, low brows, and, most important, small skulls, "wide between the parietal protuberances, prominent at the vertex, and flat on the occiput." Unsurprisingly, then, the benefits of higher culture have not been extended to them: "slow in acquiring knowledge," they are restless, vengeful, and aggressive. Blacks, or "Ethiopians," to use Morton's term, sport the predictable wooly hair, thick lips, broad noses, and narrow heads.[13]

Agassiz did not heavily annotate his copy of Morton's folio, as was his wont with books he disliked. But one passage caught his eye. *Crania Americana* came with an appendix, provided by the controversial British phrenologist George Combe, author of the bestselling treatise *The Constitution of Man*, first published in 1828 and then in many subsequent editions throughout the nineteenth century. Speculating on the "relation between the natural talents and dispositions of nations and the developments of their brains," Combe assigned "*independence, civilization,* and *political freedom*" to people with large brains, such as the British, the Anglo Americans, and—here we go!—the Swiss. No wonder Agassiz took a second look. In a note he penciled in the book's margin, he felt compelled to quibble with Combe's generalization a bit, perhaps to the benefit of the Swiss, by denying the British any rank of distinction among the large-brained: "As to the British, it is a mere historical name—today representing no peculiar & separated race—and by history all this reasonning [*sic*] can be easily overthrown." Rather than separating different Caucasian "races," Agassiz invoked the unified identity of "l'homme européen," to be found even in America.[14]

Whatever personal reasons Agassiz might have had for making race an important factor in his science after his departure from Europe, he knew too that his ideas on the subject would put him right in the vanguard of current public debates in America, more so than his fossil fish or mollusks could have done. Taking a position on race also assured Agassiz of the continuing interest of a non-academic audience, a priority that would grow in importance to him over the course of his American career. This desire to be recognized must have been part of the impetus behind his decision to address the topic in his Lowell Lectures, his first introduction to a large American audience. Asa Gray, who had given his own Lowell course two years earlier, was in the audience, listening intently, with a mixture of fascination, amusement, and alarm. Agassiz had given, Gray told his friend John Torrey, "good lectures on natural theology." Good, but not outstanding. Gray did like Agassiz's ideas on embryology, "the most original and fundamental confutation of materialism I ever heard." Agassiz had also talked about geographic distribution and expressed views that really weren't too different from those of other respected scientists, such as the Danish plant geographer Joakim Frederik Schouw. Except for one thing, and this idea instantly troubled Gray. Agassiz wanted to apply Schouw's plant geography to humans, arguing that although humans were all one species, they also, like plants, had geographically distinct origins. Agassiz also said, rather idiosyncratically, that Genesis dealt only with the origins of the Caucasians, all of whom were descended from the sons of Noah (including Ham). The devout Gray was bothered by that statement, though he felt reassured that Agassiz didn't reject the Bible: "I never heard him express an opinion or a word adverse to the claims of revealed religion." But other, more important questions led him to condemn Agassiz's argument: "We should not receive it," he told Torrey, "rejecting it on other than scientific grounds, of which he does not feel the force as we do."[15]

The meaning of that puzzling sentence becomes clearer later in the same letter, when Gray mentions his resolve to "keep" his *Manual of the Botany of the Northern United States* (which he was trying to finish then) entirely "clear of slavery." So he was including New Jersey, Pennsylvania, Ohio, Michigan, and Wisconsin, but certainly not Illinois ("which has too many Mississippi plants"), and Delaware "only if it manumits."[16] What Gray really meant when he told Torrey that Agassiz's racial views ought to be rejected "on other than scientific grounds" was quite simple: new to the American continent, Agassiz had not yet contemplated the damaging consequences of what he himself might consider a purely scientific view. But Gray did. The plants admitted to his *Manual* were Northerners only, proud denizens of a world (strange to us today) in which conscience trumped pure science. To be sure, Gray, a friend of the black man in the abstract, had his own share of racial prejudices. It was only in 1869, on a trip to Egypt, that he finally encountered some non-Caucasian people that he really liked, "dark-skinned as most American negroes, but with very handsome features." All the "disagreeable" aspects of darker skin color had vanished in the Arabs he had met there; they were, he concluded with enthusiasm, "among the best-looking and best-behaved men I ever knew." He added that he couldn't really "write about such experiences."[17]

Gray's reading of Agassiz's racism is a kind one. In truth, Agassiz relished the benefits that came with his theorizing. When he went to Charleston in the winter of 1847, attracted by the scientific reputation of the Medical School there, he basked in the warm welcome his new Southern friends extended to him. He knew that his thoughts on race were at least partially responsible for their enthusiastic feelings toward him. In December, he discussed race with the members of the Literary and Philosophical Society of Charleston, known locally as the "Conversation Club." Present that evening were John Bachman, pastor of St. John's Lutheran Church in Charleston, who had collaborated with John James Audubon on the latter's *Birds of America* and had now completely taken over the writing for the ailing Audubon's new set of volumes, *The Viviparous Quadrupeds of North America* (1846–54). Celebrated locally to this day for having promoted Christianity among the African Americans of the city, Bachman considered himself a bit of an expert on the subject of race. We know the names of other members of the "Conversation Club" who were in attendance that night: the Presbyterian minister Thomas Smyth; Frederick A. Porcher, a Yale graduate and professor of history and belles lettres at Charleston College; the banker David Ravenel; the physicians James Moultrie and Peter Gaillard; the lawyer, writer, and artist Charles Fraser; and John Edwards Holbrook, professor of anatomy at Charleston College and a leading herpetologist. Of these men, Reverends Bachman and Smyth were most unlikely to be converted to Agassiz's brand of polygenism, the view that the different human races had biologically distinct origins. But even they remained convinced that slavery was a necessity. In fact, all the members of the Conversation Club directly or indirectly profited from it: the Holbrooks, for example, at one point had no fewer than thirty-four slaves, and if John Bachman himself didn't own any, his salary as a minister came from members of a congregation whose own source of income depended on slave labor. Right into the 1850s, when the residents of Charleston sold many of their slaves to rural planters, slaves comprised the majority of the city's population, working as servants and laborers but also as blacksmiths, masons, coopers, and even in more specialized trades, such as printing and bookbinding.[18] If Bachman and Smyth objected to Agassiz's racial theory, one powerful reason was, of course, that it ran counter to the biblical narrative, "the teachings of that volume which the wisest and the best of men have regarded as the truths of heaven, revealed to an erring world by infinite wisdom and unbounded goodness."[19]

But Bachman had another reason for opposing Agassiz: he was a good enough naturalist to recognize scientific nonsense when he saw it. Over the next few years, the teetotaling pastor, who didn't suffer fools gladly, would become one of Agassiz's most formidable opponents. A portrait painted by Audubon's son John Woodhouse, about a decade before Bachman's first meeting with Agassiz, gives an indication of the minister's pertinacity: his ruddy face offset by his black clerical garb and white collar, his thin, pinched lips closed tight, he gazes steadfastly at the viewer, with knowing, steel-blue eyes. It is unclear whether he is smiling or if this is his typical expression. In the last days of the Civil War, Bachman would suffer a brutal beating

John Bachman, by John Woodhouse Audubon. Oil on canvas, c. 1837.

at the hands of federal troops, an experience that left him broken in body though not in spirit. A few months later he was back in the pulpit. He was a tough man.

Bachman's mounting irritation with polygenists like Samuel Morton and Louis Agassiz would soon find its outlet in a book-length refutation of their theories and a powerful defense of human "monospecism," based, in part, on Bachman's own excellent knowledge of ornithology and his numerous experiments with hybridized roses conducted in his own garden. Yet Bachman and Agassiz had quite a few areas of agreement. The African race, explained Bachman right at the beginning of *The Doctrine of the Unity of the Human Race*, bore "the permanent marks of inferiority." History provided abundant examples of their "incapacity for self-government." And if anyone was still confused about where in the order of things the black race belonged, "the Scriptures point out the duties both of masters and servants." While scientifically there was no obstacle to black and white intermarriage (and Bachman put his considerable expertise to work to show why this was true), the existence of mulattoes remained deplorable "in behalf of good morals." If Samuel Morton thought that natural "repugnance" stood in the way of such unions, Bachman had news for his readers: just look at what's happening all around you. It was a "melancholy" fact that if such a sense of aversion had existed on the day the slaves arrived in America, "it faded away not after the lapse of centuries but in a very few days." And, as far as Europe was concerned, Bachman recalled with a shudder the sight of a pretty white woman in Stratford-upon-Avon (Shakespeare's hometown, of all places!) leaning on the shoulder of her husband, a "full blood African." Both were surrounded by their "mulatto progeny." However revolting such an image might be "to our American feelings," *Europeans didn't seem to mind.* "We also recollect having seen well dressed young white men and women walking arm in arm with negroes in the streets of Edinburgh, London, and Paris." Bachman doesn't specify the number of children the couple in Stratford had produced, but using the word "progeny" hints ominously at their unrestrained fertility. Where Morton's essays on this subject invoke the threat of sterility, Bachman comments on the terrible prospect of limitless fecundity. Even if no scientific barriers stood in the way of such racial intermixing, Bachman suggests that human decency (or "good morals") must frown upon it.[20]

When it came to granting, in James Baldwin's terms, "human weight and complexity" to American slaves and imagining them side by side with whites, it's not only the usual suspects who fail the test. Where Agassiz saw scientific necessity, others like Bachman found at least a moral imperative. The poet Walt Whitman, who had imagined himself, in "Song of Myself," selflessly tending to the wounds of a fugitive slave, followed Agassiz in concluding that nature had "set an impassible seal" against racial amalgamation.[21] Ralph Waldo Emerson too believed that while nature loves "crosses," these relationships, among humans, should leave racial boundaries intact: "Where two shadows cross, the darkness thickens: where two lights cross, the light glows." Such glowing light manifested itself where "the Greek & Saxon geniuses" fused, as they did in John Milton and Francis Bacon. The "negro or lowest man" represented darkness, an undesirable reminder of the resemblance between the human and the nonhuman realms. No wonder, then, that Emerson felt that he had "quite other slaves to free than those negroes."[22] Taking care of his benighted white countrymen was his first order of business.

It was in Bachman's bailiwick that Agassiz—a European who, unlike those indulgent Edinburghians or Stratfordians Bachman had encountered, *did* mind indiscriminate racial mixing—officially entered the minefield of racial discourse. In March 1850, when he had been in the United States for just over three years, Agassiz listened attentively and appreciatively to a paper submitted by Josiah Nott, a slaveholder from Mobile, Alabama, during a meeting of the American Association for the Advancement of Science in Charleston. Nott was a medical doctor by training, with some expertise in the causes and treatment of yellow fever, but in the paper he delivered on this occasion, he spoke as a self-styled ethnographer. Nott declared that there was not a "particle of proof" that different races shared the same family tree. In fact, it would be impossible to "compress," into the constraints of one common origin, races that in themselves were as diverse as the Caucasians and the "endless types among the dark-skinned races of Africa." Nott announced that the science of ethnography (the cutting-edge science he represented) wasn't simply "a link in the chain of science to amuse the curious" but of "great practical importance in its bearings on the future destiny of races." He went on to add a bit of racist propaganda to clarify precisely what that future might involve for one race in particular. Blacks were, he claimed, incapable of self-government. In Haiti, for example, "barbarism advances as the white blood is expelled." And the recent Liberian experiment would fail, utterly and speedily, too; only the partially white blood of its current leaders had prevented such a disaster thus far.

Clearly energized by Nott's remarks, Agassiz got up and offered his own version of the problem: whereas men of all races were brothers and possessed "all the attributes of humanity" (another way of saying that they weren't animals), zoologically they were all distinct. It was a curiously paradoxical argument—humans aren't like animals yet should be treated as if they were. He went on to explain that animals inhabit distinct zoological provinces, "each characterized by its peculiar Fauna," and so do humans: "The principal races of men in their natural distribution, cover the same extent of ground as these zoölogical provinces," proof enough "that the differences we notice at present between the races were also primitive, and that these races did not originate from a common centre, nor from a single pair." The minister's son realized that his theory might be construed as an assault on religious orthodoxy, a charge he deflected by pointing out that the Bible itself mentions that Cain, Adam's son, finds refuge in "other lands already peopled." In other words, that's where the blacks lived.[23]

Agassiz's remarks were heard far beyond Charleston. At Down House in England, Charles Darwin, in a letter written on September 4, 1850, to his cousin William Darwin Fox, mentioned, sarcastically, "Agassiz's Lectures in the U.S. in which he has been maintaining the doctrine of several species,—much, I daresay, to the comfort of the slave-holding Southerns."[24]

Darwin was right: Agassiz did impress the "slave-holding Southerns." Right after the meeting of the American Association, a prominent South Carolinian physician, scientist, and patron of the arts, Dr. Robert W. Gibbes, invited him to tour the plantations around Columbia, where Agassiz took pleasure in identifying the tribal origins of different slaves, whether they were "Ebo, Foulah, Gullah, Guinea, Coromantee, Mandrigo and Congo Negroes."[25] But Agassiz also found corroboration of what he simply "knew" to be true: whatever their individual tribal affiliations, the men and women he encountered were alike enough—as "blacks"—to be collectively different from the white norm. After Agassiz's departure, Gibbes arranged for Joseph T. Zealy, a daguerreotypist, to take pictures of the slaves Agassiz had studied.[26] Gibbes masterminded these sessions. He had Agassiz's subjects pose in the nude, so that the anatomical features, on which "proof" of racial difference rested, were fully visible.

The photographs, meant to reveal racial types, not a sitter's individuality, were taken in Zealy's gallery in Columbia, an incongruous environment that made the finished products even more disturbing—and strange. Zealy's gallery, as a contemporary described it, was "handsomely furnished," containing a piano as well as an "anteroom, for the proper adjustment of toilette."[27] Imagine, in this ostentatiously middle-class environment, the exposed bodies of the slaves,

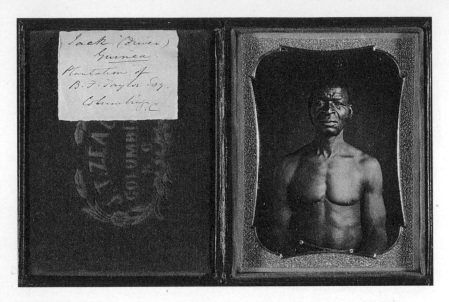

"Jack (driver) Guinea. Plantation of B. F. Taylor Esq., Columbia, S.C." Daguerreotype by Joseph T. Zealy, March 1850.

dragged there to serve someone else's racial fantasies. Zealy's "handsomely furnished" studio remains visible, at least symbolically, in the decorative frames that were laid on the plates, elevating to the status of portraiture images intended to serve as scientific proof. But the demeanor of the sitters resists this classificatory purpose. Consider the photograph of "Jack (driver) Guinea," owned by "B. F. Taylor, Esq." (The careful descriptions are Gibbes's handiwork.). Jack was a slave driver, or overseer, in charge of directing the work of other slaves on Taylor's plantation. He is powerfully built; the muscles on his biceps, bulging veins and all, are clearly visible. The light falls on his face not because Gibbes specifically requested that arrangement, but because this was how Zealy generally posed his subjects.[28] The result is a curious contrast between the nobility of Jack's facial features and the vulnerability of his naked body. Whatever limited power Jack might have enjoyed on Taylor's plantation, here he had none. But even as his slightly tilted head, his squint, and his closed lips indicate resignation, the chiseled features, deeply furrowed brow, and carefully kept beard show him to be an individual, not a generic slave. Jack's face seems older than his body, leaving the viewer to wonder about the suffering he has experienced or seen. At Gibbes's request, Zealy also produced profile views of the slaves; in Jack's image, ritual scars on his temple clearly indicate his origins in a different culture, not the one that forces him to be on display in this manner.

Hold against this photograph one of Agassiz taken around the same time, such as the studio portrait from chapter 1, with its self-conscious Napoleonic overtones. This imperial-looking Agassiz, his right hand in a pocket, is surrounded by the trappings of bourgeois comfort. The two images—one offering a successful man a stage for self-stylization, the other intended to lessen a man's individuality, to turn him into a specimen—tell a tale not of racial difference, but of social position. Nonetheless, it is amazing how much of Jack's character survives this attempt to diminish his humanity in the service of racial ideology.

After the Charleston conference, Agassiz presented his most comprehensive formulation of his views on race in a series of essays published in the *Christian Examiner*. The choice of the journal, a major forum for Unitarian thought intended to promote "spiritual and moral improvement," was not accidental. It is strange to think that Agassiz's racial fear-mongering had ever seemed innovative, but he was indeed worried about the conservative opposition he might provoke from those who regarded his views as an attack on (as Agassiz termed it) "the Mosaic account of creation." The *Christian Examiner*, which had criticized Emerson's Divinity School address and denounced transcendentalism as an un-American fad,[29] represented the more conservative side of Unitarianism, and these proper credentials could be useful for Agassiz. At the same time, he could count on finding readers who were not constrained by the more rigid forms of theological orthodoxy. Agassiz's first essay on race, misleadingly titled "The Geographical Distribution of Animals," came out in the March 1850 issue, which also contained a review of Emerson's *Representative Men*.[30] Agassiz argued that the Bible was not wrong but rather incomplete; more precisely, it had never been intended to offer a complete account of why the world came to be what it is. He aimed to establish his version of the truth as in full agreement with the biblical story (a "human construction," as he nevertheless points out) and, in fact, superior to it because it was so much more comprehensive. Much of his reasoning, though, merely appeals to the reader's common sense. Why assume that all animals originated from a common pair if so many animals themselves don't live in pairs? Take the bees in the hive, or try to imagine "a pair" (as opposed to a *herd*) of buffaloes or "a pair" (as opposed to a *shoal*) of herrings, an absurd idea if ever there was one and "as contrary to the nature and habits of those animals, as it is contrary to the nature of pines and birches to grow singly and to form forests in their isolation." Or, he asks the reader, consider the distribution of fish in three river basins "entirely unconnected with each other," the Rhine, the Rhone, and the Danube. Agassiz is now drawing on expertise he had developed in Europe and a subject that his American reader would realize he knew intimately. Most of the fish found in one of these rivers cannot be found in the others. Interestingly, among the perches, some species, *Aspro vulgaris*, for example, are common to all. Others, such as *Perca vulgaris*, can be found only in one. Why, if migration is the reason those closely allied species ended up where they are now, didn't *all* of them migrate at the same time? And why, unless they were meant to stay put, did other animals, equipped with extraordinary powers of locomotion, nevertheless remain within their often fairly circumscribed natural limits? Look also, continued Agassiz, at the problems we experience when we transport animals out of their native country into other countries.

Agassiz then offers a long digression about the intimate relationship between the distribution of animals and the atmospheric and hydrostatic pressures in their environment. This was more confirmation, if it was still needed, that animals have been placed where they ought to be. For example, the monkeys of tropical America are completely different from the monkeys of Africa or Asia, and vice versa; some, like the *Maki* of Madagascar, are even limited to just one narrowly circumscribed area. In the temperate zone, however, "the main seat of human civilizations," differences between species are less pronounced, and it is this pseudo-uniformity, argues Agassiz, that must have given rise to the notion of the idea of a common origin.

> What, indeed could be more natural for man, when for the first time reflecting upon nature around him, — when seeing, as far as he could extend his investigations, all things alike, — than to imagine that everything arose from a common centre, and spread with him over the world, as it has been the fate of the white race, and of

that only, to extend all over the globe, and that, influenced by the phenomena of the zone in which he lived, and wandered, and from which he extended farther, he took it for granted that all animals followed the same laws?[31]

Agassiz saves his most powerful argument, and his longest sentence, for last. And he takes a more psychological approach here. In order to maintain the superiority of whiteness (and render persuasive his belief in the separate creation of the white race), Agassiz must convince his readers of the limitations of whiteness. Untraveled Caucasians tend to take themselves as the norm; hence they have been blind—as Agassiz himself had been—to the existence of other races and their difference from the norm; this naiveté has made it easy for whites to assume that all humans have come from the same source. Once Caucasians leave their own zone, however, they awaken to the reality of a world in which humans of different races inhabit different zones the way animals of different species do. This thinking is both radical and reactionary: Agassiz uses a provocative human-animal analogy to prove that some humans are "less animal" than others.

Agassiz's second statement of his racial philosophy, "The Diversity of Origin of the Human Races," was printed in the *Christian Examiner* in July 1850, following an essay on "Wordsworth the Christian Poet." Portions of Agassiz's article restate positions familiar from the earlier piece, but he now also includes his own data, gathered on the plantations around Columbia. One can almost imagine him, safely back in his Oxford Street house, peering at the sorry photographs that Gibbes had procured for him: "All over Africa we have but one type, or rather we generally consider the Africans as one, because they are chiefly black. But if we take the trouble to compare their different tribes, we shall observe that there are as great differences between them as between the inhabitants of Asia."

And then, clearly referring to his South Carolina self-tutorial, he adds, "The negro of Senegal differs as much from the negro of Mozambique as he differs from the negro of Congo or of Guinea. The writer has of late devoted special attention to this subject, and has examined closely many native Africans belonging to different tribes, and has learned readily to distinguish their nations, without being told whence they came; and even when they attempted to deceive him, he could determine their origin from their physical features."[32]

This passage hides its dubious intent behind the rhetoric of scientific detachment. Its purpose, within an essay intended to question the notion that humans of different races have the same origin, is to refute the impression that Agassiz wants to pit whites against blacks (or Indians, or Asians, and so forth). Agassiz acknowledges that, far from being a monolithic category, "black" in fact serves as a label for a variety of very different tribal identities. Any sense of racial hierarchy based on simple opposition (black versus white) would thus appear to founder on the complex reality of racial diversity. However, by bringing in his own expertise based on his anthropological "fieldwork," Agassiz also cleverly reestablishes his own white superiority as a knowledgeable observer able to classify members of other races. As elsewhere in Agassiz's lectures, a sense of sportsmanship, as if ethnographic research were a kind of athletic challenge, infuses the description of his abilities and activities. While doing his fieldwork, boasts Agassiz, he was "readily" able to distinguish between the different tribes, even when his subjects—who wouldn't expect such behavior from a black man?—lied to him. When dealing with the troublesome, not-to-be-trusted, uncooperative black slave, the white scientist will always dominate.

Agassiz's July 1850 essay in the *Christian Examiner* is a rather cunning performance, a tour-de-force play on three words—*unity*, *diversity*, and *origin*—none of which, by the end of the essay, means what it used to mean. Humankind is unified, according to Agassiz, but only in a spiritual or moral sense and in contradistinction to the animal kingdom: "We recognize the fact of the Unity of Mankind. It excites a feeling that raises men to the most elevated sense of their connection with each other. It is but the reflection of that Divine nature which pervades their whole being." Agassiz then vigorously denies that he ever claimed that humans of different races belong to different species: "The writer has been in this respect strangely misrepresented." However, the human "unity of species," apparently uncontested by him, does not mean that all humans are alike or that differences between nations don't exist; even the Western ones, though strongly similar, are not alike in every detail. What works for one doesn't necessarily work for the others: "Because the French differ in many respects from the English, the Greeks, the Italians, etc., and because we see in these nations different turns of mind, does it follow that the particular degree of civilization attained by one is also the best that others could enjoy, and the best that could be introduced into their social condition?"

Having laid this theoretical groundwork, Agassiz goes on to muse that since the larger "types of races" (Caucasian, Asian, Negro) contain so many small differences or variations in themselves, how can they not be, at the level of "types," different from one another? Assuming merely that races had the same origin but then developed differently under different climatic and geographical conditions won't work. How would one explain, then, the difference between "the Old World Mongolians and Caucasians, and Indians in America," all of whom live in "the temperate zone" and therefore in similar environments? These thoughts were offered in the spirit of disinterested scientific and philosophical inquiry only, and not as a matter of politics: "It is simply with reference to the possibility of appreciating the differences existing between different men, and of eventually determining whether they have originated all over the world, and under what circumstances, that we have here tried to trace some facts respecting the human races, and the animal kingdom, in all their different classes." Nothing in his argument, he hurries to add, perhaps remembering that he was writing for a religious journal, could be construed as an attack on the account in Genesis, limited as it was to the emergence of the Caucasian race. But what was true of Adam and Eve might as well apply to other pairs elsewhere: "We have no statement relating to the origin of the inhabitants now found in those parts of the world which were unknown to the ancients."[33]

Agassiz tries to strike a scholarly pose here. The pronoun "we" and the careful qualifications ("simply"; "eventually"; "some facts") seem to underscore that the writer has no personal ax to grind. Never mind his apparent belief that the Bible is, as Emily Dickinson would put it later, "an antique volume — / Written by faded Men."[34] In Agassiz's version, the Good Book simply isn't "a text-book of natural history." But what might sound like skepticism toward revealed religion, Agassiz claims as the higher moral ground. Forget genealogy; think spirituality. Agassiz is religion's best friend: "We need not search for the highest bond of humanity," he tells his readers, "in a mere animal function, whereby we are most closely related to the brutes."

As in his previous statements, Agassiz keeps dancing around, never directly addressing the possibility that the (to him) self-evident differences between the races might indicate that they in fact constitute different species. Agassiz does suggest that the term *species* is too vague to be useful anyway. Then he reintroduces it: "There is no ornithologist, who has ever watched the natural habits of birds and their notes, who has not been surprised at the similarity of intonation of the notes of closely allied species, and the greater difference between the notes of birds belonging to different genera and families." And when Agassiz, by an ingenious sleight of hand, applies this observation about the avian world to human beings, he hopes readers will suspect that the sometimes slight differences between otherwise similar races might also be characterized as the differences between species: "Why should it be different with men? Why should not the different races of men have originally spoken distinct languages, as they do at present, differing in the same proportions as their organs of speech are variously modified? And why should not these modifications in their turn be indicative of primitive differences among them? It were giving up all induction, all power of arguing from sound premises, if the force of such evidence were to be denied." That said, Agassiz turns around again and casually denies not the evidence, but the importance of terminology: "Whether the natural groups which can be recognized in the human family are called races, varieties, or species, is of no great importance, as soon as it is understood that they present the extreme development of a peculiar diversity, already introduced to some extent among some of the higher animals."

Agassiz's affable, reasonable tone invites those who consider themselves rational and fair-minded to agree with him.[35] He seems to stand above the fray, confident and nonchalant. And if the reader by this time is convinced that humans of different races are not just *like* different species but actually *are* different species (the author's denials notwithstanding), Agassiz's work is done.

Or was it? A third *Christian Examiner* essay followed. In "Contemplations of God in the Kosmos," Agassiz proposed to lift the whole issue onto an even higher theological plane, one that he imagined would please even the most skeptical reader. If everything in the world was the divine thought made manifest, then tracing back the dizzying multiplicity of created beings to one source—or, to put it differently, the divergent human races to one original pair of humans—would be tantamount to insulting God. As is so often the case, Agassiz can be seen putting the theoretical cart before the horse. Without having properly demonstrated that the diversity of the world—"various kinds of corals growing promiscuously on the same reef," "jellyfish swimming over them in the same waters," "sea urchins and starfishes, crawling about upon the same corals"—is indeed due to God's direct intervention rather than to laws of development once instituted by God and then left alone or, worse, mere accident, he simply goes on to assume the existence of a "personal, intelligent God" whose power he then argues mustn't be questioned.[36]

Edward Lurie, his twentieth-century biographer, finds Agassiz's position "tragic" and claims that he never realized the extent to which his views served the apologists of slavery or catered to "the sensitivity of the majority of Americans to the slavery question."[37] But Agassiz's carefully crafted essays in the *Christian Examiner* and the obsessive way in which he kept revisiting the topic suggest otherwise.

In fact, Agassiz couldn't stop thinking about race. The Alabama slaveholder Josiah Nott had evidently impressed him with his Charleston paper. When Nott asked Agassiz to write an essay for the volume he had cowritten with George Gliddon, *Types of Mankind*, he readily agreed. And thus Agassiz's views, barely formed, became an integral part of one of the saddest books in the canon of nineteenth-century racial thinking.[38] Agassiz's essay, with a typically graceless title, "Sketch of the Natural Provinces of the Animal World and Their Relation to the Different Types of Man," was preceded by a quotation from a letter to Nott and Gliddon in which he asserted, somewhat misleadingly, that all he had done was restate ideas first expressed in his *Revue suisse* article of 1845, written while he was still in Neuchâtel. At that time, after carefully delineating the distinct zoological provinces that make up the animal kingdom, Agassiz had explicitly exempted man from such divisions. The differences between the animal populations of the different continents were, he declared, primordial, attributable to the same ancient cause. Was there anything comparable in humankind? For Agassiz, the answer was clear: "Évidemment non," evidently not. More proof of the superiority of the "genus" of humanity, its supreme independence in nature. Whereas different species of animals lived in carefully circumscribed zoological "provinces," humans, despite their different racial origins, all belonged to one and the same species ("une seule et même espèce"). At once the goal and the end of all creation, man was the triumphant exception in the order of living things.[39]

The essay Agassiz wrote for Nott and Gliddon revisits some of the same territory, but comes to very different conclusions. With the help of many examples, Agassiz establishes what he sees as the primordial permanence of the zoological regions in which animals are to be found. Agassiz distinguishes between the glacial zone, the temperate zone, and the tropical zone, and he goes on to argue that these geographical divisions also indicate, or "coincide with," human (or, more precisely, racial) diversity. Since the animals were originally placed where we find them now, "by the direct agency of a Creator," humans must have been put in their appropriate locations too. Now, if the different animals in their different zoological provinces can be said to have different origins, the same must be true of humans. The name for such difference in the animal kingdom is, of course, *species*, which means that the same concept will also serve to explain human racial diversity. Agassiz's understanding of species comes straight from Samuel Morton, to whose memory *Types of Mankind* was dedicated: species were, Morton had said, "primordial organic forms," even if their distinct origins might not be visible anymore. Since the donkey and horse, known to be distinct species of the same genus, can be, as Agassiz coyly remarks, "productive with one another" (as can be, he was mentally adding, the white man with the black woman), "genetic succession" isn't a good criterion for distinguishing one species from another. (Did Agassiz really not notice the circular argument he was advancing here? Since we know what species are, he seemed to be saying, there are certain criteria we shouldn't use to define species.)

Armed with Morton's "primordial" species concept, Agassiz now drops his bombshell, a radical departure indeed from the Neuchâtel essay and even from his *Christian Examiner* pieces: "I am prepared to show that the differences existing between the races of men are of the same kind as the differences observed between the different fami-

lies, genera, and species of monkeys or animals; and that these different species of animals differ in the same degree one from the other
as the races of men—nay, the differences between distinct races are
often greater than those distinguishing species of animals one from
the other." By the time he has come to the end of his sentence, he
has abandoned analogy entirely. He does backtrack a bit in the paragraphs that follow, referring to the connection between zoological
provinces and the "circumscription of the races of man" as a mere coincidence, if one that requires further investigation. But these more
carefully worded passages are at odds with the assertive tone of other
ones in the same piece: "I am prepared to show"; "I maintain distinctly."[40]

Whence this obsession with species?[41] What does Agassiz stand to
gain from making human racial groups equivalent to different animal species—a conclusion that he has been working up to, more or
less systematically, since that day in Charleston when he jumped up
to offer his support for Nott's racist ideas? On the one hand, we may
assume that Agassiz's theorizing is driven by a genuine and, in the
context of the science of his time, quite radical need to treat humans
as not fundamentally different from animals: "The laws which regu-
late the diversity of animals, and their distribution upon earth, apply
equally to man, *within the same limits* and *in the same degree*."[42] On the
other hand, though, considering human species as racially distinct
also serves a more conservative purpose—namely, that of fending off
any notion that nature might have *developed* to where it is today. What
worries Agassiz, in other words, is the idea that whatever we perceive
as diversity today must have been the product of a series of changes
over time, an assumption that would also require us to assume that
there was—horrible thought!—no general plan in place at the beginning of the Creation.

But there was yet another reason behind Agassiz's well-publicized
racism, beyond the need for order. This was the desire to align himself, as an immigrant, as firmly as he could with other whites of European descent in America, the need to construct a genealogy for
himself that would make the New World seem rather old indeed. A
prophetic hint of the worries that must have beset him after his arrival does occur, after all, in Agassiz's earlier *Revue suisse* essay. In
America, writes Agassiz, the zoological provinces are harder to keep

apart ("plus difficile à établir"), which is also why the Indians of the North look so much like the ones that live in the South. Is America the great leveler? Vaster than Europe, the American continent is also more homogeneous than the rest of the world, a terrifying prospect barely hinted at in Agassiz's elegant French prose, in phrases as elaborately positioned as the specimens in his museum display cases.

Arrived from a country as white as the glaciers whose inexorable progress he tracked, Agassiz believed in the right of the white man to lord it over "every dusky tribe," to use the caustic description provided by Melville's Ishmael.[43] But he also insisted that he was very much against slavery. As Charles Darwin would immediately point out, one couldn't really believe in the former without ending up supporting the latter. In all fairness, though, being against slavery wasn't something that could be taken for granted even in the circles in which Agassiz normally moved. Take his friend Joseph Henry of the Smithsonian, who, as late as 1860, found slavery "to be in accordance with the general tendency of modern civilization," or, for that matter, Professor Benjamin Peirce, Agassiz's Harvard colleague, who considered it "a blessing rather than a bane."[44] Agassiz's wife Elizabeth, descended from old New England stock, wasn't particularly upset either by what she glimpsed of America's "peculiar institution" when she followed her husband to Charleston. Her attitude, more than anyone else's, would have helped shape Agassiz's own emerging racial beliefs. Elizabeth's paternal grandfather, Samuel Cary, had spent eighteen years as a prosperous planter in the West Indies, and her father, after a few years of involvement in the China trade, became a treasurer of the Hamilton and Appleton Mills in Lowell, Massachusetts, an enterprise heavily dependent on Southern cotton. Elizabeth does not mention this, but we know from a memoir written by her sister Caroline Curtis that the Cary family brought a slave home with them when they returned from the West Indies. "Black Fanny," as she was known to the Cary girls, had been purchased by Elizabeth's grandmother "because she could not bear to see such a little creature left to the chances of less tender mercies than her own." Black Fanny lived in her own little cottage erected on the capacious seafront property owned by the Cary family. Usually meek and quiet, she impressed the Cary girls with her vivid recollections about how she was "seized and taken off from her home" in Africa by slave traders when she was merely a child.[45]

There's no indication, however, that Black Fanny's stories about her deportation made more than a fleeting impression on Elizabeth. In Charleston, she and her husband's Swiss-born children felt right at home, visiting the plantations of friends, attending parties, idly drifting down the rivers in boats rowed by cheerful slaves. Or so they thought. "The grim side of slavery was something they never saw," asserts Elizabeth Agassiz's biographer Mary Louise Tharp, a statement that, perhaps unintentionally, suggests that slavery also had its pleasant side. It is also incorrect.[46] Even in civilized Charleston, her husband's base of operations, Elizabeth would have had plenty of opportunity to see the uglier manifestations of Southern slavery. Uncontained by the cultural parameters of white sophistication—if they didn't serve her drinks, that is, or row her boat—black people frightened her and she kept her distance whenever possible: "The town is as empty as Boston in the middle of August," she wrote to her mother in the winter of 1851–1852. Everybody had left for their plantations for the Christmas holidays, and she was more than ready to go too: "We expect to leave tomorrow or the next day for Belmont, where we shall pass the week." When the whites left, Charleston reverted to savagery: "The town is absolutely given up to the blacks, and if any of the white population are so unfortunate as to have no refuge for the holidays in the country, they can scarcely go through the streets in safety for the firing of crackers, the shooting of pistols, playing with fire balls, and other mad pranks of the negroes, so that, I am the more glad that we have such a pleasant home for a week, which must be anything but agreeable in the city."[47] Living with blacks all the time had had an effect even on their white friends, as Elizabeth pointed out in a letter to her sister Sarah ("Sallie"). "Like their negroes," the whites of Charleston were frightened of the cold and think "the terror of the infernal regions consists in ice, not heat." They had their superstitions upside-down: "To talk of hell-fire to them would rather tempt them to sin, than keep them from it."[48]

Elizabeth Agassiz's impression of Southern blacks wouldn't change much during subsequent visits. When the Agassizes returned to Charleston the next year, their stay overlapped with that of another illustrious guest, the novelist William Makepeace Thackeray. Thackeray was in America "for 'the tin'" (to make money), as Elizabeth noted with disgust in a letter to her mother (Agassiz's lectures were free). Thackeray had already been to Boston, New York, Philadelphia, Washington, and Baltimore. In Charleston he lectured "three times a week, alternately with Agassiz." Elizabeth was afraid that the "coming of this newer star" would dampen enthusiasm for Agassiz, but that didn't happen: "The Charleston people are very constant, and they seem really fond of Agassiz." Besides, Thackeray was a poor, "monotonous" performer. "How can he help of being tired of reading the same thing through all the Cities of the United States?"[49] During his American sojourn, Thackeray was accompanied by the struggling artist and writer Eyre Crowe, his factotum and amanuensis. Together they would sit in their hotel room—which was in "awful condition," Elizabeth had heard—sketching slaves. A "negro" woman was shelling peanuts, a black boy at her side, right there in Thackeray's hotel room, while Crowe was drawing her. Elizabeth suspected he wanted to make "a book enlivened by sketches, taken on the spot."[50] And a book Crowe did make, a rather smug memoir based on notebooks he kept at the time, in which he revels in the kind of "picturesque" clichés about black life under slavery that Elizabeth preferred too.[51] Crowe knew that, thanks to "Mrs. Stowe's fiery denunciations," the debate about slavery was "at fever-heat." But that didn't keep him from finding the "negro ball" he and Thackeray attended rather "quaint" and entertaining ("we went home in high humour"). "Passing now from gay science to dull fact," Crowe goes on to report on a slave sale he witnessed, and what "fine strapping sons of toil" these slaves were. He gratefully notes that the auction was an open-air event, which "by its picturesque elements lost many of its dismal features," and includes a cheerful sketch to prove it, showing bustling activity everywhere, exotic turbans and elegant top hats intermingled as if a party, rather than a sale of human beings, was in full swing. In a series of quickly drawn portraits, Crowe records the different "negro types" offered here, revealing "varying coloured parentage," from Peter to Henry Douglass, the latter "of obscure ilk." All of that and more could be found in gallant Charleston.[52]

Elizabeth and Louis Agassiz left Charleston in the spring of 1853 to see more of the South, with George Gliddon, Dr. Josiah Nott's collaborator and co-author, acting as an informal tour guide for part of the trip. In Mobile, Alabama, the Agassizes stayed with Nott. And Louis didn't disappoint, as Elizabeth proudly reported. Many came to hear what Elizabeth provocatively described as "Agassiz' heathen views, on the diversity of the races." Agassiz's polygenism was, for lack of a better word, "in." It was cutting-edge, iconoclastic, heterodox, hard-hitting. Rodolphe's son had come a long way. As Elizabeth proudly reported, "The evening before we left, there was a very gay supper-party, given for us at Dr. Nott's, after the lecture. The last lecture was the most crowded of all the course, though all were very fully attended . . . I have never heard him so eloquent and clear on that subject, so I suppose the listeners were as much pleased or *displeased*, as they had expected to be." "The *displeased*" were likely those listeners who, along with the Reverend Bachman, believed in the common origin of all races. There couldn't have been too many Bachman fans, though, because, as Elizabeth sums it up, "The next day we had a line of friends to bid us good-bye at the boat; our visit at Mobile was so pleasant that I feel as if we could not enjoy any other part of our southern tour as much."[53]

Nevertheless, it seems that Elizabeth did find a number of other Southern places quite entertaining. The "babbles of tongues" she heard in the French part of New Orleans intrigued and amused her. But she was careful to note that the ones that remained resistant to the lure of the "foreign" were the blacks. "In the market, the negroes in the stalls sell their provisions in French, Spanish, or English according to their customer, and strange to say in every language, it is always 'nigger talk.' They carry their peculiar pronunciation into each, and 'Topsy's' lingo is the same, through every guise." Clearly, she had been reading Harriet Beecher Stowe's new novel, but whereas Stowe had seen in Topsy a soul stunted by slavery and in dire need of salvation, Elizabeth Cary Agassiz saw only racial difference or, at best, local color.[54]

Never mind what he and his wife actually thought of blacks as people. Agassiz's antislavery stance, along with his public stature, seemed to make him an ideal choice a decade later for the role of expert adviser to Samuel Gridley Howe's American Freedmen's Inquiry Commission. The commission was a direct result of Lincoln's Emancipation Proclamation of January 1, 1863. The U.S. secretary of war, Edwin

McMasters Stanton, had formed it in March 1863 to "inquire into the condition of the Colored population emancipated by acts of Congress and the proclamations of the president, and to consider and report what measures are necessary to give practical effect to those acts and proclamations, so as to place the Colored people of the United States in a condition of self-support and self-defense." Apart from the Bostonian Howe, Stanton appointed the New Yorker James McKaye and the Hoosier Robert Dale Owen to this committee.

Howe was a graduate of Brown and Harvard Medical School and the director of the New England Asylum for the Blind (later known as the Perkins Institute for the Blind). A physically imposing man once widely considered handsome, with a full beard and piercing blue eyes, Howe was sixty-one when Stanton asked him to serve. His wife, the formidable feminist Julia Ward Howe, called him "Chev," short for "Chevalier," a reference to Dr. Howe's much-noted regal bearing in public. A fan of Byron's poetry, he had fought heroically in the Greek war for independence. More recently, he was known as a vocal and courageous abolitionist; when John Brown, carrying out plans to foment an uprising of slaves, was arrested after his unsuccessful raid on Harpers Ferry in 1859, Howe had to flee to Canada. It seemed Stanton could not have found a better man to help decide what to do with America's ex-slaves.

Nevertheless, the questions he asked in his first letter to Agassiz—similar ones went out to other people whose opinion he thought mattered—were all shaped by white anxiety over what to do with black freedmen. Will the African race, "represented by less than two million blacks & a little more than two million mulattoes," be a permanent and persistent reality in the United States, or will it be "absorbed, diluted & finally be effaced" by the whites? Will abolition foster general amalgamation and bring about an increase of "unfertile," "lymphatic & scrofulous" mixed-race people? Will there be an influx of whites in the former slaveholding states to counteract the current preponderance of blacks there? Only Howe's final question appeared to favor the blacks in any way: How can we prevent whites from taking advantage of, and profiting from, the emerging black working class?[55]

This was a great moment for Agassiz. Getting Howe's letter proved that science did matter to the public and that, more important, *he* mattered, the way Humboldt had mattered to his country. In his answer to Howe, sent from his pleasant summer residence on Nahant, Agassiz stated adamantly that he wasn't a friend of slavery. In fact, he was really a friend of the blacks: if indeed a black population is to remain in North America (and Agassiz suggests, slyly, that that proposition might not be a given), then "it becomes our duty to avoid the recurrence of evils perhaps as great in a moral point of view as slavery itself." One of those evils, he explains, would be any new system of dependency that subjected the newly freed blacks to "unscrupulous managers." "Negroes" are here to stay, Agassiz concludes, an ambiguous statement at best. They're not like the Indians, who were, as Agassiz maintains, in line with prevailing ideology, destined to vanish. And they're not like the Hottentots either, who have remained where they belong. American blacks travel. They are impressionable, malleable; they accommodate themselves quickly to new sets of circumstances, and imitate, with ease, those among whom they live. For better or worse, then, they may be considered our "cotenants in the possession of this part of the world." The fact that their original home was Africa doesn't change anything, "since our own race furnishes ample evidence of the facility with which one race may settle extensive regions in which it has for ages been foreign." While Agassiz adopts the same pseudo-scientific tone that marked Jefferson's confused musings on race in *Notes on the State of Virginia*, at least he doesn't endorse the latter's assessment that blacks "should be colonized to such place as the circumstances of the time should render most proper."[56] But he shares Jefferson's concerns about "admixture," as becomes clear when Agassiz, in the next step of his argument, leaves behind any pretense of scientific reasoning: "Among the characteristic of halfbreeds one of the most important is their sterility or at least their reduced fecundity . . . Viewed from a high moral point of view the production of halfbreeds is as much a sin against nature as incest in a civilized community is a sin against purity [of] character."

Agassiz is not done yet. In reality the Civil War was fostered less by Northern horror over slavery, he writes, than by its Southern product, the offspring of confused Southern gentlemen, the halfbreeds, feeble beings who move "among us as negroes, which they are not." Racial mixing or amalgamation threatens neat categories, and although Agassiz still pretends that his position is based on physiology or a genuine concern for those whose mixed ancestry puts them in an awkward social position ("which can never be regular and settled"), it is now more than clear that what's behind all this strained theorizing is the worry that neat boundaries might become blurred, that "l'homme européen" might lose his distinctiveness. Halfbreeds jeopardize Agassiz's taxonomic system, which depends on things staying in their assigned places. But what worries Agassiz even more is the specter of sex, the great equalizer. After he has already signed his letter to Howe, he attaches a postscript in which he paints a lurid scenario intended to convince the good doctor that whereas sex between black and white is unnatural, it is, on the other hand, only too natural, which is why conditions need to be created that would prevent such encounters in the future:

> You may perhaps ask how it is that the halfbreed population is so large in the U.S., if intercourse between white and black is so unnatural. A glance at the conditions under which this takes place may suffice to settle this point. As soon as the sexual desires are awakening in the young men of the South, they find it easy to gratify them by the readiness with which they are met by colored house servants. There is no such restraint upon the early passions as exists everywhere in those communities in which both sexes are legally upon a footing of equality.

Furthermore, the "family negress" only stands to gain from her intimate connection with the "young master." And once the forbidden but oh-so-available fruit has been tasted, there is no turning back for these young men, who will look for "spicy partners" wherever they can find them.[57] Unsurprisingly, when Elizabeth reprinted the correspondence with Howe in her Agassiz biography, she removed this suggestive postscript, just as she elsewhere weeded out phrasing that seemed equally lurid, such as Agassiz's characterization of halfbreeds, in a subsequent letter, as "the ministers to the lust of other races."

Agassiz, to be sure, wasn't concerned simply with sex. What worried him was the broader concept of miscegenation. Look at any of the Central American countries, where the races are "blended," or look at Australia, Agassiz exhorts Howe in his next letter. Actually, one didn't have to go that far even: "The condition of the Indians on the borders of civilization in the United States and in Canada, in their contact with the Anglo-Saxons as well as with the French, testifies equally to the pernicious influence of amalgamation of races." Agassiz wasn't hung up on slavery either; he would have been happy to see it go. What frightened him was the prospect of complete social equality between black and white, the idea of a society in which the black waiter in Philadelphia could take his place right next to the white Harvard professor. Hence the subtle distinction he now draws between legal and social equality—for Agassiz, one doesn't imply the other. His thinking reflects the convictions that would give rise to Jim Crow: "I cannot therefore think it just, nor can it be safe, to grant at once to the negroes all the social privileges which we ourselves have acquired by long struggles." America had to be prudent now in her dealings with the "negroes" "lest it becomes necessary to deprive them by force of some of the privileges which they may use to their own & our detriment."[58]

The real solution, detailed in a third letter to Howe, was spatial separation, and the sooner, the better. "We all know," writes Agassiz, "how unfavorably ill-assorted unions influence the family circle." If blacks and whites, born in different social positions, were to begin freely marrying each other, a new element of discord would be introduced into American society: "The mere prospect is too dreadful, to allow its contemplation." While the sickly mulattoes, wanting in both "manliness and feminine virtue," are dying out, Agassiz imagines the South being re-peopled by brawny, pure blacks, working in the fields that reward "the slightest labor with a rich harvest." The Southern lowlands are uninhabitable for whites, who will invariably begin to drift North: "Abolition of slavery in the Gulf and River States coupled with identity of political rights for all the inhabitants amounts to giving over those States to the negro race." The exodus of whites from these States will be inevitable: "Since we have recognized Haity and Liberia there may be no reason why we should not admit Negro States into the Union."[59]

Upon further thought, Agassiz recognized the need to revise this plan. In a final letter to Howe, apparently never sent, Agassiz announced that he would have to think of a policy that would allow the whites to retain some control of the Southern states while still making sure that this is where the blacks stayed. All reform movements

(Agassiz refers explicitly to "Brookfarm," misspelling George Ripley's utopian experiment) ended up being "onesided" rather than broadly useful, and "there is no more onesided doctrine concerning human nature, than the idea that all men are equal, in the sense of being equaly [*sic*] capable of fostering human progeny & advancing civilization generally." Allowing a new Africa to emerge on the North American continent, allowing blacks to inhabit, without having earned the right to possess them, "some of the finest portions" of the United States now seemed counterintuitive to Agassiz, and he promised that he would sketch out a policy that would allow the whites ("our race") to retain at least partial control of the South. We should be thankful that Agassiz never got around to drafting that policy, but his letter leaves no doubt as to what it would entail: letting the blacks work long and hard for their claim to a share of the American pie, no promises made. Rarely has the duplicity at the heart of so-called Christian concern for the ex-slaves been articulated more clearly: "Let us do for the blacks all that humanity, the most active charity & the most disinterested Christian devotion may require of us, but let us not allow them to become an insuperable obstacle to our own progress."[60]

Agassiz probably knew that he wouldn't have to try all that hard to convince Howe that miscegenation was bad. When Howe thanked him, on August 18, 1863, for "the two valuable" letters he had received,[61] he engaged in some fancy verbal maneuvers regarding the "axiomatic" principles and policies he would support, "though the heavens fall": political freedom for blacks, equal rights and privileges, and "open competition for social distinction," even if that meant amalgamation. But then—while he was still pretending to be merely "gathering" facts—Howe performed an astonishing about-face, making good (if morally doubtful) use of his Unitarianism. Since the heavens weren't about to fall, couldn't one also assume God wouldn't really expect that white Americans, in their zeal to atone for the evil of slavery, would commit yet another evil and do violence to themselves? "Nemesis wields rather a guiding-rod than a scourge." In translation that meant that nothing we whites, "the more vigorous and prolific" race, had done to blacks would morally require that we live with them or condone their mating with our sons and daughters. The rights of mulattoes, to Samuel Gridley Howe, were not "axiomatic." Some might want to argue that if you dilute "black blood" with "white blood" and keep doing so, finally the "black blood" will have become so diluted that it will be in fact invisible. But they, explained the good Dr. Howe, "forget that no amount of diffusion will exterminate whatever exists; that a pint of ink diffused in a lake is still there, and the water is only the less pure." Others might say that "mulattoism" was self-limiting; physically inferior, the "halfbreeds" would just die out. Here Dr. Howe offered no refutation.

In the letters they exchanged in the summer of 1863, Agassiz and Howe identified themselves as adherents of a policy that can only be called "separate and not even close to equal." For Howe, "mulattoism" was an evil bred by slavery, and along with slavery it had to be eradicated from American soil. Like Agassiz, Howe doesn't explain why, if mulattoes are indeed feeble and infertile, we should worry about them so much. Their correspondence would be hilarious, in its parade of logical non sequiturs, tautologies, and childish anxieties, if Agassiz and Howe weren't both men who had been trained, or had at least learned, to think rigorously. In his response to Agassiz, Howe claims that it was "our duty to gather as many facts and as much knowledge as is possible, in order to throw light upon every part of the subject." But what we find instead in these letters is a confused moralizing rife with unproven assumptions (that mulattoes are feeble, that blacks are indolent, playful, sensual, and so forth), grounded not in science or any kind of data but fuzzy theology (God would not want us to punish ourselves for what we did). Not much had changed since Thomas Jefferson, eight decades before, had tremblingly described how just as the orang-utang coveted the black woman, black women in turn lusted after whites as partners.

The puzzling case of Howe the courageous abolitionist and bigoted mulatto-hater serves to put Agassiz's racism in perspective: as far less extreme, more mainstream, more calculated, and therefore perhaps even more horrifying than previous biographers and historians have assumed. James McPherson, the eminent Civil War historian, faults Agassiz with having infected the "equalitarian" Howe with the bacillus of racism.[62] But Howe, though he probably didn't realize it, had been a bigot in racial matters long before his notorious exchanges with Agassiz. In 1854, for example, a wealthy gentleman in Virginia, William Langhorne, asked him whether or not he thought that higher education for the blacks in the South was a good idea. Howe wrote back, "The plan seems to me to be fraught with grave if not insurmountable difficulties . . . My experience leads me to doubt the capacity of the blacks for such attainments as you look to." But Langhorne could be sure, added Howe, that God would look favorably upon him for having tried the experiment: "He forbade us to bury even the one poor talent in a napkin, and He will reward you for any honest and earnest effort in behalf of the unfortunate even if it should not be crowned with earthly success."[63]

Howe didn't admire Lincoln, whose Inaugural Address he thought was pro-slavery and whose Emancipation Proclamation he felt lacked *"persistent* earnestness." But there was one point where the "equalitarian" Howe and President Lincoln would not have differed, namely, in their assessment of the detrimental effects of racial mixing.[64] Listen to Lincoln, five years before Howe's initial letter to Agassiz, trying to maneuver himself out of a difficult situation as he was campaigning against Stephen Douglas, the incumbent senator for Illinois, in Charleston, Coles County, Illinois: "I am not, nor ever have been in favor of bringing about in any way the social and political equality of the white and black races," Lincoln stated, winning applause from the audience. He had never advocated "making voters or jurors of negroes, nor of qualifying them to hold office, nor to intermarry with white people; and I will say in addition to this that there is a physical difference between the white and black races which I believe will for ever forbid the two races living together on terms of social and political equality." Cohabitation of blacks and whites, in other words, was possible only if the "superior position" remained assigned to the white race. Lincoln was eager to stress that his feelings toward blacks were entirely benevolent, though the joke he attached to his comment (met with "cheers and laughter" from the audience) qualifies his expression of sympathy:

I say upon this occasion I do not perceive that because the white man is to have the superior position the negro should be denied everything. I do not understand that because I do not want a negro woman for a slave I must necessarily want her for a *wife*. [Cheers and laughter.] My understanding is that I can just let her alone. I am now in my fiftieth year, and I certainly never have had a black woman for either a slave or a wife. So it seems to me quite possible for us to get along without making either slaves or wives of negroes.

Lincoln's careful balancing—grant the "negro" his humanity, but don't let him come too close—represents his shrewd assessment of the complicated history of racial politics in Coles County, in which he himself had also played a minor (and no less complicated) part. It was here that, in 1847, some abolitionists had given shelter to a group of escaped slaves, who then sued for their freedom, and it was here too that the owner of those slaves, General Matson, had retained young Abraham Lincoln as his counsel (the court ended up ruling against Matson). At the Charleston debate, Democrats had shown up with a banner saying NEGRO EQUALITY, which featured a white man and a black woman with a mulatto boy, presumably their offspring, in the background, a message apparently not lost on Lincoln, who was at pains to establish some form of consensus.[65] If we can't agree on what to do with the blacks, we can at least all agree that we don't want them in our homes, a threat Lincoln epitomized in yet another broadside, this time directed at former vice president Richard Mentor Johnson, who had been open about his relationship with his mixed-race former slave, Julia Chinn. Even if there weren't any laws against interracial marriage, Lincoln and his friends (and presumably everyone in the audience) would never be tempted. But since there are such laws, let's observe them. Almost effortlessly, Lincoln thus manages to make Douglas seem both morally dubious (if he thinks one needs laws to keep black and white separate—what does that say about his own impulses?) and incompetent (why argue in favor of a law that at least in this state already exists):

I have never seen to my knowledge a man, woman or child who was in favor of producing a perfect equality, social and political, between negroes and white men. I recollect of but one distinguished instance that I ever heard of so frequently as to be entirely satisfied of its correctness—and that is the case of Judge Douglas' old friend Col. Richard M. Johnson. [Laughter.] I will also add to the remarks I have made, (for I am not going to enter at large upon this subject,) that I have never had the least apprehension that I or my friends would marry negroes if there was no law to keep them from it, [laughter] but as Judge Douglas and his friends seem to be in great apprehension that they might, if there were no law to keep them from it, [roars of laughter] I give him the most solemn pledge that I will to the very last stand by the law of this State, which forbids the marrying of white people with negroes. [Continued laughter and applause.][66]

As Lincoln's speech and the appreciative responses from his audience make clear, he was representing a majority position, one so well accepted that he was able to cast his opponent's fears about racial mixing as sheer paranoia. It would be easy to argue that Lincoln had to represent his position the way he did. He *wanted* to convince potential voters that there was no contradiction between his antislavery position and the desire to keep blacks in their assigned places in society—that, put differently, his racist credentials were impeccable. Having to make such an argument is not tantamount to actually believing it. However, the humor Lincoln uses here leaves a queasy feeling. Does it point to more than political expediency?

In a long footnote to his definitive biography of Lincoln, David Herbert Donald reminds his readers that Lincoln never was a "militant" racist and never spoke of African Americans as physically or mentally inferior. He also points out that even Frederick Douglass had deemed Lincoln free "from popular prejudice against the colored race." The fact remains, though, that when it came to racial coexistence his publicly articulated views differed not at all from those of the more readily vilified Agassiz or the more generally admired Howe.[67]

Nor did Agassiz's cautious approach to reconstruction deviate fundamentally from the proposals made by Herman Melville in the "Supplement" attached to *Battle-Pieces and Aspects of the War* (1866). Here Melville's paternalistic concern for the blacks "in their infant pupilage to freedom" is nearly obliterated by sympathy for "communities who stand nearer to us in nature," specifically the vanquished Southerners who are so affected by the "present perplexities" (Melville's euphemism for the Confederate defeat). Like Agassiz and Lincoln, Melville despises slavery (an "atheistical iniquity"). And again like Agassiz, Melville warns against hurriedly implementing the kind of political equality that, in his opinion, must be nurtured first: "In our natural solicitude to confirm the benefit of liberty to the blacks, let us forbear from measures of dubious constitutional rightfulness toward our white countrymen," meaning Southerners. "Graduated care" is the keyword in Melville's calculated plea for patience. "In one point of view," continues Melville, still treading cautiously but growing bolder, "the co-existence of the two races in the South—whether the negro be bond or free—seems (even as it did to Abraham Lincoln) a grave evil."[68] Some of Melville's biographers still find something to admire in this affirmation of white supremacy, arguing that Melville recognized, provocatively, that the North too had to reform itself from within and therefore wasn't in a position to tell the South what to do: "Hatred and retribution would only betray the noble aims for which the war was fought."[69] Melville's suggestion that white Americans delay granting full political rights to their fellow black citizens thus appears noble and far-sighted, an expression of paternal concern. Less generously inclined readers might consider it an argument to place strict limits on black participation in the political process.

Enfranchising blacks was certainly not the primary interest of Howe's American Freedmen's Inquiry Commission. The main focus of its opinion-collecting efforts was to determine how blacks could be put to work. In April 1863, for example, the members of the commission interviewed Frederick Law Olmsted, the executive secretary of the U.S. Sanitary Commission, an early version of the Red Cross. The organization was faced with a daunting task and hampered by inadequate resources. Olmsted had just returned from an inspection tour that had taken him, among other places, to Vicksburg, where he had looked at camps and hospital ships and talked to General Grant. En route, he had seen blacks working on fortifications, monitored by white superintendents.[70] Did he believe, the members of the commission asked him, that blacks made good soldiers? Olmsted, who admitted freely that his main interest was to hasten "the still further disorganization of plantation discipline which is equivalent to the disintegration of the peculiar structure of society at the South," seemed almost amused: "I have myself seen them manifest every quality asked for in a soldier. I believe many of them are capable of making military heroes." Recruiting the freed slaves would not only hold the government accountable for their and their families' well-being, but it would also help bring the infernal war to a speedier conclusion.[71]

In June of the same year, Howe, McKaye, and Owen submitted their preliminary report to Secretary of War Stanton. The influence of racial stereotyping is painfully evident on almost every page of this first draft.[72] As the commissioners see it, blacks, dependent like children on benevolent parental advice, need to be helped to learn to live their lives. The route to such independence would be rocky. Deprived of the "humanizing relations of civilized life," the blacks had sunk to a level of degradation that would pose a challenge to all efforts to integrate them into society. The Commission demonstrates this point through the example of the slave system of South Carolina, "where humanity is the exception." But rather than confront, head on, the responsibility of white Americans to rectify what they have caused, the commissioners, fortified by the recommendations of Olmsted and others, performed a rather self-serving maneuver: "The Commission believe that of all the present agencies for elevating the character of the colored race, for cultivating in them self-respect and self-reliance, military training, under judicious officers, who will treat them firmly and kindly, is at once the most prompt, and the most efficacious. In this respect the war, if the negro be employed by us as a soldier, becomes a blessing to him, cheaply bought at any price." In the commission's reading of the situation, it suddenly became incumbent on the "negro" to redeem himself:

> The more intelligent among these people not only feel that it is their duty to fight for their own freedom, but by proper appeal many of them can be made to understand that only by proving their manhood as soldiers, only through a baptism of blood, can they bring about such a change in public opinion as will insure for their race, from the present generation in this country, common respect and decent treatment in their social relations with whites.

Whereas Olmsted had envisioned blacks as potential military heroes, the commissioners viewed them as sacrificial lambs. Following Agassiz's advice, they recommended keeping the ex-slaves busy. Their ideas on how to achieve that goal were fairly detailed: they proposed a system of superintendents, from a superintendent-general to regional to local directors, to see that all the freedmen would be properly registered, employed, and compensated. The commissioners reckoned that as many as 200,000 freedmen could be recruited for combat or as laborers involved in a variety of support tasks. Howe drafted a separate "supplementary report" in which he outlined his plans for a "Bureau of Emancipation."

After the basic parameters of their task had been defined, the commissioners went back to their list of informants and sought more specific advice, designing a questionnaire that went out to relevant people in the field. Howe also mailed separate letters requesting information to clergymen, physicians, and even the directors of insane asylums, whom he quizzed about the comparative mortality and longevity of their black and white patients. A handful of correspondents saw through the exercise and restricted their answers to the bare essentials. Take the mayor of Leavenworth, Kansas, Daniel Read Anthony, who also happened to be the brother of the suffragist Susan B. Anthony. Once an aggressive newspaper editor, Mayor Anthony was a colorful figure widely known to prefer, in his dealings with his numerous enemies, the "meat-ax" to the "pillow."[73] Anthony scribbled his answers directly on the printed circular that Howe had sent him. No elaboration necessary. Question 11: "Do you observe any difference between blacks and mulattoes in their bodily strength, and power of endurance?" Mr. Anthony: "No." Question 12: "Are blacks more or less prolific than mulattoes?" Mr. Anthony: "The same." Question 13: "Are mulatto children as strong and healthy as black children?" Mr. Anthony: "Yes." The mayor's monosyllabic ripostes drew attention to the ridiculousness of the whole enterprise.[74]

Other correspondents were more eager to share. Captain Horace James, a well-meaning chaplain from the Twenty-fifth Massachusetts Regiment who had recently been named Superintendent of Blacks in the District of North Carolina, felt especially qualified to weigh in on the alleged difference between mulattoes and blacks. He had helped found a settlement for blacks a half mile west of Newbern, his headquarters, where he supplied them with shelter and basic health care (the area today is still known as James Town). To be sure, the Reverend James was overwhelmed: "The great amount of daily labor requiring my personal attention, as Superintendent of the Blacks in the State of North Carolina, has delayed, longer than I could have wished, a reply to the series of questions I had the honor to receive from you early in September." But where Mr. Anthony of Kansas had been monosyllabic, the good Captain James, a Civil War version of Melville's Amasa Delano, kind to "negroes" as one would be to Newfoundland dogs, waxes epic. "Even now my answers must be incomplete on many of the points suggested," he tells the members of the commission. And then he goes to town, carefully redrawing racial boundaries where the new political situation might have rendered them blurry. In physical strength and endurance, blacks are "evidently" stronger than mulattoes, though the white soldiers "are superior to either, except in bearing exposures to the hot sun." As a class, blacks were "docile and inclined to obey white people," a tendency that would always work against them and in favor of the whites, since this habit made them "slow in learning to maintain and defend their own personal rights."[75] The real trouble came from the unpredictable mulattoes. The strength of the pure blacks lay in their numbers and in sheer physical persistence. They had been, in the captain's experience, infinitely "more prolific than mulattoes," and their children were invariably more muscular and healthier than those of mulattoes. As far as the latter's much-vaunted intelligence was concerned, James felt obliged to add that some of the teachers in his school weren't even inclined to grant them that, "positively discredit[ing]" such an assumption.

A colleague of Captain James, John Eaton Jr., was equally ready to malign the mulattoes. The Reverend Eaton was a chaplain with the Twenty-seventh Ohio Infantry and had recently been selected by General Grant to run the "contraband" camps, which involved caring for and organizing the large numbers of African American men and women who had escaped from slavery. By 1863, close to seven thousand slaves had showed up at military forts behind Union lines in Mississippi, a dismal sight: half-naked, clad in wretched rags or clothes stolen from their masters, they had come driven by a "vague idea that fleeing to the enemies of their masters would make them free." About half of these people were "of mixed blood," the result of illicit or violent unions with their owners, their owners' sons, and overseers. Not allowed to form permanent unions themselves but required to mate indiscriminately with each other or with their masters, these ex-slaves had no concept of marriage. Reforming these damaged people was going to be uphill work. In the Reverend Eaton's report, the freed slaves seem like befuddled children, their black blood diluted, waiting for the benevolent white hand to guide them to the light—with an uncertain outcome.[76]

By contrast, the medical doctors Howe approached were mostly *not* able to rubber-stamp Howe's assessment of the "feeble," soon-to-be-extinct "halfbreed." John Fonerden, the medical superintendent of the Maryland Hospital for the Insane, had nothing important to report (only 8 of his 115 patients were colored, "making the proportion of colored about 7 per cent of the whole number"), and Dr. Clement A. Walker of the Boston Lunatic Asylum could not oblige either: of the 1,764 patients admitted in the thirty-five years since the hospital's establishment, only 30 had been "colored." And John E. Tyler, the superintendent of the McLean Asylum in Somerville, Massachusetts, could come up with only two such cases over the hospital's forty-year history. One of them, "a mulatto servant of Hon. Daniel Sears of Boston," was diagnosed with "acute mania," from which he made a "rapid and perfect recovery." He was, recalled Dr. Tyler, "an extremely intelligent person."[77] If any of the commissioners had hoped for confirmation that "mulattoes" were feeble-minded and would therefore crowd the cells in the country's mental institutions, these letters offered nothing to support their theory. And if mulattoes lost their marbles, they apparently did so at a much slower rate and in less alarming numbers than their white peers.

Howe also sent his new questions to Frederick Law Olmsted, who seized this second opportunity to add support for his view—quite the opposite of Agassiz's or Howe's position—that there was no inherent difference between blacks and whites or, for that matter, between "pure" blacks and mulattoes. Howe had apparently asked him to find out about life insurance issued to slaveholders for slaves, perhaps hoping that Olmsted would be able to supply him with some evidence that during the years before the war the "sicklier" mulattoes would not have qualified for coverage or would have cost more to insure. Olmsted, who was in Norfolk, Virginia, at the time, was prepared. There was only one insurance company there, the Knickerbocker, which had participated extensively in the unsavory business of insuring the slaves of Norfolk, and they limited themselves to "house-servants mechanics & steamboat men, (waiters, backers, & deck-hands), a class in which there is a large proportion of yellow men." The president of the company seemed to have "carefully studied the question whether the risk runs greater with yellow than with black men and to have come quite decidedly to the conclusion that it was not. Neither the Knickerbocker nor any other Life Insurance Company of Norfolk discriminates in its rates in favor of the pure black." In other words, not even the slaveholders shared Howe's bias. Olmsted's study of plantation slaves had not yielded any solid evidence for "the assumption of the physical debility" of mixed-race people either. "I don't mean to express a decided difference with you in this opinion which you express," Olmsted told Howe, "but merely that I do not consider it, by any means, a settled question, even at the South." As Olmsted saw it, "the ballance [sic] of facts" spoke rather against Howe's interpretation.[78]

But the commission didn't let such pesky facts get in the way of their reporting. In May 1864, it submitted the final version of its report to Stanton, a year after the preliminary one. It had taken Robert Owen three months to write it up. The actual political consequences of the two reports are difficult to assess, but as one of "the most radical attacks on slavery as a global system of labor use" yet undertaken in nineteenth-century America, they have retained considerable appeal to historians who generally praise the commissioners even as they decry their frequent "relapse into racial reasoning."[79]

In fact, that racial reasoning is part and parcel of the reports. No doubt about it, the commissioners show themselves to be deeply sympathetic to the plight of the former or soon-to-be-free slaves. Unlike Agassiz or Melville, they are also clearly in favor of immediately extending political rights to the freed blacks. They are unequivocal too in their condemnation of the slave trade, though arguably that was a battle that by 1864 did not have to be fought anymore with such passion. Yet the commissioners do have an ulterior motive, even if it takes them a while to reveal it. After pages of tables and calculations and reviews of census data, they offer a shocking, if not unexpected, conclusion regarding the importation of slaves to the Southern Hemisphere: "The 15,500,000 of poor wretches who were sentenced by the slave-trade to transportation and slavery in foreign lands are now, after three centuries of servitude, represented in these lands by less than four-fifths of their original number," a decrease entirely due to "man's crime" (and not due to the usual suspects, such as wars, disease, and natural disasters). Things were terrible in South America, then. This allows the commission to highlight the somewhat different situation in the United States. Here, by contrast, the number of slaves has increased nearly ninefold, a puzzling result that some might attribute to the fact that "slavery in the United States, even in its latter and severer phase, has been as a general rule, more merciful and lenient than in the West Indies and South America." The contrast between the development of slavery in the two hemispheres can mean two things: that, by comparison, the United States wasn't so bad when it came to the treatment of slaves (although the commissioners don't explicitly endorse that conclusion, they let it stand) or that, given the growing numbers of slaves here, the problem of what to do with them when slavery ends is much more pressing than it would be anywhere else.

And thus, after a rather arid section dealing with the constitutional aspects of emancipation, particularly the president's right to emancipate the slaves in the Southern states, the commissioners go on to consider, as the numbers have told them they should, the "future in the United States of the African race." It is here that they rehash some of the points summarized in Agassiz's letters to Howe. Additionally, much of this final section of the 1864 report relies on the fieldwork that, inspired by Agassiz's supposedly scientific approach to race, Howe had conducted in Canada during the summer of 1863. Most of the refugees Howe interviewed there had been of mixed race (and "inferior in physical power and health"), and he had found them to be very frequently "of lymphatic temperament, with marks of scrofulous or strumous disposition, as shown in the pulpy appearance of portions of the face and neck, in the spongy gums, and glistening teeth." This pseudo-medical language ("strumous" designates essentially the same condition as "scrofulous," that is, a chronic affliction of the lymphatic glands) would have reminded everyone of Dr. Howe's training, lending additional authority to his observations (published separately, as a small book, in 1864). Howe also had some good news for his white readers. He found that the experience of living in a free society had cured the Canadian ex-slaves of their "loose and incontinent habits" and had made them less likely to marry whites, for him definitive proof that an end to slavery in the United States would also mean the end of that "monstrous" practice known as "amalgamation." Marrying each other, the feeble mulattoes of Canada would thus ensure their own quick demise, as Howe observes in language borrowed, for the occasion, from Darwin: "They will dwindle and gradually disappear from the peoples of this continent, outstripped by more vigorous competitors in the struggle for life."[80] And the pure blacks would vamoose on their own. A table showing the "comparative mortality among white and colored persons" in selected cities from Boston to Memphis, included in the commission's final report, purports to demonstrate that in the Northern cities, blacks by and large had a significantly lower chance of survival. Conclusion: Allow blacks to return to the South, and they will readily go where they are better off anyway. The commissioners also threw in, for good measure, some vague Humboldtian geophysics, arguing that the former slaves by nature have no inclination at all to go North and that their movements will, in fact, follow "thermal lines."

Amalgamation, according to the report, isn't bad as such. Let the Turks and the Africans mate as much as they want. It's only the mingling of black and white that doesn't work out: "It may be that the Anglo-Saxon and the African, extreme varieties, are less suited to each other, and that the mixed race degenerates." Anglo-Saxons and Africans mustn't live together, but that doesn't mean that they can't live *next to each other*. Anglo-Saxon toughness will profit from social contact with the "genial, lively, docile" Africans, from their natural exuberance and Christian humility. Cautious friendship, not sex, is the key to peaceful coexistence.

While the sharp edge of Agassiz's recommendations—the complete segregation of black and white—had been blunted in the report, the substance (a condemnation of slavery as well as condemnation of miscegenation, as a symbol of the rapprochement of white and black) was not too different. Agassiz had provided Howe and the commissioners with specific cues, but it seems worth emphasizing that in his letters he was in fact just repeating, if in more pronounced form, the consensus view among many middle-class Americans at the time. Consider a conversation Agassiz had with Emerson in August 1866, after his return from a fact-finding expedition to Brazil. Sitting on the rocks of the Nahant Beach, Emerson and Agassiz began to talk about race. In his journal, Emerson later recorded his full agreement with Agassiz's views. Agassiz was, he said, "a man to be thankful for, always cordial, full of facts, with unsleeping observation, & perfectly communicative." A summary of Agassiz's remarks on Brazil followed suit, presumably as an example of the latter's "unsleeping" observational powers. Brazil was a country full of "excellent timber" with "not a saw mill in sight," a country "thirsting for Yankees to open & use its wealth," but badly demoralized by the lingering effects of slavery, which were visible in the "coarse features of the people showing the entire intermixing of all the races." Not slavery as such, but the evil of racial interbreeding was responsible for Brazil's current economic misery, a conclusion that the sixty-three-year-old Emerson enthusiastically embraced.[81]

Given such powerful allies, it is not surprising that Agassiz's antimiscegenation stance didn't die with him. It became the basic message of Agassiz's former assistant, Nathaniel Southgate Shaler, who was appointed professor of paleontology at Harvard in 1869 and who in the 1880s was still discussing race along the lines described by Agassiz—aged wine poured into new skins. His assessment of African inferiority Shaler mixed with a vaguely defined Lamarckian program for race improvement under which African ex-slaves, by mimicking the white master race, would slowly achieve their full—yet always limited—potential.[82] In his essay "The Negro Problem," published in 1884 in the *Atlantic Monthly* a good twenty years after the Emancipation Proclamation, Shaler pointed out that racial difference or, in the case of the blacks, racial *inferiority* was the product of environment—which didn't really mean that he had seen the light of evolution. For Shaler's racial philosophy also implied that, at least in principle, people should stay where they were born. Agassiz would have been proud. If life was hard for the ex-slaves, this was partly due to the fact that America wasn't Africa (Shaler sidesteps the inconvenient fact that the slaves hadn't left their homes voluntarily). The real evil of slavery—and Shaler carefully distinguishes "plantation slavery" from its allegedly more benign twin, "domestic slavery"—wasn't that, regrettably, some slaves "were sometimes beaten." No, slavery in its less attractive forms had kept "negroes" in a state of arrested development, a fact that had rendered the task of making them useful citizens even more daunting. On the other hand, Southern slavery, "infinitely the mildest and most decent system of slavery that ever existed," had really only perpetuated the state of "immemorial savagery" into which the slaves had been born in Africa. In this remarkably disingenuous reading, the only thing slaveholders were guilty of was not doing quite enough for their slaves.[83]

In Shaler's essay—and several others published in subsequent years—the existence of the mulatto still indicated the frightening possibility that the color line might become blurred, that America might soon be peopled by sickly, infertile people with weaker minds and shorter lives than "real" blacks or whites. Thomas Bailey Aldrich, the editor of the *Atlantic Monthly*, had asked three distinguished readers to comment on Shaler's essay: the writer and former abolitionist Thomas Wentworth Higginson; General Samuel C. Armstrong, the founder of the paternalistic Hampton Institute in Virginia; and Daniel Henry Chamberlain, the former governor of South Carolina, noted for his support of civil rights and now a professor at Cornell. He appended their responses, alongside his own, as footnotes. Among these gentlemen only Higginson was mildly critical of Shaler's opinions; generally, though, all commentators basically agreed with Shaler's main points, sometimes resoundingly so. Apropos of Shaler's observation that "halfbreeds" were inclined to vice and that he had never seen one older than fifty, Aldrich offered his support by offering a fact from the days of the "peculiar institution," pointing out that the "pure black in the former time always had a larger money value than a mulatto of the same age and general appearance."

But Shaler was also delighted to report that, at the rate things were going, there was no reason for fear in the anti-miscegenation department: "It is now rare indeed to see a child under fifteen years that the practiced eye will recognize as from a white father. This is an immense gain. Once stop the constant infusion of white blood, and the weakly, mixed race will soon disappear, leaving the pure African blood, which is far better material for the uses of the state than any admixture of black and white." Dr. Howe's dream come true—and no intervention necessary! If Frederick Douglass had shown so compellingly at the beginning of his autobiography that the white man's control over the black slave-woman destroyed both black and white families,[84] the solution envisioned by Shaler was not to imagine a dif-

ferent form of interaction between black and white (one not controlled
by a climate of fear and rape), but a geographically divided, racially
cleansed America in which black and white would be kept entirely and
permanently separate and supposedly "pure." No ink spilled. By pos-
iting white purity here and black purity over there, Agassiz and Shaler
established a kind of sham correspondence between the races, a per-
verse image of the equality they were unwilling to grant in real life.

It seems hard not to compare Agassiz's and Shaler's racial benighted-
ness with Darwin's more enlightened view of racial difference, and
while writing this chapter I have done so myself on a few occasions,
guided especially by Darwin's unequivocal condemnation of slavery.
Agassiz, to be sure, also thought slavery was wrong, but whereas his
opposition was lukewarm, driven by general considerations rather
than personal experience, Darwin's opposition was powerful, passionate, and uncompromising. Some of his biographers see Darwin
as an arch-abolitionist, a fighter not only against slavery but against
racism wherever he saw it. There is much evidence for this reading,
as there is for Darwin's antipathy toward Agassiz's racial views. But
Darwin also believed that despite the common origin of all races,
the white race in the universal struggle for survival had an edge over
others—that, for better or worse, the "white man is 'improving off
the face of the earth' even races nearly his equal."[85] Unlike Agassiz
(and like John Bachman), Darwin knew that there was no scientifically valid argument in favor of polygenism. But like Agassiz he was
uncomfortable with the idea of letting the races freely mingle, and he
took exception to Alfred Russel Wallace's "beautiful dream" of seeing
the world inhabited, at some future day, "by a single homogeneous
race, no individual of which will be inferior to the noblest specimens
of existing humanity."[86] In *The Descent of Man*, regarded by some as
his most Victorian book,[87] Darwin revived the concept of "beauty"
as a racially distinct phenomenon, as if he was looking for a new way
of dividing humans along biological lines, of making sure that the
races "stay put." In chapters 19 and 20 of the third part of *Descent*, for
example, he explains that the "negroes" and the Chinese both dislike the white man's skin and that the Siamese, Japanese, and Polyne-
sians all find facial hair disgusting. The Hottentots like big buttocks,
while the Europeans do not. And the Indians of Paraguay rip out

their eyebrows and lashes because they do not want to be like horses. Darwin rejects those of his suppliers of ethnographic evidence, such as Winwood Reade, Friedrich Gerhard Rohlfs, and Captain Burton, who believe in the *universality* of beauty and claim, for example, that the Fuegians find themselves being powerfully attracted to European women: "I cannot but think that this must be a mistake." Darwin's argument in these two chapters is complex, but the result is quite simple (and unintentionally provides a biological basis for Agassiz's disgust at that black waiter's hand in his Philadelphia hotel in 1846). While Darwin asserts, from a scientific point of view, the unity of the human species, he also endorses racial difference by emphasizing local choices, the limited and limiting role of aesthetic preferences: "In one part of Africa the eyelids are colored black; in another the nails are colored yellow or purple." Collectively, however, these local choices add up to form larger groups, the divisions between which comfortingly follow the familiar racial fault lines: "As the face with us is chiefly admired for its beauty, so with savages it is the chief seat of mutilation."[88] Darwin tosses out one kind of racism—the polygenist kind—only to introduce another, superficially more benign kind based on aesthetic preference. Where a panicking Agassiz imagines hordes of lustful black maids in bed with pimply Southern boys, wrecking America's manifest destiny one sex act at a time, Darwin tells his readers to relax: the races will remain separate, out of mutual distaste, with no racism required.

Reading Agassiz and Shaler and, yes, Darwin too, one suddenly realizes why racial mixing was so unacceptable to many of the participants in the grand palaver about race that dominated the nineteenth century. It blurred alleged biological boundaries but it also threatened to do away with the one position the black man or woman was indisputably allowed to assume in the national and international conversation about race—the object of debate, rather than debater. If American writers left "the negro" unwritten, as Daniel Aaron showed some time ago in his provocative book about the Civil War, the same is true of the various parties that chose to make him or her (or, more generally, the issue of race) a topic of intense "scientific" discussion.

As this chapter should have reminded us, there was a dizzying spectrum of possible positions on this issue: one could be an apologist for slavery and yet an opponent of polygenism (John Bachman), a defender of slavery and a polygenist (Josiah Nott), an opponent of slavery and a polygenist (Louis Agassiz), an abolitionist and a polygenist (Samuel Gridley Howe), an abolitionist and a believer in the common origin of all humankind yet a segregationist (Abraham Lincoln), a unionist and a gradualist when it came to racial integration (Herman Melville), and so forth. Having an opinion on race, even if it was the wrong opinion, was de rigueur in nineteenth-century America, and sometimes the positions people held differed only in nuance. When Agassiz first presented his views in December 1847 to the Charleston Conversation Club, the Reverend John Bachman and the Reverend Thomas Smyth were, as we have seen, not at all persuaded by his arguments. But their disagreement with Agassiz and the other members did not adversely affect their standing in the club. In fact, Thomas Smyth dedicated his refutation of Agassiz, a book called *The Unity of Human Races*, to the Conversation Club, "by whom the subject has been repeatedly and pleasantly discussed, with feelings the most harmonious, amid opinions the most discordant."[89] Smyth's grateful dedication gave "Senior," a contributor to the *National Era* (in reality, Dr. William Elder of Philadelphia), a reason to voice his disenchantment with the entire national debate on race. He had become tired of it all, the highfalutin' theorizing, the measuring, the pseudo-scientific mumbling about brain size, cranial capacities, spinal cords, and the like, and he had a message for all those racial philosophers, whether their names were Agassiz, Smyth, or Bachman. "It is of no consequence to me," he exclaimed, who "has the truth of their controversy." No one should care a fig "whether the negro's brain is large or small" or "whether his faculties are high or low." The only thing that mattered was this: these faculties "are *his* and not mine, or any other man's; and it is a sin against God and Nature to abridge their proper liberty."[90]

The intervention of "Senior" suggests that one had better take the broad view of nineteenth-century racism. Nonetheless, historians, with the laudable intention of identifying objectionable attitudes where they see them, have routinely represented Agassiz as an anomaly, an extremist, someone out of touch with both science and the people around him. This view has spilled over into popular responses to Agassiz. The eighth-grader at the Agassiz School in Cambridge, mentioned in the introduction, who made it his mission to get the name of his school changed, is one apt American example. But concerns about Agassiz's racism have also reached the country of his birth. In June 2007, the representative for the Canton Geneva, the socialist Carlo Sommaruga, expressing his disgust with Agassiz's racist ideas, asked the Swiss National Council (Nationalrat) to consider renaming a summit in the Bernese Alps, the Agassizhorn (12,946 feet), after Renty, a slave in South Carolina who had once been forced to sit for one of those dismal photographic portraits Agassiz had commissioned. Sommaruga was responding to an initiative originally launched by Hans Fässler, an author and activist from St. Gallen, who has devoted himself to uncovering Swiss complicity in the history of slavery and apartheid.

A few months later, the Swiss Nationalrat weighed in. Declining to act on Sommaruga's request, they offered a brief rebuttal that mixed sanctimoniousness with a characteristic concern for legal detail: Agassiz was, they said, "a great geologist and zoologist," and it just wouldn't do to invalidate his contributions merely because of the views he held. Furthermore, naming mountaintops wasn't a federal responsibility but had to be taken up with the regional authorities in the communities of Grindelwald, Fieschertal, and Guttannen.[91]

Sommaruga's deeply honorable renaming campaign, called Démonter Agassiz, vividly illustrates the view of history that most of us still embrace. It attributes everything to the agency of individuals and allows us to hope that washing out one "damn'd spot" will at least partially free our collective hands of the sins of the past. We are comfortable with a view of the nineteenth century that allows us to separate the good white guys from the bad white guys. But Agassiz's racism troubles that distinction. Measured by the standards of his time, his racial views were extreme mostly because he talked about them so frequently, so vehemently, and so publicly. As a whole, they reflect—as did everything else he undertook during his career—his fervent desire for science, *his* science, to be taken seriously and to be considered socially and politically relevant.

Ironically, recent revisionist initiatives have not sharpened our understanding of nineteenth-century racism. By focusing on a few memorable people (Samuel Morton, Louis Agassiz), they mask how widespread and deeply rooted opinions like Agassiz's were. Even a committed and courageous abolitionist and philanthropist like Samuel Gridley Howe and an iconoclastic philosopher like Ralph Waldo Emerson welcomed Agassiz's profoundly skewed ideas on interbreeding. Of course, not all of Agassiz's contemporaries were nervous about the potential impact of miscegenation on the future of America. The impeccable Charles Sumner, in a speech condemning the "caste" system, rhapsodized on what a "blessed sight" it would be to see "the pioneer intelligence of Europe going to blend with the gentleness of Africa," and the Virginia-born clergyman and abolitionist Moncure Conway too expected that the "mixture of the blacks and whites" would in due course produce sturdier and handsomer Americans. But in a way such arguments only reverse the racial stereotypes perpetrated by the likes of Agassiz.[92] Few and far between were those who, like Dr. Tyler of the McLean Asylum in Somerville, looked at a "mulatto" and saw not a pint, or a thimbleful, of ink, but a person, and an extremely intelligent one at that.

A DELICATE BALANCE

I N A LECTURE GIVEN at the Museum of Comparative Zoology
in October 1860, Agassiz, ever-vigilant to make science a truly
public affair, complained that the language of natural history had
become incomprehensible to anyone but the experts. Most people
were under the impression that scientists were coming up with new
names for animals or plants almost every day. In reality, though, this
was true of other disciplines too: "In the common arts of life we well
know that new names are constantly introduced." Take engineering,
for example. Here too everything was in flux: new inventions were
being produced all the time. And of course inventors had to name
what they had just created. But their names would become instantly
familiar to the public by regular use, "whereas science is so far removed from the community, at present, that its names never became
familiar."[1] Remedying this rift between science and the community
was going to be a gargantuan task. But Agassiz could always rely on
someone who made that very task her life's work, Elizabeth Agassiz, his wife, agent, and chief communicator. It is no coincidence that
Elizabeth Agassiz's handwriting was all over the drafts of the infamous letters to Howe discussed in the last chapter.

"Mrs. Agassiz," as she was known to most, was more than her husband's wife. She shared his opinions, actively participated in his scientific work, transferred much of his lectures into written form, and

oversaw the publication of his books. She became, in a sense, Agassiz's ghostwriter, a term that captures her involvement with Agassiz on many levels.[2] For this is how the public began to see Agassiz during the last decade of his life, and this is how he had increasingly come to see himself: through the eyes of his wife, the eminently capable Elizabeth Agassiz.

Elizabeth Agassiz's co-authorship or primary authorship isn't easy to document, since manuscripts for Agassiz's books, with the exception of letters, cannot be found in the archives, possibly because, anxious to guard his legacy, she destroyed them after his death.

Well, at least in most cases. A rare scientific manuscript in Elizabeth's hand, about a manatee specimen, might serve as an illustration of her commitment to Agassiz's work.[3] The undated document, a report about a meeting of the Boston Society of Natural History, carries notes apparently made by an editor and intended for the printer ("Don't put it among the local items" and "Lead one stick full," a reference to the typesetter's composing stick). But the rest of the short text is entirely in Elizabeth Agassiz's handwriting, slanting to the right, with long bars through her *t*'s and gracefully curved *d*'s ending in jaunty little loops. Elizabeth writes confidently, generously: the letters are large, and only very few of the words are crossed out. The text itself is unremarkable, but David Ames Wells, who was Agassiz's student at the time, thought it worthy of inclusion in the inaugural volume of the *Annual of Scientific Discovery*. It's the typical Agassiz story, one whose permutations would, over the years, become thoroughly familiar to Agassiz's wife: new evidence (a skeleton presented to the society by the Harvard anatomist John Collins Warren) confirms that what Humboldt had originally described as one species was in fact two, that the South American manatee had its counterpart in a North American version, an observation that beautifully supports Agassiz's theory that God had created different species in different parts of the world, according to a plan that humans are only gradually beginning to (but eventually *will*) understand.[4]

Elizabeth Cabot Cary, born in Boston on December 5, 1822, had grown up believing in compartmentalization. Her Boston was the blue-blood Boston later caustically described in the famous doggerel by Harvard graduate John Collins Bossidy as the place where "the

Boston Natural History Society

At the last meeting of the
Natural History Society, the
President, Dr. John C. Warren,
introduced a subject of particular interest to those, who have
paid some attention to the study
of the animals, which occur on
the shores of the United States.

It has long been known, that
a large marine animal occurs
about the coast of Florida,
where it is known under the
name of Sea Cow, but Naturalists have not been in possession
of precise information upon the
character, form and relations
of this singular creature. That
it is related to the Sea Cow of
the large rivers of South America appeared evident from the reports circulated about it; and
Dr Harlan of Philadelphia had
even many years since described
portions of its skull as indicating a distinct species of the

"Boston Natural History Society." Undated holograph by Elizabeth Agassiz.

Lowells talk only to Cabots / And the Cabots talk only to God," except that in her case the families involved were the Perkins and the Carys, and throughout her life she was never sure how exactly to talk to God. Her pedigree established her in the top tier of a social world in which social peers married each other and remained as restricted to their own immediate environment as the animals and plants did in Agassiz's view of the natural world. Elizabeth was the granddaughter of Colonel Thomas Handasyd Perkins, who founded the Perkins Institute for the Blind and built the first hotel on Nahant, and the daughter of Mary Perkins Cary and Thomas Graves Cary, treasurer of the Hamilton and Appleton Mills in Lowell, Massachusetts. While money was not in short supply as Elizabeth was growing up, the family's ties to society were more important than the maximizing of its fortune.

An odd mixture of aristocratic nostalgia and nouveau riche pride marked Elizabeth's upbringing in Temple Place. Her sister Emma left a short, evocative memoir, focused mostly on old Colonel Perkins's stately house, which helps us imagine the world Agassiz encountered when he was introduced to Lizzie Cary. Visitors would have entered the house, Emma recalls, through the massive oak door in front, made from wood obtained from the USS *Constitution*. Its powerful thud resounded up the broad spiral staircase inside the house and was loud enough to be heard in the other residences on Temple Place. As the door fell shut behind the visitor, she would find herself in a self-enclosed world, in which parents, as if embarrassed by their own fecundity, kept largely out of the lives of their children and left most educational decisions to governesses. The casual cosmopolitanism acquired by Elizabeth's forebears on their China trade voyages contrasted oddly with their proud parochialism, an unrepentant narrow-mindedness that rejected outside influences and ensured family cohesion. Colonel Perkins wasn't really a colonel; he had received his faux military title through a symbolic appointment to the Massachusetts volunteer militia known as the Lancers. He also wasn't primarily a businessman; he believed that it was more important that a day was a "success" — when, for example, teatime unfolded without a glitch — than that a man excel at his work and thus draw too much attention to himself. When his trading activities became too much for him, he retired. Money was what one had, not what one needed to make. And when one had it, one gave some of it to charity; hence the Perkins Institute.

Although the Colonel's riches had come from dealings with far-flung countries, he was more intent on the little colony he created around him, building houses for his daughters next to his own, among them 10 Temple Place, where Elizabeth grew up. "Cozy" then didn't yet mean, as it does in the lingo of modern realtors, a house that's too small and needs a lot of work. Rather, it signified the ultimate level of comfort attainable to a well-bred Bostonian, an appealing philosophy that nevertheless had its drawbacks for some, as Emma noted when she referred to her Aunt Sally as "wonderfully fat." Unconcerned, Emma, herself equipped with a sturdy appetite, dug in when food was made available. Her mouth still watering after all these years, Emma Cary remembered how the gingerbread was usually marked with pretty parallel lines, which the cook had produced with the prongs of her fork. After the gingerbread came perhaps some preserves from the East Indies or another unexpected delicacy. Emma went home (next door, that is) contented.[5]

Grandfather and Grandmother Perkins occupied separate quarters on the second floor of their big house. The Colonel's rooms were filled with curiosities and works of art (busts of Rubens and Raphael among them), and the children entered them only when he wasn't around. Grandmother Perkins resided in her own parlor on the same floor, propped up in a thickly upholstered rocking chair. Whenever her grandchildren passed into her realm, old Mrs. Perkins panicked. "Where's your mother?" It was only after her grandmother's death, when Colonel Perkins began wasting away too, that Emma began to understand the deep affection the two had held for each other, kept staunchly hidden from both family and strangers, because in the world of the Perkinses, admitting an emotion was tantamount to letting go.

Temple Street, in those days, was a dead end, closed on one side except for some stairs leading down to Washington Street, which created an instant playground for the enterprising offspring of the blue-bloods who resided there. People called it "the court." Emma recalls how the boys would play ball there while their sisters watched, training no doubt for their own peripheral roles in adult life. And she remembers too how those boys fared later: those who hadn't managed to get out to travel the world died, their limbs crushed, on the battlefields of the Civil War. "There were the Gardiners, George and Stanton Whitney, all bound for India and the India trade. There were Dick Cary and Louis Cabot, both destined to fight in the Civil War—Dick to die on the field of Cedar Mountain,—Jim Savage, handsome, active, high spirited, was to die fearfully shattered in a Southern prison hospital. But we thought the world was all before us . . . and the court rang with the shouts of eager ball players, and we girls looked immeasurably proud of our brothers, for whom we dreamed all sorts of ambitious dreams." The picture is astonishing to the modern reader: primly dressed girls, destined for a comfortable life on the margins, bask in their brothers' dreams and athletic successes. But the passage also points out the inevitable failures of those dreams, on the blood-drenched fields of war or in lives given up to the family business. But little Emma Cary even then had found her way out of those dilemmas: too near-sighted to excel at any physical activity, she devoted herself to the sugar plums she got at Miss Gardiner's birthday parties or to one of the big boxes of white sugar John Cushing, formerly involved in the China trade, brought to the house: "Oh, so sweet it was." Wherever those boys, handsome princes of the ball court, were now, the one who had lived to tell the tale of Temple Place was little Emma with her bad eyes and her sturdy appetite.

The world of Temple Place must have seemed strange to Louis Agassiz, the country parson's son from Switzerland, stranger than the jellyfish he saw floating in the waters of Boston Harbor. It was a realm shaped by the opportunities life provides to the privileged but laced also with the dark sense of responsibility and guilt shared by all proper Bostonians, whose social conformity often masked a quiet rebelliousness. Out of which came the woman who influenced the second half of Louis Agassiz's life like no one else.

Elizabeth Cabot Cary was twenty-three years old when the thirty-nine-year-old Agassiz became interested in her, and she in him. By some accounts, the latter happened first. If Elizabeth was not young anymore by the standards of her social environment, Louis would have been considered past middle age at least in the United States (the average life expectancy of a white American male was lower than it was in Europe, ranging, according to best estimates, around forty).[6] Considered somewhat sickly in her youth, Elizabeth received instruction at home, with particular emphasis on foreign languages. She enjoyed going to the opera, read Dickens and the Brontës, took singing lessons, spent her evenings attending parties at the homes of relatives and friends, and otherwise wasn't overly worried about her future. The summer months she passed in a stone cottage on Nahant, overlooking the bay. When she was sixteen, she described marriage—in a letter to a cousin to whom she was rumored to be romantically linked—as a *"slough of despond."*[7] Elizabeth Cary liked her life, and if she hadn't found a suitable husband yet in 1846, this wasn't because she didn't appeal to men.

A photograph taken a few years after her marriage shows her in a pose eerily similar to that of a self-portrait by Agassiz's first wife, Cecilie. Her hair is neatly parted in the middle and tied in the back, with long curls trailing down on either side of her head; her face is focused on her new stepdaughter Ida, who is sitting on her left—in marked contrast with Cecilie, whose clear, sad eyes are fully trained on the viewer in her 1829 self-portrait.

Perhaps less than conventionally beautiful because of her longish nose, Elizabeth Cary still would have turned more than a few heads when Louis Agassiz showed up in Boston to hold forth on the "plan of creation." Her sister Caroline Gardiner Curtis described Elizabeth's nature as "always sweet and unruffled," a statement that was dictated more by family piety than fact.[8] For Elizabeth was clearly able to show fierce determination when needed, and she would likely have kept her eyes firmly on the prize when she was introduced, at her sister Mary Felton's house, to the interesting foreign professor, with whom she was able to converse in French, a language she spoke better than Cecilie Braun. In some versions of the story, Mrs. Cary had been the first to spot Louis Agassiz, in the church pew of the Lowells, as a good match for her daughter.[9]

Cecilie's recent lonely death in faraway Freiburg allowed Agassiz to pursue the desirable Elizabeth Cary. When news of his engagement reached his new American friends (who had never met Cecilie), the consensus was that Agassiz was once again complete, as it were. "Now you will have no feeling unemployed," wrote Harriet Holbrook, the wife of his Charleston friend John Edwards Holbrook, on

Elizabeth Cary Agassiz, with her stepdaughters Pauline (left) and Ida (right), c. 1851–1852.

January 6, 1850. "In spite of what you have told me of the chains in which science binds you I think I have devined [*sic*] in you the strongest capacity for all the domestic affections." Referring to Agassiz's son, she added, "One could not caress Alex as you do without a fountain within." Holbrook regretted that Agassiz's marriage would now virtually guarantee that Agassiz stayed at Harvard, "at the North," rather than coming to teach in Charleston, but she reconciled herself to that prospect by imagining the "parlor in Oxford St. bright with happy faces and noisy with sweet children's voices."[10]

But then again, that was not about to happen. Cecilie Braun and Elizabeth Cary were worlds apart. Miss Cary had other plans for her marriage to the famous foreign scientist than to be the ensurer of domestic bliss and compliant producer of additional children. Not that she wasn't devoted to him. In her biography of Agassiz, referring to herself in the third person ("Elizabeth Cabot Cary, daughter of Thomas Graves Cary, of Boston"), she speaks of her marriage purely in terms of convenience — her husband's, that is: "It connected him by the closest ties with a large family circle, of which he was henceforth a beloved and honored member, and made him the brother-in-law of one of his most intimate friends in Cambridge, Professor C. C. Felton."[11]

Her correspondence, however, does hint at a deeper emotional engagement, characteristically by indirection rather than confession. Once, in an undated letter to Louis, written during the brief period of their engagement, Elizabeth alluded to a day spent on Nahant when they walked along the beach and, instead of gazing at the ocean, apparently gazed mostly at each other. A missed opportunity, as it now seemed to Elizabeth — for natural history, that is, not for romance: "I know that your study of nature must have originated in a deep love of it, yet we have spoken but little of such things, and except on the day at Nahant when we strolled on the beach and thought more of each other than of the ocean."[12] When she talked to others and even to Agassiz himself about her relationship, Elizabeth Cary would adopt a deliberately businesslike language, as if her marriage were a contract to be worked out, an impression not inconsiderably heightened by the fact that she regularly called Agassiz, as she would for the rest of her life, by his last name only. Thus, a letter dated "Wednesday morning" and written during the winter 1849, when Agassiz had traveled south, sounds much like a promissory note detailing the kind of payment Agassiz will receive (an impeccable, always truthful wife, who will make him happy) for the value that he has to offer (especially trustworthiness). Elizabeth promised "dear Agassiz" that he will be "satisfied" and that he won't be "disappointed." She begins by recalling how pleased she was when one of the maids ("the girls") told her she had not one, but two letters by him waiting for her:

> The girls know so well my delight when there comes anything in your handwriting, for me, that they run to tell me the good news . . . Ah, dear Agassiz, if it is but in my power to make you as happy as you hope to be, and I feel confident that it will be, for I know that the letters which have given you such faith, and especially the one that you speak of so often were written most truthfully, and with the desire not to mislead you in the least as to my own state of mind. Therefore if it will satisfy you that my conduct as a wife should be consistent with what I have expressed there, I think you will not be disappointed.

To the rational mind, even negative experiences, such as a lover's prolonged absence, can be made to appear beneficial. Her temporary period of independence reinforced her dependence on Agassiz and made her a "safer" wife:

> Perhaps though our separation was so great a trial, your absence has not been without its good influence, since I have been left to think out for myself all these questions, and though I have sometimes longed so impatiently for your help that if you were only here, all would seem right to me, yet this very suffering and the loneliness I could not but feel, while you are away, has but given me the stronger conviction, that my only safety is in the most complete reliance and trust in you.[13]

Hidden behind the strenuously rational language, there was true, lasting affection. Twenty years later, when Agassiz had gone west to lecture, Mrs. Agassiz admitted, in a letter to her sister, that she missed him terribly: "This absence of Agassiz only makes me the more certain that the romance of life does not diminish with time, and so I find the weeks of waiting rather long."[14] If Elizabeth offered Agassiz social entré and financial security, he gave her a sense of purpose and, above all, adventure—the "romance of life," indeed.

In many ways, their relationship, loving as it was, must have seemed an unlikely one to their contemporaries. The age difference of fifteen years was not the only potential hazard. Class was a factor too, and the inquiries about Agassiz that Mr. Cary made on his daughter's behalf did not focus only on the rumors of inappropriate behavior that his jealous associate Édouard Desor said Agassiz had shown toward his servant, Jane. Agassiz, the descendant of Swiss mountain folk, the penniless son of a pastor from the provinces, was hardly the groom-made-in-heaven for a girl from Boston's Temple Place. In a letter to her future husband, Elizabeth spoke openly of "my difference from you." But she also promised that that problem would be moot once they had been formally married, when she would be happy to "yield" and give up "the responsibility of all important decisions."[15]

But in fact she never did. When Charles Darwin, in his late twenties, contemplated marriage, he noted among other benefits the prospect of "a nice soft wife on a sofa with good fire, & books & music perhaps."[16] Emma Wedgwood Darwin, self-effacing and tolerant to a fault, proved to be such a wife. Though she did worry about the "painful void" that separated her, the pious descendant of a long line of Wedgwoods, from her heterodox husband, she bridged that gulf by embracing the role of nurse to her husband, mother to his children, and housekeeper to all. That was not the part Elizabeth Cabot Cary envisioned for herself. Despite her Temple Place pedigree and her repeated assurances that she was not a scientist and that she had no ability to understand "technical scientific work,"[17] a life spent merely watching the boys play was not for her. Watch she did, but she would also *write* about her experiences.[18]

Agassiz liked his women to be cultivated. Both his sister Cécile and his first wife Cecilie drew illustrations for him. Elizabeth Agassiz soon realized she had a different, even more important gift to give; to Agassiz's science, she gave the power of words. During her marriage, Elizabeth gradually emerged from the larger-than-life shadow of her husband, taking responsibility for his health and finances and, most important, his writing. She became far more than his ghostwriter; in Agassiz's final years, *she* was the public face of the Agassiz enterprise, through books and essays in magazines, letters she wrote to family and friends, and finally through the official biography she published. If she doesn't fit the classic mold of the humble helpmeet, the faint feminine voice drowned out by male bluster (the way the British ornithologist and artist John Gould marginalized his wife Elizabeth Coxon's contributions to his magnificent plates), this is not because she ever rebelled against the conventions of her upbringing or her marriage or because her own views ever became more tolerant or liberal than those held by her husband. Elizabeth Agassiz made a virtue out of the obvious limitations of her amateur status. Superficially nonthreatening to the male scientific community, her writing both publicly (in her books and articles) and privately (in her family letters, some of which she recycled for publication) pushed aside her husband's more authoritative pronouncements. If the great Agassiz went out with a whimper, that was at least in part because of his wife's chatty, nonheroic musings on nature and on her husband's curious, infinitely interesting little dealings with it. Elizabeth easily ranged from strange animals, food, and beautiful plants to acceptable behavior and the places best to be avoided in foreign lands. Ultimately, the artistic and intellectual choices Elizabeth Agassiz made when she wrote about accompanying her husband to the tide pools of Nahant, the rivers of Brazil, and the Straits of Magellan contributed significantly to the tradition of popular science writing in America. What Elizabeth Agassiz wrote was not science itself. Instead, she presented the scientific enterprise as a commodity, a product to be neatly packaged in the form of books and entertaining essays, part of the enticing surface of life. If Agassiz couldn't stop amassing stuff and thus never really completed the projects he advertised to the American public, leaving both his multivolume *Contributions* and his museum unfinished, Elizabeth Agassiz did deliver, and she did so increasingly under her own name and in her own way. Paradoxically, in becoming Agassiz's public voice, she learned to speak for herself, which laid the seeds for her commitment to women's education and the success of the Harvard Annex, later renamed Radcliffe College, whose first president she became.

It seems strange that someone who flaunted his uncompromising belief in the personal, direct observation of nature would leave so much of the writing to someone not directly involved in his fieldwork. Characteristically, Agassiz came up with a high-minded explanation for this: there was so much to do, and so little time. "You are right, my dear Dana," he wrote to his Yale colleague on January 26, 1855, "I have not only an excellent wife, but in her an excellent assistant and but for her a large amount of what I am doing would be altogether lost, since I generally leave a subject when I have got all I can out of it, without caring much to record my observations in a regular manner." After all, nothing really changes in nature, and if one couldn't properly finish one's discussion of a particular subject, one could always return to it later. "Our studies," Agassiz added, "ought only to be preparations for a better appreciation of Nature and her great Author."[19] What this in fact meant was that he absolved himself from any blame for relinquishing control over his publications to others. If his essays weren't perfect, well, they were all approximations of the great truth about nature that would be revealed fully at some point in the near future, as a result of scientists' collective efforts.

The difference between Agassiz's argument and a seemingly similar one advanced by Darwin at the beginning of *On the Origin of Species* is instructive. Describing the time it had taken him to assemble and reflect "on all sorts of facts which could possibly have any bearing" on the question he had been asking himself, Darwin cast the answer he was now providing in provisional terms, as an "Abstract" that was "necessarily . . . imperfect." Darwin maps out the genesis of his book—from some speculative "short notes" he had drawn up after five years of fact collecting, to a preliminary "sketch of the conclusions" he had composed in 1844, to the prolonged period of drafting that led, finally, to the completion of the current, as yet unfinished version of his theory. Like nature itself—and, more precisely, the geological record whose imperfection Darwin points out later—his book has a history; it has grown and is now close to reaching maturity. The reason that the book is a fragment, a promise of a fuller explanation yet to be written, has nothing to do with the mountain of work that still awaits the scientist's busy hands (as Agassiz would insist), but with the enormous dimensions of Darwin's archive, the sheer amount of data that, like the barnacles he once studied, had attached themselves to the core of an idea he had decades ago. "My work is now nearly finished," writes Darwin, suggesting that whatever gaps a skeptical reader might find are not due to any flaws in his thinking but to the simple reality that, rushing his book into print, he hadn't been able to publish "in detail all the facts, with references, on which my conclusions have been grounded." The reason for the hurry? Darwin mentions it on the very first page: he was about to be scooped, if he hadn't been already, by Alfred Russel Wallace, who had arrived at "almost the same general conclusions that I have on the origin of species." Unlike Agassiz, then, Darwin has a very clear sense of authorship, involving his individual rights to both his discovery and his book, and is adamantly holding on to it.[20]

On September 26, 1855, Elizabeth Agassiz opened a private girls' school in the reconfigured attic of her home on Quincy Street, to help defray some of the costs of her husband's scientific endeavors, expenses that couldn't be offset by the lecture tours and public appearances that appeared to exhaust Agassiz more and more. Whatever assets Elizabeth might have brought into the marriage (recorded is a share in the summer house on Nahant), money was always in short supply. All of Agassiz's earnings went toward his scientific pursuits. Additionally, there was a large mortgage — held by Harvard University — on the new Quincy Street house.[21] The idea for the school was emphatically hers, and she waited to tell Agassiz about it until she had discussed the plan with other family members, among them Alex and Ida, but most of all her father: "Your approbation and sympathy about the plan have made me really strong and indeed if you had not listened to it so kindly I should never have dared to propose it."[22] And a good plan it was: opportunities for girls to receive a formal education were rather limited even in New England. Wealthier families would send their daughters away to boarding school, an experience recorded in Fanny Fern's novel *Ruth Hall* (1854), in which the protagonist makes fun of the brainlessness of her fellow students who are more interested in prospective future husbands than their lessons. Or they would delegate female education to governesses (the way Elizabeth had been raised) and, if need be, hire tutors for specific tasks (the way Elizabeth had enjoyed her own singing instructor). Sometimes family governesses would instruct the daughters of neighbors for pay. Miss Davie, for example, ran a "school" in the upstairs study at Craigie House, the Longfellow family mansion. Among her pupils were not only Longfellow's own daughters but the children of their neighbors, Fanny Horsford, Henrietta Dana, and Josie Ames. Such informal establishments emphasized, as the proper subjects for girls, literary skills and useful habits such as good posture, which in Miss

Davie's school the girls practiced by balancing beanbags on their head while studying and stacks of books while walking around the room.[23] In her bestselling society novel *The Barclays of Boston* (1854), Mrs. Harrison Gray Otis mentions the gentleman who told a lady that he considered her education perfectly finished, with one important exception, and that oversight would be remedied after she had given proper attention "to a certain little volume which he would send her." The eagerly awaited work contained instructions on how to tie one's cravat in thirty-six different ways.[24]

By comparison, the material covered in Mrs. Agassiz's school included geography, natural history, mathematics, and botany, as well as English composition (taught by Mrs. Agassiz herself). Louis Agassiz, who had enthusiastically embraced the plan once informed of it, was her selling point. The circular announcing the new school had gone out under Professor Agassiz's name and with the promise of his active involvement: "I shall myself superintend the methods of instruction and tuition, and while maintaining that regularity and precision in the studies so important to mental training shall endeavor to prevent the necessary discipline from falling into a lifeless routine, alike deadening to the spirit of teacher and pupil."[25] Apart from Agassiz himself, who taught physical geography and natural history, Agassiz's brother-in-law, Cornelius Felton, and even the nineteen-year-old Alexander Agassiz acted as instructors. In his efforts to teach mathematics to the young girls, Alex was often aided by the illustrious Benjamin Peirce of Harvard.[26] One particularly interesting feature was the degree of flexibility built into the curriculum. Agassiz was, he said in the circular, against "binding every mind to the same kind of training" and promised attention to "individual character." The enormous popularity of the school, and the continuing ties between him and many of his former students, suggests that this approach worked.

Agassiz himself, in a letter to his Charleston friend Holbrook, admitted how much work Elizabeth was doing for the school, especially after Felton became unexpectedly ill: "Lizzie was very anxious & overworked having herself taken up part of his recitations. I had of course to step in." When Felton remained unwell for a time, Agassiz knew he would have to become even more involved, "for I cannot afford to kill my Milk cow."[27]

Among the sixty or so girls from Boston, Brookline, Cambridge, and Concord who attended the Agassiz School were some well-known names, such as Alice S. Hooper, daughter of a Massachusetts senator; Ellen and Edith Emerson, the philosopher's daughters; and Melusina Fay (who would subsequently marry the philosopher and mathematician Charles Sanders Peirce, and as "Zina Peirce" embark on her own career as a feminist proponent of cooperative housekeeping). Agassiz himself felt close ties with his girls; in a letter written to her Uncle William shortly after Agassiz's death, Elizabeth Agassiz observed, "Of all the memories of Agassiz's public life I think the experience of the school was one of the most unmixed happiness—and what friendships he brought away from it—His relation with his school girls would never have ended but with his life,—at least with many of them."[28]

Elizabeth's educational experiment, which lasted eight years and brought in about $19,000 dollars (more than $342,000 in today's money), was the germ of the Harvard "Annex" that she helped found after her husband's death, the first incarnation of Radcliffe College. While Elizabeth and Louis Agassiz might have seen her School for Young Ladies as primarily a moneymaking venture (tuition was $150 a year),[29] her efforts came at a time when even some women were still wondering, or encouraged to wonder, if their health "could stand the strain of education."[30] The concept of the school, which for a price made top-drawer scholars available to young female students, had broken down some important walls, not only between secondary education and college education but also between men and women. In April 1873, Agassiz received a letter, signed by 173 of his former pupils, announcing that they had gathered $4,050 (more than $76,000 today) in support of his museum, "an earnest expression of grateful and lasting interest from your students." The list of names reads like a Who's Who of Boston and Cambridge. Next to the Emerson daughters and Miss Alice Hooper, former students such as Mary Bancroft, Bessie Bigelow, Carrie Chickering, Kate Gannett (now Mrs. Wells), Sallie Howe, Lillie Lodge (Mrs. James), Sarah Lowell, and Lizzie Washburn (now Mrs. Grinnell) had appended their signatures. While some of the former students added their married names, the sheer number of those who, like Ellen Emerson, had apparently remained single is striking.[31]

The "Agassiz girls" would continue to wield influence in public life. As the centennial of Agassiz's birth was approaching in May 1907, a letter in the *New York Times* stressed that the event was "arousing fully as much interest among women as among the men." Although many of Louis Agassiz's disciples had passed away,[32] Mrs. Agassiz's former students were still around, scattered over the United States and Europe. For example, the author of the note, Frank Gaylord Cook, mentioned Anna Lea Merritt, the Philadelphia-born painter who had resided in London since 1871.

The year 1859 marked Elizabeth Agassiz's first public appearance as an author in her own right. *A First Lesson in Natural History*, by "Actaea," was written expressly for children and parents who "share the general juvenile delight in Aquariums."[33] The short book was not intended to compete with Louis Agassiz's weightier publications. It follows a popular format for natural history instruction: in a series of letters, the author introduces her young readers to the creatures found at the edge of the sea, in tide pools, on New England beaches, or in the aquariums that were now in vogue: sea anemones, corals, hydroids, jellyfish, starfish, and sea urchins. None of the insights Elizabeth offered were based on her own original research, and as if to further disavow her stake in the book's authorship, she chose a pseudonym, and a rather unlikely one at that: Actaea was one of the daughters of Nereus, usually represented as rather sparsely clothed, even naked, and riding on tritons or dolphins. Perhaps Elizabeth wanted her readers to think of the name more etymologically, as designating, in the original Greek, one who lives close to the ocean. Either way, "Actaea" had limited value as a pseudonym, since the author, in a short prefatory note, thanked "Professor Agassiz" for having offered "direction," "advice," and "assistance," and then, on the first two pages of the first chapter, went on to identify herself as "Aunt Lizzie," who was writing "true stories" about the sea for her niece "Lisa" (Louisa) and her nephew "Connie" (Cornelius), the Felton children, who had enjoyed walks with her on the beach of Nahant and were also the proud owners of an aquarium. A collective effort, the book was intended for a collective audience, not for the individual reader burning the midnight oil in his study chamber.[34]

Perhaps with her young audience in mind, "Aunt Lizzie" unashamedly anthropomorphized all on which she could lay her hands, or rather her pen. Throughout the book she adopts an intimate tone, that of a friend speaking to friends about . . . other friends: "We will begin with an old friend of yours, — the five-armed Star-Fish that you have often collected on the beaches." The weirdness of the subject is already evident in this sentence; what typical New England boy or girl would have a five-armed friend? But what "Aunt Lizzie" really wants to point out is not the strangeness of the starfish; it is the strangeness that resides in our calling it a "friend" at all. As "Aunt Lizzie" will show, we really don't know all that much about these creatures. Addressing her young readers directly, she writes that they would probably take it for granted that starfish eat, "but you do not know where their mouth is." Such obvious differences aside, the starfish's aquatic world isn't so very different from ours. The same social hierarchies that Elizabeth Agassiz and her niece Lisa and nephew Connie would take for granted in their lives apply under water too, and there is no need to let go of cultural or aesthetic prejudices either. Corals, the "little masons of the sea," which had built the reefs of Florida and the mountains of Switzerland, are like families, dominated by the larger individuals (in the case of the *Madrepora* coral), "the patriarchal heads of the family, occupying the seat of honor at the summit." And what seems ugly to us doesn't seem to attract anyone down there either: the sea anemone, for example, can rest assured that no enemies will find him because "he," a dark, soft ball, looks so uninviting. But then that same animal is good for some surprises too. Once pulled from its hiding place and put in a glass bowl, the unsightly creature will do things that aren't humanlike at all. It will stick out its feelers, pretty fringes that are deadly lassoes meant for catching food: "Little shrimps swimming near them, full of activity, are suddenly struck dead at the mere contact with these poisonous whips, and may be seen hanging lifeless on the feelers." Believe it or not, some people like to munch on these soft creatures — the Chinese, for example — but serious naturalists are driven by desires other than culinary ones. How about sea cucumber for dinner? "I doubt whether you or I would like it very much."[35]

A variation of the same strategy shapes Elizabeth Agassiz's discussion of the movements of the starfish, which she at first describes rather condescendingly as comparable to humans only in a rather distant way: "To be sure, it is a slow and clumsy way of moving, but then the Star-Fish is rather a dull fellow, and he is as well satisfied if he has walked an inch or two in an hour as you would be if you had walked a mile in half that time." What seems remarkable at first—the fact that starfish have five eyes—turns out to be no big deal at all: "Let me tell you that five of their eyes are by no means so good as one of yours, and indeed though these red specks are essentially organs of sight, it is very doubtful how much they see with them." The superiority of the human observer remains unchallenged: *we* see *them*, and not vice versa, at least for now. Immediately, however, Elizabeth Agassiz goes on to a story that is exactly about how a starfish *does* see. Starfish carry their eggs near their mouth, and a friend of hers (we may assume that this was Louis Agassiz himself) once pried them off and kept them in a jar for a while. When he was finished examining them, he returned them to the jar in which he kept the starfish, and at once the bereft animal moved toward them at top speed, "placed itself over them, folded its suckers once more around them, and so took them up again." The friend repeated the experiment, placing the eggs at the other end of the receptacle, as far away from the parent as possible, again with the same result. The obvious moral of the story: even the lowest animals partake in the life of the emotions that distinguishes humankind. Elizabeth Agassiz's account of the five-eyed, five-armed, offspring-loving starfish thus presents at least a small challenge to the idea that the two-eyed, two-armed offspring-loving humans are unique in nature.[36] Louis Agassiz, who spent his scientific life both upholding and poking holes into the notion of human superiority, would have approved.

Among the other creatures treated in the book, the inevitable jellyfish, elegantly subversive and stubbornly sturdy at the same time, had by now become a family enterprise. Elizabeth Agassiz devotes a full chapter to them. In great detail, she describes finding a cluster of hydroids on the beach, taking them home, placing them in the aquarium, and watching a medusa, *Sarsia* in this case, detach itself from the cluster. The excitement of the narrator faced with such a sight is reflected in the palpable delight this new—new to us, that is—animal takes in life: "Up and down, and on every side it darts about, and no bird can enjoy its flight through the air more than this animal, which scarcely seems to have a material body, so frail and unsubstantial is it." If the motions of the jellyfish cannot be compared to those of birds, other analogies fail too: "It is perfectly transparent; a drop of water, a bubble of air, a spider's web, a fly's wing, anything that has form and shape at all, can hardly be more slight in texture than this little creature." Addressing the newborn medusa as "our fairy friend," Elizabeth Agassiz makes heavy weather of the fact that it is so unlike its parent, an observation that seems intended to bolster Agassiz's anti-evolutionary stance.[37]

For Elizabeth Agassiz, jellyfish were the "the lamps of the sea," literally light brought into the dark. Note how she employs the language of visual display, encouraging her young readers to keep them in glass jars in a dark place: "If you trouble the water by passing your hand through it, they will begin to shine, and sometimes, if you have one of the larger ones, you may see the light run along the more highly organized parts of the whole body. He seems to tell you thus, in fiery characters, the story of his own structure."[38] Here it is again, Louis Agassiz's confidence that the world is fully legible, and that any gaps that still exist in the story are not because nature's record is broken or "imperfect," to use Darwin's phrase. Agassiz's jellyfish literally shed light upon themselves.[39]

Notwithstanding the delight she took in their beauty, Elizabeth Agassiz wasn't too squeamish when it came to dissecting her underwater creatures. This was an important part of her husband's public message too: science isn't for the contemplators but for the doers, those who practice it. "If we could make a cut across our little friend, so as to get a glimpse of his internal arrangement," she writes in the section on the sea anemone, implying that she has done so on previous occasions, "we should see this sac which makes a cavity in the middle of the body, and we should find that the rest of the body is divided by a number of partitions, running from top to bottom, and radiating from this central sac to the outside." Such a simple dissection will even convince a child that her husband's classification of these animals as Radiates is basically correct. And what about the sea urchin? "Though it looks very unlike a Star-Fish," she lectures her readers, "it is almost exactly like it in the number and arrangement of its parts." Think of an orange, similar in shape to a sea urchin: when you cut five equal divisions into its skin, "leaving them united at the base," then peel off the skin and pull it out—voilà, you have a starfish. Later, she suggests that her readers try a similar experiment in connection with the sea cucumber, an elongated, soft animal that looks like a worm. Take a sea urchin (presumably not the one that the child has just sliced up as if it were an orange). Pretend for a moment that the creature is elastic, she proposes, and grab each end firmly. Then stretch it out till it is no longer a round, compressed ball (like a sea urchin) but long and cylindrical (precisely like a sea cucumber). "You would then have an animal like the one of which I speak." As Elizabeth Agassiz's young readers stretch, pull, and knead their way through the invertebrate world, they experience, playfully and visually, the truth of one of the cornerstones of Agassiz's theory: the homology of the creatures inside the same class (Radiates, in this case).[40]

That is not to say that Elizabeth Agassiz adopts the voice of institutional authority throughout the book. She does admit to gaps in her knowledge. How the sea urchin makes its hole in the rock, for example, "is not known." And, while *First Lesson* is certainly framed by a conventional understanding of God's design for the world as Agassiz had explained it to everyone who'd care to listen (the book's last word is *plan*), Elizabeth also makes clear that her real interest is not in grand concepts but in the little things: "It seems difficult to believe that a substance so soft and delicate as the vibrating fringes on these animals should produce any effect on a substance hard as granite, yet we know that the constant dropping of water wears away a stone, and it may be that the continual friction even of the soft parts of the Sea-Urchin would be equally effectual."[41]

Elizabeth Agassiz's next book, *Seaside Studies in Natural History*, another volume focused on marine creatures, was published by Ticknor and Fields, Agassiz's (and Longfellow's and Emerson's) publisher in 1865. Intended for a more advanced audience, the book offered more straightforward scientific information. Her stepson, Alexander, had advised her as she was writing it; though the tone and style of the volume are distinctly Elizabeth's own, his name appears on the title page alongside hers.[42] In her preface, Elizabeth declared that her work was going to accomplish for the American (actually, the New England) coast what books published abroad had already done for the English seaside. She was probably thinking of books like Philip Henry Gosse's *Tenby: A Sea-Side Holiday* (1856) or *Actinologia Britannica: A*

History of the British Sea-Anemones and Corals (1860). Elizabeth Agassiz hoped too that references to classification and scientific principles would help make her book more of a natural history manual than the collection of "stories" her earlier book had been — a work, then, "useful not only to the general reader, but also to teachers and to persons desirous of obtaining a more intimate knowledge of the subjects discussed in it."[43] Her intended audience was those amateur collectors who find dead jellyfish on the beach after a storm and would like to know what these creatures really *look* like: "In such a condition the Cyanea is far from being an attractive object; to form an idea of his true appearance, one must meet him as he swims along at midday, rather lazily withal, his huge semi-transparent disk, with its flexible lobed margin, glittering in the sun, and his tentacles floating to a distance of many yards behind him."[44]

Seaside Studies begins with an overview of the history of invertebrate research, in which Elizabeth Agassiz also mentions, as if her husband had never quarreled with these men, Darwin's "fascinating book," the *Voyage of the* Beagle, and Haeckel's "valuable" descriptions, which "have all the vividness and freshness which nothing but familiarity with the living specimens can give." However, like *First Lesson, Seaside Studies* is insistently local in emphasis, sometimes directing the reader to particular places that the author herself knew really well. Go to East Point at Nahant and seek out the rock pools where the sea anemones live, Elizabeth Agassiz encourages the reader, "even at the risk of wet feet," and even if getting there means "a slippery scramble over rocks covered with damp sea-weed." You may need to crawl on your hands and knees to get to the grotto where they are, but you will be rewarded with a sight you won't forget. The rocks are "studded" with the animals,

> and as they are of various hues, pink, brown, orange, purple, or pure white, the effect is like that of brightly colored mosaics set in the roof and walls. When the sun strikes through from the opposite extremity of this grotto, which is open at both ends, lighting up its living mosaic work, and showing the play of the soft fringes wherever the animals are open, it would be difficult to find any artificial grotto to compare with it in beauty.[45]

But Elizabeth Agassiz has also mastered the more straightforward discourse of scientific description, as in the passage devoted to the embryo of the sea anemone, a "little planula, semi-transparent, oblong, entirely covered with vibratile cilia." The mature animal's "inner sac," marked *s* in the accompanying illustration, is the "digestive cavity," with an opening at the bottom, marked *b*. It is contained in a larger sac, the body's main cavity. This animal consists of nothing but enclosures and openings—a challenge for any writer, though not for Elizabeth Agassiz, who can weigh and measure things that would seem to elude everyone else's grasp. A large specimen of *Cyanea arctica*, which weighed about thirty-four pounds when alive, after being left to dry in the sun for some days, was found to have lost about $99/_{100}$ of its original weight, "only the merest film remaining on the paper upon which it had been laid."[46]

Next to the marvelous jellyfish and pliable sea anemones captured so elegantly in Elizabeth Agassiz's pages, the world of professional science, with its rivalries and petty feuds, intrudes only briefly in *Seaside Studies*. Some of the names scientists give to living things are evocative (*Goethea semperflorens*, for example) but from the ponderous to the silly it's only a short step, and soon we have the weed Linnaeus christened *Buffonia*, after the man he bitterly hated. That said, Lizzie Agassiz does like a genus of "pretty, graceful" jellyfish named *Lizzia* by the Manx naturalist Edward Forbes.[47]

Professional science is not, after all, the realm in which Elizabeth Agassiz was most comfortable. Her comical attempt to measure the *Cyanea* by laying one of her boat's oars, approximately eight feet in length, across the disk of the animal, which "did not seem in the least disturbed by the proceeding," reminds one of Thoreau's clumsy effort to determine the length of a Maine moose with the help of his umbrella.[48] The jellyfish's diameter turned out to be a little shorter than the oar, but not by much: seven feet! "Backing the boat slowly along the line of the tentacles, which were floating at their utmost extension behind him, we then measured these in the same manner, and found them to be rather more than fourteen times the length of the oar, thus covering a space of some hundred and twelve feet." Concludes Elizabeth Agassiz: "This sounds so marvellous that it may be taken as an exaggeration; but though such an estimate could not of course be absolutely accurate, yet the facts are rather understated than overstated in the dimensions here given." In other words, the efforts of scientists to measure and classify pale next to the wonderful reality of the animal in the flesh as it reveals itself to the attentive observer's eye. This is true of all of the creatures in her book: Elizabeth Agassiz fulsomely praises the "slow, undulating motion" of *Bolina*, "its delicacy of tint and texture, and its rows of vibrating fringes," a "very beautiful object," indeed, and one that "well rewards the extreme care without which it dies at once in confinement." And she goes out of her way to celebrate *Oceania*, which is "so delicate and unsubstantial," a mere "web of threads in the water, without our being able to discern by what means they are held together." No one is really prepared for the sight of multitudes of these medusae floating in the water in good weather: "The number of these animals is amazing. At certain seasons, when the weather is favorable, the surface of the sea may be covered with them, for several miles, so thickly that their disks touch each other. Thus they remain packed together in a dense mass, allowing themselves to be gently drifted along by the tide till the sun loses its intensity, when they retire to deeper waters."[49] Or take the wonderfully named *Zygodactyla*, with its fringed tentacles and "light-violet colored disk," so "exceedingly delicate and transparent" that the human observer is inclined to forgive the animal's "graceful indolence." The motions of the jellyfish are not so different from those of humans: "Indeed, one cannot help being reminded . . . of the difference of temperament in human beings. There are the alert and active ones, ever on the watch, ready to seize the opportunity as it comes, but missing it sometimes from too great impatience." And then there are "the slow, steady people, with very regular movements, not so quick perhaps, but as successful in the long run." And finally, the dreamy ones, never surprised by anything that happens around them.[50] Darwin would have approved, if not of the rampant personifications in these lines, then at least the sentiment behind them. The first part of his *Descent of Man* was entirely devoted to the proposition that the difference between man and the rest of nature was one of degree rather than category.

Like her husband, whose presence is palpable in every line she writes, Elizabeth Agassiz was painfully aware of the limitations of human systems of representation when describing the true nature or, rather, "the different degrees of consistency" in the substance of a jellyfish: "One's vocabulary is soon exhausted." But there was a solution: don't just talk about them, touch them. "If, for instance, you place your hand upon a Zygodactyla," you will feel that you have touched something that has at least a shape. "But if you dip your finger into a bowl where a Tima is swimming, and touch its disk, you will feel no difference between it and the water in which it floats, and will not be aware that you have reached it till the animal shrinks away from the contact." Visual evidence comes in handy when tactile experiences cannot be shared, and it is offered as a kind of fantasy intended to make readers forget that Elizabeth Agassiz had in fact *not* seen all of these creatures in real life either: "To judge of their beauty," she writes about the Portuguese man-of-war, a marine invertebrate known for its painful sting, go ahead and "see them in the Gulf of Mexico, sailing along with their brilliant float fully expanded, their crest raised, and their long tentacles trailing after them." But sometimes leaving these animals in their own habitat isn't enough. Look at the *Cuvieria*, for example, a solid red lump, "with neither grace of form nor beauty of color," when we find it on the beach. When you pick it up, its red tint grows dull, and the creature seems perfectly dead, devoid of any charms, even hidden ones. But if you place it in a glass bowl with fresh seawater, "the dull red changes to deep vivid crimson, the tentacles creep out," the creature stretches, and soon its mouth will be surrounded by a delicately traced wreath comparable in beauty to the richest of seaweeds.[51]

A proper Bostonian to the core, Elizabeth Agassiz would profess immense satisfaction that the ocean too was controlled by the "same beneficent order" that rules the distribution of animals on land. And she reassuringly repeats, in simplified form, Agassiz's notion of the threefold parallelism in nature—namely, that the taxonomic order of nature, ranging from simple to complex forms, is reflected in the history of life as it manifests itself in the fossil record (ancient, simple forms of life superseded by ever more complex ones, culminating in man) as well as in the development of the individual from egg to adult. The Acalephs, for example, "in their first stages of growth . . . remind us of the adult forms among Polyps, showing the structural rank of the Acalephs to be the highest," since they obviously develop beyond the highest stage reached by the polyps. However, adult Acalephs resemble the embryonic phases of the class next above them, the Echinoderms. And so on. Wouldn't anyone find comforting the knowledge that someone had assigned to all those colorfully named *Sarsias, Bolinas, Cyaneas,* and *Cuvierias* "their fitting home in the dim waste of waters"? Each living thing stays—like the boys and girls of Temple Place—in its appointed place and class.[52]

It's perhaps no coincidence that Mrs. Agassiz likes best those animals that have a sense of decorum. She particularly admires the sea urchins, painfully private animals who find ever new ways of avoiding our attempts to see them. And the sea anemones have a way of getting rid of their excrement that meets Elizabeth's rapt approval. Using the forklike ends of their external appendages, they pass on the body's waste until it is dropped off in the water. Thus, a normally disagreeable event becomes a sight to see. Says Elizabeth, entranced by such neatness, "Nothing is more curious and entertaining than to watch the . . . accuracy with which this process is performed."[53] Elizabeth's writing, in both *First Lesson* and *Seaside Studies,* reflects her husband's science liberated from the deadly pressure for competition that Louis now faced daily in his professional life, as he attempted to stem the tide of Darwinism, which had claimed one student after another and had even arrived at the doorstep of his Cambridge museum. While Louis participated in these larger debates, Elizabeth focused on how much fun it was to be a scientist.

As Elizabeth Agassiz was becoming known as an author in her own right, both her excitement and her nervousness about the share she had in her husband's activities began to increase. From the 1860s onward, Louis Agassiz's popular essays typically started as transcripts, produced by Elizabeth, of his public lectures. Apparently, Elizabeth did not know shorthand but had developed a system of her own that helped her write down more or less precisely what Agassiz said (and he was, by all accounts, a fast talker).[54] One of his assets as a lecturer was his tendency to extemporize, rather than speak from a set of notes. This, no doubt, made his appearances more fun for audiences. But one can imagine that Agassiz's waywardness as a public speaker would have created significant problems for his faithful transcriber as she tried to follow the various trains of thought he seemed to pursue at the same time. The tough Elizabeth was unfazed, though: rather than criticize her husband for his rhetorical eccentricities, she embraced them. Sometimes she wanted him to loosen up even more. For example, thinking of Agassiz's upcoming anniversary lecture on Humboldt, which she realized would be one of the most important public lectures her husband would ever give, she told her stepdaughter Pauline that she was in fact hoping he would "throw aside his notes and trust memory and impulse . . . You know how impulsive and emotional he is."[55] Truth be told, Agassiz's unpredictability as a public speaker created more opportunities for her to shape the final product.

But with that freedom came anxieties. Elizabeth revealed as much in a letter to her sister Sarah Cary, who had praised a series of articles by Agassiz, "Methods of Study in Natural History," which had been appearing in the *Atlantic Monthly* since January 1862.[56] Written in what was recognizably Louis Agassiz's voice, and reflecting his penchant for grand declarations ("It is my intention, in this series of papers, to give the history of the progress of Natural History"), the essays were nevertheless entirely Elizabeth's work. While still maintaining the guise of Agassiz's authorship, Elizabeth's choice of personal pronouns in her letter to Sarah betrayed how she really felt about her stake in these writings: "Every now and then I am seized with doubts and fears about the articles by Agassiz, and *I* like to be propped up with a friendly word about them. Agassiz says at his club Whipple, Lowell, and Holmes praised *him* highly." Public praise was Agassiz's due; to her belonged, in private, the anxiety of authorship. Elizabeth Agassiz was concerned about one article in particular. Titled "Formation of Coral Reefs," it later became chapter 11 of Agassiz's *Methods of Study in Natural History*. This was a subject that she felt she had understood particularly well, and therefore the finished product had worried her even more than usual: "I am conscious that what is beautiful and picturesque in his studies interests me more than what is purely scientific, and sometimes I am afraid that in my appreciation of that side of the subject I shall weaken his thought and give it a rather feminine character." But she concluded her paragraph with a sentence that left the question of agency deliberately vague (who, in fact, *is* the author here?) while it also asserted her right to be considered an equal partner in Agassiz's dealings with the publisher: "It grows every month more fascinating to me to write them" (the articles, that is), "and I hope *we* shall make another arrangement with

Ticknor and Fields next year." Nervousness or not, the days of silent partnership were over.[57]

In 1868, Elizabeth Agassiz published *A Journey in Brazil*, a vivid account of her husband's research trip to Brazil from April 1865 to August 1866. Here there was no more ventriloquizing for Agassiz. He was no longer her mask; instead, he had become her topic. The volume reflects a "double experience," she said, drawing on the observations made by both herself and her husband (the cover identified the book as having been written by both "Professor and Mrs. Agassiz"). This dual authorship, she conceded, "makes it occasionally difficult to draw the exact line marking the boundaries of authorship; the division being indeed somewhat vague in the minds of the writers themselves." But in reality this interweaving of narratives was a fiction. Agassiz, speaking in his own voice at the end of the book, himself admitted that the book was written "for the most part by another hand." He had explored collaborative authorship previously, in his report about *Lake Superior*. But the success of that earlier volume had depended less on J. Elliot Cabot's often self-deprecating narrative asides than on the actual results of the expedition, which were documented in over three hundred impressive pages of geological, ichthyological, and ornithological commentary and nine scientific plates. In *Journey in Brazil*, Elizabeth's voice dominates, framing and putting into place any and all scientific statements made by Agassiz, which are usually included in the form of quotations: footnotes, passages culled from his lectures, short essays. In the journal entries that make up the bulk of the book, science appears as a distinct and definable activity, fully observable and describable by nonscientists.

Journey in Brazil also has a well-defined narrative trajectory, in which the scientist as sage and harbinger of democratic values who appears at the beginning is gradually replaced by a more mundane portrait of the scientist as a collector of facts dependent on a network of dedicated helpers, the members of his expedition, the native people, and, of course, Mrs. Agassiz. Some of this was a deliberate strategy. The trip had been funded by the wealthy Bostonian Nathaniel Thayer, and the emphasis on Agassiz's entrepreneurial qualities was a message intended for future sponsors. But attentive readers will also remember the grand statement Agassiz made at the beginning of the voyage, when, the unwitting prophet of his own doom, he warned his party that one could collect too much: "We must, above all, try not to be led away from the more important aims of our study . . . by trying to cover too much ground,—by becoming collectors rather than investigators." If only he had stuck to his own advice.[58]

At first, though, things went well. When the steamer *Colorado* left New York Harbor on April 1, 1865, Agassiz still felt reasonably secure in his opposition to Darwin, whom he ridiculed for thinking he could explain the world without assuming that there was some divine agency: "Until we have some facts to prove that the power, whatever it was, which originated the first animals has ceased to act, I see no reason for referring the origin of life to any other cause."[59] After his arrival in Brazil, Agassiz originally did his best to set himself up as the representative of that divine agency. His goal was clear: Brazil, the Shangri-La of biodiversity, was to be the ultimate testing ground in his quest to prove that although humans can travel, nature really does not—species originated where they are found, and therefore Darwin must have been wrong. It was hardly a progressive agenda even by Agassiz's standards, but it was one he hoped to implement by thoroughly modern means. The strong, fishy smell of his traveling laboratory attracted the local fishermen wherever he went, and Agassiz readily delegated the collecting to them, "remaining himself on board to superintend the drawing and putting up of the specimens as they arrive."[60] Increasingly Agassiz in Brazil seemed less like God-turned-scientist and more like the general manager of a corporation, whose salesmen (assistants, that is), among them the young Harvard student William James, would fan out over the country (in this case the vast Amazonian basin, with all its tributaries) and report back to him with their profits.

The ideological preconceptions that marred, indeed doomed, Agassiz's enterprise have received plenty of attention in recent years, but the degree to which it involved serious fieldwork is perhaps less recognized. William James's letters and personal diary entries, for example, have been reprinted numerous times; his collecting notes have not. They contain instructions on what should be preserved in alcohol and how ("for marine animals add 2 oz. of salt per quart"), what to do in case of snake bite, and the best way of packing small insects for transportation (stack them in layers with paper moistened with alcohol and camphor). The tedium of such an existence is well-captured in a note James made while camping on the shores of the Solimões River: "After a most narrow escape from dying of old age at Tonantins we got off at 6 P.M. and went all night."[61] In *Journey in Brazil*, natural history collecting plays a prominent, even excessive, role, and Elizabeth Agassiz remains focused on the quantitative rather than the qualitative aspects of Agassiz's activities, the logistics rather than the scientific relevance. If Darwin's empirical research consisted in slicing living things under a microscope or unwrapping specimens others had collected for him, Agassiz was right there, *in the field:*

> *December 6th* (Manaos). Mr. Thayer returned to-day from Lake Alexo, bringing a valuable collection of fish, obtained with some difficulty on account of the height of water; it is rapidly rising now, and the fish are in consequence daily scattered over a wider space. This addition with the collections brought in by Mr. Bourget and Mr. Thayer from Cudajas, by Mr. James from Manacapuru, and by Major Coutinho from Lake Hyanuary, José Fernandez Curupira, &c., &c., brings the number of Amazonian species up to something over thirteen hundred. Mr. Agassiz still carries out his plan of dispersing his working force in such a manner as to determine the limits of the distribution of species; to ascertain, for instance, whether those which are in the Amazons at one season may be in the Solimoens at another or at the same time, and also whether those which are found about Manaos extend higher up in the Rio Negro.[62]

And not only specimens were being hoarded: Agassiz's draftsman Jacques Burkhardt, suffering tremendously from the heat and the mosquitoes, made nearly two thousand watercolor drawings of fresh fishes and local habitats, a virtually untapped resource to this day. There are piles of these beautiful drawings in the archives of the Museum of Comparative Zoology in Cambridge. None of the scientific illustrations made it into *Journey in Brazil*, even though Burkhardt's quaint sketches of palm trees, landscapes, and Brazilian homes did—standard travel-book fare, in other words. This is a pity,

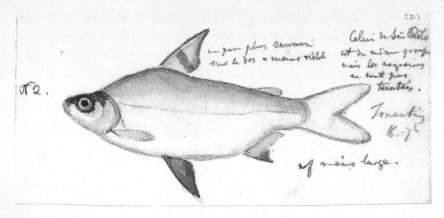

Anodus. Watercolor and ink illustration by Jacques Burkhardt, 1865.

since Burkhardt's fish wonderfully exemplify the scientist's point of view and give us a glimpse into Agassiz's workshop. Artistic effect, in these drawings, is always subservient to the scientific purpose (to help the scientist differentiate between a particular specimen and other similar ones), but somehow Burkhardt still manages to make his fish shine. Incredibly, Agassiz's comments, scribbled in the margins, urge Burkhardt to be even subtler. "Un peu plus saumon sur les dos et moins violet"—a bit more salmon-colored on the back and less violet, he orders his draftsman, right on the drawing of a fish belonging to the genus *Anodus*, harvested precisely where William James thought he would be dying of old age. In the right margin Agassiz added, also in French, "The one from Sao Paolo belongs to the same group, but its fins ('nagéoires') are less colored." The back fin he wanted "moins large," less big.

By contrast, the illustrations that did make it into the book, such as the lithograph "Veranda and Dining-room at Teffé," based on one of Burkhardt's watercolors, dramatize Elizabeth Agassiz's point of view. In the passage that immediately follows the drawing, Elizabeth describes how comfortable she felt in the house a Brazilian member of Agassiz's team, Major Coutinho, had found for them in the pleasant village of Teffé on the Amazon. The setting was as beautiful as she could have wished. From the window of her room, "looking into the court behind," she wrote, "I get a glimpse of some lovely Assai palms and one or two orange-trees in full flower." And this is precisely what Burkhardt's drawing shows: a leafy court, where, to the left, a cou-

"Veranda and Dining-room at Teffé." Lithograph after Jacques Burkhardt; published in *Journey in Brazil*, by Louis and Elizabeth Agassiz, 1868.

ple, apparently sitting in chairs, are engrossed in conversation. Right next to it is the veranda, the only place where work is going on, represented by the dark-skinned servant who is carrying a large vessel on her head. In the background, a man appears to be resting casually on the banister, looking out, his legs crossed, an image replicated in the more immediate foreground, where a little pet monkey is perched, his limbs wrapped around a post, seeming to mock the man's contemplative pose.[63]

The young William James, Agassiz's assistant, wrote in his diary that Elizabeth Agassiz seemed "to fancy that we are mere figures walking about in strange costume on a stage with appropriate scenery," and indeed there is something self-consciously staged about Elizabeth's writing in this book too.[64] In the slow-moving drama of scientific investigation Elizabeth Agassiz enacts for her readers, she plays the role of the educated laywoman who realizes the need for, and relies on, the work scientists do. And yet she is no longer so awed by the mystique surrounding her husband's science that she dare not make light of it. In her narrative, the scientist and the amateur curious about science, interested in answers "that may fitly be introduced into the privacy of domestic life" (as opposed to those that require an advanced understanding of Latin taxonomy), play complementary roles, a division of labor that anticipates twentieth-century developments. But this is a relationship in which the amateur now has a distinct edge: she is the one wielding the pen.[65]

Consider the beginning of *Journey in Brazil*, where Agassiz alludes again, as he did so often in public, to his own health problems: "In the winter of 1865 it became necessary for me, on account of some disturbance of my health, to seek a change of scene and climate, with rest from work." Agassiz here speaks *in propria persona*, as he won't again for most of the book, ceding his voice and authority to that of the educated amateur. But even in this passage he is not really, first and foremost, a scientist. What he acknowledges is that he gets sick like everybody else, the only difference being that he has the resources, or knows how to get the resources, to go elsewhere for rest and relaxation. It is only then that his being a naturalist enters into the equation: "Europe was proposed; but though there is much enjoyment for a naturalist in contact with the active scientific life of the Old World, there is little intellectual rest." Hence the decision to go to Brazil, the fulfillment of a "lifelong desire." Note how Agassiz's primary reason for going there (before more scientific reasons are given) is identified as the result of a "desire," a motivation instantly recognizable to the ordinary reader planning a vacation or an adventure abroad.[66]

Another good example of how these different ways of talking about science — that of the professional and the amateur — shade into each other is Elizabeth's amused description of Agassiz's appearance upon his return from a botanizing excursion. The passage is framed by Elizabeth's obvious pleasure that, upon their return, a breakfast buffet was ready for them, of which, we may assume, the scientist was going to partake heartily: "At the close of our ramble, from which the Professor returned looking not unlike an ambulatory representative of tropical vegetation, being loaded down with palm-branches, tree-ferns, and the like, we found breakfast awaiting us." Amateurs may reasonably expect to understand professionals. What decides whether you are one or the other is the degree to which you devote yourself to an activity — whether you are the one staggering under the weight of specimens or the one holding the coffee cup.[67]

Elizabeth Agassiz is so secure in the role of the gifted lay observer that she makes no attempt to spruce up her comparative assessments of Brazilian and American culture as anything other than the off-the-cuff observations of a casual traveler without any aspirations to intellectual sophistication. Here's the recipe she offers — a little late, in 1868 — for coping with emancipation in America, modeled on something they apparently do right in slaveholding Brazil: "I have wondered, on our Southern plantations, that more pains was not taken to make clever seamstresses of the women. Here plain sewing is taught to all the little girls, and many of them are quite expert in embroidery and lace-making." The effects of such "clever" skills were evident in the attachments even ex-slaves felt toward their former masters in Brazil, such as the old woman who had been given her liberty but chose to stay with her family anyway and "never" would have thought of leaving them. Needlework as a panacea for slave ennui?[68]

When it comes to Brazil and the Brazilians, Elizabeth Agassiz similarly doesn't restrain herself, offering unabashed speculations un-contaminated by closer acquaintance with the facts: "I do not know whether it is in consequence of the climate, but a healthy, vigorous child is a rare sight in Rio de Janeiro." No fan of the American Civil War, Elizabeth is smart enough to realize that the end of slave ex-ploitation in Brazil is coming at too leisurely a pace: "Unhappily, the process is a slow one, and in the mean while slavery is doing its evil work, debasing and enfeebling alike whites and blacks." None of this, however, prevents her from enjoying the ride a few "negro-bearers" give her from the boat to the beach, an enjoyment she stipulates was shared by those who carried her: "So I seated myself, and with one arm around the neck of each of my black bearers, they laughing as heartily as I did, I was landed triumphantly on the sands." She appreciates the fact that the natives of the Amazons are so full of "geniality" and therefore so different from "our sombre, sullen Indians." But Brazilian women, with the exception of those pioneers living close to the Indians of the Upper Amazons, are usually "indolent and languid," leading stifled, empty, vapid lives, shut up in their own homes, nuns without a religion to lend fire to their lives. The luckier ones among them smoke pipes while swinging in their hammocks, a pleasure they share with the common women of the country. As Elizabeth saw it, the deplorable chaos of race relations was only another manifestation of the paralyzing slovenliness of life in Brazil: "Notwithstanding their fondness for bathing, order and neatness in their houses are not a virtue among the Brazilians."[69]

Mrs. Agassiz's more self-consciously scientific descriptions also proudly fly the flag of rampant amateurism. The medusae that float by their steamer have the rich color of dark chocolate or look as if they had been traced delicately with seaweed, their lobed edges tinged with "an intensely brilliant dark blue," and it seems to Elizabeth that she could hear them pant with the effort their hardscrabble lives require. It is left to the Professor to identify two different-looking individuals, in a footnote added at the end of the entry. Characteristically, the note, like so much of Agassiz's work, is cast in the mode of future promise rather than delivering the finality more scientifically inclined readers might have preferred: "These two Medusae belong to the Rhizostomidae, and I shall take an early opportunity to publish a description of them, with the drawings of Mr. Burkhardt. — L. A."[70]

When Elizabeth comes across a beautiful mushroom in Pará, she takes the initiative and offers some more precise measurements, but even then she feels compelled to top the passage off with a literary reference: "The stem was pure white, three or four inches in height, and about half an inch in diameter, surmounted by a club-shaped head, brown in color, with a blunt point, and from the base of this head was suspended an open white net of exquisitely delicate texture, falling to within about an inch of the ground; a fairy web that looked fit for Queen Mab herself."[71] As if induced by that reference to the fairy queen who drives her chariot across the faces of sleeping people, giving them dreams in which their wishes come true, Elizabeth seems to want to distinguish her lazy approach to nature from that of the always-busy Louis: "The week, so peaceful for me, has been one, if not of rest, at least of intense interest for Mr. Agassiz . . . specimens have poured in upon him from all quarters." And this is how Agassiz indeed appears here: as an eager child constantly caught off guard by the richness of his environment. Surely a somewhat disingenuous characterization in view of the many other passages in the book that document Agassiz's organizational talents. Ironically, the result of both types of passages is that Agassiz's activities appear as less categorically distinct from what we nonscientific readers would do in such an environment. The difference is, perhaps, that Agassiz is more intense. While Elizabeth can lean back and appreciate, Louis needs to hold and handle. More than six hundred fish he had collected from the waters of the Amazon alone—a truly staggering number that caused problems at home. Meanwhile, Elizabeth was dozing, "without remorse or ennui," in the comfortable shade of trees, book in hand.[72]

The blissfully intermediate position Elizabeth occupied between her husband's science and an ignorant, uncomprehending public (as illustrated, for example, by the pipe-smoking Senhoras of Brazil) allowed her to understand also what another group, namely the native people of Brazil, thought of her husband's doings. Or so she thought. Like her, these "children of the forest" intuitively know much about the plants, fish, birds, and insects around them and are able to identify species just by looking at Monsieur Burkhardt's new sketches. "They scarcely make a mistake,—even the children giving the name instantly, and often adding, 'É filho d'este,' (it is the child of such an one,) thus distinguishing the young from the adult." Such folk knowledge clearly delimits the claims of science, redefining it as a more formalized account of what careful observers—those in the field or equipped with sufficient curiosity—know anyway. Elizabeth's book thus both returns science to its roots in natural history and gives it a more mundane, circumscribed role in modern society, as something that earns its right of existence not through *what* it does but *how* it does it: with intensity and concern for whether the objects it captures, studies, and preserves are pretty or not.[73]

But the modern scientific amateur is not like the natural historian of yore. Content to lean and loaf at her ease, she gains her insights in the parlor or as a visitor in a museum, not exposed to the rigors of the field (with Theodore Roosevelt, that older tradition would enjoy a brief revival, as intense as it was unique). As an amateur Elizabeth is fully within her rights to recoil from an ugly, enormous, menacing-looking centipede she encounters: "These animals are not only hideous to look upon, but their bite is very painful." But look what happens when "science" (here represented as an impersonal force) takes over: "I crept softly away from my sofa without disturbing my ugly neighbor, who presently fell victim to science; being very adroitly caught under a large tumbler, and consigned to a glass jar filled with alcohol." And consider what the scientist's tool is—a tumbler. Never too far removed from the domestic realm, science remains an ordinary enough pursuit.[74]

None of this is, of course, accidental. Elizabeth Agassiz is a supremely self-conscious writer, capable of considerable self-irony, which she applies in such a manner that it actually reinforces the larger point she is trying to make. For example, she relishes the addition of a sloth to the expanding menagerie on board their ship. "I am never tired of watching him," she writes. "He looks so deliciously lazy." The animal radiates indifference; "he seems to ask only for rest." When pushed or tapped, the sloth "lifts his head and drops his arms so slowly, so deliberately, that they hardly seem to move, raises his heavy lids and lets his large eyes rest upon your face for a moment with appealing, hopeless indolence." Then it will again close its lids softly; the head droops, and he assumes his previous state of serene repose. This attractive embodiment of what in the Christian tradition is a cardinal sin caricatures Elizabeth Agassiz's own penchant for doing nothing (except taking notes for this book) during her Brazilian sojourn, a languid, informed laziness that is different from the paralyzing inertness she encounters among the Brazilian senhoras, whose lives are marked by repression and constraint and who do not even have access to books, except of the most insipid kind. Once, while staying on a *fazenda*, the master of the house comes upon Elizabeth as she is looking at a romance novel she has found lying on the family piano. This is not suitable reading for ladies, her host tells her, and thrusts in her hand a work more appropriate for women, in his opinion. "I opened it, and found it to be a sort of text-book of morals, filled with commonplace sentiments, copy-book phrases, written in a tone of condescending indulgence for the feminine intellect, women being, after all, the mothers of men, and understood to have some little influence on their education." The irony of this passage is withering. "I could hardly wonder," concludes Elizabeth, "that the wife and daughters of our host were not greatly addicted to reading."[75]

Elizabeth later said that she had a kind of fondness for what she called "the Brazilian book," just as she had for the school she ran in Cambridge, "because I had worked at it with Agassiz, and we have had so much pleasure with it together."[76] What she neglects to say is that in both cases she had been the actual originator, the author. Ironically, *Journey in Brazil* has become the one book in the canon of Agassiz's works—or, should we say, of works associated with Agassiz?—that is still read frequently today, though mostly in terms of how far-sighted the young William James proved when it came to recognizing the perniciousness of Agassiz's racism, and how complicit Elizabeth Agassiz was in the latter.[77] But there's also another way of looking at *Journey in Brazil:* as an extended meditation on Elizabeth Agassiz's part about her role as writer vis-à-vis her husband's science, and as an important step in the direction of bringing not just science itself but also the activity of writing about science down to the "level of popular intelligence," which is what Oliver Wendell Holmes had claimed Agassiz had wanted to do (see chapter 1). Though Elizabeth called herself Agassiz's "Scribe," she was in fact so much more, and her ability to do what she wants, within limits, was driven home by the dependent condition of Brazilian women she saw everywhere she went, women who were, she wrote in a letter, "more to be pitied than blamed." Writing books was a "perilous business," she knew that. But in Brazil, she was an "exponent . . . of a freer kind of life" than her Brazilian peers had ever known. Interestingly, the unpredictable and unreliable William James, a "fellow of vivid, keen intellect," was a special favorite of hers during the Brazilian journey.[78]

Agassiz's Brazilian junket was a failure, from the scientific point of view at least, but Elizabeth's readers wouldn't have known that from her book. What the expedition yielded most was specimens, hundreds and hundreds of fish that, despite the alcohol in which they had been preserved on site, often looked rather the worse for wear by the time they reached the Museum of Comparative Zoology and were piled up in the basement corridors because no one had the time or space to unpack them. The hope Agassiz mentions at the end of his preface to *Journey in Brazil*—that he would soon complete a more technical book, "already begun," dealing with the natural history of Brazil and especially "the Fishes of Brazil, in which will be recorded not only my investigations during the journey and those of my assistants in their independent excursions, but also the researches now regularly carried on in connection with the immense Brazilian collections stored in the Museum at Cambridge"—that hope never materialized. In 1870, the Canadian Charles Frederick Hartt, a member of the original Thayer expedition, published a volume devoted to what the title page identified as "Scientific Results of a Journey in Brazil, by Louis Agassiz and His Travel Companions." While it seems that he was still toeing the party line in the book ("I believe, with Professor Agassiz . . ."), Hartt was in reality increasingly troubled by the absence of glacial scratches (which Agassiz had noticed too, though he blamed their lack on "decomposition") and found it difficult to endorse fully Agassiz's assumption of wholesale glacial activity in the Amazon valley. For poor Mr. Hartt, Brazil was not merely a temporary diversion, something to be explored in a month or two; he was hooked. Agassiz finagled a position at Cornell for him, but Hartt kept returning to Brazil, refusing to leave the country even when his wife had become pregnant with twins and promptly left him (she lost the babies after her return to Buffalo). Hartt died in 1878 in Rio, at age thirty-eight, of yellow fever, another life left unfinished in the shadow of Agassiz's overpowering presence. Agassiz never responded publicly to Hartt's critique, though neither did he reiterate his claims regarding glaciation in Brazil.[79]

Meanwhile, Elizabeth Agassiz pressed on, perfecting the genre that we today would call the science essay, balancing state-of-the-art scientific knowledge with the stance of the outsider usually not privy to the things real scientists see. The first two *Atlantic Monthly* essays she proudly signed as "Mrs. E. C. Agassiz" appeared in 1869, a year after *Journey in Brazil*.[80] Again, the underlying genre was a travel narrative: a report about what she had seen during an excursion aboard the Coast Survey steamer *Bibb* (off the coast of Cuba, on the Bahama Banks, and among the coral reefs of Florida), in which she and Agassiz had participated at the invitation of Agassiz's former student, Louis François de Pourtalès.[81] In the new *Atlantic Monthly* essays, Elizabeth refers to a coral, *Theocyathus*, found near the Cuban coast, as "the prettiest thing to see in the world." She is offering the reader both that trivial assessment *and* the Latin name. Likewise we find her sitting under a tree in Cuba, enjoying the picturesque view of the men collecting specimens in the hot sun: "Here, while the others made collections along the shore, I sat and rested, pondering dreamily the old stories of pirates and robbers connected with these regions."[82] And she will describe the ocean creatures as if they were staring at her in an "exquisite aquarium,"[83] live demonstrations included: porpoises are jumping out of the water; sea anemones are softly stirring; gorgonias sway to and fro in the water, "their elastic branches in constant gentle motion"; brightly colored fish frolic in limpid waters; mollusks fly; and seals roll. But then comes, on the other end of the spectrum, the jarring reminder that she, because she has done her homework, at least for now knows more than the general reader, such as the right manner in which to catch a Portuguese man-of-war. Hence the need to pay attention to her: "You must capture him in a net," she writes about the stinging animal, "and plunge him at once into a deep glass vase filled with sea-water: then you will see the full beauty of his pearly float."[84]

Science writing, as the science columnist Natalie Angier phrased it in her introduction to *The Best American Science Writing 2009*, throws wide the door to the scientific enterprise: "It gives you a sense of entitlement. You've met science, you've understood it, you're ready to do it again. Science becomes like music or art. You may not be able to play an instrument or draw a straight line. But you can trust your eyes and ears, and your hungry, inquiring mind."[85] What Angier finds at work in the science writing of 2009, Elizabeth Agassiz already practiced in the middle of the nineteenth century. She came to the genre as a proud nonscientist, if with a more than average understanding of science and an "inside" view of the scientific process. She was a blessed amateur, writing not quite amateurishly, not quite professionally, for other amateurs, the not-so-blessed ones. This was amateurism as a conscious strategy, raised to the level of fine art. If Louis Agassiz professionalized American science, Elizabeth Agassiz amateurized it—a delicate balance, indeed.

· 8 ·

A GALÁPAGOS PICNIC

GASSIZ'S REIGN OVER American science was now a shared one. Whatever he undertook, Elizabeth was at his side, no longer as scribe, but as an increasingly independent, at times even skeptical voice. He needed her even more than she needed him. In September 1869, at the age of sixty-two, Agassiz suffered his first stroke. Though eventually he was able to resume work, he had Elizabeth to thank for that: during his enforced absence from Cambridge, she spoke, wrote, and thought for him. When he returned to his museum a year later, he must have realized that he had lost even more ground in his fight against Darwinism. Even his own son had gradually transitioned to the evolutionist camp; soon Alex would admit publicly what Darwin had been saying for a long time, namely, that we "can no longer define species as has been customary."[1] Imagine, then, Agassiz's elation when Benjamin Peirce, the mathematician and now also superintendent of the U.S. Coast Survey, asked him if he might be interested in getting a new expedition under way: "My dear friend . . . I am going to send a new iron surveying steamer round to California in the course of the summer. She will probably start at the end of June. Would you and Lizzie go in her, and do deep sea dredging all the way round?"[2] Agassiz was delighted at this new sign of his continuing relevance to science. Besides being Agassiz's unfailingly supportive colleague at the Lawrence Scientific School, Peirce was an ardent fan of *Journey in Brazil*,[3] so that it is certainly no co-incidence that his invitation to Louis included Elizabeth too. The new, fully equipped U.S. Coast Survey steamer *Hassler*, named after the survey's first superintendent, Ferdinand R. Hassler, an expatri-ate Swiss like Agassiz, was due in San Francisco, and Peirce's brilliant idea was that Agassiz could take advantage of the scheduled trip along the South American coastline and stop to make collections wherever this seemed promising and convenient. Peirce did make it clear that the government could not pay for the Agassizes' expenses, but that did not put a damper on his friend's enthusiasm. "I am overjoyed at the prospect your letter opens before me," he told Peirce on Febru-ary 20, 1871.[4] Thus, Agassiz once again asked wealthy Bostonians to reach deep into their pockets—with a result that must have warmed his heart. Through private subscriptions alone, he was able to raise $17,450 (more than $310,000 in today's money) to cover the cost of collecting and transportation.

When Darwin heard, via Alexander Agassiz, about the elder Agas-siz's plan for a new South American expedition, he could barely con-ceal his amazement: "Pray give my most sincere respects to your father. What a wonderful man he is to think of going round Cape Horn; if he does go, I wish he could go through the Strait of Magel-lan."[5] Darwin always chose his words carefully. "Wonderful" was per-haps less a reference to Agassiz's superb resilience than an expression of Darwin's own wonder that Agassiz, now in his sixties, hadn't given up yet. Indeed, the prospect of retracing part of his arch-opponent Darwin's South American journey appeared as enticing to Agassiz as did the opportunity of extending his hunt for glacial abrasions to yet another part of the world and adding yet more specimens to his over-flowing museum collections.

And Darwin certainly remained on Agassiz's mind every minute during the expedition. Notably, he *did* go through the Straits of Ma-gellan. "Wasn't it on a similar voyage that Darwin's current views were awakened in him?" he wrote, feigning ignorance, to the anato-mist Carl Gegenbaur on July 28, 1872, when he was already off the coast of Guatemala. "I have taken only a few books with me, to keep my mind free of too specialized research," he continued. Among those few books were, as it happened, Darwin's major works—*The Voyage of the* Beagle, *On the Origin of Species, The Variation of Animals and Plants*

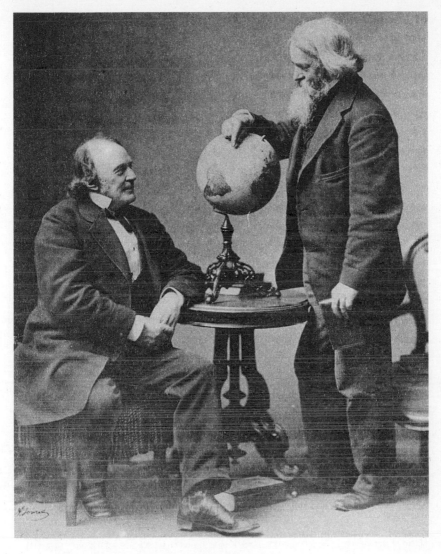

Louis Agassiz and Benjamin Peirce, 1869. Photograph by Antoine Sonrel.

Under Domestication, and *The Descent of Man*—and Gegenbaur's own anatomy textbook (*Grundzüge der Vergleichenden Anatomie,* 1859) as well as Ernst Haeckel's *Generelle Morphologie der Organismen* (1866). Lest Gegenbaur or, for that matter, anyone else construe his reading list as a softening in his opposition to evolutionary theory, Agassiz added a short postscript: "Do you find no deeper meaning in nature? I am not talking about the results of the combined intellectual activities of humankind, but nature as it exists outside the realm of humanity?" How does one get from mollusk to man? No evolutionary theory had ever explained that, which is why Agassiz had always kept his distance from such ideas.[6] Agassiz was now less focused on refuting Darwin in regard to specific matters (such as geological record and taxonomy). He was interested in the Big Picture. As he saw it, this voyage would bring him a step closer to that comprehensive understanding of the world that he associated with the divine mind, that grand plan for the world of which all his scientific efforts had been only so many approximations. He told Peirce, "If this world of ours is the work of intelligence and not merely the product of force and matter, the human mind, as part of the whole, should so chime with it, that from what is known it may reach the unknown."[7] Though Louis Agassiz could not have foreseen it, it seems oddly fitting that the final grand act of his life as a scientist should be framed as a recasting of the first act of Charles Darwin's career.

The ideological premises of the *Hassler* expedition are vividly illustrated in a famous photograph that shows Agassiz and Peirce contemplating the globe, with Peirce's index finger resting comfortably somewhere in the eastern United States, perhaps even on that hub of the universe, Boston. Agassiz, looking quite satisfied with himself, remains seated. Agassiz's science, joined with Brahmin self-confidence, surely had the capacity to unlock the mysteries of the world! But, as this chapter will show, the results of the expedition were somewhat underwhelming, and Agassiz's wife kept her own counsel. The delicate balance between the two of them had shifted, and not in Agassiz's favor.

The *Hassler* was a three-masted, double-hulled steamer of 350 tons, built in Camden, New Jersey, and the first Coast Survey vessel made of iron. At 151 feet in length, it was much smaller than the *Colorado*, the ship that had transported the Agassizes to Brazil. But the *Hassler*'s compact size and innovative technology—it was propelled by a three-masted-schooner sailing rig as well as by a modern 125-horsepower engine—made it suitable for rough offshore sailing as well as surveying in shallower coastal waters. For Agassiz's trip, new dredges had been installed, which would allow him to explore the ocean at greater depths than anyone had done before. The *Hassler*'s crew of

The *Hassler*. From the scrapbook of James Henry Blake.

forty-five was under the command of Captain Philip Carrigan Johnson Jr., an experienced career navy officer who had served honorably
in both the Mexican American War and the Civil War; he had joined
the Coast Survey in 1871. As it turned out, the *Hassler* was just a bit
too cutting-edge to be useful for Agassiz: while the engine was more
economical than that of comparable steamers, it gave the crew no end
of trouble, as did the dredging equipment.[8]

Agassiz's hand-picked scientific team included the inevitable Pourtalès, who was to oversee the deep-sea dredging; the equally ubiquitous ex-president of Harvard, Dr. Hill, who came along as physicist;
a young physician from Philadelphia, Dr. William White, who acted
as general scientific factotum; Dr. Franz Steindachner of the Natural
History Museum in Vienna, who served as the official natural history collector; and James Henry Blake, the official natural history
artist. Mrs. Agassiz and Mrs. Johnson, the captain's wife, completed
the motley group.

A rough sketch by Blake, drawn on coarse brown paper, represents
the members of Agassiz's party in outline only. Interestingly, Eliza-

beth, whom he respectfully called "Mrs. A.," grown sturdily stout, is third on the left, right in the foreground, dominating the rest of the group both in bulk and position, right next to her husband, who is leaning comfortably against the ship's railing.[9] Blake pasted the drawing into a scrapbook that he compiled and continued to add to until long after the expedition.[10] Oddly, Blake left some of the faces blank, his own as well as that of the young Dr. White—a reflection of their status on board? Dr. White, who had just graduated from medical school when he signed on for the trip, later remembered that he knew from the beginning that Agassiz was "down on the Darwinian theory," which White personally had found pretty convincing. But the young physician decided to forgo his skepticism in view of Agassiz's promise to buy him a shotgun. "Which is the most expensive kind?" Dr. White asked his father.[11]

After some delays, harbingers of future engine trouble, Agassiz's ship left Boston on December 4, 1871, a day before Elizabeth Agassiz's forty-ninth birthday. It arrived in San Francisco on August 31, 1872. After a weather-related delay in Barbados, the *Hassler* reached the coast of South America by mid-January, stopping at Pernambuco

The *Hassler* party. Sketch from the scrapbook of James Henry Blake, with the following legend: "1. Prof. Louis Agassiz; 2. Dr. Thomas Hill; 3. Mrs. Louis Agassiz; 4. Franz Steindachner; 5. Commander Philip C. Johnson; 6. Lieut. Commander C. Kennedy; 7. Mrs. Philip C. Johnson; 8. Dr. William White; 9. J. Henry Blake; 10. Ct. L. de Pourtalès."

for coal on January 15. Agassiz's party stayed in Rio for a month. By the end of February, they were in Montevideo and the La Plata area. Rounding Cape Virgin, they anchored in the Straits of Magellan. By the end of March, they had traversed the Straits. On April 25, Agassiz, his wife, and Dr. Steindachner separated from the group and went overland to Santiago and Valparaiso, where they met up with the rest of their party again, continuing north on the *Hassler*—via Caldera, Pisco, Callao, and Payta—to the Galápagos, the ideological heart of the voyage. The *Hassler* then sailed on to Panama, Acapulco, the Gulf of California, and finally San Diego, where Agassiz remained from August 18 to 28. After his arrival in San Francisco, Agassiz continued his collecting in the Bay area. Dr. White noted that it was a blessing the expedition ended when it did. Agassiz had recently learned to play solitaire, a game he pursued, muttering to himself in four languages, with the same intensity he brought to finding a new tadpole. From there he had progressed to poker: "Heaven knows what further temptations lay in wait for this straight-living scientific gentleman, if the harbour of San Francisco had not put an end to the sport."[12]

In copious letters sent during the voyage to her mother and sisters Sallie and Mollie, many of them signed "with heaps of love" or "bestest love," Elizabeth Agassiz continued the interest in her husband's scientific activities she had displayed so publicly in *Journey in Brazil*. But this was a project of a different kind: her voice was no longer bracketed by, and filtered through, her husband's science. From the beginning of the trip, she had written her supposedly private letters, informally known as the "*Hassler* Letters,"[13] with publication in mind. This was to be Agassiz's *Voyage of the* Beagle, or rather his *Voyage of the* Hassler, but told by her. (Agassiz's death in December 1873 thwarted Elizabeth's publication plans, though excerpts from the letters found their way into a series of essays Elizabeth published in the *Atlantic Monthly*, and then, finally, her artfully self-effacing biography of Agassiz.)[14]

Other members of the expedition wrote about the trip too: Dr. Hill dispatched articles to the *New-York Tribune*, while Dr. White, not to be outdone, sent his to the *New-York Herald* (which published them under lurid but no doubt effective titles: "Millions of Skeletons at the Bottom of the Sea," "Oysters a Foot in Diameter," "Beautiful

Tempest-Defying Creatures Dancing on the Crests of the Waves").[15] And James Henry Blake kept a careful record of the trip in his journals, three volumes filled from cover to cover with mostly scientific observations, weather data, and notes on some of the elderly Agassiz's unreasonably strenuous activities during the trip ("I felt frightened for him").[16] Louis Agassiz, by comparison, remained silent; the public heard from him only through a few letters to Benjamin Peirce, which the *New-York Tribune* printed in irregular intervals, interspersed with Hill's fuller accounts. In a final note to Peirce of July 29, 1872, written off the coast of Guatemala and printed in the San Francisco *Evening Bulletin*, Agassiz commented a bit sheepishly on his near-erasure by these other commentators: "Do not be surprised at my few messages. It is about all I can do to take advantage of every opportunity that offers for study and collection: but I rarely feel sufficiently collected to do any connected writing."[17]

Not driven by her husband's need to settle old ideological scores as to scientific ideology, Elizabeth Agassiz was free to present herself in *her* letters as the ever-curious observer, sometimes wide-eyed, sometimes wryly skeptical, always ready to enjoy the landscape, the creatures Agassiz's men collected, and the food, which was rather different from the accustomed offerings at her own dinner table. The semi-official nature of the prior Brazilian venture, combined with a deeply felt need to salvage her husband's crumbling reputation, had cramped her style then. But now, in the "*Hassler* Letters," Elizabeth is unstoppable. More often than not, her New England haughtiness gives way to unabashed admiration for all things foreign. Game to offer humorous asides and literary references whenever they seem appropriate, she casually establishes and then emphasizes her point of view as distinct from that of her scientist husband; in her pages, he is another interesting specimen ripe for observation, rather than the powerful mover and shaker who appears in *Journey in Brazil*. This is, then, how Agassiz's science ends—as a curiosity in the eyes of both his Darwinian detractors and the woman who used to be his "Scribe." The role Elizabeth carves out for herself in these letters is deliberately harmless, often self-mocking, nonthreatening. And yet it allows her—in a world dominated by male scientists—to perfect her own unmistakable voice, buoyed by the confidence that she too has something to contribute to the scientific debates of the day.

A good example of Elizabeth's newfound independence appears right at the beginning of the "*Hassler* Letters." The "negroes" selling their goods in the market of St. Thomas, Virgin Islands, did not elicit from her a reflection on their relative place in the order of nature, musings that would have been typical of her husband. Instead, these women and men reminded her of Wilkie Collins's recent play, *Black and White* (1869). She imitated their speech ("I make you my Compliment sir and I wish for a very good morning") and envied them their apparent carefree attitude. And she was very much taken with the "swarms of negro women around their trays of fruit and Cakes—gathering, laughing, joking, seeming to care little whether they sold anything so long as they had their fun."[18]

If this passage still sounds a bit patronizing, there is no trace of condescension in Elizabeth's dealings with the first Latin American woman she had ever gotten to know closely: Elvira Johnson, the captain's wife, a native of Talcahuano on the coast of Chile and on her way home. Elizabeth fell in love with her and unabashedly admitted it. "As a South American woman she is a revelation to me," Elizabeth Agassiz told her mother on December 29. "I had no idea that a woman of that type was to be found from one end to another of S. America." Pining for her Quincy Street home, barely recovered from the seasickness the Caribbean winds had brought with them, and feeling quite lost in the wilderness of the enormous rooms at the governor's mansion in Barbados, where the ferns were kept moist by the play of a fountain raining a fine mist on them, Elizabeth was grateful for Mrs. Johnson's gentle presence. "Mrs. Johnson proves a perfect blessing to me—such a sweet sympathetic person—I hope now she will keep on the whole way, at least as far as her home in the Pacific, with us. I should feel quite lost without her. She is pretty sea-sick but her power of reaction is wonderful; the moment the anchor drops, all her woes are forgotten; she is gay as a lark with every faculty ready for enjoyment and eyes and ears open to every impression." To while away the time, Elizabeth began to read *Jane Eyre* to her.[19]

In her letters Elizabeth Agassiz also reported her impressions of other fellow travelers. She developed a mild crush on Lieutenant Commander Kennedy, a man with "cold manners" but an expressive face. Among Agassiz's assistants she liked best the hardworking Steindachner ("kind and unobtrusive") and the unflappable Pourtalès ("a man of deeds not words"), and she recorded, with relish, her intense dislike of pompous Dr. Hill, who had so ineptly handled the Clark affair. Dr. Hill was "a queer combination of qualities," self-obsessed and slow, yet endowed with a considerable intellect, Elizabeth told her sister. Personally she never found him interesting, his abilities notwithstanding. Hill would regularly wear a cardigan, instead of more suitable crab gear, even when sailing the high seas, and with his odd clothes and gaunt appearance, "he is a singular picture."[20]

Meanwhile, Agassiz's dredging had begun in earnest. The scientific work absorbed all of his attention, and so Elizabeth left the boat whenever she could and went for walks on the shore. Sometimes Mrs. Johnson accompanied her, and Elizabeth began to dread her new friend's imminent departure from the ship: "She will be a real loss to me not only for her pleasant society . . . I can do many things with her that I could not do without her." Elizabeth distracted herself with reading and studying, activities that became somewhat complicated, thanks to the unpredictable weather, as she told her sister Mollie during the rather stormy passage from Rio to Montevideo: "The 'Hassler' is pitching about in such a way that no one can stand who does not know how to take the attitude of the Colossus of Rhodes on a steep slant."[21] But while Agassiz's nets went deep, dredging up strange creatures from the bottom of the ocean (when the equipment was working well, which wasn't often the case), Elizabeth Agassiz stayed cheerfully in the world above, rocky as it was, and she began to develop a distinct preference for those animals that skated across the ocean's surface. For example, she was entranced with the little pteropod, or "sea butterfly," she saw gliding along, "a perfect little beauty." It had "its mantle all spread out and folding the sides upward it used them just like wings flapping them with the greatest rapidity & flying through the water like an arrow."[22]

The happy world of speedy little creatures favored by Elizabeth Agassiz offered a direct contrast to the image of nature as the site of competition and strife in Darwin's books, which Elizabeth's husband, his forehead furrowed in disapproval, was studying below deck. Elizabeth did appreciate Dr. White's skepticism regarding her specimen-collecting husband's apparent inability to leave living things alone. Agassiz was dropping "everything of value into alcohol," White drily observed (he often had to photograph specimens that Agassiz hauled in till dusk, lamenting his own inexperience and the complexity of the task). But while White found it difficult to like the "ugly little fishes" their nets yielded,[23] Elizabeth always gave in to Agassiz's excitement about nature's beauty. Nevertheless, she never pretended to know all about it. In a subtle dig against the very premise of Agassiz's activities, she pointed out "how little after all we know of the life and enjoyments of these creatures which we see preserved in Museums."[24]

Elizabeth's comment came as Agassiz was ready "to jump overboard with joy" about the results of his dredging: "If he had not thought the dredge would do it better, I verily believe he would have gone down himself to see what he could find. Among other things he found a very rare shell,—and *two specimens, the young & the old* one would say, from the relative size,—and only known heretofore from the Straits of Magellan where he had had a faint hope he might find it, though even there it's not easy." Elizabeth Agassiz, for her part, kept her eyes at water level or slightly above, admiring an albatross, for example, which she was able to see quite without the literary references, as if Coleridge and Melville had never invoked it: "It is a beautiful bird on the water—sitting so gracefully with the body half sunk in the waves, the large head with soft glittering white plumage resting above the surface, it looks as much at home and as secure as any bird in its nest on land,—when it rises it scuds along on the water for a little way, then soars away on wide spread wings, as easy in its motion as in its rest." This is a lovely passage, remarkable also for its emphasis on the albatross being "at home" here. But in fact all the animals Elizabeth Agassiz liked were moving thus elegantly over the water, a place where Elizabeth realized humans definitely didn't belong. Whereas Agassiz looked down, into water forty fathoms deep, and the astronomically minded Dr. Hill looked up (in these southern skies, the stars seemed "multiplied a hundred fold"), Elizabeth Agassiz focused on the surface, viewing her husband's enthusiasm for the secrets of the sea with mixed emotions: "I am . . . afraid that he will be tempted by the immense number & variety of new facts and objects to study more than he might."[25]

The abridged snippets from the *Hassler* correspondence Lucy Allen Paton published in her biography of Elizabeth Agassiz do not reveal how effusive and nuanced these letters are, with paragraphs and entries running into each other, just as the days at sea, punctuated only by bursts of bad weather, would blur together. Elizabeth Agassiz's prose delights in the obvious, not shying away from commonplace observations like this one: "One thinks so much more of weather at sea than on land."[26] Of course she exercised her mind too, occasionally dipping into her copy of the *Voyage of the* Beagle, as Darwin's *Journal of Researches* is now known (she notes with satisfaction that since Darwin did not go on shore in the gulf of San Matías, it really was terra incognita). However, surrounded by specimens yielded up by Agassiz's dredging and the crew's fishing, Elizabeth—or the persona she crafts in these letters—was equally preoccupied with food: "Lunched on delicious fresh fish,—for science for once was generous & yielded part of her loot to the mess,—a most acceptable gift—since we have had nothing fresh for some time."[27] One evening, accompanied by Elvira Johnson, she ascended a sandy slope somewhere in the gulf of San Matías to get a better view of the country behind the beach—and then she heard Agassiz and others on the beach shouting after her. Apparently, Steindachner had killed a poisonous snake (a "serpent") exactly where she was now standing: "I immediately consented to postpone a farther investigation of the scenery and returned with remarkable celerity to the shore. Here we sat down on the clean dry shells and watched them draw the seine and enjoyed the sunset over the lonely beach and bay; as the light died out the men built bonfires on the beach and their fitful blaze succeeded the twilight glow." Back on board the ship, champagne was brought out in celebration of someone's birthday. "There is nothing to bring men here—neither wood nor water," she concluded, as if to justify her persistent focus on her own creature comforts, "so that I suppose it will remain deserted for many a year to come." As they were leaving the bay, she could see their group's beach fires still burning, ghostly reminders of their presence: "We wondered who would light the next fire in this solitary place."[28]

En route to the Straits of Magellan, the storms became so strong that Louis and Elizabeth jumped on their beds for safety—a bad choice, since the structure broke free of its iron moorings and began to drift violently around the cabin. After clamoring for help for a while, they realized that no one could hear them over the din caused by the storm. "Agassiz undertook to hold the bed while I climbed over it." The "grandeur" of storms, especially when they whacked about not just things but people, was not for her. But she had to admit that some of the creatures that Agassiz was netting *were* quite amazing: a starfish more than a foot in diameter, its ten arms "subdivided a hundredfold into countless delicate fibrouslike branches winding & coiling into an endless variety of curves"; another one shaped like an "immense sunflower" (she counted thirty-seven arms on this one!); "many beautiful sea-urchins," and so on.[29]

When they finally entered the Straits, nature obligingly delivered what Elizabeth Agassiz had been longing for, evidence of mammalian life. A whale spouted "quite near the ship" and a sea lion clumsily lolled on the Patagonian shore, so close that Elizabeth was able to follow its every motion; boobies were floating by on islands of kelp. Finally, the weather lightened up again, like the best of balmy October days back home at Nahant. Agassiz too was "on the top wave of life," Elizabeth said, resorting to a nautical metaphor for the occasion. He was happy with the results of his work, and his mood improved even more after he came across a terminal moraine, proof that here too the glaciers had done their work.[30]

But Elizabeth again immediately felt the need to distance herself from Agassiz's scientific exploits, reminding herself that the salt pond teeming with marine shells Agassiz discovered some two hundred feet above sea level was in fact confirmation of his rival's theories too: "This will please Darwin, if he does not already know it, because it illustrates a statement he made many years ago that the geology of this coast was connected with upheaval." And she mocked Agassiz's penchant for collecting whatever he found, describing how his men returned from the shore carrying, of all things, a dead skunk: "It may be interesting to you as a scientific fact to know that skunks smell in Patagonia exactly as they do in New England." Luckily, Agassiz's men had killed some other animals too, enough at least for the cook, who prepared a great feast from the spoils, a social event in grand style, "with a center ornament which was thought could not be matched at any dinner party on Beacon Street or Fifth Avenue." A guanaco skull sat in the middle of the table, crowned by an arrangement of ostrich plumes, with fronds of kelp delicately placed around it. As for the meal, a course of mussels roasted on the shell was followed by Patagonian snipe on toast, accompanied by a selection of fine wines, sherry,

Sauternes, and Champagne. A skinned guanaco supplied the steaks for breakfast the next morning. Very much like beef, reported Elizabeth. Later in the day, while Agassiz was getting busy with the animal's brain, Elizabeth ran her fingers over its skin, which was lying on the ship's deck: very soft and excellent material for a robe. The men told her that these graceful animals, when disturbed, "hurry close together and stand startled & alert with their pretty heads lifted listening & whimpering to each other like young colts."[31]

Charles Darwin had admired the guanacos too ("elegant animals," he had called them, "with long slender necks and fine legs"), but unlike Elizabeth, he had actually heard them utter "their peculiar shrill neighing note of alarm" and seen them prance and leap nervously when approached.[32] When Darwin wrote about the glaciers of Tierra del Fuego, however, Elizabeth Agassiz still felt she had the upper hand, if only because she was traveling with the Ice King himself, the "glacier-mad" (if Darwin was to be believed)[33] Louis Agassiz.

Elizabeth was not given to the descriptive flights of fancy that characterized Darwin's writing. When he looked at Mount Sarmiento in 1834, he beheld "vast piles of snow, which never melt, and seem destined to last as long as the world holds together" and waxed ecstatic about this "noble and even sublime spectacle."[34] Elizabeth, in March 1872, took pleasure in the landscape's "cleanliness." Thanks to

"Mount Sarmiento." Ink drawing from a letter by Elizabeth Cary Agassiz to Mary Perkins Cary, 1872.

Agassiz, everyone knew that glaciers did not stay put. And who could look at those mountains and not think of all that Agassiz had accomplished in Switzerland? Elizabeth asked her mother. They looked like the Alps and the Jura, but one would have to imagine water in place of the valleys. And there were flowers galore, as many fuchsias as there were mountain laurels in New England. "I think one of the great charms to Agassiz in all this scenery has been a kind of home feeling;— though they rise from the ocean instead of from the plain of Switzerland the snow fields & glaciers of the Straits have carried him back to his Youth and he said the sunset the other evg. — the singular transparent rose color on the snow and then the deadly pallor, was the very reproduction of an Alpine sunset."

But while Agassiz continued to find his glacial scratches and striations everywhere, transforming this exotic landscape into a version of what he already knew, Elizabeth made an effort to appreciate the glaciers for what they were, something utterly strange and different. She was especially impressed by the field of ice in Glacier Bay, which seemed to pour directly into the water, though it was in fact surrounded by a belt of trees "as luxuriant in vegetation as any wood I have ever seen." Every trunk and branch, every log and the ground itself were covered with damp moss; ferns of the most exquisite beauty grew everywhere; and from branches dripping with moisture hung trumpet-shaped flowers. The devoted Lieutenant Kennedy's ax cleared the way for the ladies.[35] Balancing on fallen logs to cross streams of water that increased in volume as they drew near, Mrs. Agassiz and Mrs. Johnson, wearing "overhauls" and rubber boots borrowed from their respective husbands, finally made it to the glacier. "You don't know," Elizabeth would write to her sister Mollie a few days later, still relishing the experience, "how satisfactory it is to get on a pair of waterproof overhauls and your husband's boots and go splash through any water that is not over your knees. I feel like little boys let loose in puddles."[36] The glacier was indeed remarkable, even by the standards of the veteran glaciologist Agassiz — a mile and a half in width and dotted with caves of blue transparent ice. "I have heard Agassiz lecture & talk so much about glacial phenomena it seemed very strange & interesting to me to see him measuring & examining the movement & action of a new glacier." Elizabeth tried out Agassiz's game for a bit too, mentally tracking the glacier's "ancient course" by way of the boulders it had left behind and counting the furrows and scratches the ice had engraved on the rocky walls through which it ground its way. Finally, she stepped into one of the mysterious caves, where she saw, "between the lower surface of the ice and the ground the accumulated mass of loose material, stones, pebbles, and boulders which I have so often heard Agassiz describe as 'ground moraine.'"

But the brief taste she got of glaciology-in-action did not appease the pangs of hunger Elizabeth suddenly felt. To her and Mrs. Johnson's great relief, they heard a shout coming from the woods: the lunch baskets had arrived. Perched on Agassiz's terminal moraine, Mrs. Agassiz and Mrs. Johnson munched on sardines and potato salad and helped themselves to port wine ("poetry, potatoes & port, see how well they go together," quipped Elizabeth). An excellent meal, which Elizabeth topped off with a few sips out of her sherry flask. At dinner, to toasts of champagne, they christened the glacier the "Hassler." Strange that Darwin hadn't visited it.[37]

Into this culinary idyll erupted the Fuegians, a band of half-naked savages (as Elizabeth perceived them at first). She had seen them a few days earlier, when three men and three women, with their infants strapped to them, approached the *Hassler* in their canoes. They shouted and made weird gestures; Agassiz's party, bundled in winter coats, looked on in disbelief. The native women continued to nurse their babies while lustily paddling with both arms in the water! Over and over again during the voyage, the childless Elizabeth Agassiz would find herself attracted to such casual displays of fecundity and seemingly uncomplicated maternity. When Elizabeth Agassiz and her party were enjoying one of their famous picnics a few days later, resting comfortably on blankets that they had spread out on the shore next to their lunch baskets, the Fuegians—a group of men, women, children, and dogs—finally ventured near them. Elizabeth was appalled by their "low and degraded" appearance, noting that each man wore a sealskin loosely tied around his neck, which barely covered his "shockingly dirty" body. However, after she had watched the Fuegians for a while, revulsion yielded to interest and the native Fuegians appeared "much more human" to her.

Elizabeth and her shipmates shared their crackers and pork with them, and, as if to thank them, one of the men, the chief, began to sing "in a strange monotone, a kind of chanting song which was really not without expression." Intuitively, Elizabeth knew that he was singing about *them*. She listened closely enough to recognize patterns and she suspected that he was dividing his song into units, resembling the stanzas of an actual poem. Like a true performer, the chief afterward paused for applause, which the startled audience at first failed to deliver. Elizabeth admired the handsome face of a boy she thought to be around eighteen, who might have been taken for an Italian—a definite crack in the surface of the tidy racial categories her husband had developed. As they left, Mrs. Agassiz and Mrs. Johnson waved their handkerchiefs; the Fuegians pulled out an old rag and waved back.[38]

Compared to Darwin's response to the Fuegians he met not far from Cape Horn nearly forty years earlier ("The most abject and miserable creatures I any where beheld. . . . one can hardly make oneself believe they are fellow-creatures, and inhabitants of the same world") and his assumption that the natives did not know the pleasures of home or "domestic affection," the handkerchief-waving Mrs. Agassiz, with her appreciation of Fuegian improvisational poetry, looks like a beacon of cultural enlightenment.[39] If Agassiz, the self-styled expert on all things racial, weighed in on the Fuegians, Elizabeth did not record it. But if the entries about these encounters in James Henry Blake's journal are any indication, she might have been the most open-minded of her shipmates. Blake found the Fuegians "hideous-looking" and "disgusting" and couldn't get over the fact that one of them, "in the presence of the ladies," loosened the string that held his sealskin garment and showed himself to Agassiz's party the way he was born.[40]

On April 11, 1872, the Agassiz expedition reached Talcahuano, Chile. Agassiz, Elizabeth, and Dr. Steindachner left the *Hassler* to continue overland to Santiago by carriage and rail. Elizabeth, though saddened by the departure of Elvira Johnson, was pleased "to be living on land again,"[41] while Agassiz merely shifted the focus of his collecting impulses: "It would entertain you," wrote Elizabeth to Sallie, "to see the groups of ragged dark-eyed dark skinned children coming with snakes, toads, spiders, starfishes, sea urchins, fossils, every thing living they can lay their hands upon to sell them to Agassiz—He has given it out that he will buy every living thing and he is followed by a mob of dirty urchins wherever he goes—all Talcahuano is collecting for him and he is really getting very valuable things." And although he was doing what he always did, it was good for Agassiz to be away from his museum and the "chronic anxiety" as to whether or not enough money could be raised to maintain it.[42] It lifted his spirits to see how famous he was even here, on the dusty roads of Chile, surrounded by beggars and children asking for necklaces. The German innkeeper in Curicá, for example, who had fled to Chile after his involvement in the revolution of 1848, "knew all about Agassiz, had heard that he was on the road, had our rooms all ready for us and gave us a hearty welcome." And in Santiago, there was even more buzz about Agassiz's presence: "If we could stay and if Agassiz were well enough we should see all there is of society & luxury here!" But Elizabeth knew he wouldn't be up to the strain: "He can bear his regular scientific work but the fatigue of society and the talking with heaps of people are exciting & exhausting." One of the naturalists at the Universidad de Chile, Dr. Rudolf Amandus Philippi (or Rodolfo Amando Philippi, as he now called himself), had long ago made a pilgrimage to the young Agassiz in Neuchâtel—small world indeed. Elizabeth Agassiz clearly regretted not being able to be up and about town, but she compensated herself with "the gorgeous symbolism of the Catholic Church," which she appreciated for the first time as she was gazing at the city's magnificent marble buildings. In retrospect, the churches in Brazil seemed so "tawdry & full of tinsel."[43]

When the Agassizes and Steindachner got to Valparaiso, the *Hassler* was waiting for them and they set sail for the Galápagos, in many ways the heart of the voyage. During stops in Peru, Agassiz continued his industrial-scale collecting. While the frequent failure of the complicated dredging equipment continued to annoy him, the crew did what they could to make up for it. "We hardly get the anchor down in a collecting place," Elizabeth wrote from the Peruvian coastal town of Pisco, "before Kennedy . . . has every thing ready for the most extensive fishing—nets out, seine prepared, parties organized, every thing arranged to make the most of the time." Meanwhile, those not involved in the fishing went on shore with their guns. In Pisco, for example, Dr. Pitkin, the ship's surgeon, left by himself "and brought back one seal two flamingos 1 immense pelican a number of scissor bills & some other birds. Meantime Kennedy was hauling the seine—and the result of the day was some 8 species of sharks, a number of skates . . . sea turtles & any number of small fish crabs & the like." They got so much in this particular place that Elizabeth and Steindachner had to go inland to obtain more barrels. To their surprise, they discovered that this part of Peru was quite the wine-growing region. The proprietor of a well-stocked wine cellar insisted that they taste some of his products, an offer Elizabeth readily took advantage of, until she, in her own words, "began to feel a little muddled in my ideas" and worried about the condition in which she would return to the ship. She wasn't muddled enough, however, to ignore the discrepancy between such luxury and the poverty in which most of the residents of Pisco lived.[44]

On June 10, 1872, the *Hassler*—freshly stocked with empty barrels—reached Charles Island (now Floreana) in the Galápagos. The letters Elizabeth sent home from the Galápagos are not with the rest of the *"Hassler"* manuscripts but an article published in the *Atlantic Monthly* supplies at least a portion of those missing installments (it is conceivable that Elizabeth kept the original letters separately as she was working them up for publication, and that they were subsequently lost).

The very title of her piece, "A Cruise Through the Galápagos," already suggests that it wasn't primarily a scientific exercise.[45] Yet Mrs. Agassiz certainly didn't lack an agenda. She started her observations with a celebration of marine life, assuring her readers that "physical enjoyment and the mere delight of living was provided for the tenants of the sea as well as for those of the forest." Casually she set up a playful underwater scene, which resists the compulsive greed of Agassiz's collecting as much as it defies the explanatory power of Darwin's model of natural selection. Look how many perfect hiding places nature holds in store for its creatures: "Occasionally a barracuda or a huge garupa"—a grouper—"would loom up in the neighborhood of such a crowd of small fry, and instantly they would disperse and be gone among the thousand nooks and crevices of coral growth. There they would be hidden until their enemy had disappeared, when they would come out again and resume their play." Sea anemones bask in the sunlight and starfish crawl on corals, all part of a "living, glowing picture" of underwater life that seems intended to show how good cheer reigns in the marine world, from the tiniest sea creatures to the largest, the whales: "Seeing these animals in numbers, as one meets them in the Pacific Ocean or about Cape Horn, you cannot resist the impression that they have an excellent time in their way; that they romp and frolic and enjoy life and each other immensely." No rude struggle for survival is apparent in this happy scene.

Even on arid and scorched Charles Island, Elizabeth found cause for optimism and celebration: "A few mangrove-trees had found foothold along the shore, and, throwing down, their long, stilt-like roots, had bordered the beach with a scanty rim of verdure and shade." Sitting on a gnarled root, she passed the time till her husband's collectors were done with their work by watching "armies of brilliant red crabs swarming on the rocks and sand." There was, she concluded, abundance in unlikely places. Take the glossy sea lions she saw from a distance. Not unexpectedly, Agassiz's men killed one, and as they were transporting their prize back to the ship, hundreds of others followed them, a crowd of mourners "crying and howling, whether in anger, fear, or lamentation we could not tell." As Elizabeth Agassiz described it, this was an unlikely, surreal scene, "a strange funeral procession, to which the twilight fading into night upon the sea, the black rocks fringed with surf, the white sand beach with its dark background of mangroves added a wild picturesqueness." The narrative grows even more peculiar when a native of Ecuador—a dubious ex-colonel fallen on hard times—boarded the *Hassler*, begging for food and supplies for the failing colony he had attempted to set up on Charles Island. Elizabeth Agassiz, motivated by the same naive charity as Melville's Captain Delano, gave what she could.

The landscape of Albemarle (now Isabela Island), formed by molten lava, served as a backdrop for one of Elizabeth Agassiz's famous picnics, with claret and all. In the *Atlantic Monthly* essay, Elizabeth's description of the repast is preceded by a fantasy in which Elizabeth's hiking companion—Steindachner (never Agassiz, by the way)—appears as a reincarnation of the ancient god Vulcan:

> I missed my companion, but suddenly heard him calling to me in a stifled voice that seemed to come from below. I looked around vainly, and it was only after a little search that I discovered him standing at the black opening of one of these underground tunnels.

Heated and dusty with his walk, a large club in his hand, he seemed the very subterranean Vulcan my fancy had predicted. Climbing over the huge *débris* of the ancient fire-time, I followed his invitation and entered the mouth of the cave, expecting to find, at the least, a one-eyed Cyclops at his forge hewing out a thunderbolt for imperial Jove.

The allusions to Darwin's *Voyage of the* Beagle are obvious. If Darwin had encountered a "Cyclopian scene" in the Galápagos, an archaic landscape that reminded him of the iron foundries of Staffordshire,[46] Elizabeth finds not a mythological creature risen from the depths of the past, but rather Dr. Steindachner from Vienna, holding a lunch basket. Resting on the seats formed, as if for her comfort, by ancient lava flows, she partook heartily of the assembled refreshments. Sipping wine atop this geological furniture, which comfortably stood in for upholstered chairs in a Boston salon, Elizabeth was ready to doubt the notion that Darwin had popularized — that these islands were simply nature's ongoing evolutionary workshop.

This was, of course, Louis Agassiz's main concern. His draftsman James Henry Blake records, in some detail, an improvised lecture Agassiz gave in Panama Bay, ten miles off Capa Mala, a summary of his feelings about Darwin's Galápagos experience. "I do love him," he said about Darwin, with uncharacteristic generosity, and yet he feared that no one would do more damage to "the progress of science." Darwin had been on a "wild goose chase" in the Galápagos and had brought us "not an inch" nearer a proper understanding of why nature took the forms it did there. "Knowledge is not advanced by argument," he said.[47] Agassiz apparently didn't notice how argumenta tive, rather than fact-based, his own lecture was. Elizabeth, who was in the audience when Agassiz held forth, did.

She tried a different approach to the mysteries of the Galápagos, one that left scientific squabbling behind and replaced it with personal exhilaration and, where appropriate, befuddlement. In her essay, the landscape appears as both strangely familiar (and therefore not really surprising) and safely distant, both knowable and entirely unknown, the site of claret-soaked picnics and mysteries hidden in lava. In fact, her text rather delights in the superficiality of her experience of these islands, as if she had intended to both imitate and parody certain parts of Darwin's *Beagle* narrative—those in which he is simply having fun, riding, for example, on the shell of a lumbering tortoise that didn't even take notice of him. Elizabeth's encounter with the flamingos on James Island (now Santiago) was perhaps written in response to such a scene in *Voyage of the* Beagle: Darwin was halfway through munching on a cooked emu when he realized that his dinner might in fact be a new species—*Rhea darwinii*, as it has come to be known—a funny comment, in retrospect, on Darwin's later attempt to tear down essentialist concepts regarding species. In this passage from Darwin's travelogue, the idea of species concerned the stomach more than the mind.[48] Likewise Elizabeth Agassiz, after commenting at length on the beauty of these birds, revealed her passion for flamingo flesh. Hidden behind the trees, she took a seat:

> Two of them promenaded near me, walking along the edge of the surf. They stepped high, with a certain dainty caution, an aristocratic deliberateness of movement, which seemed to imply that haste was vulgar. The curve of the neck was no less graceful in walking than in swimming; but in flight, though their color is wonderfully brilliant and shows to great advantage, their position, with the legs and neck stretched out, is awkward. Shall I confess that, beautiful as they were, and seemingly unfit for coarser uses, we dined on roasted flamingo that evening? Very tender and delicate it was, and of a delicious flavor. In the somewhat monotonous state of our reduced larder, the temptation was irresistible.

But not to worry. A convenient comfort of believing in God's plan for the world was that you never had to be concerned about running out of God-ordained sources of meat: though some species (like the dodo) might become extinct, others stood at the ready to take over. James Island abounded in game, such as "ducks, snipes, and other small birds,—so that for a day or two our table was not without its luxuries."

Elizabeth found even more evidence on Jervis Island (now Rábida) that nature wasn't just a mad scramble for survival. This time a "happy family" of seals exemplified this idea: "As we approached they looked curiously at us, and then waddled into the water, remaining, however, in the surf, sometimes coming up on the sand, sometimes rolling over and over in the waves, playing with one another, rubbing their heads together, and indulging in endless gambols and fun." As so often in her letters written during the voyage, Elizabeth Agassiz showed herself to be impressed by a display of maternal nurturance, held in store for her by "uncivilized" nature: "A mother had made a kind of nursery for herself and her two little cubs in a green arbor formed by the low-growing branches of a tree a few yards from the beach. Though they looked at us with inquiring wonder, they were perfectly unconcerned at our approach; allowed us to sit down close by them, and pat them, and they would even smell of the bread and crackers with which we tried to tempt them to feed from our hands." Not only did these seals have a taste for human snack food, but they also welcomed the intruders with open hands, ahem, fins. Any indication of strife among them reflected the kind of squabbling that happens in human families: "It was amusing to watch them in their home; the little ones cuddling up to the mother, quarrelling for the nearest, warmest place with that selfish instinct of dependence and affection which startles us in animals as something strangely human." Perhaps attracted by this intra-species benevolence, members of other species lined up to join the fold: "The 'happy family,' so often represented in menageries, was to be seen here in nature. Small lizards crawled over the mother seal and ate flies from her back, and little birds hopped close over her head and between her and her little ones, without the slightest fear."

In a vignette that comically anticipates the experiments with the sensory abilities of earthworms that Darwin would conduct a few years later, Elizabeth Agassiz describes herself testing the musical talents of the Galápagos lizards, those grotesque "red and orange colored terrestrial iguanas which haunt this island in numbers." The ground was burrowed in every direction with their holes:

> As I was returning through the ravine in advance of my companions, I saw an iguana running very actively around the foot of a tree. I had heard one of our party say that these animals were easily attracted by music, and could be quieted and caught in that way. Remembering the charm, I began to sing. Suddenly he stood quite still; and, delighted with my own success and with the susceptibility of the uncouth creature, I drew gently nearer, always singing,

and beckoning meanwhile—though not without a certain self-reproach for taking such unfair advantage of his love of music—to one of our sportsmen behind to come up cautiously and give the fatal blow.

Was Elizabeth trying to help the crew in their collecting efforts? One of Agassiz's men approached silently, but suddenly stopped in his tracks and exclaimed, "Why, Mrs. Agassiz, he's tied!" As it turned out, the iguana's seemingly breathless appreciation of Mrs. Agassiz's music was mainly due to the fact that he had inadvertently twisted the rope around the tree in such a manner that he was unable to move. Instead of a latter-day siren, Mrs. Agassiz became her party's laughingstock. Or as she put it, with humor: "A more mortified *prima donna* was never hissed off the stage."

One might interpret such episodes as a fawning tribute to Agassiz's patriarchal hold on scientific truth: when women try their hand at experiments, things go wrong. A more compelling way of reading the scene would be to assume that Elizabeth Agassiz is making fun of the pretensions of scientific authority. She gives us "science lite," a way of writing that freely expresses the author's own (sometimes wrongheaded) opinions yet manages to avoid the dogmatic inflexibility that marred her husband's scientific pontifications as well as Darwin's allegedly superior claim to the scientific truth. In fact, her Galápagos essay ends with a little surprise. Elizabeth finally confronts the question, posing it as if no one had ever asked it before, that had dominated debates about evolution for quite some time: Whence did the fauna of the islands, so distinct from that of the mainland, really come? Almost disingenuously, she mentions the "odd coincidence" that the Galápagos Islands, obviously of such recent origin, had become so intimately associated with Darwin's theory. And she summarizes the two competing ways of explaining the diversity of life in these isolated regions: (1) that all these species were created by God in the very location where we find them now, or (2) the less likely theory, at least from her husband's perspective, that natural selection, a rapid transformation and adaptation of species to new environments, was somehow responsible.

Agassiz had been emphatic about the absurdity of the latter idea.

The Galápagos "belong to our times, geologically speaking," he wrote, with considerable exaggeration, to Benjamin Peirce on July 29, 1872. If the animals and plants found there are indeed descended from other types, "belonging to some neighboring land," then the transformation of species must have happened much faster than the adherents of evolution claim. And if that was the case, "the mystery of change, with such marked and characteristic differences between existing species, is only increased, and brought to a level with that of creation." If Darwin found the key to evolution on the Galápagos, Agassiz again finds God—or at least a humbling reminder that science isn't ready to understand what has been going on here.[49]

Elizabeth Agassiz agrees, but only up to a point. Perhaps, she muses, it would have been better if their party had spent less time collecting and more observing: "Our collections, were, indeed, large and various, because our small corps of naturalists was multiplied by the whole working force of the ship, officers and men joining in the search with a hearty good-will which trebled and quadrupled the strength of the scientific party; but they would have been far more interesting had we been less hurried." And though Agassiz would have argued (as he in fact did) that the absence of transitional forms between different species of animals on the Galápagos was proof enough that Darwin was wrong, Elizabeth's own conclusion, especially in light of her complaint that not sufficient time was spent on fieldwork, seems to acknowledge that the matter might not be settled yet. Sure enough, those transitional types the Darwinians constantly invoke, if they do indeed exist, "should not elude the patient student or the alert and watchful spirit of the age." But then, Agassiz's men had just proved that they were less than patient. By contrast, Darwin had done some of his "best work" here. Obviously, Elizabeth Agassiz is not entirely in her husband's pocket. Perhaps some proof might yet be found for Darwin's "subtle, imperceptible alchemy." For Louis, the questions raised by the Galápagos Islands pointed the observer to God and the mystery of "creation." Elizabeth, taking no definitive stance at all, unless one regards the phrase "subtle . . . alchemy" as a slight, delegates the solution to this conundrum to people or agencies other than herself or the readers of the *Atlantic Monthly*.[50] Where Darwin's account of the Galápagos in *Voyage of the* Beagle gives us science on the brink of a breakthrough—the islands, he claims, are nature's *"work-shop"*—the retracing of the voyage by Louis and Elizabeth Agassiz in 1871–1872 yields nothing remarkable: a picnic or two, and otherwise more questions than answers.[51]

Even from a collecting point of view, the voyage of the *Hassler* was a decidedly mixed success. Agassiz claimed that they gathered some thirty thousand specimens and used thirty-five hundred gallons of alcohol in packing them. Franz Steindachner needed eight months after his return to work his way through the fish collections. However, according to the Museum of Comparative Zoology's Ichthyology Department, only seven thousand specimens from the *Hassler* expedition actually remained at Harvard. It appears that the good Dr. Steindachner rewarded himself for all his hard work. Taking his cue from the greedy Master himself, he took untold numbers with him when he went back to Vienna in 1873.[52]

Agassiz died a little more than a year after their return. "It is over," wrote Elizabeth on January 5, 1874, to her favorite uncle, William. "A life that grew daily fuller & richer in happiness for twenty three years and was only clouded at last by my anxiety for him" had ended. "I can never tell anyone how delightful it was to live by the side of a mind so suggestive, so fresh & original, so prodigal of its intellectual capital—There was never a day that I did not feel this powerful stimulus and it seems to me now that I am in danger of mental starvation." But her daughter-in-law had died too, leaving her with an enormous responsibility, a second set of stepchildren to raise, three boys. Never having given birth herself, she didn't expect that she would have to go through the experience of mothering twice. "My life after Agassiz should be gone had always seemed to me very clear & simple,—to gather up the lovely scattered threads of our past, to live on my recollections and to watch over Mother if she outlived him,—that was the quiet end I pictured for myself." How little did she know what was ahead of her, apart from her responsibility for her stepson, Alexander, and his now motherless boys: "A mother never had a more tender affectionate delightful son—If I can do something also to comfort him, and make his life less desolate, I shall think myself very happy." Agassiz's science now was Alex's concern, not hers. "He takes the deepest interest in perfecting and completing his father's scientific objects," which included the museum as well as the new summer school at Penikese.[53]

But Elizabeth Agassiz's writing days, despite her newfound domestic role, weren't yet over. Almost four years after Agassiz's death, she did take it upon herself to compile Agassiz's biography, a move that was not unusual for the literate spouse of a famous writer or artist, though it was perhaps less common for a scientist's wife to undertake such a task.[54]

Louis Agassiz: His Life and Correspondence, published eight years later by Houghton Mifflin, the preferred publisher of both Mr. and Mrs. Agassiz, became Elizabeth's last book, and in a sense it would turn out to be the hardest of them all. She was trying, she told Longfellow in 1877, to let Agassiz's "letters & reminiscences and those of his early friends tell the story as far as they can be made to do so."[55] She already had discovered what the writer of this book has found too — that Agassiz, on paper, did not reveal all that much about himself. Much of what he had accomplished happened in personal interactions with his students, friends, and family. And then there was the question of how much of his science had in fact survived the impact of Darwinism, which almost every self-respecting American academic, including her stepson, Alexander, had embraced in one form or another. Elizabeth Agassiz was no fool. She knew the tide had turned, and not just in natural history. As racial conflicts in the post–Civil War decade were intensifying, race relations simply couldn't be discussed as authoritatively as Agassiz had once hoped; hence her careful editing of Agassiz's letters to Howe. On May 15, 1876, Elizabeth explained to Cecilie Mettenius, the daughter of Agassiz's former brother-in-law, Alexander Braun, that she didn't want her Agassiz book to be too "controversial" and that she was hoping to avoid any claims or assertions that would only awaken counterclaims. "I believe we should not be in haste about this biography; as a general thing I believe biographies are written too soon and have a certain crudeness in consequence."[56] But write she did, though in doing so she was going "through much doubt and perplexity," as she told Longfellow, and kept asking herself whether she was indeed the right person to undertake such a biography, "if indeed it be important to have a biography at all."[57]

In the final version of Elizabeth's biography, not much remained

Elizabeth Cary Agassiz. Gelatin silver print, 1885–1890.

of the graceful, witty, playful stylist of the earlier essays and books. Her *Life and Correspondence* had become a balancing act that she herself astutely defined, right in the first sentence of her preface, in negative terms: "I am aware that this book has neither the fullness of personal narrative, nor the closeness of scientific analysis, which its too comprehensive title might lead the reader to expect." If the book was neither autobiographical nor scientific, what was it then? Elizabeth

Agassiz presented her work not in terms of responding to the demand for more information about her late husband, but as loss prevention: "My chief object was to prevent the dispersion and final loss of scattered papers which had an unquestionable family value."[58] Since her biography became, in fact, a compilation of texts by others (by Agassiz himself, his family, his friends and colleagues), Elizabeth Agassiz found it easy to downplay not only her own involvement in his life but her authorship, too. The index lists her name but once, a reference to that dispassionate sentence about her marriage to Agassiz already mentioned. The Galápagos experience received barely four pages, with special emphasis on the alleged recent geological origin of Albemarle Island—the party line, as it were. Mindful of the genre, Elizabeth reimagined the days they spent there entirely from Agassiz's perspective, even reversing the opinion she had stated at the time; now she claimed that the islands had provided "admirable collecting grounds."[59] Agassiz's science, throughout the book, appears in quotation marks—it is not her story, but *his*. What she had wanted to tell, she explained to William James somewhat cryptically, was a story "of unswerving steadfastness of purpose muted to a rare enthusiasm." But whether the "muted . . . enthusiasm" was Agassiz's or hers (as seems more likely) she left open to interpretation. William James, for one, had liked the book, even if he had grown disenchanted with Agassiz's science,[60] and Elizabeth Agassiz had liked hearing about how much he enjoyed it. When she thanked James for writing her "in the first freshness of your feeling on finishing the book," she suggested that Agassiz's biography, the final joint product of the Agassiz couple, was best read jointly by yet another couple: "I like to think that you & your wife were reading it together."[61] James had been one of Agassiz's most skeptical students, as Elizabeth well knew. But the substance of Agassiz's science was no longer at stake; in its place, she was offering a *reading experience*.

In 1894, Elizabeth Agassiz became the first president of the newly founded Radcliffe College, the higher-education version of her school for girls. Elizabeth had been associated with what was long called the "Annex" since 1879, when a group of women got together at the house of Mr. Arthur Gilman at 5 Phillips Place in Cambridge and plotted how they might get Harvard faculty to teach women students. Mrs.

Agassiz, who had learned to assert herself without being assertive, was ideally suited to represent an institution that, instead of being "founded" in the traditional way, merely continued to grow. As a Radcliffe alumna, Anna Carret Dunlap observed, "The older business men saw that a woman could care for 'higher education' without being a blue stocking." Mrs. Dunlap also remembered that Mrs. Agassiz dropped and scattered all the diplomas at graduation but remained "composed and gracious" despite the lapse. "Someone said at the time that this trait of Mrs. Agassiz was an advantage" to the Annex, where everyone went out of their way, during those early years, not to alienate anyone important at Harvard.[62]

The Annex, chartered as Radcliffe College in 1894, proved a magnet for students not afraid to flaunt their individuality. Gertrude Stein attended from 1893 to 1897, attracting the interest of her teachers (among them William James). Interestingly, one of the subjects she studied at the college presided over by Louis Agassiz's wife was biology, specifically evolution, as Stein recalled in *Everbody's Autobiography*. A fellow student, Leslie W. Hopkinson, decades later still remembered Stein's presence at a meeting of the Philosophy Club at student Sarah Folsom's home: "I can *see* Gertrude Stein sitting monumentally in one corner, her eyes fixed on a spot in the floor in the opposite corner, to which she talked, exclusively—but *very* ably—quite the cleverest person there."[63]

At the beginning of the new century, Elizabeth Agassiz stepped down as president of Radcliffe. But she continued to take an active interest in the world around her. Her mind sharp as ever, she read William James's *Varieties of Religious Experience*, hot off the press in 1902, and found herself intrigued by the comparative material on the eccentricities of religious life he had gathered, and by his eloquent evocation of "that outlying border of our daylight consciousness which we are beginning to call subconscious or subliminal," a region of the mind that she had rarely focused on. She couldn't find *subliminal* in her two-volume dictionary, she told James. Undaunted, she ventured her own criticism of his readings. It is so difficult, she pointed out, to separate that "material" realm from "the personality of the narrator," a shrewd description of the way in which she had managed her own writing, where point of view was everything and whatever seemed dark and inexplicable was soon quenched by yet another occasion to gather for lunch. There was, to be sure, "a something outside of our life here and yet in direct touch with it." Always aware of the existence of that "great secret" and much less confident than her husband that she could definitively name and understand it, she had stayed clear of it, offering her readers shiny surfaces of lucid, cheerfully controlled prose — some of the best science writing for a popular audience in the American tradition.[64]

Before the year ended, she wrote to William James again, this time to thank him for his good wishes on the occasion of her eightieth birthday. Her letter seems like an epilogue to what had been, in retrospect, a happy life — happy because of the many memories she could now summon at will: "What a precious possession friendship is and so enduring." James's lines had unleashed in her a "rush of memories," for she associated him with some of the "most interesting times & events of her life." Did he too remember that afternoon in Brazil when "you & I passed each other on our separate boats, as I floated out of the Igarapé into the sunset glow over the great river and you floated into the hidden water-way into the forest?" A wonderful scene, if ever there was one. When James was rowing past her, he had asked, "Is it real or a dream?" And thus it appeared now to her indeed, a dream, but "of what abiding power & beauty"! The same day, a gift had been dropped into her hands "from the sky," $116,000 (more than $3 million today) for the building of the Elizabeth Cary Agassiz House at Radcliffe College. Life was good. "Good bye, — best wishes for you & yours from one who dearly values your friendship. — Elizabeth C. Agassiz."[65]

Elizabeth Cabot Cary Agassiz died on June 27, 1907, in Arlington, Massachusetts, age eighty-four, at the home of her niece Lisa Felton, after suffering a stroke, as Louis Agassiz had too.[66] She had survived him by a quarter of a century, not a minute of which had she wasted. Almost to the day, she died a month after Louis Agassiz, the prophet of the kind of education she had institutionalized in Radcliffe College, would have turned one hundred.

Epilogue

URING THE GREAT California earthquake of 1906, the stone shelf supporting a marble statue of Louis Agassiz on the second story of the north wall of Stanford University's Zoology building failed, and the statue plunged headfirst into the ground below. And when people came running to see what had happened, there he was: head buried to his shoulders, feet in the air. According to an eyewitness account, they "couldn't help laughing, and one fellow went up and shook hands with him."[1] Among the stories that circulated about Agassiz's graceless fall from a great height was a charitable if cheeky one that attributed the accident to scientific curiosity: when the earthquake occurred, Agassiz, ever the determined geologist, stuck his head underground to find out what was going on; his finger pointed at an imaginary audience as if to say "Hark! Listen!" (No other marble celebrities then represented on the wall were similarly inclined: Gutenberg, Franklin, and Humboldt stayed right where they belonged.) An edgier campus joke, reported by none other than Stanford president David Starr Jordan, one of Agassiz's former pupils, claimed the calamity proved that "Agassiz was great in the abstract but not in the concrete."[2] Miraculously, when the deeply imbedded statue was recovered, it was found that only the nose had shattered. The outstretched hand remained intact.

The dramatic photograph of the marble scientist, head firmly

Agassiz in the ground, 1906. Picture postcard.

lodged in the concrete, became one of the most iconic images associated with the earthquake. Although Mr. Agassiz's statue was eventually restored to its rightful place next to his mentor Humboldt,
any image search for Agassiz on Google will yield this photograph
within the first dozen hits. And this indeed is how he is most often
remembered—a somewhat comical version of Mozart's marble Com-
mendatore, intent on having his revenge, but, with his head stuck
in the ground and his historical nose broken, unable to drag anyone
down with him. My own Agassiz, the one I have tried to portray in
this book, is different: not pitiful but still wrong, a man and scientist
possessed of great personal charisma as well as great personal flaws.
What interests me about the fallen Agassiz—as it did the unnamed
Stanford student—is less his broken nose than the extended finger,
still pointing, still telling others what to do, even as its owner was
lodged upside-down in the ground, his head surrounded by darkness.
"Hark! Listen!"

As early as 1906, though, no one had harked for a while. Shortly
after Agassiz's death, his scientific goals enjoyed a brief revival in the
Agassiz Association, founded by the Massachusetts librarian Harlan Hoge Ballard. It spawned close to a thousand local chapters, or
science clubs, from Lenox, Massachusetts, to Traverse City, Michigan, all the way to Garden Grove, California. In the end, though,

this movement, devoted to introducing young people to nature study and the basics of natural history collecting, had little measurable impact on mainstream science.[3] To be sure, Agassiz's Stanford statue was quickly restored to its former place. But at the time of the earthquake, his specimen-stuffed, incomplete museum, a grand attempt to represent nature as completely as possible, had become a thing of the past. While his son, Alexander, expanded the museum to facilitate research carried out by the experts, he abandoned his father's Humboldtian ambitions, replacing the idea of a great synoptic hall with a sequence of interconnected smaller rooms, filled with representative specimens—luminous details. "When taken together," said Alexander about his selections, "they illustrate the animal kingdom as a whole in its general relations, and in its geographical and palaeontological range and distribution." Where Agassiz had wanted to look widely, his son echoed his picnicking stepmother's comment on Agassiz's investigations in the Galápagos. He emphasized the need to look deeply. Nothing here could be comprehended at a glance. The truth requires a third look. And a fourth. And a fifth.[4]

When Alfred Russel Wallace, whose own work on natural selection had forced Darwin to go public with his theory before he felt quite ready, visited Agassiz's museum in 1886, he found not a complete library of the works of God, as the elder Agassiz had hoped. He saw instead carefully chosen pages from it, a deliberately incomplete record that cried out for visitors to put two and two together and tell the whole story themselves: "The rodents, for example, are illustrated by means of stuffed specimens and skeletons of an agouti, a porcupine, a rabbit, a squirrel, a jerboa . . . the ungulates by a small tapir and a young hippopotamus," and so on. But that was just fine by Wallace. He appreciated the extensive textual commentary Alexander and his staff had provided and lavished praise on the economy of their displays, which were so different from the disorganized heaps of bones and jaws and teeth a visitor would see displayed in British museums.[5] What Alexander Agassiz's museum revealed to Wallace was not nature itself, but an *idea* about it, a narrative—ironically, the one the elder Agassiz had opposed all his life, with all his might—namely, that life on earth is in constant flux, that the more things change, the less they remain the same. Instead of suggesting to visitors that nature itself was present here, needing no further explanation than what a pair of eyes could see, Alex Agassiz's exhibition rooms represented a human intellectual construction, an "abstract," like Darwin's famous book, not the full truth about nature.

And yet, as Louis Agassiz drifts into the sunset of this narrative, it is worth remembering how his struggles, problems, and aspirations are still with us. Yes, we haven't moved beyond his biases and blindnesses as much as we would like to think we have, but that isn't all. In my view, Louis Agassiz was never more interesting than when he argued that science ought to be part of the general fabric of society. Here, we have fallen far short. A 2009 survey conducted by the Pew Research Center and the American Association for the Advancement of Science revealed that only 52 percent of Americans knew how stem cells differ from other kinds of cells and that just 46 percent of those polled were aware that atoms are larger than electrons. On a highly controversial topic such as global warming, the gap between scientists and the public was remarkable: 84 percent of scientists, but just 49 percent of ordinary citizens, thought emissions attributed to human activities are causing global warming.[6] Agassiz's glaciers are melting fast, but half of the American population doesn't know why. Nor do they seem to care too much. But such ignorance doesn't seem to prevent them from weighing in on issues they know little about: "On politicized issues like climate change, embryonic stem cell research, the teaching of evolution, and the safety of vaccines, many Americans not only question scientific expertise but even feel entitled to discard it completely," write Chris Mooney and Sheril Kirshenbaum, authors of *Unscientific America*, a recent study that recommends that scientists spend more time on public outreach and sketches out opportunities for an entirely new relationship between them and the public. In the current stalemate (overspecialized scientists on one side, turning their backs to the bovine masses of passive consumers clutching their television remotes on the other), it's up to the scientists to be creative. Or at least that's how Mooney and Kirshenbaum envision it: "No longer merely a distant voice of authority, the scientist could . . . become an everyday guide and ally, a listener as much as a lecturer. There's no doubt members of the public must become much more knowledgeable about science and its importance. But scientists must also become far more involved with—and knowledgeable about—the public."[7]

But this lovely dream has pitfalls. If the professionals begin to mingle with the amateurs, how does one separate one from the other? Can one hide behind the other and vice versa? Friendship means familiarity. Will scientists begin to feel confident about assessing the needs of ordinary Americans, just as those ordinary Americans feel free to judge the actions of the scientific community? That was the vision Rachel Carson promoted in *Silent Spring* (1962), her hugely successful indictment of a cadre of specialists who had become isolated, with lethal consequences, from the rest of the world.[8] Agassiz's utopian hope, throughout his life, had been to avoid such a split. He firmly believed that, yes, God—any God worth our worship—worked according to something like human intellectual powers and that therefore the only obstacles to our understanding were the ones we imposed on ourselves. Science to Louis Agassiz had always been a grand affair, not a matter of bits and pieces, parts of a whole. At the same time it was a little thing too, as tiny as a moon snail in our hand, as easy as a child's puzzle-game.[9]

Today, we live in a world of ecological and economic limits now, whereas to Louis Agassiz the world had seemed limitless. In his opinion, all lay people, as long as they followed his guidance, could turn themselves into scientists; all amateurs (particularly those who agreed with him) were, he hoped, potential professionals. According to Elizabeth's slightly different view, it was fine, even empowering, to remain an amateur, as long as there was a cooperative scientist nearby to provide information and perspective: an "everyday guide and ally" like her husband. To some extent, that was the principle behind her commitment to the Agassiz School for Young Ladies and Radcliffe College: the ambition to provide an outlet for the female desire for high-quality education that would not seem to threaten the male establishment, though it would profit from it and permanently change it. One important result of her demotion of Agassiz to a bit player in her writings on the *Hassler* expedition was her own promotion to amateur arbiter and judge, giving carte blanche to all those who, like herself, wanted to think and voice their opinions on science but did not conduct actual fieldwork or experiments.[10] Elizabeth Agassiz thus contributed substantially to the emergence of popular science writing, a genre that flourishes despite the fact that mainstream science continues to see itself as a heroic, specialist enterprise.[11]

The history of science is unforgiving: it remembers those who were right and commits to the dustbin those who were wrong. And wrong Agassiz certainly was, dead wrong, about evolution and about race. Nevertheless, his formula for work in science even today continues to seem both noxious and weirdly seductive: Do your science while beholden both to God and the world of facts, and the "connected picture," the truth, will reveal itself, coherently, completely, beautifully.[12]

"SPLENDOUR! IT ALL COHERES!" wrote the poet Ezra Pound, one of Agassiz's great twentieth-century admirers, in his notes to *The Women of Trachis*, a play by Sophocles that he translated in 1954. He was celebrating the heroic Heracles, a man who had spent his life moving from one adventure to the next, taking advantage of everyone and everything around him, but who was now, finally, luminous in death. But when Pound, some years later, was hoping to bring *The Cantos* to a close, his gigantic attempt to, in his own words, "make Cosmos" and to do for poetry what Agassiz had tried to do for science, he found himself pleading only for a "little light"—any light, really—that would lead him, and us, "back to splendour."[13]

Acknowledgments

Louis Agassiz enjoyed nothing more than spending time with his friends. Well, almost nothing. I do suspect that jellyfish, for example, did interest him quite a bit more. But they are hard to keep at the table with you, and so Agassiz, a devotee of good food and wine, settled for human company instead. As I struggled to understand the less appealing sides of Agassiz's character—his impatience, his racial prejudices, his treatment of his first wife—I was often heartened by the frank delight Agassiz took in friendship. Fortunately, during the many years I spent working on his book I was never without friends myself, never without my family, and never without excellent advice. I salute Frank Kearful, my friend for more than two decades, who read many drafts of this book and sustained me when I lost courage; Daniel Weinstock, who knows natural history as well as medicine and helped me rewrite some knotty passages; Scott Russell Sanders, one of my favorite living writers and a fountain of good advice, whose presence can be felt on every page I write; and, especially, my editor at Houghton Mifflin Harcourt, Deanne Urmy, who believed in this book, saved me from numerous errors and missteps, and sharpened my thinking as well as my prose. Her vision is evident on every page of this book. Susanna Brougham was a congenial manuscript editor; she treated this book as if she had written it herself. Lisa Glover efficiently oversaw the production process. I am also grateful to Nicole Angeloro and Ashley Gilliam for much editorial support, and to Gail Cohen for her expert proofreading. Tom Cronin, of the Department of Biological Sciences at the University of Maryland Baltimore County, an internationally known expert on marine invertebrates, corrected my science as well as my grammar. Alan Braddock of Temple University kept my art history honest. Edward McCarthy of Johns Hopkins Medical Institutions explained Agassiz's autopsy records to me. My dear friend Raphael Falco helped me make some tough and much-needed decisions when I thought I was almost done; the final version of this book is immeasurably improved because of my conversations with him. John T. Bethell, with infinite patience and kindness answered numerous questions about the history of Harvard, a subject he knows better than anyone. And nothing of what you have just read would have ever seen the light of day had it not been for Robert Meitus, who stepped in and lifted me up when things looked dark and hopeless. One of the best things that has come out of the decade-long process of my preoccupation with a dead man's life is what happened at the end: the beginning of my friendship with Robert and his wife, the singer Carrie Newcomer.

Among the many friends who have given me advice and support I want to acknowledge Jessica Berman, Lawrence Buell, Jordi Cat, Christopher Corbett, Jonathan Elmer, Sandy Gliboff, Donald Gray, Susan Gubar, Paul Gutjahr, Michael Hamburger, George Hutchinson, and Linda Lear. My deep gratitude also to the endlessly creative Alita Hornick at Indiana University, who always saw to it that I had what I needed for my work, and to Stephen Burt at Harvard University, who obtained a much-needed resource for me from the Schlesinger Library. Jackson Lears and Stephanie Volmer again allowed me to try out some of my ideas in the pages of *Raritan*. In the early stages of my work on this book, Polly Winsor, who created the foundation on which most current work on Agassiz must rest, provided me with articles and references. I would also like to thank my students at Indiana University, graduate and undergraduate, for putting up with my interest in jellyfish, turtles, and autopsy reports when I should have been discussing Emerson or Whitman with them. They have helped me think through the ideas in this book so many times that I am often no longer sure which ones were mine originally. I am particularly indebted to Robert Arbour and Emer Vaughn for their expert research assistance. Two anonymous reviewers read this manuscript in an earlier incarnation and gave excellent advice.

Work on this book was supported by several grants: a full-year faculty fellowship of the National Endowment for the Humanities that gave me more time for my writing than I'd ever had; the Rodney G. Dennis Fellowship in the Study of Manuscripts awarded by Houghton Library; and generous support from the Dedicated Research Initiative Fund (DRIF) of the University of Maryland Baltimore County, which allowed me to hire two excellent research assistants, Asynith Palmer and Ilse Schweitzer, who have since become wonderful scholars in their own right. A grant-in-aid from the Folger Shakespeare Library in Washington, D.C., allowed me to attend a highly productive seminar on "Writing Scientific Biography," directed by Steven Shapin. I was more than fortunate to be able to complete my work in the perfect setting of Indiana University's Lilly Library, with daily access to the most knowledgeable library staff I know: Rebecca Cape, David Frasier, Breon Mitchell, Joel Silver, Gabriel Swift, and Cherry Williams, among others. I challenge everyone who doesn't believe me when I say that this is the single best place in the world for the study of rare books and manuscripts to spend a day in the Lilly's Reading Room.

Librarians and curators at other institutions have facilitated my research and answered multiple inquiries (some of them quite annoying, I'm sure). Among many others I want to single out Dana Fisher at the Museum of Comparative Zoology in Cambridge, who readily provided me with images, sources, and other assistance; Leslie Morris and Peter Accardo of Harvard's Houghton Library, who responded to numerous pleas for help; Lisa DiCesare of the Arnold Arboretum at Harvard; Jack Eckert of the Countway Library of Medicine at Harvard; as well as Malcolm Beasley and Andrea Hart on the staff of the Museum of Natural History in London. Diana Carey at the Schlesinger Library for the History of Women in America and Robin G. McElheny at the Harvard University Archives provided generous assistance at the eleventh hour. Two brilliant photographers, Tim Ford of the Department of Biological Sciences at the University of Maryland Baltimore County and Zach Downey of the Lilly Library, prepared the majority of the images in this book.

I truly could not have written these pages without the people closest to me: the ageless Daniel Aaron, who knows me better than anyone else and has been my mentor and teacher for longer than I can remember; Lauren Bernofsky, my wife and loveliest critic, who cheered me on when I most needed it; our beautiful, wonderful children Nick and Julia; my beloved mother Elisabeth; and Jeremy, my old Maine Coon cat, who constantly reminds me of something Agassiz knew too, though his theology forced him occasionally to suppress that knowledge: that the boundaries between human and nonhuman animals are fleeting at best.

Finally, I do want to commemorate those who are no longer here to see this book finished: my beloved great-aunt Elisabeth Mueller, who many years ago instilled in me the love of travel, languages, and rare books; Janice Thaddeus, whose voice I still hear every time I start a new semester; Tom Ford, a gentle soul if ever there was one, whom illness prevented from finishing his own book; and, of course, my dear father, Hans Dietrich Irmscher, whose death two years ago tore a hole in my heart and my life that no one and nothing can ever fill. Like my previous books and like anything I will do hereafter, this one is for him too.

Chronology

1807 May 28: Jean Louis Rodolphe Agassiz born in Môtier, Switzerland, to Jean Louis Rodolphe Benjamin Agassiz, a Protestant minister, and his wife, Rose Mayor Agassiz.

1809 July 29: Cecilie Braun born in Karlsruhe, Germany.

1817 Attends grade school at the Collège de Bienne.

1822–24 Continues studies at Academy of Lausanne. Reads Lamarck and Cuvier.

1822 December 5: Elizabeth Cabot Cary born in Boston.

1824 Begins, at insistence of family, study of medicine at the University of Zurich but takes classes in natural history.

1826 Transfers to Heidelberg University. Studies with Friedrich Tiedemann (comparative anatomy) and Rudolf Leuckart (zoology).

1827 Begins study of medicine and natural history at the University of Munich. Studies with the explorer of Brazil, Carl Friedrich Philipp von Martius.

1829 Receives degree of doctor of philosophy. Publishes first part of first book, about Brazilian fish, *Selecta genera et species piscium . . .* , dedicated to Georges Cuvier.

1830 Receives degree of doctor of medicine and surgery.

1831 December 16: Goes to Paris to study fossil fish with Georges Cuvier.

1832 Begins friendship with Alexander von Humboldt. Accepts professorship at preparatory school in Neuchâtel.

1833 October 26: Marries Cecilie Braun. Begins publication of *Recherches sur les poissons fossiles*.

1835 December 17: Birth of son, Alexander (Alex).

1837 August 8: Birth of daughter, Ida. December 6: Death of father, Rodolphe.

1840 Sets up scientific field station ("Hôtel des Neuchâtelois") on the Lower Aar Glacier; *Études sur les glaciers*.

1841 February 8: Birth of daughter, Pauline.

1845 Cecilie Agassiz and daughters leave Agassiz; Alex follows a year later.

1846 October 3: Arrives in the United States and gives the Lowell Lectures in Boston's Tremont Temple.

1847 Moves, with assistants, into house on Webster Street in East Boston. September: Accepts professorship at Lawrence Scientific School at Harvard University.

1848 June 15: Undertakes expedition to Lake Superior. July 27: Cecilie Agassiz dies from tuberculosis in Freiburg, Germany.

1850 March: Argues at the meeting of the American Association for the Advancement of Science that different races of humans are "zoologically distinct." April 5: Marries Elizabeth Cabot Cary. Publication of *Lake Superior*.

1855 September 26: Elizabeth Agassiz opens the Agassiz School for Young Ladies.

1857 Publishes *Essay on Classification* as the first volume of *Contributions to the Natural History of the United States of America*.

1859 Begins building Museum of Comparative Zoology at Harvard University. Darwin sends a copy of *On the Origin of Species*. May 6: Alexander von Humboldt dies in Berlin.

1860 Harvard botanist Asa Gray begins open attacks on Agassiz's anti-evolutionary science.

1862 Publishes fourth and final volume of *Contributions*.

1863 March 20: Has altercation with favorite student Henry James Clark, which leads to permanent rift. Later that year, mass exodus of student assistants. August: Corresponds with Samuel Gridley Howe regarding the freedmen. November: Publishes *Methods of Study in Natural History*.

1865 April 1: Leaves for Brazil on Thayer expedition (with William James as volunteer).

1866 August 6: Returns from Thayer expedition. Publishes *Geological Sketches: First Series.*

1867 September 11: Death of mother, Rose Mayor Agassiz.

1868 Publishes *Journey in Brazil* with Elizabeth Agassiz.

1869 Spring: Does deep-sea dredging off the coast of Florida and Cuba on the U.S. Coast Survey steamer U.S.S. *Bibb.* September 14: Delivers the Humboldt Centennial Lecture in Boston. Suffers cerebral hemorrhage immediately after.

1870 Recuperates in Deerfield, Massachusetts. Returns to museum in November.

1871 December 4: Leaves Boston on the *Hassler* for deep-sea dredging expedition along the coast of South America and through the Straits of Magellan.

1872 June: Visits the Galápagos Islands. August 31: Returns to San Francisco.

1873 July 8: Opens Anderson Summer School of Natural History on Penikese Island. December 14: Dies in his house on Quincy Street, Cambridge, from the results of a stroke. December 18: Buried in Mount Auburn Cemetery, Cambridge.

1874 January: "Evolution and Permanence of Type" posthumously published in *Atlantic Monthly.*

1885 Elizabeth Agassiz publishes *Louis Agassiz: His Life and Correspondence.*

1894 Elizabeth Agassiz named first president of Radcliffe College.

1907 June 27: Elizabeth Agassiz dies in Arlington, Massachusetts.

Abbreviations and Notes

AG Asa Gray
AP Louis Agassiz, Correspondence and Other Papers, Houghton Library, Harvard University
CD Charles Darwin
Contributions Louis Agassiz, *Contributions to the Natural History of the United States of America*, 4 vols. (Boston: Little, Brown, 1857–1862)
DCP Darwin Correspondence Project: http://www.darwinproject.ac.uk/home
EAP Elizabeth Cary Agassiz Papers, 1838–1920, Schlesinger Library, Radcliffe Institute, Harvard University
ECA Elizabeth Cary Agassiz
FLA Fonds Louis Agassiz, Archives de l'État de Neuchâtel, Switzerland
HJC Henry James Clark
HL Houghton Library, Harvard
Journey Louis and Elizabeth Agassiz, *Journey in Brazil*, 6th ed. (Boston: Ticknor and Fields, 1869)
LA Louis Agassiz
Life Elizabeth Cary Agassiz, *Louis Agassiz: His Life and Correspondence*, 2 vols., 3rd ed. (1885; Boston: Houghton Mifflin, 1886)
Marcou Jules Marcou, *The Life, Letters, and Works of Louis Agassiz*, 2 vols. (New York: Macmillan, 1896)
MCZ Museum of Comparative Zoology, Harvard University, Cambridge, MA
Origin Charles Darwin, *On the Origin of Species: A Facsimile of the First Edition* (1859; Cambridge, MA: Harvard University Press, 1964)
SL Schlesinger Library on the History of Women, Radcliffe Institute, Harvard University

All translations are my own unless otherwise noted. Quotations from unpublished sources generally follow the original text. I have not altered spelling, punctuation, or capitalization, except where the sense was affected, and I present only the final wording as intended by the author of each source.

INTRODUCTION

1   Edward Waldo Emerson, *The Early Years of the Saturday Club, 1855–1870* (Boston: Houghton Mifflin, 1918), 417. The consul, the Reverend R.W.G. Mellen, had in fact just resigned his position; his arrival in the States and return to his former pulpit at the Independent Christian Church in Gloucester, MA, are reported by the *Salem Register,* 4 October 1866. Agassiz's curator of birds, Joel Asaph Allen, does indeed record the acquisition of a dodo skeleton in his report for the year 1868, and it seems that Mr. Mellen got himself some money for at least one of his birds: "1 dodo, from Mauritius, (through Mr. Mellers [sic], U.S. Consul at Mauritius," notes Allen in a list of items acquired "by purchase." *Annual Report of the Trustees of the Museum of Comparative Zoology, at Harvard College, in Cambridge, Together with the Report of the Director, 1868* (Boston: Wright and Potter, 1869), 26. The dodo skeleton on display in the museum today (MCZ#340825) cannot be linked to Agassiz. Personal communication, Dana Fisher, Ernst Mayr Library, Museum of Comparative Zoology, 15 February 2012.

2   Oliver Wendell Holmes, "At the Saturday Club," in *The Poetical Works of Oliver Wendell Holmes,* vol. 2 (Cambridge, MA: Houghton, Mifflin, 1892), 267.

3   *James T. Fields: Biographical Notes and Personal Sketches, with Unpublished Fragments and Tributes from Men and Women of Letters,* edited by Annie Fields (Boston: Houghton Mifflin, 1881), 212.

4   James Russell Lowell, "Agassiz," in *The Complete Poems of James Russell Lowell: Cabinet Edition* (Cambridge: Houghton Mifflin, 1899), 501–11; see 510.

5   David C. Smith and Harold W. Borns Jr., "Louis Agassiz, the Great Deluge, and Early Maine Geology." *Northeastern Naturalist* 7, no. 2 (2000): 157–77, 167.

6   Elizabeth Higgins Gladfelter, *Agassiz's Legacy: Scientists' Reflections on the Value of Field Experience* (New York: Oxford University Press, 2002).

7   The phrase is actually Walt Whitman's, but it characterizes the white anxiety about race in America that Agassiz helped to epitomize. See Daniel Aaron, *The Unwritten War: American Writers and the Civil War* (New York: Knopf, 1973), 60–61. Whitman's remark is quoted in chapter 6.

8   See Lauren R. Dorgan, "Committee Renames Local Agassiz School," *Harvard Crimson,* 22 May 2002; "Darwin the Abolitionist," *Living on Earth,* 6 February 2009. For a transcript of the show, see http://www.livingonearth.org/shows/segments.htm?programID=09-P13-00006&segmentID=4.

9   *Louis Menand, The Metaphysical Club: A Story of Ideas in America* (New York: Farrar, Straus and Giroux, 2001), 141.

10   Adrian Desmond and James Moore, *Darwin's Sacred Cause: How a Hatred of Slavery Shaped Darwin's View on Human Evolution* (Boston: Houghton Mifflin Harcourt, 2009).

11 George Levine, *Darwin Loves You: Natural Selection and the Re-Enchantment of the World* (Princeton, NJ: Princeton University Press, 2006).

12 Lurie's *Louis Agassiz: A Life in Science* (Chicago: University of Chicago Press, 1960) was reprinted in 1988 by Johns Hopkins University Press. A successful fictionalized retelling of Agassiz's life comes from the pen of the historian of science Marc-Antoine Kaeser, who has also written a biography of Agassiz's former assistant and later enemy Édouard Desor: see Kaeser, *Un savant séducteur: Louis Agassiz (1807–1873), prophète de la science* (Lausanne: Les Éditions de l'Aire, 2007). Kaeser's account is the latest and most self-consciously ambivalent of the many fictional portraits of LA, which also include a number of adoring biographies for young adults: Mabel L. Robinson, *Runner of the Mountain Tops: The Life of Louis Agassiz* (New York: Random, 1939), winner of a Newbery Honor designation; Catherine Owens Peare, *A Scientist of Two Worlds: Louis Agassiz* (Philadelphia: J. B. Lippincott, 1958); Aylesa Forsee, *Louis Agassiz: Pied Piper of Science* (New York: Viking, 1958); Louise Hall Tharp, *Louis Agassiz: Adventurous Scientist* (Boston: Little, Brown, 1961).

I. AGASSIZ AT REST

1 The *Boston Daily Advertiser* of December 6, 1873, reported "cloudiness, and continued low temperatures."

2 Henry James, *The Bostonians* (1886; New York: New American Library, 1980), 197.

3 Ralph Waldo Emerson, "An Address to the Senior Class in Divinity College, Cambridge, 15 July 1838," in *Essays and Lectures*, edited by Joel Porte (New York: Library of America, 1983), 89.

4 See "Zoological Hall: Occupants 1867–'73," the map drawn by LA's draftsman-assistant James Henry Blake, now kept in the archives of the Ernst Mayr Library, MCZ; reproduced as figure 5 in Mary P. Winsor, *Reading the Shape of Nature: Comparative Zoology at the Agassiz Museum* (Chicago: University of Chicago Press, 1991), 32.

5 *Annual Report of the Trustees of the Museum of Comparative Zoology, at Harvard College in Cambridge: Together with the Report of the Director for 1871* (Boston: Wright and Potter, 1872), 11.

6 Marcou, vol. 2, 219.

7 William Dean Howells, *Literary Friends and Acquaintance: A Personal Retrospect of American Authorship*, edited by David F. Hiatt and Edwin H. Cady (1900; Bloomington: Indiana University Press, 1968), 227.

8 Unattributed fragment, preceded by a quotation from Psalm 85:11: "Truth shall spring out of the earth: and righteousness shall look down from heaven." EAP, SL, A-3/33.

9 Ernst Haeckel, *Ziele und Wege der heutigen Entwickelungsgeschichte* (Jena: Hermann Dufft, 1875): "Louis Agassiz war der genialste und thätigste Industrieritter auf dem Gesammtgebiete der Naturwissenschaft" (80). Karl Marx, in "Der Achtzehnte Brumaire des Louis Bonaparte" (1852), uses the term *Industrieritter* for the swindlers who have hijacked the French nation into a system of monarchical oppression.

10 Theodore Lyman, "Recollections of Agassiz," *Atlantic Monthly*, vol. 33, no. 196 (February 1874): 221–29; see 226 and 227–28.

11 Oliver Wendell Holmes to LA, 20 October 1863, AP, HL, MS Am 1419 (406). See also Holmes, *Ralph Waldo Emerson* (1898; New York: Chelsea, 1980), 172.

12 See A. Fields, *James T. Fields*, 87.

13 LA to Baird, 10 October 1873; Baird to LA, 25 November 1873, in *Correspondence Between Spencer Fullerton Baird and Louis Agassiz: Two Pioneer American Naturalists*, edited by Elmer Charles Herber (Washington, DC: Smithsonian, 1963), 224–25, 228.

14 "Professor Agassiz," *Boston Advertiser*, vol. 122, no. 142 (12 December 1873).

15 Longfellow to Charles Sumner, 1 February 1871, *The Letters of Henry Wadsworth Longfellow*, edited by Andrew Hilen, 6 vols. (Cambridge, MA: Belknap, 1966–1982), vol. 5, 396.

16 Charles William Eliot, "Personal Recollections of Dr. Morrill Wyman, Professor Dunbar, Professor Sophocles, and Professor Shaler," in *Cambridge Historical Society Publications, VII: Proceedings for the Year 1917* (Cambridge, MA: The Society, 1925), 25–45. See also T.E.C., "Dr. Morrill Wyman's Treatment of the Oldest Son of President Eliot of Harvard About 1870," *Pediatrics*, vol. 66, no. 1 (July 1980): 4.

17 "Professor Agassiz: No Amelioration in His Condition. Paralysis of the Throat Prevents Swallowing," *New York Times*, 13 December 1873.

18 Agassiz once told Longfellow that he was "so loveable [*sic*] that I should like to have you all to myself"; see Henry Wadsworth Longfellow, 18 August 1871, Longfellow Papers, HL, bMS Am 1340.2 (45). I discuss the relationship between Longfellow and Agassiz in more detail in *Public Poet, Private Man: Henry Wadsworth Longfellow at 200* (Amherst: University of Massachusetts Press, 2009), 88–97.

19 Henry Wadsworth Longfellow to George Washington Greene, 13 December 1873, in *The Letters of Henry Wadsworth Longfellow*, vol. 5, 698.

20 "Prof. Agassiz: His Condition Extremely Dangerous, but Not Hopeless," *New York Times*, 12 December 1873.

21 A. Fields, *James T. Fields*, 122.

22 LA to Nathaniel Southgate Shaler, 8 June 1870, in LA, Letters to N. S. Shaler, MCZ 024.

23 The photograph is likely from one of the "classbooks" assembled for Harvard undergraduates at their specific request. A pencil signature indicates that the former owner was John Codman Ropes, (Harvard) A.S. 1857, LL.B. 1861, LL.D. 1897 and an overseer of Harvard in 1868. Whipple made his first class album in 1852 and continued to produce them till 1860. Communication from Daniel Weinstock, M.D., Geneva, NY, 6 November 2010. See also Sally Pierce, *Whipple and Black: Commercial Photographers in Boston* (Boston: The Boston Athenaeum, 1987), 24.

24 My dating of this photograph is approximate. Cartes de visite became fashionable around 1859. The stamp verso identifies the photographer as "John Adams Whipple, 96 Washington Street"; by July 1, 1865, Whipple had moved to 296 Washington Street. See Pierce, *Whipple and Black*, 28, 32.

25 Marcou, vol. 2, 50.

26 Louise Hall Tharp, *The Appletons of Beacon Hill* (Boston: Little, Brown, 1973), 328.

27 Fanny Appleton Longfellow to Emmeline Austin Wadsworth, 15 May 1860, in *Mrs. Longfellow: Selected Letters and Journals of Fanny Appleton Longfellow (1817–1861)*, edited by Edward Wagenknecht (New York: Longmans, Green, and Co., 1956), 221.

28 Ralph Waldo Emerson, journal entry, November 1852, in *Emerson in His Journals*, edited by Joel Porte (Cambridge, MA: Belknap Press, 1982), 441.

29 *Letters of Longfellow*, vol. 4, 239.

30 Janet Browne, "I Could Have Retched All Night: Charles Darwin and His Body," in *Science Incarnate: Historical Embodiments of Natural Knowledge*, edited by Christopher Lawrence and Steven Shapin (Chicago: University of Chicago Press, 1998), 240–87.

31 LA to Baird, 10 April 1847 and 26 April 1847, in Herber, *Spencer Fullerton Baird and Louis Agassiz*, 24, 25.

32 LA to James Dwight Dana, 8 July 1853; LA, draft of letter to Abbott Lawrence, 20 May 1854; LA to Dana, 4 October 1859; LA to Harriott Pinckney Rutledge Holbrook, 30 January 1855; all in AP, HL, MS Am 1419 (122), (125), (141), (128).

33 LA to Baird, 30 July 1854, 1 November 1858 (?), and 12 April 1860, in Herber, *Spencer Fullerton Baird and Louis Agassiz*, 76, 145, 155.

34 Baird to Agassiz, 8 April 1873 and LA to Baird, 13 April 1873, ibid., 214–16.

35 A. Fields, *James T. Fields*, 177.

36 Addison Emery Verrill, entry for June 1859, Private Journal of A. E. Verrill for 1859, Harvard University Archives, HUD 859.90. For more on Verrill, see chapter 5.

37 ECA to Baird, 31 December 1851, in Herber, *Spencer Fullerton Baird and Louis Agassiz*, 49–50.

38 ECA to Mary Perkins Cary, 11 March 1853, EAP, SL, A-3/10 (the transcript of the letter in the collection is misdated). Elizabeth Cary Agassiz was thinking of Charles Dickens's novel *The Haunted Man and the Ghost's Bargain*, published in 1848, in which Professor Redlaw, a chemist, loses all recollection of painful incidents in his past. Surprisingly, this doesn't make him a happier man. He turns bitter and angry instead; in giving up his "memory of sorrow, wrong, and trouble," he has also "lost all, man would remember." See Charles Dickens, *The Haunted Man and the Ghost's Bargain* (London: Bradbury and Evans, 1848), 172.

39 *The Complete Writings of Henry Wadsworth Longfellow*, Craigie edition, 11 vols. (Boston: Houghton Mifflin, 1904), vol. 6, 147, 427. The death scene, later discarded, was written just a few months after LA's death, on March 3, 1874.

40 LA to Rose Mayor Agassiz, 22 March 1865, AP, HL, MS Am 1419 (156).

41 Whittier, "The Prayer of Agassiz" (1874), in *The Complete Works of John Greenleaf Whittier: Household Edition* (Boston: Houghton, Mifflin, 1904), 552. The best description of the Penikese venture comes from David Starr Jordan, who was one of the participants: "Agassiz at Penikese," *Popular Science Monthly*, vol. 40 (1898): 721–29. A list of enrolled students appears in

Burt G. Wilder, "Agassiz at Penikese," *American Naturalist*, vol. 32, no. 375 (March 1898): 189–96.

42 LA to Leo Lesquereux, 28 October 1873, AP, HL, MS Am 1419 (177).

43 LA to Longfellow, December 1873, Longfellow Papers, HL, bMS Am 1340.2 (45).

44 *Origin*, 1.

45 LA, "Evolution and Permanence of Type," *Atlantic Monthly*, vol. 33, no. 195 (1874): 92–101.

46 Marcel Proust, *Remembrance of Things Past*, translated by C. K. Scott Moncrieff, 2 vols. (New York: Random House, 1934), vol. 1, 941.

47 Lyman, "Recollections of Agassiz," 227.

48 *Life*, vol. 2, 782–83.

49 Pauline Agassiz Shaw to Henry Wadsworth Longfellow, 14 December 1873, Letters to Henry Wadsworth Longfellow, HL, MS Am 13402 (5027).

50 "The Late Prof. Agassiz: The Last Hours of the Great Naturalist," *New York Times*, 16 December 1873.

51 Longfellow, *Letters*, vol. 5, 99.

52 Marcou, vol. 2, 215.

53 Janet Browne, *Charles Darwin: The Power of Place* (Princeton, NJ: Princeton University Press, 2002), 495.

54 Marcou, vol. 2, 215n1. The (disputed) final sentence uttered by Rabelais is alleged to have been the following: "Tirez le rideau, la farce est jouée." Lower the curtain; the farce is over.

55 Or so his associate and (unreliable) biographer Anton Schindler reports. What Beethoven did or didn't say before his death was also hotly contested; see Alexander Wheelock Thayer, *Ludwig van Beethoven*, 3 vols., edited by Henry Edward Krehbiel (New York: Beethoven Association, 1921), vol. 3, 303–5.

56 ECA to Henry Cary, 10 February 1896, EAP, A-3, folder 32.

57 Morrill Wyman to ECA, 12 February 1896, EAP, A-3, folder 32.

58 Herman Melville, *Moby-Dick; or, The Whale* (1851; New York: Modern Library, 1992), 8.

59 *Contributions*, vol. 1, 88. Agassiz's *Essay on Classification* appeared in the first volume of *Contributions* as well as separately (London: Longman, Brown, Green, Longmans and Roberts, 1859).

60 Alexander Agassiz to Sir John Murray, March 1875, in Murray, "Alexander Agassiz: His Life and Scientific Work," *Bulletin of the Museum of Comparative Zoology*, vol. 54, no. 3 (1911): 139–58, see 146.

61 See Horace, *Carmina*, 1:34. Longfellow, Journal, 1 March 1847–31 December 1848, entry for 11 June 1848, Longfellow Papers, HL, MS Am 1340 (201).

62 LA to Eben N. Horsford, 8 May 1848, Horsford Family Papers, Institute Archives and Special Collections, Rensselaer Polytechnic Institute, MC # 05.

63 Tayler Lewis, professor of Greek at Union College, argued for a complete harmony between the scriptural record and geology; see *The Six Days of Creation; Or, The Scriptural Cosmology, with The Ancient Idea of Time-Worlds*,

in Distinction from Worlds in Space (Schenectady, NY: Van Debogert, 1855).

64 LA to James Dwight Dana, 18 July 1856, AP, HL, MS Am 1419 (123). Dana's "Science and the Bible: A Review of 'The Six Days of Creation of Prof. Tayler Lewis,'" first appeared in the January 1856 issue of *Bibliotheca Sacra* and was published separately later that year by Warren F. Draper in Andover, MA.

65 "Agassiz: Obsequies of the Naturalist," *New York Times*, 19 December 1873.

66 "The Death of Prof. Agassiz," *New York Tribune*, 17 December 1873.

67 Robert D. Lyons, *A Handbook of Hospital Practice* (New York: 1860), cited in Michael Sappol, *A Traffic of Dead Bodies: Anatomy and Embodied Social Identity in Nineteenth-Century America* (Princeton, NJ: Princeton University Press, 2002), 319.

68 See personal communications from Jack Eckert, public services librarian, Francis A. Countway Library of Medicine, 24 August 2010; Jeff Mifflin, archivist, Massachusetts General Hospital, 25 August 2010; and David M. Louis, pathologist-in-chief, Massachusetts General Hospital, 30 August 2010. According to Jack Eckert, "There are very few Harvard Medical School records extant from the nineteenth century (probably the result of a number of moves before relocation to its current site in 1906) and certainly no autopsies" (personal communication, 10 November 2010).

69 See George Prochnik, *Putnam Camp: Sigmund Freud, James Jackson Putnam, and the Purpose of American Psychology* (New York: The Other Press, 2006).

70 John E. Loveland, "Reginald Heber Fitz, the Exponent of Appendicitis," *Yale Journal of Biology and Medicine*, vol. 9, no. 6 (July 1937): 509–20.

71 Cited in Burt G. Wilder, "Jeffries Wyman," in *Leading American Men of Science*, edited by David Starr Jordan (New York: Henry Holt and Company, 1910), 171–209; 194.

72 See Asa Gray's address delivered to the Boston Natural History Society on 7 October 1874, "Jeffries Wyman," in *Scientific Papers of Asa Gray*, edited by Charles Sprague Sargent, 2 vols. (Boston: Houghton Mifflin, 1889), vol. 2, 385.

73 See *Dear Jeffie: Being the Letters from Jeffries Wyman, First Director of the Peabody Museum, to His Son, Jeffries Wyman, Jr.*, edited by George E. Gifford Jr. (Cambridge, MA: Peabody Museum Press, 1978), especially 36.

74 See Stephen Jay Gould on the French craniometrist Paul Broca (1824–1880), in *The Mismeasure of Man* (1981; New York: Norton, 1993), 99.

75 The autopsy report had first appeared in the *New York Tribune*, 16 December 1873, and was reprinted, either in full or in excerpts, numerous times; see "The Brain of Agassiz," *Medical and Surgical Reporter*, vol. 30, no. 6 (7 February 1874): 131; "The Autopsy of Professor Agassiz," *Scientific American*, vol. 30, no. 17 (14 February 1874): 96; "Autopsy of Agassiz," *Popular Science Monthly* (March 1874): 633–34.

76 I owe my reading of the autopsy reports to Edward McCarthy, professor of pathology, Johns Hopkins Medical Institutions (personal communication, 2 June 2008), and the internist Daniel Weinstock, M.D., Geneva, NY (multiple communications, November 2010). Autopsy findings should always be

evaluated in the light of a patient's medical history, which, in Agassiz's case, is, of course, conjectural, though some of his habits (lack of rest, fondness for good food and drink, and the cigar smoking) would be among the typical risk factors.

77 See Sappol, *A Traffic in Dead Bodies*, 2.

78 "Avoirdupois" refers to a system of weights based on the pound, which contains sixteen ounces.

79 See, for example, "Items of Interest," *Saturday Evening Post* (21 February 1874), 7. Morrill Wyman first reported these measurements in a letter to Putnam, 19 December 1873, in which he also argued that, given the likely "decrease in the weight of the brain from the age of 35 or 40 years, at the rate of one avoirdupois ounce for each ten years elapsed," the weight of Agassiz's brain "at its greatest weight" had been 56.5 ounces avoirdupois (Morrill Wyman to J. J. Putnam, 19 December 1873, Countway Library of Medicine, Harvard University). However, Wilder ("Jeffries Wyman") claims that the published figure was slightly exaggerated and that 52.7 was closer to the truth (197).

80 Morris Longstreth to J. J. Putnam, 29 January 1874, Countway Library of Medicine, Harvard University. Longstreth (1846–1914), Harvard class of 1866, was appointed pathologist to the Pennsylvania Hospital in 1870 and later became its first chairman of pathology.

81 Josiah C. Nott and George R. Gliddon, *Types of Mankind; or, Ethnological Researches, Based Upon the Ancient Monuments, Paintings, Sculptures, and Crania of Races, and Upon Their Natural, Geographical, Philological, and Biblical History: Illustrated by Selections from the Inedited Papers of Samuel George Morton, M.D.*, 2nd ed. (Philadelphia: J. B. Lippincott, Grambo, and Co., 1854), 299n.

82 See Friedrich Tiedemann's remarkable book *Das Hirn des Negers mit dem des Europäers und Orang-Outangs verglichen* (Heidelberg: Winter 1837), 18, 63–64; Edward Anthony Spitzka, "A Study of the Brains of Six Eminent Scientists Belonging to the American Anthropometric Society, Together with a Description of the Skull of Professor E. D. Cope," *Transactions of the American Philosophical Society*, New Series, vol. 21, no. 4 (1907): 175–308.

83 Thomas Hill, *The Life Is More than Meat. Sermon Preached in 1st Parish Church, Portland, Me., 21 December 1873* (Portland: Stephen Berry, 1874).

84 Henry Ward Beecher, "Agassiz," *Christian Union* (24 December 1873): 8, 26.

85 "The Will of Prof. Agassiz," *New York Times*, 10 January 1874.

86 *Life*, vol. 1, v–vi; Marcou, vol. 2, 216.

87 ECA to Longfellow, 12 April 1876, Longfellow Papers, HL, MS Am 1340.2 (44).

88 See, for example, Charles Lyell, *Principles of Geology, Being an Attempt to Explain the Former Changes of the Earth's Surface, by Reference to Causes Now in Operation*, vol. 1 (London: John Murray, 1830), 299–300, and vol. 3 (London: John Murray, 1833) 149–50.

89 CD, *Journal of Researches into the Geology and Natural History of the Various Countries Visited by the H.M.S. Beagle, Under the Command of Captain Fitz-Roy, R.N., from 1832–36* (London: Colburn, 1839), 616–21.

90 LA, *Geological Sketches: Second Series* (1876; Boston: Houghton Mifflin, 1887), 102.

91 A. Fields, *James T. Fields*, 119–20.

2. THE ICE KING

1 Louis Rodolphe Agassiz to LA, 25 March 1828, AP, HL, MS Am 1419 (179).

2 Louis Rodolphe Agassiz to LA, 16 November 1830, AP, HL, MS Am 1419 (182).

3 Louis Rodolphe Agassiz to LA, 25 March 1828 (see note 1).

4 Louis Rodolphe Agassiz to LA, 31 August 1829, AP, HL, MS Am 1419 (181).

5 LA to Cécile Agassiz, 28 October 1828, AP, HL, MS Am 1416 (27).

6 LA to Cécile Agassiz, 20 November 1828, AP, HL, MS Am 1419 (20).

7 M. H. Sabaj and C. J. Ferraris Jr., "Doradidae (Thorny catfishes)," in *Checklist of the Freshwater Fishes of South and Central America*, edited by R. E. Reis, S. O. Kullander, and C. J. Ferraris Jr. (Porto Alegre, Brazil: EDIPUCRS, 2004), 456–69.

8 *Selecta genera et species piscium: Quos in itinere per Brasiliam annis MDCCCX-VII–MDCCCXX jussu et auspiciis Maximiliani Josephi I. Bavariae Regis augustissimi peracto collegit et pingendos curavit Dr. J. B. de Spix . . . digessit descripsit et observationibus anatomicis illustravit Dr. L. Agassiz, praefatus est et edidit itineris socius, F. C. Ph. de Martius* (Munich: C. Wolff, 1829–31), 14–15.

9 *Voyage de Humboldt et Bonpland. Recueil d'observations de zoologie et d'anatomie comparée faites dans l'Océan Atlantique, dans l'intérieur du nouveau continent et dans la mer du sud pendant les années 1799–1803, 2ème Partie Zoologie*, 2 vols. (Paris: Schoell, 1805–1809), vol. 2, 184. Agassiz did encounter *Doras humboldti* when he traveled to Brazil in 1865, but even then "not in the flesh": the note in *Journey in Brazil* refers only to the fish's skeleton (see *Journey*, 274n).

10 See Jürgen Hamel and Klaus-Harro Tiemann, "Vorwort," in *Alexander von Humboldt über das Universum: Die Kosmosvorträge 1827/28 in der Berliner Singakademie*, edited by Jürgen Hamel and Klaus-Harro Tiemann (Frankfurt am Main, 1993), 11–36; 11.

11 LA to Louis Rodolphe and Rose Mayor Agassiz, 14 February 1829, AP, HL, MS Am 1419 (31).

12 Louis Rodolphe Agassiz to LA, 23 February 1829, AP, HL, MS Am 1419 (180).

13 LA, *Address Delivered on the Centennial Anniversary of the Birth of Alexander von Humboldt Under the Auspices of the Boston Natural History Society, with an Account of the Evening Reception* (Boston: Boston Natural History Society, 1869), 35–36.

14 Louis Rodolphe Agassiz to LA, 16 November 1830 (n. 2).

15 See William Coleman, *Biology in the Nineteenth Century: Problems of Form, Function, and Transformation* (1971; Cambridge, UK: Cambridge University Press, 1977), 1.

16 LA, *Address Delivered on the Centennial*, 45–46.

17 While the literature refers to the Académie de Neuchâtel as a "college," Agassiz was in fact teaching at a *Gymnasium* or *lycée*, a school reserved for the upper grades, which means that his older pupils were probably around the same age as the Harvard undergraduates he encountered later. That this was a less than ideal appointment for a scientist of Agassiz's potential must have been as evident to him as it was clear to his colleagues. In a letter dated December 4, 1832, Agassiz's former professor, the distinguished Heidelberg anatomist Friedrich Tiedemann, encourages Agassiz to consider an appointment in Heidelberg and advises him not to commit to teaching at a "Lyceum or Gymnasium," which was, he said, not a suitable place for a scientist of Agassiz's sophistication to build a career. Tiedemann to LA, 8 December 1832, AP, HL, MS Am 1419 (681).

18 Marcou, vol. 1, 57.

19 Cecilie's long-lost portfolio contains about a hundred drawings and two exercise books with perspective drawings. See Cecilie ("Cécile") Braun, Portfolio of Pencil Drawings, &c / by J. L. R. Agassiz's first wife, Cécile Braun. fol. BOTANY LIBRARY DRAWINGS BRA. National Museum of Natural History, London. Some of the sketches carry notes in the handwriting of Cecilie's daughter Ida, which suggests that she might have collected them, though the circumstances under which they ended up in London remain unclear. On Cecilie Braun Agassiz as an artist, see Cecilie Mettenius, *Alexander Braun's Leben nach seinem handschriftlichen Nachlass dargestellt* (Berlin: Reimer, 1882), 42.

20 Cecilie Braun first signed her name as Cecile (without the accent) in a drawing of a flowering plant from 1823 and then later (and correctly) on the cover of an exercise book with perspective drawings from 1829. I have found no instance of her using Cecilie after her marriage. The confusion about her name is made even greater by the fact that in her few extant letters she seems to prefer the spelling Silli to Silly, the version of her nickname used by her husband and also adopted by her family. For all these details see Alexander Braun's biography, written by his daughter, who, confusingly enough, is also named Cécile, though this was done perhaps less as a tribute to his sister than to the young Cécile Guyot, with whom Alexander had once fallen in love. See Mettenius, *Alexander Braun's Leben*, especially 44–46. Need I remind the reader that Agassiz's sister was also called Cécile? Poor Cecilie Braun, transformed into Cécile and named like virtually every other woman around her, barely had a chance to develop her own individual identity.

21 For the most sympathetic portrait of Cecilie (based on secondary sources), see David Dobbs, *Reef Madness: Charles Darwin, Alexander Agassiz, and the Meaning of Coral* (New York: Pantheon, 2005).

22 LA to Cecilie Braun, May 1830, FLA, 5/2.8. For a description of the collection, see Maryse Surdez, *Catalogue des archives de Louis Agassiz, 1807–1873, Bulletin de la Société Neuchâteloise des Sciences Naturelles*, vol. 97 (1974).

23 LA to Cecilie Braun [1830?], FLA, Surdez 5/2.14.

24 Cecilie Braun to LA, 27 October 1832, FLA, Surdez 7/1.7. For the original poem (which Cecilie copied faithfully), see Novalis (Friedrich von Harden-

berg), *Schriften*, edited by Jacob Minor (Jena: Diederichs, 1907), vol. 1, 219.

25 Schmidt von Lübeck (Georg Philipp Schmidt), *Lieder*, 3rd ed. (Altona: Hammerich, 1847),143–45.

26 LA, "L'histoire de l'espéce humaine," FLA, Surdez 17/3.3 (b). The first page of the manuscript carries the note "lu le 14 Ocr. 1833" (read on 14 October 1833), not "Janvier" (January), as indicated in Surdez.

27 The identification is a bit tentative, since the only extensive samples of Cecilie's handwriting we have are in old German script. But especially the capital letters accord well with the captions under Cecilie's drawings, as do occasional mistakes that point to a writer not entirely comfortable with French (*tems* for *temps* or *ossemens* instead of *ossements*).

28 Cecilie Braun Agassiz to Karl Braun, 5 December 1833, FLA, Surdez 5/1.9.

29 See LA to Karl Braun, 22 December 1834 and 1 July 1835, FLA, Surdez 5/1.10 and 5/1.11.

30 I have not been able to locate the drawings for Agassiz's *Poissons fossiles*. A footnote in G. R. Agassiz's *Letters and Recollections of Alexander Agassiz* states that these had been sold to the British Museum "at one of Louis Agassiz's frequent moments of financial need. Some years ago when his daughter, Mrs. H. L. Higginson, was examining them there, the young assistant who had been detailed to show her the drawings remarked, 'I notice that those signed by the artist "C. A.," are much the most beautiful'" (4).

31 Dinkel's remarks are quoted in *Life*, vol. 1, 93.

32 On Agassiz's threefold parallelism, see Stephen Jay Gould, *Ontogeny and Phylogeny* (Cambridge, MA: Belknap Press, 1977), 63–68.

33 LA and Cecilie Braun Agassiz to Karl Braun, 23 April 1836, FLA, Surdez 5/1.15.

34 Jordan, "Agassiz at Penikese," 721–29; see 29.

35 Humboldt to LA, 27 March 1832, AP, HL, MS Am 1412 (417).

36 Humboldt to LA, 4 July 1833, AP, HL, MS Am 1419 (422).

37 LA to Humboldt, October 1835, AP, HL, MS Am 1419 (100).

38 Humboldt to LA, 19 July 1837, AP, HL, MS Am 1419 (423).

39 "Ureises Spätrest, älter als Alpen sind! / Ureis von damals, als die Gewalt des Frost's/ Berghoch verschüttet selbst den Süden, / Eben verhüllt so Gebirg als Meere!" ("Ye late rest of Ur-ice, older than Alps! / Ur-ice of yore when frost's power / Mountain-high covered the South, too / Veiled the mountains as well as the seas!"). Karl Friedrich Schimper, "Die Eiszeit. Wissenschaftliches Document, zum erstenmal abgedruckt und in fliegenden Blättern ausgetheilt in Neuschatel am Geburstage Galilei's 1837," in *Gedichte* (Erlangen: Ferdinand Enke, 1840), 301–4; here 302.

40 "Discours prononcé à l'ouverture des séances de la Société Helvétique des sciences naturelles, à Neuchâtel, le 24 juillet, 1837, par L. Agassiz, Président," in Marcou, vol. 1, 89–108; see 101.

41 Buckland is the subject of a smart, brief essay by Stephen Jay Gould, "The Freezing of Noah," in Gould, *The Flamingo's Smile: Reflections in Natural History* (1985; New York: Norton, 1987), 114–25.

42 LA to William Buckland, 1838?, AP, HL, MS Am 1419 (107).

43 LA, "On Glaciers and Boulders in Switzerland," *Report of the Tenth Meet-*

ing of the British Association for the Advancement of Science; Held at Glasgow in August 1840 (London: John Murray, 1841), 113–14; see 114.

44 William Buckland to LA, 15 October 1840; in *Life*, vol. 1, 309–10.

45 LA, *Études sur les glaciers par L. Agassiz. Ouvrage accompagné d'un Atlas de 32 planches, dessinés d'après nature par Joseph Bettannier* (Neuchâtel: Aux frais de l'Auteur, 1840). I will be quoting throughout this chapter the English translation by Albert V. Carozzi, in LA, *Studies on Glaciers, Preceded by the Discourse of Neuchâtel, by Louis Agassiz*, edited by Carozzi (New York: Hafner, 1967).

46 LA to Jean de Charpentier, 28 June 1841, in Marcou, vol. 1, 162–63.

47 LA, *Studies on Glaciers*, 57.

48 Ibid., 71–72.

49 Ibid., 85.

50 Ibid.

51 LA, *Études sur les glaciers*, 235; *Studies on Glaciers*, 130.

52 Humboldt to LA, 2 December 1837, AP, HL, MS Am 1419 (106).

53 Marcou, vol. 1, 190. The transformations of the "Hôtel" are well-described in Charles Gos, *L'Hôtel des Neuchâtelois: Un épisode de la conquête des alpes* (Lausanne: Librairie Payot & Cie, 1928), which also includes the engraving of Cecilie's visit. The climb to his father's mountain retreat was young Alexander Agassiz's "earliest recorded adventure"; see G. R. Agassiz, *Letters and Recollections of Alexander Agassiz*, 6–7.

54 Humboldt to LA, 2 December 1837, AP, HL, MS Am 1419 (106).

55 Humboldt to LA, 2 December 1842, AP, HL, MS Am 1419 (427).

56 Humboldt to LA, March 2, 1842, AP, HL, MS Am 1419 (426).

57 John Imbrie and Katherine Palmer Imbrie, *Ice Ages: Solving the Mystery* (Cambridge, MA: Harvard University Press, 1979), 21.

58 *Life*, vol. 1, 338.

59 Emily Dickinson, "The Zeros taught Us—Phosphorus," *The Poems of Emily Dickinson: Reading Edition*, edited by R. W. Franklin (Cambridge, MA: Belknap Press, 1999), 126–27. Hitchcock soon lost faith in Agassiz and argued for the combined influence of water and ice on the rocky landscapes of the New World, something he called, rather mysteriously, "glacio-aqueous action." Edward Hitchcock, "Postscript: Glacio-Aqueous Action Between the Tertiary and Historic Periods, Denominated in My Report, Diluvial Action," in Hitchcock, *Final Report of the Geology of Massachusetts: In Four Parts, Vol. I, Containing I. Economical Geology. II. Scenographical Geology* (Northampton, MA: J. H. Butler, 1841), 3a–9a.

60 LA, "Physical History of the Valley of the Amazons," *Atlantic Monthly*, vol. 18, no. 105 (July and August 1866): 49–60, 159–69.

61 CD to Charles Lyell, 8–9 September 1866, DCP 5208.

62 Humboldt to LA, 15 August 1840, AP, HL, MS Am 1416 (425).

63 Alexander Braun to "Silli" Agassiz, 14 May 1844, in Mettenius, *Alexander Braun's Leben*, 376–77.

64 Karl Friedrich Schimper, "Gebirgsbildung," in *Gedichte*, 300.

65 Jane M. Oppenheimer, "Louis Agassiz as an Early Embryologist in America," in *Science and Society in Early America: Essays in Honor of Whitfield J.*

Bell Jr., edited by Randolph S. Klein (Philadelphia: American Philosophical Society, 1986), 393–414. See *Histoire naturelle des poissons d'eau douce par L. Agassiz. Embryologie des salmones* (Neuchâtel: Aux frais d l'auteur, 1842). Agassiz's name is the only one that appears on the spine of the volume; the title page mentions his name first and only then identifies Vogt as the author of the volume. The same applies to the atlas accompanying the volume.

66 Karl Marx's *Economic and Philosophic Manuscripts* appeared in 1844.

67 Alexander Braun to Cecilie Braun Agassiz, 14 May 1844 and 16 May 1845, in Mettenius, *Alexander Braun's Leben*, 376–79. As Mettenius, Braun's daughter, remembers her childhood, Braun did not really live by his own advice: he was a kind, tolerant father (see Mettenius, 402). Apparently he, like his college friend Agassiz, felt the need to lord it over the less self-assured Cecilie.

68 G. R. Agassiz, *Letters and Recollections of Alexander Agassiz*, 10.

69 See, for example, Philippe de Champaigne's *The Repentant Magdalene* (1648; Palazzo Pitti, Florence) or Guido Reni's *Penitent Magdalene* (1620, The Walters Art Museum, Baltimore, MD). I owe this description to Alan Braddock, Temple University.

70 LA to Augustus Addison Gould, Gould Papers, HL, MS Am 210 (37).

71 LA to John Lowell, unsigned draft, 6 July 1864, AP, HL, MS Am 1419 (65). Dinkel, who had spent two decades working for Agassiz, decided against going with him to the States, a blow to Agassiz's ego remedied later when two other loyal illustrators, Jacques Burkhardt and Antoine Sonrel, joined him.

72 Humboldt to LA, 16 June 1846, AP, HL, MS Am 1419 (430).

3. HUMBOLDT'S GIFT

1 "I should say that those New England rocks on the sea-coast, which Agassiz imagines to bear the marks of violent scraping contact with vast floating icebergs—I should say, that those rocks must not a little resemble the Sperm Whale in this particular." (Agassiz, of course, had taken issue with the iceberg theory—see chapter 1.) See Herman Melville, chapter 68 ("The Blanket") of *Moby-Dick; or, The Whale* (1851; New York: Modern Library, 1992), 443.

2 LA, "Ice Period in America," *Geological Sketches: Second Series*, 77.

3 *Trumpet and Universalist Magazine*, vol. 19, no. 17 (10 October 1846): 67.

4 LA to Rose Mayor Agassiz, 2 December 1846, AP, HL, MS Am 1419 (66).

5 See G. Frederick Wright, "Agassiz and the Ice Age," *American Naturalist*, vol. 32, no. 375 (March 1898): 165–71.

6 LA, *An Introduction to the Study of Natural History, in a Series of Lectures Delivered in the Hall of the College of Physicians and Surgeons, New York. Illustrated with Numerous Engravings* (New York: Greeley and McElrath, 1847). The actual title of the lectures given in the book is "The Animal Kingdom." On Houston, a colorful personality with close ties to antislavery

circles who reported for both New York and Washington newspapers, see the Guide to the James Alexander Houston Incoming Correspondence in the Manuscripts Division of the Stanford University Libraries, M 1711.

7   LA, *Introduction to the Study*, 4, 5.

8   Ibid., 5.

9   LA and A. A. Gould, *Principles of Zoölogy: Touching the Structure, Development, Distribution, and Natural Arrangement of the Races of Animals, Living and Extinct, with Numerous Illustrations. Part I: Comparative Physiology* (1848; Boston: Gould and Lincoln, 1867, rev. ed.), 26.

10 LA, *Introduction to the Study*, 9–10, 13.

11 Ibid., 9, 20.

12 Ibid., 54, 50, 6.

13 Ibid., 6.

14 "From the Evening Post: Lectures on Natural History: Professor Agassiz's Third Lecture," *Connecticut Courant*, supplement (18 January 1848): 6.

15 LA, *Introduction to the Study*, 41.

16 Ibid. Ernest Wadsworth Longfellow, the poet's son and a professional (though not lavishly talented) painter himself, recalled what a "treat" it was to "see a perfect fish or skeleton" develop under Agassiz's hand, "with extraordinary sureness and perfect knowledge, without any hesitation or correcting, like a Japanese drawing in its truth to nature, and it seemed a shame that such beautiful drawings were only in chalk and had to be rubbed out again." Longfellow, *Random Memories* (Boston: Houghton Mifflin, 1922), 27.

17 LA, *Introduction to the Study*, 42.

18 Lucy Allen Paton, *Elizabeth Cary Agassiz: A Biography* (Boston: Houghton Mifflin, 1919), 34.

19 LA, *Introduction to the Study*, 44, 46, 21, 53.

20 Ibid., 25.

21 Norman Allison Calkins, *Manual of Object-Teaching, with Illustrative Lessons in Methods and the Science of Education* (New York: American Book Company, 1881), 27. See Sarah Anne Carter's unpublished paper given at the annual convention of the Organization of American Historians in Seattle, March 26, 2009, "Object Lessons into Science: Objects and Pictures in the Nineteenth-Century Classroom."

22 See Lurie, *Louis Agassiz*, 137–41.

23 LA, *Lake Superior: Its Physical Character, Vegetation, and Animals Compared with Those of Other and Similar Regions* (with a narrative of the tour by J. Elliot Cabot) (Boston: Gould, Kendall and Lincoln, 1850), 24, 12.

24 Willis Goth Regier, *Quotology* (Lincoln, NE: University of Nebraska Press, 2010), xiv.

25 LA, *Lake Superior*, 23–24, 38.

26 Ibid., 62, 70.

27 Ibid., 124, 83, 109.

28 Ibid., 39, 32, 50–52, 417.

29 George Adams, *The Boston Directory: Containing the City Record, a General Directory of All Citizens, and a Special Directory of Trades, Professions, &c. 1848–49* (Boston: James French and Charles Stimpson, 1848), 58.

30 Marcou, vol. 2, 20.

31 Ibid., vol. 1, 271.

32 LA to John A. Lowell, 18 January 1849, AP, HL, MS Am 1419 (712). See Édouard Desor and Louis Agassiz, *Catalogue raisonné des familles, des genres, et des espèces de la classe des échinodermes,* in *Annales des sciences naturelles. Zoologie,* 3rd ser. 6 (1846): 305–74; 7 (1847): 129–68; 8 (1847): 5–35, 355–88; Desor, "Account of the Development of the Embryo of the Starfish," *Proceedings of the Boston Society of Natural History,* vol. 3 (1848–50): 13–14 and 17–18.

33 See LA v. Desor, "Agreement to Submit Their Difficulties to Arbitration," autographed notes signed by Desor and LA, Cambridge, 5 December 1848, AP, HL, MS Am 1419 (710), as well as "Mr. Agassiz's Accusations Against Mr. Desor as Written Down by Him at East Boston," Ms. transcript, 1849, AP, HL, MS Am 1419 (712).

34 Marc-Antoine Kaeser, *L'Univers du préhistorien: Science, foi, et politique dans l'oeuvre et la vie d'Édouard Desor, 1811–1882* (Paris: L'Harmattan, 2004), 115.

35 LA v. Desor, "Proces verbal of the case of Desor vs. Agassiz," autograph ms. by John A. Lowell, 1849, signed by Thomas B. Curtis, J. A. Lowell, D. Humphreys Storer, AP, HL, MS Am 1419 (713); see also "Agassiz v. Desor. Award," Ms. transcript, Boston, 9 February 1849, AP, HL, MS Am 1419 (714).

36 Nevertheless, in 1856, Thomas Curtis, upon returning all the papers concerning the affair to LA, said he felt "reluctance in calling to your mind a subject that has happily gone by." See Thomas B. Curtis to LA, 23 November 1856, AP, HL, MS Am 1419 (713).

37 G. R. Agassiz, *Letters and Recollections of Alexander Agassiz,* 13.

38 "Letters of Charles Girard to Prof. Agassiz, accompanied with statements in reference to them by Charles Girard," part A, Charles Frédéric Girard Papers, c. 1846–1860, Smithsonian Institution Archives, Record Unit 7190.

39 Girard to LA, 26 January 1850, Girard Papers, Smithsonian.

40 Girard to LA, 20 November 1850, Girard Papers, Smithsonian.

41 LA to Baird, June 27, 1853, in Herber, *Spencer Fullerton Baird and Louis Agassiz,* 55.

42 Marcou, vol. 2, 227.

43 Thomas Hill, "A Collecting Trip with Louis Agassiz," in *The Harvard Book: Selections from Three Centuries,* rev. ed. (1953; Cambridge: Harvard University Press, 1982), 54–58. The date given for the essay (1848) is incorrect; Alexander Agassiz did not arrive in the United States before June 1849.

44 LA to Achille de Valenciennes, draft [1856], AP, HL, MS Am 1419 (130). LA's assessment of Flourens, a pioneer in experimental brain science who first demonstrated that the main divisions of the brain served different functions, is manifestly off the mark.

45 LA, fragment of a letter to Sir P. de M. Grey-Egerton, 1856–1857(?), AP, HL, MS Am 1419 (133).

46 Edwin Percy Whipple, "Recollections of Agassiz," *Harper's New Monthly Magazine,* vol. 59, no. 349 (June 1879): 97–110; see 109.

47 Lyman, "Recollections of Agassiz," 225.

48 See Nancy Pick and Mark Sloan, *Rarest of the Rare: Stories Behind the Trea-*

sures at the Harvard Museum of Natural History (New York: HarperCollins, 2004), 50.

49 William Chauvenet to LA, 24 August 1853, AP, HL, MS 1419 (248).

50 J. Milton Sanders to LA, 25 August 1853, AP, HL, MS Am 1419 (584).

51 Silvanus Thayer Abert to LA, 30 August 1853, AP, HL, MS Am 1419 (1).

52 E. R. Andrews to LA, 27 September 1853, AP, HL, MS Am 1419 (197).

53 The name in fact derives from the Wampanoag word for "big river."

54 See Christoph Irmscher, *The Poetics of Natural History: From John Bartram to William James* (New Brunswick, NJ: Rutgers University Press, 1999), 131.

55 Charles Sumner to LA, 10 October 1854, AP, HL, MS Am 1419 (617).

56 Sumner to LA 20 October 1863, AP, HL, MS Am 1419 (622): "I send to you a box of *St. Georges*, recd direct from Mr. Gordon, who is the owner of the choicest vineyard of this name, near the village [of Montpellier]—rough, strong & unpromising to a common eye, but producing the best wine. Montesquieu in commending his wine to some of his English correspondents said that they would receive it 'first as he received it from the good God,' & I think I may say the same of this St. Georges."

57 See Lurie, *Louis Agassiz*, 214.

58 To calculate the relative value of historical dollar amounts (and since I am mostly interested in the purchasing power money would have had then) I rely on tools like the one available through www.measuringworth.com and specifically the one giving Consumer Price Index equivalents. Of course, such conversion calculators are not exact, and I remain aware that the impact of such sums was likely greater than I can account for here. Thanks to Michael McGerr, Department of History, Indiana University Bloomington, for helping me figure this out.

59 LA to Abbott Lawrence, draft, 20 May 1854, AP, HL, MS Am 1419 (125).

60 See Mary Pickard Winsor, "Agassiz's Notions of a Museum: The Vision and the Myth," in *Cultures and Institutions of Natural History*, edited by Michael T. Ghiselin and Alan E. Leviton, *Memoirs of the California Academy of Sciences* (San Francisco: California Academy of Sciences, 2000), 240–71.

61 Harriet Beecher Stowe, *Uncle Tom's Cabin; or, Life Among the Lowly*, edited by Ann Douglas (Harmondsworth: Penguin, 1981), 229. On Agassiz's use of the library analogy, see Louise Hall Tharp, *Adventurous Alliance: The Story of the Agassiz Family of Boston* (Boston: Little, Brown, 1959), 134.

62 See Humboldt, "Ideen zu einer Physiognomik der Gewächse," in *Ansichten der Natur*, edited by Adolf Meyer-Abich (3rd ed. 1849; Stuttgart: Reclam, 1969), 86. See also Humboldt's *Kosmos*, wherein he likens the ideal scientist to the painter "who comprehends nature at *a single glance.*" *Cosmos: A Sketch of the Physical Description of the Universe*, translated by E. C. Otté, 2 vols. (New York: Harper, 1858), vol. 2, 96.

63 Addison Emery Verrill, 7 January 1860, from Verrill, Journal, 1 January 1860–December 1863, Harvard University Archives, HUD 860.90.

64 "Science in America: Professor Agassiz's New Museum," *New York Times*, 11 May 1868.

65 LA to Nathaniel Southgate Shaler, 19 May 1870; Agassiz, Letters to Shaler, Archives, Ernst Mayr Library, MCZ, MCZ 024.

66 Verrill, Journal 1860–1863, 8 January 1860.

67 Winsor, "Agassiz's Notions," 263.

68 Three years before his death, Agassiz told Shaler, "You will get your synop-tic series only after you have worked up in detail the systematic collections *as a whole*, the faunal collections *in their totality*, the geological sequence of the *whole group* under consideration, as well as its embryology and geo-graphical distribution." 21 May 1870, LA, Letters to Shaler, MCZ 024; my emphasis.

69 LA to Thomas Cary, 26 March 1860, AP, HL, MS Am 1419 (146).

70 The report of the committee, signed by George Ticknor and Jacob Big-elow, dated 26 October 1864, appears in *Annual Report of the Trustees of the Museum of Comparative Zoology, at Harvard College, in Cambridge, To-gether with the Report of the Director, 1864* (Boston: Wright and Potter, 1865), 5–6.

71 Alexander Agassiz, "Seventh Annual Report," *Annual Report of the Trust-ees of the Museum of Comparative Zoology at Harvard College in Cambridge, Together with the Report of the Director, 1865* (Boston: Wright and Potter, 1866), 12.

72 LA, "Special Report of the Director," *Annual Report of the Trustees of the Museum of Comparative Zoology, at Harvard College in Cambridge, Together with the Report of the Director for 1866* (Boston: Wright and Potter, 1867), 9, and LA, "Report of the Director of the Museum of Comparative Zoology, for the Year 1869," *Annual Report of the Trustees of the Museum of Compara-tive Zoology, at Harvard College, in Cambridge, Together with the Report of the Director for 1869* (Boston: Wright and Potter, 1870), 5.

73 LA, "Report of the Director of the Museum of Comparative Zoology, for the Year 1870," *Annual Report of the Trustees of the Museum of Comparative Zoology at Harvard College, in Cambridge: Together with the Report of the Di-rector for 1870* (Boston: Wright and Potter, 1871), 5; LA, "Report of the Di-rector of the Museum of Comparative Zoology, for the Year 1871," *Annual Report of the Trustees of the Museum of Comparative Zoology, at Harvard Col-lege, in Cambridge: Together with the Report of the Director for 1871* (Boston: Wright and Potter, 1872), 8.

74 Goethe would receive a similar posthumous honor a few years later, in 1875. Humboldt's popular success in America is sketched out in Cora Lee Nollendorfs, "Alexander von Humboldt Celebrations in the United States: Controversies Concerning His Work," *Monatshefte*, vol. 80, no. 1 (Spring 1988): 54–66, and Laura Dassow Walls, "'Hero of Knowledge, Be Our Tribute Thine': Alexander von Humboldt in Victorian America," *Northeast-ern Naturalist*, vol. 8, no. 1 (2001): 121–34, as well as, most recently, Laura Dassow Walls, *Passage to Cosmos: Alexander von Humboldt and the Shaping of America* (Chicago: Chicago University Press, 2009). Aaron Sachs paints, in bold strokes, Humboldt's influence on nineteenth-century notions of the "environment": *The Humboldt Current: Nineteenth-Century Exploration and the Roots of American Environmentalism* (New York: Viking, 2008).

75 *Louis Agassiz: Memorial Meeting of the Boston Society of Natural History, Janu-ary 7, 1874* (Boston: privately printed, 1874), 31–32.

76 LA, *Address Delivered on the Centennial*, 23.

77 LA's undated note to Waterston is cited in "Agassiz and the Humboldt Celebration," in *Louis Agassiz: Memorial Meeting*, 37.

78 Whipple, "Recollections of Agassiz," 106.

79 James T. Fields, *Ballads and Other Verses* (Boston: Houghton Mifflin, 1880), 42–44.

4. DARWIN'S BARNACLES, AGASSIZ'S JELLYFISH

1 See George Henry Lewes, *Sea-Side Studies at Ilfracombe, Tenby, the Scilly Isles, & Jersey* (Edinburgh: William Blackwood and Sons, 1858), 115–16; Lynn Barber, *The Heyday of Natural History, 1820–1870* (London: Cape, 1980), 121.

2 LA, "Contributions to the Natural History of the Acalephae of North America. Part I: On the Naked-Eyed Medusae of the Shores of Massachusetts," *Memoirs of the American Academy of Arts and Sciences*, New Series, vol. 4 (1850): 221–316.

3 Ibid., 223. See also 256: "It is really an unexpected circumstance, that the investigations of the lowest animals should lead to the most appropriate and natural method of studying, describing, and depicting animals at large."

4 Ibid., 226, 229, 232, 230.

5 Ibid., 259–60.

6 Ibid., 244, 245, 254, 289, 290, 294.

7 CD to LA, 22 October 1848, AP, HL, MS Am 1419 (274); see also CD to J. E. Gray, 18 December 1847, DCP 1139.

8 CD to LA, 22 October 1848. See n7.

9 CD to LA, 25 June 1850, AP, HL, MS Am 1419 (278).

10 *Origin*, 310–11.

11 See Gould, *Ontogeny and Phylogeny*, 47–49.

12 CD to Huxley, 13 March 1853, DCP 2430.

13 See Gray's unkind characterization of Agassiz from a letter to the American expatriate Francis Boott, a doctor and physician who lived in London: "He is a sort of demagogue and likes to talk to the rabble." 15 January 1860, Darwin-Lyell Papers, American Philosophical Society.

14 AG to John Torrey, 13 October 1846, in *Letters of Asa Gray*, edited by Jane Loring Gray, 2 vols. (Boston: Houghton Mifflin, 1893), vol. 1, 344.

15 James Russell Lowell, "To A. G.: On His Seventy-Fifth Birthday": "Just Fate, prolong his life well-spent / Whose indefatigable hours / Have been as gaily innocent / And fragrant as his flowers!" (dated 18 November 1885). *Botanical Gazette*, vol. 11 (1886): 9.

16 AG, *Letters*, vol. 1, 321–22.

17 See A. L. Perry, *Scotch-Irish in New England* (Boston: J. S. Cushing, 1891), 18–20. Perry, like Asa Gray a great-great grandson of Matthew Gray of Worcester, notes that the traits of Gray's intellect ("canny, absorbed, analytic, comprehensive, religiously consecrated") reflected his ancestry.

18 AG, *Letters*, vol. 1, 161, 162, 183, 205.

19 1 March 1844. Ibid., vol. 1, 316.

20 AG, *How Plants Grow: A Simple Introduction to Structural Botany* (New York: American Book Company, 1858), 1.

21 Ibid., 2.

22 Ibid., 4. See also 34: "Those who would learn more of the structure and morphology of plants should study the Lessons in Botany."

23 Ibid., 6, 78, 22, 33; Thoreau's journal, 20 May 1851, in *The Writings of Henry David Thoreau: Journal II*, edited by Bradford Torrey (Boston: Houghton Mifflin, 1906), vol. 8, 294. See A. Hunter Dupree, *Asa Gray: American Botanist, Friend of Darwin* (1959; Baltimore: Johns Hopkins University Press, 1988), 222.

24 CD to J. D. Hooker, 26 March 1854, DCP 1562. Lyell was in Boston in 1852 to deliver the Lowell lectures and would have had occasion to attend one of Agassiz's lectures too; see Leonard G. Wilson, *Lyell in America: Transatlantic Geology, 1841–1853* (Baltimore: Johns Hopkins University Press, 1998), 372–79.

25 CD to AG, 25 April 1855, DCP 1674; AG to CD, 22 May 1855, DCP 1685.

26 AG to CD, 30 June 1855, DCP 1707. "Silliman's journal" refers to the *American Journal of Science*, inaugurated in 1818 by Professor Benjamin Silliman of Yale and subsequently edited by his son, Benjamin Silliman Jr.

27 CD to AG, 2 May 1856, DCP 1863.

28 AG to CD, 23 September 1856, DCP 1959.

29 CD to AG, 1 January 1857, DCP 2034.

30 AG to CD, 16 February 1857, DCP 2053.

31 See AG's seminal paper "Diagnostic Characters of New Species of Phaenogamous Plants Collected in Japan by Charles Wright, Botanist of the U.S. North Pacific Exploring Expedition," *Memoirs of the American Academy of Arts and Sciences*, New Series, vol. 6 (1859): 377–452. An excerpt from that paper appears under the title "The Flora of Japan" in *Scientific Papers of Asa Gray*, vol. 2, 124–41.

32 CD to AG, 29 November 1857, DCP 2176.

33 CD to AG, 9 May 1857, DCP 2089; AG to CD, 1 June 1857, DCP 2098; CD to AG, 18 June 1857, DCP 2109. CD also quotes LA's purported remark in letters to Hooker, 21 March 1857 and 3 January 1860 (DCP 2067 and 2635).

34 AG, *Darwiniana: Essays and Reviews Pertaining to Darwinism*, edited by A. Hunter Dupree (1876; Cambridge, MA: Belknap Press, 1963), 122. Agassiz's essay had first appeared in the *Atlantic Monthly*, vol. 6, no. 36 (1860): 406 25. See also Paul Jerome Croce, "Probabilistic Darwinism: Louis Agassiz vs. Asa Gray on Science, Religion, and Certainty," *Journal of Religious History*, vol. 22 (February 1995): 35–58, and Croce, *Science and Religion in the Era of William James. Vol. 1: The Eclipse of Certainty, 1820–1880* (Chapel Hill: University of North Carolina Press, 1995), 124–34. For Croce, the differences between Agassiz and Gray are not a product of the eternal conflict between religion and science but rather the result of different ways of looking at the same thing, "the fault line of certainty in both science and religion." For earlier, sympathetic treatments of Gray's thought and his relationship with Agassiz, see also Elaine Claire Daughetee Wolfe, "Acceptance of the Theory of Evolution in America: Louis Agassiz vs. Asa Gray," *American Biology Teacher*, vol. 37 (1975): 244–47, and William E. Phipps, "Asa Gray's Theology of Nature," *American Presbyterians*, vol. 66, no. 3

(Fall 1988): 167–75. Phipps argues that "Gray's theology of nature is still largely unassimilated in our culture" (174).

35 CD to AG, 26 September 1860, DCP 2930. See AG, *Darwiniana*, 129.

36 AG, "Review of *Explanations: A Sequel to the Vestiges of the Natural History of Creation*," *North American Review*, vol. 52 (1846): 465–506.

37 Quoted in Dupree, *Asa Gray*, 259.

38 AG to J. D. Hooker, 5 January 1860, DCP 2638.

39 *Origin*, 365. "Gmelin" refers to Johann Georg Gmelin (1709–1755), German explorer and botanist.

40 Ibid., 295, 391.

41 AG, "Darwin on the Origin of Species," *Atlantic Monthly*, vol. 6, no. 34 (August 1860): 229–39; see AG, *Darwiniana*, 96. For the quotation from "Darwin and His Reviewers," see *Darwiniana*, 316.

42 Ibid., 78. I owe the last observation to Scott Russell Sanders.

43 CD to Jeffries Wyman, 3 December 1860, DCP 3005.

44 The original of Gray's letter is lost, but Darwin cites this passage in a letter to Charles Lyell, 2 February 1861, DCP 3054. At a meeting of the American Academy of Arts and Sciences on January 8, 1861, Agassiz had voiced his "general disbelief in the supposed derivation of later languages from earlier ones, he regarding each language and each race as substantially primordial, and ascribing the resemblances and coincidences of language to a similarity in the mental organization of the races." See *Proceedings of the American Academy of Arts and Sciences*, vol. 5 (1860–62), 102, and n3 to letter 3054 in DCP. Agassiz was also taking on his friend Cornelius Felton, who also happened to be his wife's brother-in-law. The classicist Felton had gone on record as believing that a common primordial language was the root of all "Aryan" languages. For Gray's literary inclinations, see AG, *Letters*, vol. 1, 12n1.

45 Dupree, *Asa Gray*, 323.

46 As Wayne Hanley put it succinctly, "Gray, working at great risk against the public figure of Agassiz as the greatest American naturalist, convinced American scientists of the worth of Darwin's theory." *Natural History in America: From Mark Catesby to Rachel Carson* (New York: Quadrangle, 1977), 194.

47 AG to LA, 21 July 1863, DCP 4248.

48 AG's letter to CD is lost, but CD quotes this passage in a letter to H. W. Bates; see CD to Bates, 4 March 1863, DCP 4022.

49 AG to CD, 26 May 1863, DCP 4186.

50 AG to CD, 23 November 1863, DCP 4346.

51 LA, "The Formation of Glaciers," in *Geological Sketches*, 19th ed. (1866; Boston: Houghton Mifflin, 1896), 208. The essay first appeared in the *Atlantic Monthly*, vol. 12, no. 72 (November 1863): 568–76.

52 Sir Michael Faraday to LA, 20 October 1863, AP, HL, MS Am 1419 (343).

53 Hooker to AG, 16 March 1860, Gray Herbarium, Harvard University.

54 AG to CD, 21 July 1863, DCP 4248.

55 William Winwood Reade to CD, 26 December 1869, DCP 7036.

56 CD to AG, 23 November 1862, DCP 3820.

57 AG to CD, 6 November 1866, DCP 5268.

58 Joseph Henry to AG, 31 October 1866, Gray Herbarium, Harvard University.

59 CD to LA, 19 August 1868, AP, HL, MS Am 1419 (278).

60 CD, *The Descent of Man, and Selection in Relation to Sex*, 2nd ed. (1879; New York: Appleton, 1927), 346–47. The passage about the "conspicuous protuberance" on the head of a species belonging to the genus *Geophagus*—a fish also more colorfully known as the red hump eartheater—from Agassiz's letter reads in full: "I have often observed these fishes at the time of spawning when the protuberance is largest and also at other seasons when it is totally wanting and the sexes show no difference whatever in the outline of the profile of the head; but I could never ascertain that they subserve any special function. The Indians know nothing about its use. They say however that during the spawning season they are often seen rubbing their head against submerged stumps of trees. The fact that these protuberances are transient brings them into the category of those swellings which appear about the head in some birds during the breeding season; they resemble still more the swellings of the head of some Batrachians with which they hold their female during copulation." LA to CD, 22 July 1868, Agassiz Letter Books, IV: 169–70, MCZ. CD also mentions the analogy with the "fleshy carbuncles on the heads of certain birds" but doesn't attribute it to Agassiz—and he leaves the frogs and toads ("Batrachians") alone.

61 AG to CD, 26 and 29 October 1869, DCP 6957.

62 AG to CD, 14 February 1870, DCP 7105.

63 AG to CD, 27 February and 1 March 1870, DCP 7119.

64 CD to Alexander Agassiz, 1 June 1871, in G. R. Agassiz, *Letters and Recollections of Alexander Agassiz*, 118–19. "Pedicellariae" are clawlike appendages found on sea urchins and starfish.

65 *Contributions*, vol. 3, 89, 91. Thoreau uses the term "insect view" in his essay "The Natural History of Massachusetts" (1842). For Darwin's use of *grandeur*, see *Origin*, 490.

66 *Contributions*, vol. 3, 91–92n1.

67 See chapter 4 ("Language") of *Nature* (1836) and "The Poet" (1844) in Emerson, *Essays and Lectures*, 20–25 and 459.

68 *Contributions*, vol. 3, 92n1.

69 Ibid., 93.

70 Ibid., 4.

71 For Descartes, visualization was a source of error in the sciences; he argued that our perceptions have merely mental status and sensation is an unreliable source of knowledge. See Brian Baigrie, "Descartes's Scientific Illustrations and 'la grande mécanique de la nature,'" in *Picturing Knowledge: Historical and Philosophical Problems Concerning the Use of Art in Science*, edited by Brian Baigrie (Toronto: University of Toronto Press, 1996), 86–134; see also 129n3.

72 *Contributions*, vol. 3, 71, 69, 78.

73 "Fifth Annual Report of the Director of the Museum of Comparative

Zoology, by Louis Agassiz," *Annual Report of the Trustees of the Museum of Comparative Zoology, Together with the Report of the Director, 1863* (Boston: Wright and Potter, 1864), 7.

74 On Agassiz's "shabby" books, see Paton, *Elizabeth Cary Agassiz*, 45. Agassiz's marginalia are discussed by Stephen Jay Gould in *I Have Landed: The End of a Beginning in Natural History* (New York: Harmony, 2002), 314–18.

75 LA, *Methods of Study in Natural History* (Boston: Ticknor and Fields, 1863), 297–98.

76 See Julia Voss, *Darwins Bilder: Ansichten der Evolutionstheorie, 1837–1874* (Frankfurt am Main: Fischer 2007).

77 Samuel H. Scudder, "In the Laboratory with Agassiz," *Every Saturday*, vol. 16 (4 April 1874): 369–70.

78 Lyman, "Recollections of Agassiz," 225.

79 Ibid.

80 While Agassiz continued to be his chief employer, Sonrel also worked for Spencer Fullerton Baird of the Smithsonian Institution. Indications of his versatility are the steel plates he contributed to the revised edition of Thaddeus William Harris's *Treatise on Some Insects Injurious to Vegetation* (Boston: Crosby and Nichols, 1862). For more on Sonrel, see Ann Shelby Blum and Sarah Landry, "In Loving Detail," *Harvard Magazine*, vol. 79 (May–June 1977): 38–51; Bettina A. Norton, "Tappan and Bradford: Boston Lithographers with Essex County Associations," *Essex Institute Historical Collections*, vol. 114 (July 1978): 149–60; Sally Pierce and Catharina Slautterback, *Boston Lithography, 1825–1880: The Boston Athenaeum Collection* (Boston: The Boston Athenaeum, 1991), 180–81; Ann Shelby Blum, *Picturing Nature: American Nineteenth-Century Zoological Illustration* (Princeton: Princeton University Press, 1993), 369n34.

81 LA, "Naked-Eyed Medusae," 222.

82 *Contributions*, vol. 4, 87.

83 Ibid., 88–89.

84 *Origin*, 485.

85 Lewes, *Sea-Side Studies*, 255–56, 341–42.

86 *Contributions*, vol. 3, 125.

87 "Explanation of the Plates," appendix to *Contributions*, vol. 3, 7.

88 *Contributions*, vol. 4, 101–2.

89 Ibid., 92.

90 Manfred Laubichler, "Nature's Beauty and Haeckel's Talents," *Science*, vol. 308 (17 June 2005): 1746.

91 Ernst Haeckel, *Das System der Medusen: Erster Theil einer Monographie der Medusen*, 3 vols. (Jena: Gustav Fischer, 1879–80), vol. 1, 189, 527.

92 Ernst Haeckel, *Kunstformen der Natur* (1904; Wiesbaden: Marix, 2004), 22.

93 See plate 8 in *Kunstformen der Natur* as well as plate 30 ("Desmonema") in vol. 3 ("Atlas") of *System der Medusen*. On Haeckel's falsifications, see the chapter "Le Darwinisme: Classification de Haeckel," which Agassiz added to the French translation of his *Essay on Classification: De l'Espèce et de la classification en Zoologie*, translated by Félix Vogeli (Paris: Baillière, 1869), 375–91, as well as, more recently, Stephen Jay Gould, "Haeckel's 'Artforms

of Nature': Either or Neither? Fused or Misused?" in *The Hedgehog, the Fox, and the Magister's Pox: Mending the Gap Between Science and the Humanities* (New York: Three Rivers, 2003), 157–63, and Gould, *I Have Landed*, 305–20.

94 See Michael Huey, "Medusa Man," *World of Interiors*, vol. 19, no. 8 (August 1999): 54–63.

95 Haeckel, *Ziele und Wege*, 80; Haeckel, *System der Medusen*, 519.

96 Haeckel, *Kunstformen*, 4. See Stephen Jay Gould's critique of the "Whiggish" view of history in "Agassiz's Later, Private Thoughts on Evolution: His Marginalia in Haeckel's *Natürliche Schöpfungsgeschichte*," in *Two Hundred Years of Geology in America*, edited by Cecil J. Schneer (Hanover, NH: University Press of New England, 1979), 277–82. Lorraine Daston and Peter Galison, in *Objectivity* (New York: Zone, 2007), contrast Haeckel's "truth-to-nature" with the newly emerging regimen of "mechanical objectivity," as represented by Haeckel's opponent, the embryologist Wilhelm His, who employed a drawing prism and stereoscope to project and then trace meticulously "objective" representations of his specimens (193–95). Sonrel's version of "objectivity" was more comprehensive—but, in a sense, no less accurate and "unprejudiced"—than the "unthinking, blind sight" (16) Daston and Galison regard as the hallmark of objectivity. He had found a different way of eliminating "the knower" from his images.

97 See   http://hermes.mbl.edu/marine_org/images/animals/images/C.capil lata5.JPG.

98 See Michael Behe, *Darwin's Black Box: The Biochemical Challenge to Evolution* (New York: Free Press, 1996), 42. For a trenchant critique of Behe's mousetrap model, see Michael Ruse, *Darwin and Design: Does Evolution Have a Purpose?* (Cambridge, MA: Harvard University Press, 2003), 313–36.

99 Alexander Agassiz, "Mode of Catching Jelly-Fishes," *Atlantic Monthly*, vol. 16, no. 93 (December 1865): 736–39. The essay also appears in Elizabeth Agassiz and Alexander Agassiz, *Seaside Studies in Natural History, Marine Animals of Massachusetts Bay: Radiates*, 2nd ed. (1865; Boston: Osgood and Co., 1871), 85–90.

100 E. W. Longfellow, *Random Memories*, 28.

101 The two standard surveys of Anglo-American natural history illustration were written by, respectively, an antiquarian bookseller with scientific interests and the archivist of a natural history museum. See S. Peter Dance, *The Art of Natural History* (1978; New York: Arch Cape, 1990), and Blum, *Picturing Nature*. For the use of pictorial devices in scientific discourse, see Baigree, *Picturing Knowledge*, and Daston and Galison, *Objectivity*.

102 Walter Benjamin, "The Work of Art in the Age of Mechanical Reproduction" (1936), translated by Harry Zohn, in *The Norton Anthology of Theory and Criticism*, gen. ed. Vincent B. Leitch (New York: Norton, 2001), 1166–86; see especially 1168.

103 The devices used to expose half of the negative at a time included special plate-holders and rotating partial lens caps. For other examples of the genre, see the online exhibition of the American Museum of Photography, "Seeing Double: Creating Clones with a Camera," http://www.photography-museum.com/seeingdouble.html.

5. MR. CLARK'S HEADACHE

1   *Contributions*, vol. 1, xvi.

2   CD to Benjamin D. Walsh, 20 August 1866, Special Collections, Field Museum Chicago. Walsh (1808–1869), a self-taught Illinois entomologist originally from Britain, over several years carried on a lively correspondence with Charles Darwin, in which he left no doubt where his sympathies lay. In a letter of March, 1865, he compared Agassiz to "a dishonest lawyer pettifogging a hard case." Later in the letter, he extended this folksy simile: in his defense of separate creations for otherwise identical species, Agassiz reminded him of "the Western lawyer, whose client was sued for a kettle which he had borrowed and [returned] with a large crack in it and who put in three pleas: 1st that his client had never borrowed the kettle, 2nd that it was already cracked when he borrowed it, & 3rd that it was perfectly sound when he returned it." On July 17, 1866, Walsh asked Darwin if he had read Clark's *Mind in Nature* and added an unflattering comment about the author: "He strikes me as having almost as illogical a mind as Prof. Aggasiz [*sic*]. From one end to the other of the Book I don't see a single new fact or argument to carry out his thesis." As Darwin's response on 20 August shows, Walsh was preaching to the converted. See David M. Walsten, "Darwin's Backwoods Correspondent: Letters Between Charles Darwin and Illinois Naturalist Benjamin D. Walsh," *Field Museum of Natural History Bulletin*, vol. 45, no. 1 (January 1974): 8–9, 9–15.

3   HJC, *Mind in Nature; or, The Origin of Life, and the Mode of Development of Animals* (New York: Appleton, 1865), 61 and 279. See Mario A. DiGregorio, with the assistance of N. W. Gill, *Charles Darwin's Marginalia, Vol. 1* (New York: Garland, 1990), 166–67.

4   All the quotes from HJC's diaries are from the six manuscript volumes in the archives of the Ernst Mayr Library, MCZ (sMu 612.41.1). They will be referenced by the date of the entry rather than by volume number. My interest in Clark was awakened by Mary Winsor; see her *Reading the Shape of Nature*, 49–58.

5   For biographical information, I have relied on Xenos Y. Clark, letter to Alpheus Spring Packard Jr., 11 July 1873, Archives, Ernst Mayr Library, MCZ; Alpheus Spring Packard Jr., "Memoir of Henry James Clark, 1826–1873. Read before the National Academy, 23 April 1874," *National Academy of Sciences, Washington, DC: Biographical Memoirs* (Washington, DC: National Academy of Sciences, 1874) vol. 1, 317–28; "Henry James Clark, 1826–1873," *General Catalogue of the Massachusetts Agricultural College, 1862–1886* (Amherst, MA: J. E. Williams, 1886), 103–7.

6   Packard, "Memoir," 319.

7   Mary Holbrook Clark to Alpheus Hyatt, 18 November 1873, Henry James Clark Papers (FS 048), Special Collections and University Archives, W.E.B. Du Bois Library, University of Massachusetts Amherst.

8   AG to HJC, 7 February 1850, Collection of Daniel Weinstock, M.D., Geneva, NY.

9   See Edward Orton, *An Account of the Descendants of Thomas Orton of Wind-*

sor, Connecticut, 1641, Principally in the Male Line (Columbus, OH: Nitschke Brothers, 1896), 194. *Trow's New York City Directory for the Year Ending May 1, 1872*, compiled by H. Wilson, lists a "Thomas Edward Clark, physician" living at 154 East 56th Street (New York: Trow, 1871), 20. See also the reference to Thomas E. Clark in Mary Holbrook Clark's letter to Alpheus Hyatt, 18 November 1873, n7. Ned Clark later retired to a "life of leisure" in Los Angeles, California, where he died in 1921, age ninety-three; "Scientific Notes and News," *Science*, vol. 55 (24 March 1922): 314–15.

10 The original image, long thought to be extant only in reproductions, was recently acquired by Daniel Weinstock, M.D., Geneva, NY.

11 See Edward Laurens Mark, "Zoology," in *The Development of Harvard University Since the Inauguration of President Eliot, 1869–1929*, edited by Samuel Eliot Morison (Cambridge, MA: Harvard University Press, 1930), 378–99; see 380; Winsor, *Reading the Shape of Nature*, 5.

12 HJC, Journal, 24 March 1857. Xenos's obituary inaccurately gives May 1853 as the date of his birth; see R.E.C.S. [Robert Edwards Carter Stearns], "The Late Xenos Y. Clark," *American Naturalist*, vol. 23 (August 1889): 749–50.

13 HJC, Journal, 16 May 1857.

14 HJC, Journal, 17 April 1857.

15 HJC, Journal, 3 May 1857.

16 HJC to LA, 15 July 1856, Archives, Ernst Mayr Library, MCZ, bMU 612.10.

17 *Contributions*, vol. 1, 390n2.

18 HJC, Journal, 14 May 1857.

19 Putnam became the first director of the Peabody Academy of Science in Salem, Massachusetts (now the Peabody Essex Museum) and, in 1874, was appointed curator of Harvard University's Peabody Museum of Anthropology and Archaeology. Tenney, who held the first chair of natural history at Vassar, subsequently accepted a professorship at Williams College.

20 HJC, Journal, 19 May 1857.

21 HJC, Journal, 26 January 1859, and HJC, "Some Remarks upon the Use of the Microscope in the Investigation of the Minute Organization of Living Bodies," *American Journal of Science and Arts*, vol. 28, no. 82 (November 1859): 37–48, 40.

22 HJC, Journal, 26 January 1859.

23 HJC, "On the Origin of Vibrio," *American Journal of Science and Arts*, vol. 28, no. 82 (1859): 107–9; HJC, Journal, 12 April 1859.

24 LA with A. A. Gould, *Principles of Zoölogy*, 132.

25 HJC, "On Apparent Equivocal Generation," *American Journal of Science and Arts*, vol. 28, no. 2 (1859): 154–55.

26 HJC's official title was assistant professor. See the minutes of a special meeting of the President and Fellows of Harvard College, 14 June 1860, *Corporation Records of Harvard University*, Harvard University Archives, vol. 10 (1857–1866), 125: "Voted. That Mr. Henry James Clarke [*sic*] be appointed Assistant Professor of Zoology, without any existing funds of the University." Present were President Felton and the Fellows of the Corporation, Chief Justice Lemuel Shaw (Herman Melville's father-in-law); Professor of Surgery George Hayward; John Amory Lowell; the Reverend

George Putnam; Judge Ebenezer Rockwood Hoar; and Treasurer Amos Abbott Lawrence, a nephew of the very Abbott Lawrence whose donation to Harvard had secured Agassiz's appointment. Clark's title notwithstanding, the designation of adjunct professor more accurately describes the reality of his appointment (communication from Mårten Liander, associate secretary to Harvard University, 10 April 2006).

27 HJC, Journal, 16 August 1860.

28 Fields, "Agassiz," in *Ballads and Other Verses*, 108–10.

29 HJC, Journal, 23 and 25 August 1860.

30 HJC, Journal, 18 and 30 August 1860. The proper German plural is *Semmeln*.

31 HJC, Journal, 1 and 2 September 1860 and 1 and 2 October 1860.

32 HJC, Journal, 4 October 1860. Clark misspells the German word *Platz*, "public square."

33 HJC, Journal, 5 October 1860.

34 HJC, Journal, 17 September 1860. Haeckel had read Agassiz's *Essay on Classification* in the summer of 1860, at the same time that he studied and annotated *On the Origin of Species*. His book *Radiolaria* (1862) commented favorably upon Darwin, although according to Sander Gliboff it is unlikely that he would have used a formal talk for grandstanding against Agassiz. Haeckel's reading notes don't reveal that, in the summer of 1860, he looked at the *Essay* as anything other than an ideological alternative to *Origin*. Mario A. DiGregorio, *Ernst Haeckel and Scientific Faith* (Göttingen: Vandenhoeck and Ruprecht, 2005), 83–85. An abstract of Haeckel's paper was printed in *Amtlicher Bericht über die fünf und dreissigste Versammlung deutscher Naturforscher und Ärzte in Königsberg in Preussen* (Königsberg: Hartungsche Buchdruckerei, 1861), 107. The conference proceedings also record "Clark, H.J. Professor der Zoologie" as one of the participants in the conference (7). Personal communication from Sander Gliboff, Department of the History and Philosophy of Science, Indiana University Bloomington, 20 August 2011.

35 HJC, Journal, 19 September 1860.

36 HJC, Journal, 28 September 1860; 4 and 7 September 1860.

37 HJC, Journal, 16 and 17 October 1860.

38 HJC, Journal, 17 and 18 October 1860.

39 HJC, Journal, 23 and 25 October 1860.

40 CD to AG, 26 September 1860, DCP, Letter 2930.

41 See Dorothy G. Wayman, *Edward Sylvester Morse: A Biography* (Cambridge, MA: Harvard University Press, 1942), 181.

42 See Lurie, *Louis Agassiz*, 314.

43 HJC, "To the Honorable Committee for visiting the Lawrence Scientific School," Archives, Ernst Mayr Library, MCZ, bMU 612.10.1.

44 LA to HJC, 24 March 1863, Harvard College Papers, second series, UAI 5_125, vol. 30, no. 67, Harvard University Archives. The letter is cited in Clark's Journal, 25 March 1863, though without Agassiz's conciliatory reference to his "independent career."

45 HJC, Journal, 30 March 1863. When Darwin, a few years after the incident, asked him about Clark, Asa Gray called him "a capital observer"

though with a "lumbering sort of mind." Clark was, he said, "quite incapable of understanding what Natural Selection meant," though, unlike his master, Agassiz, he had really made an effort. But even in this not altogether flattering context, Gray left no doubt about what he thought of Agassiz's treatment of his former assistant: "A. used him very unfairly as soon as he no longer wanted him." AG to CD, 7 August 1866; DCP 5184.

46 Thomas Hill, *The Annual Address Before the Harvard Natural History Society, Delivered by the Reverend Thomas Hill, Thursday, 19 May 1853* (Cambridge: John Bartlett, 1853), 15.

47 HJC, Journal, 30 March 1863.

48 See 30 May 1863, *Corporation Records of Harvard University*, vol. 10 (1857–1866), 310.

49 LA to Joseph Henry, 2 June 1863, Agassiz Letter Books, MCZ, vol. 2, 253–54.

50 See Winsor, *Reading the Shape of Nature*, 58.

51 LA to HJC, 25 June 1863, Agassiz Letter Books, MCZ, vol. 2, 265–66.

52 HJC, *A Claim for Scientific Property* (Cambridge, MA: privately printed, 1863), Harvard University Archives, HUG 300.

53 HJC, Journal, 9 September 1863.

54 28 November 1863, *Corporation Records of Harvard University*, vol. 10 (1857–1866), 335. See HJC, Journal, 14 December 1863.

55 HJC, Journal, 5 January 1864.

56 Verrill's relationship with Agassiz is amply documented in his journals: Private Journal of A. E. Verrill for 1859 (18 March–31 December), Harvard University Archives, HUD 859.90, and Journal, 1 January 1860–December 1863, Harvard University Archives, HUD 860.90.

57 Verrill, Private Journal, 15 November 1859 and 21 December 1859. The reference is to Henri Milne-Edwards's *Histoire naturelle des coralliaires, ou polypes proprement dits*, 3 vols. (Paris: Roret, 1867–60).

58 Verrill, Private Journal, 31 December 1859.

59 Verrill, Journal 1860–1863, 6 January 1860.

60 Verrill, Journal 1860–1863, 23 April 1860.

61 Verrill, Journal 1860–1863, 19 April 1863.

62 Verrill, Journal 1860–1863, 8 January 1860. I have not been able to confirm the existence of this institution. Somerville High School, which is still on Highland Street, opened its doors in 1852.

63 A photograph that creates a positive image on a sheet of glass. Less expensive than the daguerreotype, ambrotypes were all the fashion during the early 1860s.

64 Verrill, Journal 1860–1863, 25 July 1860; 1 August 1860. On 15 June 1865, Flora Louisa Smith became Verrill's wife. They had six children, among them Alpheus Hyatt Verrill, named after Verrill's Harvard classmate. See Wesley R. Coe, *Biographical Memoir of Addison Emery Verrill, 1839–1926, National Academy of Sciences of the United States of America 14: Second Memoir* (1929).

65 Verrill, Journal 1860–1863, 14 June 1860.

66 Verrill, Journal 1860–1863, 6 and 9 January 1860.

67 Verrill, Journal 1860–1863, 14 June 1860.

68 Morse's patience wore thin barely a month later and he left the museum: "I can do better with my time at home than I can do here." Agassiz refused to return Morse's collection of shells to him, thus depriving him of the opportunity to sell it. See Ralph W. Dexter, "The Salem Secession of Agassiz Zoologists," *Essex Institute Historical Collections*, vol. 101 (1965): 27–39; here 31. The quotations are from Morse's unpublished journal. A year later, though, Agassiz sent Morse $250—almost $7,000 today—to pay for the shells.

69 Addison Emery Verrill, "Revision of the Polyps of the Eastern Coast of the United States," *Memoirs Read Before the Boston Society of Natural History*, vol. 1 (1864): 1–64.

70 Verrill, Journal 1860–1863, 2 December 1862.

71 Verrill, Journal 1860–1863, 3 December 1862.

72 Verrill, Journal 1860–1863, 12 December 1862.

73 Verrill, Journal 1860–1863, 23 February, 8 March, 29 March 1863; 19 April 1863; 9 and 10 February 1863.

74 Verrill, Journal 1860–1863, 19 December 1863.

75 Josiah Gilbert Holland, *Bitter-sweet: A Poem*, 11th ed. (1858; New York: Scribner's, 1860), 168.

76 Verrill, Journal 1860–1863, 21 December 1863. When his "Revision of the Polyps" was published in 1864, Verrill thanked Agassiz profusely: "In the preparation of this paper, I have been greatly indebted to Prof. Agassiz, who has not only allowed me the unrestricted use of the extensive collection of the museum, but has also, with characteristic liberality, placed in my hands his magnificent series of drawings, made from life by Mr. J. Burkhardt" (2).

77 Coe, *Verrill*, 26.

78 HJC, *Mind*, 5n4.

79 "Notices of New Books: *Mind in Nature*, by Prof. H. J. Clark," *New Englander and Yale Review*, vol. 25, no. 96 (July 1866): 581–82.

80 HJC, *Mind*, 236, 9.

81 George Louis Leclerc, comte de Buffon (1707–1788), had proposed his theory of the degeneracy of the New World in volume 5 of his *Histoire naturelle générale et particulière* (1766).

82 HJC, *Mind*, 209.

83 Ibid., 112, 14–15, 54.

84 "Reviews and Literary Notices," *Atlantic Monthly*, vol. 17, no. 103 (May 1866): 649–50.

85 HJC, *Mind*, 315.

86 See also HJC's "Polarity and Polycephalism: An Essay on Individuality," *American Journal of Science and Arts*, vol. 49 (1870): 69–75, wherein Clark explains his new definition of individuality, one not based on monocephalism (the existence of one head) but on polarity, "the controlling influence of a power which . . . radiates itself through the whole organism" (71).

87 See HJC, "Conclusive Proofs of the Animality of the Ciliate Sponges, and of Their Affinities with the Infusoria Flagellata," *American Journal of Science and Arts*, vol. 42 (1866): 320–24.

88 H. James-Clark [HJC], "The American Spongilla, a Craspedote, Flagellate Infusorian," *American Journal of Science and Arts*, 3rd series, vol. 2, no. 12 (December 1871): 426–36.

89 See Iñaki Ruiz-Trillo, Gertraud Burger, Peter W. H. Holland, Nicole King, B. Franz Lang, Andrew J. Roger and Michael W. Gray, "The Origins of Multicellularity: A Multi-Taxon Genome Initiative," *Trends in Genetics*, vol. 23, no. 3 (2007): 113–18. In the article, HJC is given credit for being the first scientist to recognize the importance of choanoflagellates in the investigation of animal origins.

90 HJC, "American Spongilla," 434, 426.

91 Henry J. Slack, "The Nature of Sponges (Researches of Clark and Carter)," *Popular Science Review*, vol. 11 (1872): 167–76.

92 HJC to Henry Porter Clark and Abigail Orton Clark, 24 May 1869, Archives, Ernst Mayr Library, MCZ, bMU 612.10.2

93 AG to HJC, 16 March 1872, Collection of Daniel Weinstock, M.D., Geneva, NY.

94 "Contract Between L. N. Grainger and Henry James Clark, According to Plans and Specifications This Day Signed by Both Parties," 21 October 1872, Henry James Clark Papers (FS 048), Special Collections and University Archives, W.E.B. Du Bois Library, University of Massachusetts Amherst. The contract is in Clark's handwriting (not in Grainger's, as listed in the library's Finding Aid). In today's money, the house would have cost around $92,000.

95 Thomas Edward Clark, handwritten note attached to letter by Mary Holbrook Clark to Alpheus Hyatt, 18 November 1873 (note 7).

96 *The Amherst Directory, 1895. A Complete Index to the Residents, Businesses, Streets, etc. of the Town* (Shirley Village, MA: A. B. Sparrow, 1895), 58. See also Mary Holbrook Clark's letter to Alpheus Hyatt, 18 November 1873 (note 7).

97 HJC, *Lucernariae and Their Allies: A Memoir on the Anatomy and Physiology of Haliclystus Auricula, and Other Lucernarians, with a Discussion of Their Relations to Other Acalephae, to Beroids, and Polypi, Smithsonian Contributions to Knowledge*, vol. 242 (Washington: Smithsonian Institution, 1878).

98 HJC, *Lucernariae*, 15.

99 Ibid., 14.

100 Ibid., 63.

101 Ibid., 70.

102 Ibid., 74n1, 96.

103 Ibid., 97, 105.

104 *Annual Report of the Trustees of the Museum of Comparative Zoology, Together with the Report of the Director, 1863* (Boston: Wright and Potter, 1864), 9.

105 Corynne McSherry, *Who Owns Academic Work? Battling for Control of Intellectual Property* (Cambridge, MA: Harvard University Press, 2001).

106 LA to Frederic Ward Putnam, 24 March 1864; Agassiz Letter Books, vol. 2, MCZ, Houghton Deposit MCZ F 890. See also "Regulations for the Museum of Comparative Zoology," passed by the faculty of the MCZ on 5 November 1863, which state that "whatever is done by any one connected

with the Museum . . . is considered as the property of the Museum"; *Annual Report of the Trustees of the Museum of Comparative Zoology . . . 1864*, (Boston: Wright and Potter, 1865), 48–49.

107 Josiah Royce, "The Present Ideals of American Life," *Scribner's Magazine*, vol. 10 (1891): 376–88; see 383.

108 See, for example, Stephen Jay Gould, "In a Jumbled Drawer," in *Bully for Brontosaurus: Further Reflections in Natural History* (1991; London: Penguin, 1992), 309–24.

109 Cited in William Clark, *Academic Charisma and the Origins of the Research* (Chicago: University of Chicago Press, 2006), 468–69.

110 *Annual Report . . . 1863*, 9.

111 Xenos Clark to Benjamin Paul Blood, 3 October 1880, Autograph File, C, HL.

112 See Dmitri Tymoczko, "The Nitrous Oxide Philosopher," *Atlantic Monthly*, vol. 277, No. 5 (May 1996): 93–101.

113 See Clark's letter to William James, as quoted in James, *The Varieties of Religious Experience: A Study in Human Nature* (1901–1902; London: Fontana, 1975), 375n1.

114 Xenos Clark to Benjamin Paul Blood, 9 November 1880; 3 October 1880, both Autograph File C, HL.

115 Xenos Clark to Benjamin Paul Blood, 9 November 1880, HL, Autograph File C, HL.

116 James, *Varieties*, 375n1.

117 Xenos Clark to Benjamin Paul Blood, 21 July 1882, HL, Autograph File C, HL.

118 Xenos Y. Clark's obituary reported the official cause of death as Bright's disease and "some affection of the heart." See "The Late Xenos Y. Clark," 750.

6. A PINT OF INK

1 HJC to Henry Porter Clark and Abigail Orton Clark, 24 May 1869, Archives of Ernst Mayr Library, MCZ, bMU 612.10.2.

2 See LA, *Selecta genera et species piscium*, xi–xv and Tab. A–G.

3 See LA, "L'histoire de l' espèce humaine," FLA, Surdez, 17/3.3 See also the discussion of this lecture in chapter 2.

4 See LA, *Notice sur la géographie des animaux*, Extrait de la Revue Suisse, août 1845 (Neuchâtel: Henri Wolfrath, 1845).

5 Humboldt, *Cosmos*, vol. 1, 356, 358.

6 Gould, *Mismeasure of Man*, 76.

7 LA to Rose Mayor Agassiz, transcript, 2 December 1846, AP, HL, MS Am 1419 (66).

8 Elizabeth does not reliably indicate omissions from the letters. For Jefferson's comments on the "immovable veil of black" separating whites from their slaves, see Query XIV of his *Notes on the State of Virginia* (1784), in *The Life and Selected Writings of Thomas Jefferson*, edited by Adrienne Koch and William Peden (New York: Modern Library, 1944), 256.

9 LA to Rose Mayor Agassiz, 2 December 1846, AP, HL, MS Am 1419 (66).

10 James Baldwin, "Stranger in the Village," in *Notes of a Native Son* (1964; London: Corgi, 1974), 148–49.

11 Melville, *Moby-Dick*, 282.

12 He also mentions that he was completely taken with some bones found at Natchez, Mississippi, by one Dr. Dickson (for four hours he stared at them, finding it hard to believe what he saw): "I wish I could describe to you what I felt," he wrote to his mother, "when I realized that these were indeed human bones, and those of another race than ours." LA to Rose Mayor Agassiz, 2 December 1846; see note 7.

13 Samuel Morton, *Crania Americana; or, A Comparative View of the Skulls of Various Aboriginal Nations of North and South America* (Philadelphia: J. Dobson, 1839), 5, 6. Agassiz's copy in the Special Collections of the MCZ carries the following dedication in Morton's own hand: "M. Louis Agassiz, with the profound respect of the Author. Philadelphia, October 28, 1846."

14 Ibid., 283.

15 AG to Torrey, 24 January 1847, AG, *Letters*, vol. 1, 345–47.

16 Ibid., 347. Gray also excluded Indiana, which had inexcusably waffled on the slavery question, from the first edition of his abolitionist *Manual*. See AG, *Manual of the Botany of the Northern United States, from New England to Wisconsin and South to Ohio and Pennsylvania Inclusive* (Boston: Munroe, 1848). An amusing response to this decision is the copiously annotated copy of Gray's *Manual* in the Lilly Library, Indiana University Bloomington, once owned by Indiana's first resident botanist, Dr. Asahel Clapp. Inserted into the book are Dr. Clapp's own additions to Gray's *Manual*, lists of species found on the north side of the Ohio. Indiana had abolished slavery in its constitution of 1816. However, since 1824 the state also had its own fugitive slave law, delineating the steps slaveholders and officials had to follow in order to claim their "property." In practice, the law was used against those helping slaves escape. In 1850 the legislature, justifying Gray's doubts, passed another law, the Exclusion Act, making it illegal for African Americans to enter Indiana. Charles H. Money, "The Fugitive Slave Law of 1850 in Indiana," *Indiana Magazine of History*, vol. 17 (1921): 159–98, 257–97. For more on Dr. Clapp's copy, see Christoph Irmscher, *Music for the Worms: A Darwin Exhibit at Lilly Library, Indiana University Bloomington* (Bloomington: The Lilly Library, 2009), 8–9.

17 AG, *Letters*, vol. 2, 583, 584.

18 On the number of Holbrook's slaves, see Lester Stephens, *Science, Race, and Religion in the American South: John Bachman and the Charleston Circle of Naturalists, 1815–1859* (Chapel Hill: The University of North Carolina Press, 2000), 100. See also Michael P. Johnson, "Slavery in Charleston, SC," *Dictionary of Afro-American Slavery: Updated with a New Introduction and Bibliography* (Westport, CT: Greenwood, 1997), 96–98.

19 John Bachman, *The Doctrine of the Unity of the Human Race Examined on the Principles of Science* (Charleston, SC: C. Canning, 1850), 292. The definitive account of the discussions among Bachman and his Southern colleagues is Stephens, *Science, Race, and Religion.*

20 Bachman, *Doctrine of the Unity*, 8, 104–5.

21 Walt Whitman, *I Sit and Look Out: Editorials from the* Brooklyn Daily

Times, edited by Emory Holloway and Vernolian Schwarz (New York: Columbia University Press, 1932), 90. See also Aaron, *The Unwritten War*, 60–61.

22 *Emerson in His Journals*, 369 (March–April 1847), 463 (August 1855), 437 (August 1852).

23 See Josiah Nott, "An Examination of the Physical History of the Jews, in Its Bearings on the Question of the Unity of Races," in *Proceedings of the American Association for the Advancement of Science. Third Meeting, Held at Charleston, S.C., 1850* (Charleston: Walker & James, 1850), 98–107. Agassiz's comments are reprinted at the end of the article.

24 CD to William Darwin Fox, 4 September 1850, DCP 1352.

25 Robert W. Gibbes to Samuel G. Morton, 31 March 1850, Morton Papers, The Library Company of Philadelphia.

26 Agassiz's photographic studies of slaves were rediscovered in 1976 by Elinor Reichlin, a staff member of Harvard's Peabody Museum of Archaeology and Ethnology, in an unused storage cabinet in the museum's attic. Each daguerreotype case was embossed with the notation J. T. ZEALY, PHOTOGRAPHER, COLUMBIA, and several had handwritten labels. See Elinor Reichlin, "Faces of Slavery: A Historical Find," *American Heritage*, vol. 28, no. 4 (June 1977), 4–11; Brian Wallis, "Black Bodies, White Science: Louis Agassiz's Slave Daguerreotypes," *American Art*, vol. 9, no. 2 (Summer 1995): 39–61; and Gwyneira Isaacs, "Louis Agassiz's Photographs in Brazil: Separate Creations," *History of Photography*, vol. 21, no. 1 (1997): 3–12. The history of Zealy's photographs and the stories surrounding them is told (and in part creatively imagined) in Molly Rogers, *Delia's Tears: Race, Science, and Photography in Nineteenth-Century America* (New Haven: Yale University Press, 2010).

27 Quoted in Wallis, "Black Bodies," 60n13.

28 See, for example, Zealy's daguerreotype of the South Carolina Militia general Paul Quattlebaum, produced during the same year; Harvey S. Teal, *Partners with the Sun: South Carolina Photographers, 1840–1940* (Columbia: University of South Carolina Press, 2001), 30.

29 In January 1837, the young Harvard tutor Francis Bowen (mentioned in chapter 5 as a critic of Darwin) had panned Emerson's *Nature* in the pages of the journal. See his essay "Transcendentalism" in the *Christian Examiner and General Review*, vol. 21, no. 1 (January 1837): 371–85.

30 LA, "The Geographical Distribution of Animals," *Christian Examiner and Religious Miscellany*, vol. 48, no. 2 (March 1850): 181–204.

31 Ibid., 201.

32 LA, "The Diversity of Origin of the Human Races," *Christian Examiner and Religious Miscellany*, vol. 49, no. 1 (July 1850): 110–45; here 125.

33 Ibid., 110, 112–13, 111.

34 *The Poems of Emily Dickinson*, ed. Franklin, 581.

35 LA, "Diversity," 119, 136, 140, 141.

36 LA, "Contemplations of God in the Kosmos," *Christian Examiner and Religious Miscellany*, vol. 50, no. 1 (January 1851): 1–17.

37 Edward Lurie, "Louis Agassiz and the Races of Man," *Isis*, vol. 45, no. 3 (September 1954): 227–42; see 236.

38 LA, "Sketch of the Natural Provinces of the Animal World and Their Relation to the Different Types of Man," in Nott and Gliddon, *Types of Mankind* (2nd ed., 1854), lviii–lxxviii.

39 LA, *Notice sur la géographie des animaux*, 31.

40 LA, "Sketch," lxxiii, lxxiv, lxxiv–lxxv.

41 The most comprehensive treatment of Agassiz's concept of species is Mary P. Winsor, "Louis Agassiz and the Species Question," *Studies in History of Biology*, vol. 3 (1979): 89–117. Winsor ascribes Agassiz's insistence on the fixity of species to his "authoritarianism and the unwillingness to entertain alternative explanations."

42 LA, "Sketch," lxxvi. Having ventured that far, Agassiz immediately, and quite characteristically, takes a step backward: if our much-vaunted "liberty and moral responsibility" may thus seem less "spontaneous" and more "instinctive" than usually assumed, all this is still directed and ordered by God, the "All-wise and Omnipotent," so that the "great harmonies established in Nature" are fulfilled.

43 Melville, *Moby-Dick*, 273.

44 Quoted in Robert V. Bruce, *The Launching of Modern American Science: 1846–1876* (New York: Knopf, 1987), 271.

45 Caroline Gardiner Curtis, *Memories of Fifty Years in the Last Century: Written for Her Grandchildren* (Boston: privately printed, 1947), 37–38.

46 Tharp, *Adventurous Alliance*, 114. In his 1960 biography of Louis Agassiz, Edward Lurie does not mention Elizabeth's Southern letters at all. Paton and Tharp, writing about Elizabeth in 1919 and 1959, respectively, do cite them, but they cut several crucial passages, including those that reveal Elizabeth's racial prejudices.

47 ECA to Mary Perkins Cary, 22 December 1851, EAP, SL, A-3/10.

48 ECA to Sarah G. Cary, undated, winter 1851–1852, EAP, SL, A-3/10.

49 ECA to Mary Perkins Cary, 11 March 1853, EAP, SL, A-3/10.

50 ECA to Mary Perkins Cary, 11 March 1853. See also Thackeray to Anna Smith Strong Baxter, 12 March 1853, in *Thackeray's Letters to an American Family* (New York: Century, 1904), 53–54. In the same letter, Thackeray describes Agassiz as a "delightful *bonhomious* person as frank and unpretending as he is learned and illustrious in his own branch." He also mentions that he received $665 (almost $20,000 today) for three lectures.

51 Eyre Crowe, *With Thackeray in America* (London: Cassell, 1893).

52 Ibid., 134, 148, 150, 151, 152; see the sketch on page 151.

53 ECA to Mary Perkins Cary, 15 April [1853], EAP, SL, A-3/10.

54 ECA to Mary Perkins Cary, 17 April [1853], EAP, SL, A-3/10.

55 S. G. Howe to LA, 3 August 1863, AP, HL, MS 1419 (415).

56 Thomas Jefferson, *Notes on the State of Virginia*, Query XIV, *Selected Writings*, 255.

57 LA, Transcript of Letter to S. G. Howe, 9 August 1863, AP, HL, MS Am 1419 (150).

58 LA, Transcript of Letter to S. G. Howe, 10 August 1863, AP, HL, MS Am 1419 (151).

59 LA, Transcript of Letter to S. G. Howe, 11 August 1863, AP, HL, MS Am 1419 (152).

60   LA to S. G. Howe, 15 August 1863, AP, HL, MS Am 1419 (153).

61   S. G. Howe to LA, 18 August 1863, AP, HL, MS Am 1419 (416). In her biography, Elizabeth reprints only two letters, those of August 6 and 10, 1863, and mentions a third, unfinished one "which was never forwarded to Dr. Howe." But there are, aside from Agassiz's initial acknowledgment of Howe's inquiry (6 August 1863, HL, Autograph File A), in fact, *two* more, dated August 11 and 15, and she incorporated material from both, without further acknowledgment, into her version of the August 10 letter. It is not entirely clear which of Agassiz's letters Howe did receive, since the manuscripts we do have are, with the exception of the letter written on August 15, 1863 (which carries a note in his wife's handwriting that it had remained "unfinished"), transcripts written by Elizabeth and by an unidentified second hand. The content of Howe's response, which is almost entirely devoted to an analysis of "mulattoism," does create the impression that he received only the first two Agassiz letters.

62   James McPherson, *The Struggle for Equality: Abolitionists and the Negro in the Civil War and Reconstruction* (Princeton, NJ: Princeton University Press, 1967), 146–47.

63   *Letters and Journals of Samuel Gridley Howe*, edited by Laura E. Richards, 2 vols. (London: John Lane, 1906–1909), vol. 2, 41–42.

64   S. G. Howe to Francis W. Bird, 14 June 1876. Cited in Harold Schwartz, *Samuel Gridley Howe, Social Reformer, 1801–1876* (Cambridge, MA: Harvard University Press, 1956), 252, 257.

65   David Herbert Donald, *Lincoln* (London: Cape, 1995), 220.

66   18 September 1858, in *The Complete Lincoln-Douglas Debates of 1858*, edited by Paul M. Angle (1958; Chicago: University of Chicago Press, 1991), 235–36.

67   Ibid., 633–34.

68   Herman Melville, *Battle-Pieces and Aspects of the War* (New York: Harper and Brothers, 1866), 268–69.

69   Laurie Robertson-Lorant, *Melville: A Biography* (1996; Amherst: University of Massachusetts Press, 1998), 495.

70   Laura Wood Roper, *FLO: A Biography of Frederick Law Olmsted* (1973; Baltimore: Johns Hopkins University Press, 1983), 221–22.

71   "Testimony of Fred. Law Olmstead [*sic*], Esq., Secretary of Sanitary Commission, Before the Special Inquiry Commission, April 22, '63," American Freedmen's Inquiry Commission Records, HL, MS Am 702 (74). The manuscript appears to be in the handwriting of George Chapman, the secretary of the American Freedmen's Inquiry Commission.

72   *Preliminary Report Touching the Condition and Management of Emancipated Refugees, Made to the Secretary of War, June 30, 1863* (New York, 1863), available at http://www.civilwarhome.com/prelimcommissionreport.htm. All quotations are from this easily accessible web version.

73   See the account of a lawsuit brought against Anthony, "An Astonishing Plea," *Law Notes*, vol. 21 (July 1917): 70–71.

74   D. R. Anthony, "Answers to General Circular," 30 August 1863, American Freedmen's Inquiry Commission Records, HL, MS Am 702 (5).

75 Horace James to the Commission, 13 November 1863, American Freedmen's Inquiry Commission Records, HL, MS Am 702 (55). The letter is misdated as April 1, 1863, in the Houghton Finding Aid.

76 S. G. Howe, "Abstract of Mr. Eatons [*sic*] Report," American Freedmen's Inquiry Commission Records, HL, MS Am 702 (37).

77 See John Fonerden to George T. Chapman, 26 August 1863, American Freedmen's Inquiry Commission Records, HL, MS Am 702 (137); C. A. Walker to S. G. Howe, 22 April 1864, American Freedmen's Inquiry Commission Records, HL, MS Am 702 (156). Dr. Walker is misidentified as "C. N. Wolker" in the Houghton Finding Aid. John E. Tyler to the Commission, 24 August 1863, American Freedmen's Inquiry Commission Records, HL, MS Am 702 (153).

78 Frederick Law Olmsted to S. G. Howe, 13 August 1863, American Freedmen's Inquiry Commission Records, HL, MS Am 702 (74). "Backers" are porters or unloaders at the dock. A penciled note in Howe's handwriting on Olmsted's manuscript identifies the topic of the letter as the "Question of the vitality of blacks + yellows."

79 See most recently Oz Frankel, "The Predicament of Racial Knowledge: Government Studying the Freedmen During the Civil War," *Social Research*, vol. 70, no. 1 (Spring 2003): 45–81. Harold Schwartz, in *Samuel Gridley Howe*, praises the commission's "masterly indictment of the white race" but adds that the "*Report* was quietly shelved and no notice of it was taken" (267). The final version, published in *Sen. Exec. Doc.*, 38 Cong., 1 sess., no. 53, can be accessed at http://www.civilwarhome.com/commis sionreport.htm.

80 Samuel Gridley Howe, *The Refugees from Slavery in Canada West: Report to the Freedmen's Inquiry Commission* (Boston: Wright & Potter, 1864), 33.

81 31 August 1866, *Emerson in His Journals*, 541–42.

82 See the excellent discussion of Shaler's racial ideology in chapter 5 of David N. Livingstone, *Nathaniel Southgate Shaler and the Culture of American Science* (Tuscaloosa: University of Alabama Press, 1987).

83 Nathaniel Southgate Shaler, "The Negro Problem," *Atlantic Monthly*, vol. 54, no. 325 (1884): 696–709.

84 *Narrative of the Life of Frederick Douglass, an American Slave* (1845).

85 Darwin to Charles Lyell, 23 September 1860, DCP 2925. Darwin might have come across that phrase in an article—an unabashed celebration of British colonial rule in India—published in 1856. The phrase is used entirely without irony. The French, had they gone to India, would have quickly become "Hindooized," but not the British, the author argues: "The British race are the Romans of the modern world . . . They go forth dominating and civilizing . . . ever tending to a policy not unaptly expressed by the American phrase 'improving off the face of the earth.'" "India Under Lord Dalhousie," *Blackwood's Edinburgh Magazine*, vol. 80 (1856): 233–56; here 243.

86 Wallace did not envision racial mixing as the way by which such homogeneity would be achieved. The process he described was almost mystical, a gradual process of purification and improvement by which "the passions

and animal propensities" of humans will be "restrained within those limits which most conduce to happiness." Alfred Russel Wallace, "The Origin of Human Races and the Antiquity of Man Deduced from the Theory of 'Natural Selection,'" *Anthropological Review and Journal of the Anthropological Society of London*, vol. 2 (1864): clviii–clxxxvii. Wallace's positions and Darwin's response are lucidly described in Ross A. Slotten, *The Heretic in Darwin's Court: The Life of Alfred Russel Wallace* (New York: Columbia University Press, 2004), 209–16.

87 See Ruse, *Darwin and Design*, 105–6.

88 See the section "The Influence of Beauty in Determining the Marriages of Mankind," in Darwin's *Descent of Man*, 586–98. For Darwin's remark on the Fuegians, see 595n68.

89 Thomas Smyth, *The Unity of Human Races Proved to Be the Doctrine of Scripture, Reason, and Science; with a Review of the Present Position and Theory of Professor Agassiz* (New York: Putnam, 1850).

90 "Senior," "Orthodoxy vs. Slavery," *National Era*, vol. 6, no. 307 (18 November 1852): 187.

91 Schweizer Nationalrat, 18. Sitzung, 10-05-2007, 07.3486: Interpellation Sommaruga, Carlo: "Louis Agassiz vom Sockel holen und dem Sklaven Renty die Würde zurückgeben" / Interpellation Sommaruga, Carlo, "Démonter Louis Agassiz et redonner la dignité à l'esclave Renty," and Reply Nationalrat, 09-12-2007; see the official documents on the website of the Swiss parliament: http://www.parlament.ch/F/Suche/Pages/geschaefte .aspx?gesch_id=20073486. Sommaruga's motion was inspired by Hans Fässler, *Reise in Schwarz-Weiss: Schweizer Ortstermine in Sachen Sklaverei* (Zürich: Rotpunktverlag, 2005). On Agassiz, see 145–53.

92 Charles Sumner, *The Question of Caste: Lecture by the Hon. Charles Sumner* (Boston: Wright and Potter, 1869); Werner Sollors, *Neither Black nor White Yet Both: Thematic Explorations of Interracial Literature* (New York: Oxford University Press, 1997), 134.

7. A DELICATE BALANCE

1 The lecture was among several transcribed by Adelaide Edmands, the fiancée of Agassiz's student Frederic W. Putnam. Excerpts from these lectures appear in Ralph Dexter, "Agassiz on Zoological Classification and Nomenclature," *Bios*, vol. 50, no. 4 (December 1979): 218–22; see 221.

2 See Nina Baym's pioneering chapter "Elizabeth Cary Agassiz and Heroic Science," in Baym, *American Women of Letters and the Nineteenth-Century Sciences: Styles of Affiliation* (New Brunswick, NJ: Rutgers University Press, 2002), 91–112. I am also indebted to the work of Linda Bergmann; see her "'Troubled Marriage of Discourses': Science Writing and Travel Narrative in Louis and Elizabeth Cary Agassiz's *A Journey in Brazil*," *Journal of American Culture*, vol. 18 (1995): 83–88; and "Widows, Hacks, and Biographers: The Voice of Professionalism in Elizabeth Agassiz's *Louis Agassiz: His Life and Correspondence*," *Auto/Biography Studies*, vol. 12 (1997): 1–21.

3 I acquired the autograph from the bookseller Mark Stirling of Up-Country Letters in 2009 but have not been able to find out details about its provenance.

4 "The Sea-Cow," *The Annual of Scientific Discovery, or Yearbook of Facts in Science and Art*, edited by David A. Wells and George Bliss Jr. (Boston: Gould, Kendall, and Lincoln, 1850), 313–14. Agassiz's portrait serves as the frontispiece of the volume, and the editors, after thanking him for his help, include a laudatory biographical note, praising him for the "large number of communications" he had made to the American Academy of Arts and Sciences and "other scientific bodies." Wells, who graduated from the Lawrence Scientific School in 1851, went on to become a noted economist, with special expertise on tariffs and taxation.

5 Emma F. Cary, "Memories, Old Temple Place," Gardiner Family Papers A-70/M-59 (6).

6 See Herbert S. Klein, *A Population History of the United States* (Cambridge, UK: Cambridge University Press, 2004), 100–101.

7 Paton, *Elizabeth Cary Agassiz*, 22.

8 Curtis, *Memories of Fifty Years*, 132.

9 See Paton, *Elizabeth Cary Agassiz*, 31.

10 Harriet P. Holbrook to LA, 6 January 1850, AP, HL, MS Am 1419 (401).

11 *Life*, vol. 2, 477.

12 The letter is simply dated "Tuesday evening Temple Place." Elizabeth Cary to LA, EAP, SL, A 3/9.

13 Elizabeth Cary to LA, Winter 1849, EAP, SL, A 3/9.

14 ECA to Sarah Gray Cary, 11 September 1868; Paton, *Elizabeth Cary Agassiz*, 113.

15 Elizabeth Cary to LA, 1849/1850, EAP, SL, A 3/9. The letter is dated "Thursday morning," but Elizabeth refers to Agassiz's stay in Columbia, which took place in March 1850 (he was "exploring" the plantations in the area then; see chapter 6).

16 CD, "Second Note on Marriage," Darwin Archive, Cambridge University Library, DAR 210.10 [July 1838?], http://www.darwinproject.ac.uk/darwins-notes-on-marriage.

17 Paton, *Elizabeth Cary Agassiz*, 185.

18 For ECA's "impact" on scientific culture, see also Debra Lindsay, "Intimate Inmates: Wives, Households, and Science in Nineteenth-Century America," *Isis*, vol. 89 (1998): 631–52.

19 LA to James Dwight Dana, 26 January 1855, AP, HL, MS Am 1419 (127).

20 *Origin*, 1.

21 Tharp, *Adventurous Alliance*, 138.

22 Quoted in Tharp, *Adventurous Alliance*, 139–40.

23 Mary King Longfellow, Diary, 7 and 26 May 1866, Mary King Longfellow Papers, Longfellow House-Washington's Headquarters National Historic Site, box 1, folder 1.

24 Mrs. Harrison Gray Otis [Eliza Henderson Bordman], *The Barclays of Boston* (Boston: Ticknor, Reed, and Fields, 1854), 15.

25 *Life*, vol. 2, 526–27.

26 ECA to William H. Gardiner, 5 January 1874, Gardiner Family Papers, SL, A-70/M-59.

27 LA to J. E. Holbrook, 1858, AP, HL, MS Am 1419 (137).

28 ECA to William H. Gardiner, 5 January 1874, Gardiner Family Papers, SL, A-70/M-59.

29 More than $4,000 in today's money.

30 Thus the retrospective comment by M. Carey Thomas, the second president of Bryn Mawr College. Quoted in Tiffany K. Wayne, *Women's Roles in Nineteenth-Century America* (Westport, CT: Greenwood, 2007), 84.

31 Alice Hooper et al. to LA, 22 April 1873, AP, HL, MS Am 1419 (412).

32 Having said that, Cook provides an impressive list of survivors: Joel Asaph Allen and A. S. Bickmore of the American Museum of Natural History in New York; W. K. Brooks of Johns Hopkins University; David Starr Jordan, the president of Stanford University; Edward S. Morse of Salem; William H. Niles of MIT; P. R. Uhler of the Peabody Institute in Baltimore; Samuel H. Scudder of Cambridge; A. E. Verrill of Yale University; and Burt G. Wilder of Cornell University. "Forthcoming Celebration of the Centenary of Louis Agassiz by the Cambridge Mass. Historical Society," *New York Times*, 18 May 1907.

33 *A First Lesson in Natural History, by Actaea* [ECA] (Boston: Little, Brown, 1859), 3.

34 *First Lesson*, 3, 7–8. My own copy once belonged to three brothers, Edward, Matthew, and John Harkins, of 18 Florence Street in Boston (one of them, Matthew, would later rise to prominence as the bishop of Providence, Rhode Island).

35 *First Lesson*, 62, 63, 36, 26, 23, 12–13, 80.

36 Ibid., 65–67.

37 Ibid., 47, 48. Haeckel, however, uses the very same observation as proof that Darwin's theory is true: "The whole organization of the Medusa rises far above its low ancestral form, the polyp," he notes with satisfaction in his *History of Creation*. "Those who, like myself, have for many years studied the natural history of the splendid Medusae, and their alternation of generation with the adherent polyps, may from this alone even become firmly convinced of the truth of the Theory of Descent. For it alone can explain in the simplest manner the numerous and wonderful phenomena of the Medusae, which without the doctrine of descent would be utterly inexplicable." Haeckel, *The History of Creation; or, the Development of the Earth and Its Inhabitants by the Action of Natural Causes*, translated by E. Ray Lankester, 4th ed., 2 vols. (London: Kegan Paul, Trench, Trübner & Co., 1899), vol. 2, 184–85.

38 *First Lesson*, 59–60.

39 In her biography of Agassiz, Elizabeth later remembered how especially the smaller jellyfish would fill up the deep glass bowls in the laboratory at Nahant, and she repeated her praise for the strange animals: "Their structure is so delicate, yet so clearly defined, their color so soft, yet often so brilliant, their texture so transparent, that you seek in vain among terrestrial forms for terms of comparison, and are tempted to say that nature has done her finest work in the sea rather than on land." *Life*, vol. 2, 548–49.

40 *First Lesson*, 14, 73, 74, 78.

41 Ibid., 75, 76.

42 A second edition of *Seaside Studies* was published in 1871 by James Osgood, the successor of James Fields.

43 Ibid., v. In his preface to his *Actinologia Britannica: A History of the British Sea-Anemones and Corals*, Gosse said that he had wanted to write a book "a student can work with" (London: Van Voorst, 1860), v.

44 ECA, *Seaside Studies*, 38–39.

45 Ibid., 2–3, 9.

46 Ibid., 10–11, 37–38.

47 Ibid., 25.

48 See Thoreau's "Chesuncook" (1858), later incorporated into *The Maine Woods* (1864).

49 ECA, *Seaside Studies*, 39, 32, 53, 56.

50 Ibid., 58, 60.

51 Ibid., 60, 61, 84, 98.

52 Ibid., 153, 139.

53 Ibid., 105.

54 See "Mrs. Agassiz Dies at Arlington Home," *Boston Journal*, 28 June 1907.

55 ECA to Mrs. Quincy A. Shaw, not dated; quoted in Paton, *Elizabeth Cary Agassiz*, 114–15.

56 The first installment was LA, "Methods of Study in Natural History," *Atlantic Monthly* 9, no. 51 (January 1862): 1–14.

57 ECA to Sarah Gray Cary, 29 April 1862; quoted in Paton, *Elizabeth Cary Agassiz*, 65–66. My emphasis. The installment appeared in the *Atlantic Monthly*, vol. 9, no. 55 (May 1862): 570–78.

58 *Journey*, 290n, 495, 25.

59 Ibid., 43.

60 Ibid., 59, 160.

61 William James, Brazil diary, 1865, Archives, Ernst Mayr Library, MCZ, bMu 1556.41.1; see entry for 6 October 1865.

62 *Journey*, 294.

63 Ibid., 214.

64 James, Brazilian Diary, 1865–1866, Notebook 4, William James Papers, HL, bMS Am 1092.9 (4498).

65 *Journey*, 90.

66 Ibid., v.

67 Ibid., 110.

68 Ibid., 120.

69 Ibid., 124, 129, 133, 226, 232, 135.

70 Ibid., 136–38.

71 Ibid., 143–44. See Mercutio's speech in Shakespeare's *Romeo and Juliet*, act 1, scene 4.

72 *Journey*, 144, 259.

73 Ibid., 274.

74 Ibid., 327.

75 Ibid., 361, 480.

76 ECA to Mary Perkins Cary, 18 November 1867, in Paton, *Elizabeth Cary Agassiz*, 105.

77 William James's complicated dealings with Mr. and Mrs. Agassiz and his participation in the Brazilian excursion have been the subject of several studies, including my *Poetics of Natural History;* see chapter 5, "Agassiz Agonistes." Menand, *The Metaphysical Club*, devotes a chapter to James and Agassiz. All these accounts, not excepting my own, stress how "uninspiring" (Menand, 137) James found his Brazilian experience. The most forceful recent treatment of James's Brazilian episode is Maria Helena P. T. Machado's bilingual, definitive edition, *Brazil Through the Eyes of William James: Letters, Diaries, Drawings, 1865–1866* (Cambridge, MA: Harvard University Press, 2006). Machado believes that James's writings on Brazil show the kind of empathy for the regions and its inhabitants the other participants in the expedition sorely lacked, thus transcending the "conventional, stereotypical repertory of tropical narratives" that shapes the book written about the same trip by Mrs. Agassiz, who, according to James, "can't describe landscape, or in fact anything, worth a damn." Letter to Thomas Wren Ward, 24 May 1868, in *The Correspondence of William James*, edited by Ignas K. Skrupselis, vol. 4 (Charlottesville: University of Virginia Press, 1996), 309; quoted also by Machado, 21. In her analysis of the passage, Machado says that James found *Journey* to be "pleasant reading" though he "was not at all convinced by its contents." But in fact he reports being "*very much* pleased" with the book (which he had expected to be duller); the criticism cited earlier pertains to style, not content.

78 ECA to Sarah ("Sallie") Gray Cary, 8 March 1866; ECA to Mary Perkins Cary, 18 November 1865; ECA to Sarah Gray Cary, 8 January 1866; ECA to Mary Perkins Cary, 11 December 1865; ECA to Pauline Agassiz Shaw, 8 September 1865; all in Paton, *Elizabeth Cary Agassiz*, 96, 90, 95, 91, 88.

79 *Journey*, x. Charles Frederick Hartt, *Scientific Results of a Journey in Brazil, by Louis Agassiz and His Traveling Companions: Geology and Physical Geography of Brazil* (Boston: Fields, Osgood and Co., 1870), 23. For a brilliant analysis of Hartt's defection from the Agassiz camp, see William R. Brice and Silvia F. de M. Figueirôa, "Charles Hartt, Louis Agassiz, and the Controversy Over Pleistocene Glaciation in Brazil," *History of Science*, vol. 39 (2001): 161–83.

80 The author of ECA's earlier article, "An Amazonian Picnic," *Atlantic Monthly*, vol. 17, no. 101 (March 1866): 313–23, was only identified as "Mrs. Agassiz."

81 For LA's own account, see "Report upon Deep-Sea Dredgings in the Gulf Stream, During the Third Cruise of the U.S. Steamer *Bibb*," *Bulletin of the Museum of Comparative Zoology*, vol. 13 (1869): 363–85.

82 ECA, "A Dredging Excursion in the Gulf Stream, I," *Atlantic Monthly*, vol. 24, no. 144 (October 1864): 507–51; see 516. ECA, "A Dredging Excursion in the Gulf of Mexico, II," *Atlantic Monthly*, vol. 24, no. 145 (November 1869): 571–78; see 572.

83 ECA, "A Dredging Excursion, I," 507–16; see 509.

84 ECA, "A Dredging Excursion, II," 574, 579, 572.

85 *The Best American Science Writing 2009*, edited by Natalie Angier (New York: Ecco, 2009), x.

8. A GALÁPAGOS PICNIC

1 Alexander Agassiz, *Revision of the Echini, Parts I and II. Illustrated Catalogue of the Museum of Comparative Zoology at Harvard College*, no. 7 (Cambridge, MA: University Press, 1872), 16.

2 Benjamin Peirce to LA, 18 February 1871, AP, HL, MS Am 1419 (567).

3 See Benjamin Peirce to ECA, 18 December 1867: "During the short time that I have been able to keep your book in my hands, from the ravenous demands of my wife and children, I have examined it enough to feel sure that it will be a very great success. It is elegant in style—in the much refined good taste—and in all ways worthy of science, our country and our age. But its highest attraction is that it contains such a perfect portrait of our beloved and great-hearted Agassiz. I did not know that you were such an artiste." AP, HL, MS Am 1419 (566).

4 *Life*, vol. 2, 690.

5 CD to Alexander Agassiz, 1 June 1871, in A. Agassiz, *Letters and Recollections*, 118–19.

6 LA to Carl Gegenbaur, 28 July 1872, AP, HL, MS Am 1419 (171).

7 *Life*, vol. 2, 692.

8 Philip C. Johnson, born on November 21, 1828, was the brother of the well-known painter Eastman Johnson, cofounder of the Metropolitan Museum of Art. Captain Johnson died on January 28, 1887, in Portsmouth, NH. His wife was Elvira Lindsay (1838–1908), from Talcahuano, Chile, the daughter of a Scotsman and a Chilean woman. See Philip Johnson's death notice in *The Record* (Valparaiso), vol. 16, no. 243 (24 March 1887): 4, as well as his obituary in *United States Naval Academy Graduates Association: Fourth Annual Reunion, June 6, 1884* (Baltimore: Isaac Friedenwald, 1890), 24–25; and ECA to Sarah ("Sallie") Gray Cary, *Hassler* Letters, 25 April 1871, EAP, SL, A-3/19. The *Hassler* was decommissioned in 1895 after its maintenance became too expensive for the Coast Survey. Rechristened *Clara Nevada*, it hit a rock and sank off the coast of Alaska in February 1898. The submerged wreck has recently attracted new interest. See the excellent project website maintained by the National Marine Sanctuaries: www.sanctuaries .noaa.gov/maritime/expeditions/hassler/mission/html.

9 The drawing is based on a photograph now in the collections of the MCZ, with the names of the group's members listed verso. The numbers on the drawing reflect the list supplied on the photograph, which also carries the handwritten caption, in Blake's hand, "on board the Hassler after coming from a visit to the Hass glacier. 1872." For the group's visit to the Hassler Glacier, see pages 325–26 in this book.

10 J. H. Blake, Scrapbook of Clippings, Photographs, Cartes-de-Visite Studio Portraits, Manuscripts and Other Materials, Archives, Ernst Mayr Library, MCZ, Harvard University, sMu 326.43.1.

11 Agnes Repplier, *J. William White, M.D.: A Biography* (Boston: Houghton Mifflin, 1919), 8.

12 Ibid., 25.

13 All the following quotations are from the autograph letters at the Schlesinger Library: ECA, *Hassler* Letters (1871–1872), 27 items, EAP, SL, A-3/19.

14 See ECA, "The Hassler Glacier in the Straits of Magellan," *Atlantic Monthly*, vol. 30, no. 180 (October 1872): 472–78; "In the Straits of Magellan," *Atlantic Monthly*, vol. 31, no. 183 (January 1873): 89–95; "A Cruise Through the Galápagos," *Atlantic Monthly*, vol. 31, no. 187 (March 1873): 579–84.

15 Hill's and White's dispatches are collected in a scrapbook erroneously identified as containing Elizabeth Agassiz's work: *Narrative of the Voyage of the* Hassler *in the Form of Letters Written on Board by Mrs. Agassiz and Published in the Boston Transcript and the New York Tribune, 1871–1872*, Archives, Ernst Mayr Library, MCZ, Harvard University, MCZ 023.

16 Entry for 23 March 1872, J. H. Blake, *Hassler* Journal, 1871–1872, vol. 2. Archives, Ernst Mayr Library, MCZ, Harvard University, sMu 326.41.1.

17 "The *Hassler* Expedition: A Letter from Professor Agassiz," *San Francisco Evening Bulletin* (29 July 1872): 1. The original is in AP, HL, MS Am 1419 (172). Agassiz's other letters appeared in the *New-York Tribune*: "The *Hassler* Expedition: Professor Agassiz Reports on the Gulf Weed" (4 January 1872): 2 (for a transcript of the original letter, see LA to Peirce, 15 December 1872, AP, HL, MS Am 1419 [170]); "The *Hassler* Expedition: Professor Agassiz Justifies His Prophecies" (12 February 1872): 3; "The *Hassler* Expedition: Letter from Prof. Agassiz—Signs of Glacial Action in the Southern Hemisphere" (18 April 1872): 5.

18 ECA to Sarah Gray Cary, *Hassler* Letters, 18 December 1871.

19 ECA to Mary Perkins Cary, 29 December 1871 and 12 January 1872.

20 ECA to Sarah Gray Cary, *Hassler* Letters, 10 February 1872.

21 ECA to Sarah Gray Cary and Mary ("Mollie") Cary Felton, *Hassler* Letters, 10 and 26 February 1872.

22 ECA to Mary Perkins Cary, *Hassler* Letters, 3 March 1872.

23 Repplier, *William White*, 13–14.

24 ECA to Mary Perkins Cary, *Hassler* Letters, 3 March 1872.

25 ECA to Mary Perkins Cary, *Hassler* Letters, 4 March 1872.

26 ECA to Mary Perkins Cary, *Hassler* Letters, 4 March 1872.

27 ECA to Mary Perkins Cary, *Hassler* Letters, 5 March 1872.

28 ECA to Mary Perkins Cary, *Hassler* Letters, 6 March 1872.

29 ECA to Mary Perkins Cary, *Hassler* Letters, 9 March 1872.

30 ECA to Mary Perkins Cary, *Hassler* Letters, 13 and 15 March 1872.

31 ECA to Mary Perkins Cary, *Hassler* Letters, 15 March 1872.

32 CD, *Journal of Researches*, 196 (Patagonia, December 1833).

33 See page 78 in this book.

34 CD, *Journal of Researches*, 306 (Tierra del Fuego, June 1834).

35 ECA to Mary Perkins Cary, *Hassler* Letters, 23 March 1872 and 12 April 1872.

36 ECA to Mary Cary Felton, *Hassler* Letters, 28 March 1872.

37 ECA to Mary Perkins Cary, *Hassler* Letters, 23 March 1872.

38 ECA to Mary Perkins Cary, *Hassler* Letters, 20 and 27 March 1872.

39 See CD, *Journal of Researches*, 235–36 (December 1832).

40 J. H. Blake, *Journal*, vol. 2, 20 and 27 March 1872.

41 ECA to Mary Cary Felton, *Hassler* Letters, 12 April 1872.

42 ECA to Sarah Gray Cary, *Hassler* Letters, 13 April 1872.

43 ECA to Mary Perkins Cary, *Hassler* Letters, 4 and 7 May 1872.

44 ECA to Mary Perkins Cary, *Hassler* Letters, 24 May 1872.

45 ECA, "A Cruise Through the Galapagos," see n14.

46 CD, *Journal of Researches*, 455–56 (September 1835).

47 Entry for 23 June 1872, J. H. Blake, *Hassler* Journal, vol. 2.

48 See CD, *Journal of Researches*, 109 (August 1833). The incident happened at Port Desire in Patagonia (now Argentina). The species name was John Gould's idea.

49 LA to Benjamin Peirce, AP, HL, MS Am 1419 (172). Agassiz ignores Darwin's main point, namely, that God, had he produced such diversity, would have had no reason to create the inhabitants of these islands so that they would resemble other species to be found, in close proximity, on the South American mainland. See Stephen Jay Gould, "Agassiz in the Galápagos," in *Hen's Teeth and Horse's Toes: Further Reflections in Natural History* (New York: Norton, 1983), 107–19.

50 But see Edward J. Larson, *Evolution's Workshop: Science and God on the Galápagos Islands* (New York: Basic, 2001), who argues that Elizabeth "bluntly" agreed with her husband's anti-evolutionist stance (265n10). In *Methods*, largely ghostwritten by Elizabeth, "alchemy" still appears as a derogatory term for Darwin's theory of evolution: "The philosopher's stone is no more to be found in the organic than the inorganic world; and we shall seek as vainly to transform the lower animal types into the higher ones by any of our theories, as did the alchemists of old to change their base metals into gold" (319). How interesting, then, to see her, just a few years later, at least grant "subtlety" to Darwin's view.

51 CD, *Journal of Researches*, 455.

52 See Winsor, *Reading the Shape of Nature*, 76n. The official report about the expedition was provided by Louis François de Pourtalès as Appendix 11. "Voyage of the Steamer *Hassler* from Boston to San Francisco," in *The Report of the Superintendent of the United States Coast Survey, Showing the Progress of the Survey During the Year 1872* (Washington: Government Printing Office, 1872), 213–22. For more on the scientific results of the expedition, see Alexander Agassiz and L. F. de Pourtalès, *Echini, Crinoids, and Corals: Memoirs of the Museum of Comparative Zoology*, vol. 4, pt. 1 of *Zoological Results of the* Hassler *Expedition*, 1 (Cambridge, UK: Cambridge University Press, 1874).

53 ECA to William H. Gardiner, 5 January 1874, Gardiner Family Papers, SL, A-70/M-59.

54 Lucy Audubon's *Life of John James Audubon* (1869) or Annie Fields's compilation of James Fields's *Biographical Notes and Sketches* (1881) come to mind. Richard Holmes recounts the interesting case of Sir Humphry Davy's widow, Lady Jane Davy, who "made no attempt to publish anything of Davy's, or about him, though she dined out for the next twenty years on her amusing tales of 'dear, great Sir Humphry.'" See Richard Holmes, *The*

Age of Wonder: How the Romantic Generation Discovered the Beauty and Terror of Science (London: HarperPress, 2008), 433.

55 ECA to Henry Wadsworth Longfellow, Longfellow Papers, HL, bMS Am 1340.2 (44).

56 Paton, *Elizabeth Cary Agassiz*, 184.

57 ECA to Longfellow, 26 July 1877, Longfellow Papers, HL, bMS Am 1340.2 (44). See Longfellow's diary for October 8, 1877: "Mrs. Agassiz reads to me the Life of Agassiz she is writing, the beginning only. Very interesting. Childhood." And October 10: "Then to Mrs. Agassiz. Letters and Life at Munich." Longfellow, Journal, 1 January 1874–31 January 1882, Longfellow Papers, HL, MS Am 1340 (214).

58 *Life*, vol. 1, iii.

59 Ibid., 762.

60 See pages 298–99 in this book.

61 ECA to William James, 28 October 1885, Letters to William James, HL, MS Am 1092 (10).

62 Anna Weld Carret (Mrs. Charles B. Dunlap), "Radcliffe College—1870 [*sic*]," Papers of Annie Ware Winsor Allen, 1880–1950, SL, SC 35.

63 Gertrude Stein, *Everybody's Autobiography* (New York: Random House, 1938); Leslie W. Hopkinson to Annie Allen, 20 November 1942, Papers of Annie Ware Winsor Allen, SL, SC 35.

64 ECA to William James, 22 July 1902, Letters to William James, HL, MS Am 1092 (6). In *The Varieties of Religious Experience*, James had declared that we cannot "avoid the conclusion that in religion we have a department of human nature with unusually close relations to the transmarginal or subliminal region" (462). Given the sometimes rocky relationship between her husband and his former student, Elizabeth would have appreciated the methodological advice James quoted at the beginning of a chapter with case studies of religious conversion: "As Professor Agassiz used to say, one can see no farther into a generalization than just so far as one's previous acquaintance with particulars enable one to take it in" (219). Study the facts, not the books.

65 ECA to William James, 14 December 1902, transcript, Letters to William James, HL, MS Am 1902 (7).

66 "Mrs. Agassiz Dies at Arlington Home," *Boston Journal*, 28 June 1907.

EPILOGUE

1 See the Centennial Exhibition, "Stanford and the 1906 Earthquake," by the Stanford University Archives, http://quake06.stanford.edu/centennial/tour/stop3.html.

2 David Starr Jordan, *The Days of a Man: Being Memories of a Naturalist, Teacher, and Minor Prophet of Democracy*, 2 vols. (Yonkers-on-Hudson, NY: World Book Company, 1922), vol. 2, 173. There are different theories as to who first came up with the quip. Jordan credits Frank Angell, professor of psychology at Stanford.

3 See Harlan H. Ballard, *Hand-Book of the St. Nicholas Agassiz Association*, 2nd

ed. (Lenox, MA: privately printed, 1884), for a list of local chapters (81–111).

4   Alexander Agassiz, "Report to the President and Fellows of Harvard College," *Annual Report of the Curator of the Museum of Comparative Zoology at Harvard College, to the President and Fellows of Harvard College, for 1882–83* (Cambridge: University Press, 1883), 3.

5   Alfred Russel Wallace, "American Museums: The Museum of Comparative Zoology, Harvard," *The Fortnightly Review*, vol. 48 (1 September 1887): 347–59.

6   See http://people-press.org/2009/07/09/public-praises-science-scientists -fault-public-media/.

7   Chris Mooney and Sheril Kirshenbaum, "The Formula," *Boston Globe*, 26 July 2009. See also Mooney and Kirshenbaum, *Unscientific America: How Scientific Illiteracy Threatens Our Future* (New York: Basic, 2009).

8   Rachel Carson, *Silent Spring* (1962; Boston: Mariner, 2002): "This is an era of specialists, each of whom sees his own problem and is unaware or intolerant of the larger frame into which it fits . . . The public must decide whether it wishes to continue on the present road, and it can do so only when in full possession of the facts" (13).

9   LA, "America the Old World," *Geological Sketches*, 11.

10   See Tharp, *Adventurous Alliance*, 294.

11   See Rachel Carson, *The Sea Around Us* (New York: Oxford University Press, 1951); *The Edge of the Sea* (Boston: Houghton Mifflin, 1955).

12   LA, "America the Old World," 11.

13   *Sophocles, Women of Trachis. A Version* by Ezra Pound (New York, 1957), 54; and Pound, Canto 116, *The Cantos*, 4th ed. (London: Faber, 1987), 795. For Pound's use of Agassiz, see chapter 1 of his *ABC of Reading* (1951; London: Faber, 1961), 17–18.

Select Bibliography

MANUSCRIPTS AND ARCHIVES

The major repositories of Agassiz's papers are the Archives de' l'État de Neuchâtel, Switzerland, and Harvard University, with significant collections held by the Houghton Library, the University Archives, and the Museum of Comparative Zoology. Agassiz's Letter Books at the Ernst Mayr Library of the Museum of Comparative Zoology at Harvard contain some thirteen hundred letters by Agassiz. They have recently been digitized through the Harvard University Library Open Access Program; see http://ocp.hul.harvard.edu/dl/ expeditions/009696477. At the Mayr Library, I have also had access to Agassiz's letters to Nathaniel Southgate Shaler, the journals and letters of Henry James Clark, and the scrapbook and journals of James Henry Blake. Agassiz's "ethnographic" albums of photographs taken in South Carolina and Brazil are in the archives of the Peabody Museum at Harvard University. Among the collections at Houghton Library I have used are the Augustus Addison Gould Papers; the William James Papers; the Henry Wadsworth Longfellow Papers; the Letters to Henry Wadsworth Longfellow; the James Russell Lowell Papers; and the American Freedmen's Inquiry Commission Records. At the Arthur and Elizabeth Schlesinger Library on the History of Women in America I have consulted the Elizabeth Cary Agassiz Papers; the Gardiner Family Papers; and the Papers of Annie Ware Winsor Allen. From the Countway Library of Medicine,

Harvard University, I obtained autograph letters by Morrill Wyman and Morris Longstreth. I have also relied on the journals of Addison Emery Verrill at the Harvard University Archives. Other collections from which I have drawn include the Asa Gray Papers at the Gray Herbarium, Harvard University; the Horsford Family Papers in the Institute Archives and Special Collections of the Rensselaer Polytechnic Institute; the Charles Frédéric Girard Papers at the Smithsonian Institution Archives; the Darwin-Lyell Papers at the American Philosophical Society; and the Henry James Clark Papers in the Special Collections and University Archives, W.E.B. Du Bois Library, University of Massachusetts Amherst.

Cecilie Braun Agassiz's portfolio of over a hundred original drawings and sketches is at the Botany Library of the Natural History Museum in London. It was a special pleasure for me to discover this album, long considered lost, and to spend a rainy day in London leafing through it. The Darwin correspondence collected and made available online by Cambridge University Library's Darwin Correspondence Project has been invaluable to me throughout my work on this book. I have also relied on the private collection of Daniel Weinstock, M.D., in Geneva, New York, and on the archives of the Longfellow House–George Washington's National Headquarters Historic Site, notably the Mary King Longfellow Papers.

ANNUAL REPORTS OF THE MUSEUM OF COMPARATIVE ZOOLOGY, CAMBRIDGE, MA

Annual Report of the Trustees of the Museum of Comparative Zoology, Together with the Report of the Director, 1863. Boston: Wright and Potter, 1864.

Annual Report of the Trustees of the Museum of Comparative Zoology, at Harvard College, in Cambridge, Together with the Report of the Director, 1864. Boston: Wright and Potter, 1865.

Annual Report of the Trustees of the Museum of Comparative Zoology, at Harvard College, in Cambridge, Together with the Report of the Director, 1865. Boston: Wright and Potter, 1866.

Annual Report of the Trustees of the Museum of Comparative Zoology, at Harvard College, in Cambridge, Together with the Report of the Director for 1866. Boston: Wright and Potter, 1867.

Annual Report of the Trustees of the Museum of Comparative Zoology, at Harvard College, in Cambridge, Together with the Report of the Director for 1869. Boston: Wright and Potter, 1870.

Annual Report of the Trustees of the Museum of Comparative Zoology, at Harvard College, in Cambridge, Together with the Report of the Director for 1870. Boston: Wright and Potter, 1871.

Annual Report of the Trustees of the Museum of Comparative Zoology, at Harvard College, in Cambridge, Together with the Report of the Director for 1871. Boston: Wright and Potter, 1872.

Annual Report of the Curator of the Museum of Comparative Zoology at Harvard College, to the President and Fellows of Harvard College, for 1882–83. Cambridge: University Press, 1883.

SELECTED BOOKS / MONOGRAPHS BY LOUIS AGASSIZ:

Agassiz's published oeuvre (monographs, articles, essays, notes) is vast. There is no single complete bibliography. However, a good, if not always reliable start is the appendix to Jules Marcou's *Life and Letters* (Marcou), volume 2, 258–303, which lists 425 books and articles.

Selecta genera et species piscium: Quos in itinere per Brasiliam annis MDCCCXVII–MDCCCXX jussu et auspiciis Maximiliani Josephi I. Bavariae Regis augustissimi peracto collegit et pingendoes curavit Dr. J. B. de Spix . . . digessit descripsit et observationibus anatomicis illustravit Dr. L. Agassiz, praefatus est et editit itineris socius, F. C. Ph. De Martius. Munich: C. Wolf, 1829-31.

Recherches sur les poissons fossiles. 5 vols. of texts and 5 atlases [18 parts]. Neuchâtel: Petitpierre, 1833–1843.

Monographies d'échinodermes, vivants et fossiles (with Édouard Desor and G. Valentin). 4 pts. Neuchâtel: Aux frais de l'auteur, 1838–1842.

Histoire naturelle des poissons d'eau douce de l'Europe centrale (with Carl Vogt). Atlas of 41 plates and 2 vols. of text (*Embryologie des salmones; Anatomie des salmones*). Neuchâtel: Aux frais de l'auteur, 1839–1845.

Études sur les glaciers par L. Agassiz. Ouvrage accompagné d'un Atlas de 32 planches, dessinés après nature par Joseph Bettannier. Neuchâtel: Aux frais de l'auteur, 1840.

Études critiques sur les mollusques fossiles. 2 parts. Neuchâtel: Petitpierre; Wolfrath, 1840–1845.

Nomenclator zoologicus. 26 parts. Solothurn: Jent et Gassmann, 1842–1846.

Monographie des poissons fossiles du Vieux Grés-rouge ou Système Dévonien [Old Red Sandstone] des îles Britanniques et de Russie. 3 parts. Neuchâtel: A. Sonrel, 1844–1845.

Notice sur la géographie des animaux. Extrait de la *Revue suisse*, août 1845. Neuchâtel: Henri Wolfrath, 1845.

An Introduction to the Study of Natural History, in a Series of Lectures Delivered in the Hall of the College of Physicians and Surgeons, New York. Illustrated with Numerous Engravings. New York: Greeley and McElrath, 1847.

Nouvelles études et experiences sur les glaciers actuels, leur structure, leur progression, et leur action physique sur le sol. Paris: V. Masson, 1847.

Principles of Zoölogy: Touching the Structure, Development, Distribution, and Natural

Arrangement of the Races of Animals, Living and Extinct, with Numerous Illustrations: Part I: Comparative Physiology (with A. A. Gould). 1848. Rev. ed. 1851. Boston: Gould and Lincoln, 1867.

Bibliographia zoologicae et geologicae: A General Catalogue of All Books, Tracts, and Memoirs on Zoology and Geology. Edited by H. E. Strickland. 4 vols. London: Ray Society, 1848–1854.

Twelve Lectures on Comparative Embryology, Delivered Before the Lowell Institute, in Boston, December and January, 1848–1849. Boston: Henry Flanders, 1849.

Lake Superior: Its Physical Character, Vegetation, and Animals, Compared with Those of Other and Similar Regions (with a narrative of the tour by J. Elliot Cabot). Boston: Gould, Kendall, and Lincoln, 1850.

Contributions to the Natural History of the United States of America. 4 vols. Boston: Little, Brown, 1857–1862.

An Essay on Classification. London: Longman, Brown, Green, etc., 1859.

Methods of Study in Natural History. Boston: Ticknor and Fields, 1863.

Geological Sketches. 1866. 19th ed. Boston: Houghton Mifflin, 1896.

The Structure of Animal Life: Six Lectures Delivered at the Brooklyn Academy of Music in January and February 1862. New York: Charles Scribner, 1866.

A Journey in Brazil (with Elizabeth Agassiz). Boston: Ticknor and Fields, 1868.

Address Delivered on the Centennial Anniversary of the Birth of Alexander von Humboldt Under the Auspices of the Boston Natural History Society, with an Account of the Evening Reception. Boston: Boston Natural History Society, 1869.

De l'espèce et de la classification en zoologie. Translated by Félix Vogeli. Paris: Baillière, 1869.

Geological Sketches: Second Series. 1876. New York: James R. Osgood, 1886.

Studies on Glaciers, Preceded by the Discourse of Neuchâtel, by Louis Agassiz. Edited and translated by Albert V. Carozzi. New York: Hafner, 1967.

SELECTED ARTICLES BY AGASSIZ IN PERIODICALS:

"On Glaciers and Boulders in Switzerland." *Report of the Tenth Meeting of the British Association for the Advancement of Science; Held at Glasgow in August 1840.* London: John Murray, 1841. 113–14.

"The Geographical Distribution of Animals." *Christian Examiner and Religious Miscellany,* vol. 48, no. 2 (March 1850): 181–204.

"The Diversity of Origin of the Human Races." *Christian Examiner and Religious Miscellany,* vol. 49, no. 1 (July 1850): 110–45.

"Contributions to the Natural History of the Acalephae of North America. Part I: On the Naked-Eyed Medusae of the Shores of Massachusetts." *Memoirs of the American Academy of Arts and Sciences,* New Series 4 (1850): 221–316.

"Contemplations of God in the Kosmos." *Christian Examiner and Religious Miscellany,* vol. 50, no. 1 (January 1851): 1–17.

"Prof. Agassiz on the Origin of Species." *American Journal of Science and Arts,* vol. 30 (July 1860): 142–55.

"Physical History of the Valley of the Amazons." *Atlantic Monthly,* vol. 18, no. 105 (July and August 1866): 49–60, 159–69.

"Report upon Deep-Sea Dredgings in the Gulf Stream, During the Third Cruise of the U.S. Steamer *Bibb.*" *Bulletin of the Museum of Comparative Zoology*, vol. 13 (1869): 363–85.

"Evolution and Permanence of Type." *Atlantic Monthly*, vol. 33, no. 195 (1874): 92–101.

BOOKS AND ARTICLES

Aaron, Daniel. *The Unwritten War: American Writers and the Civil War.* 1973. New York: Oxford, 1975.

Agassiz, Alexander. "Mode of Catching Jelly-Fishes." *Atlantic Monthly*, vol. 16, no. 93 (December 1865): 736–39.

———. *Revision of the Echini. Parts I and II, Illustrated Catalogue of the Museum of Comparative Zoology at Harvard College. No. 7.* Cambridge, MA: University Press, 1872.

———. *Revision of the Echini, Parts III and IV. Illustrated Catalogue of the Museum of Comparative Zoology, at Harvard College. No. 7.* Cambridge, MA: University Press, 1873–1874.

———. *Letters and Recollections of Alexander Agassiz.* Edited by G. R. Agassiz. Boston: Houghton Mifflin, 1913.

[Agassiz, Elizabeth Cary]. *A First Lesson in Natural History, by Actaea.* Boston: Little, Brown, 1859.

Agassiz, Elizabeth Cary, and Alexander Agassiz. *Seaside Studies in Natural History. Marine Animals of Massachusetts Bay: Radiates.* 2nd ed. 1865. Boston: Osgood and Co., 1871.

Agassiz, Elizabeth Cary. "An Amazonian Picnic." *Atlantic Monthly*, vol. 17, no. 101 (March 1866): 313–23.

———. "A Dredging Excursion in the Gulf Stream, I." *Atlantic Monthly*, vol. 24, no. 144 (October 1869): 507–16.

———. "A Dredging Excursion in the Gulf Stream, II." *Atlantic Monthly*, vol. 24, no. 145 (November 1869): 571–78.

———. "The Hassler Glacier in the Straits of Magellan." *Atlantic Monthly*, vol. 30, no. 180 (October 1872): 472–78.

———. "In the Straits of Magellan." *Atlantic Monthly*, vol. 31, no. 183 (January 1873): 89–95.

———. "A Cruise Through the Galápagos," *Atlantic Monthly*, vol. 31, no. 187 (March 1873): 579–84.

———. *Louis Agassiz: His Life and Correspondence.* 2 vols. Boston: Houghton Mifflin, 1886.

Bachman, John. *The Doctrine of the Unity of the Human Race Examined on the Principles of Science.* Charleston, SC: C. Canning, 1850.

Baigrie, Brian. "Descartes's Scientific Illustrations and 'La Grande Mécanique de la Nature.'" *Picturing Knowledge: Historical and Philosophical Problems Concerning the Use of Art in Science.* Edited by Brian Baigrie. Toronto: University of Toronto Press, 1996. 86–134.

Baldwin, James. *Notes of a Native Son.* 1964. London: Corgi, 1974.

Baym, Nina. *American Women of Letters and the Nineteenth-Century Sciences: Styles of Affiliation.* New Brunswick, NJ: Rutgers University Press, 2002.

Bergmann, Linda. "'A Troubled Marriage of Discourse's: Science Writing and Travel Narrative in Louis and Elizabeth Cary Agassiz's *A Journey in Brazil*." *Journal of American Culture*, vol. 18 (1995): 83–88.

———. "Widows, Hacks, and Biographers: The Voice of Professionalism in Elizabeth Agassiz's *Louis Agassiz: His Life and Correspondence*." *Auto/Biography Studies*, vol. 12 (1997): 1–21.

Blum, Ann Shelby, and Sarah Landry. "In Loving Detail." *Harvard Magazine*, vol. 79 (May–June 1977): 38–51.

Blum, Ann Shelby. *Picturing Nature: American Nineteenth-Century Zoological Illustration*. Princeton: Princeton University Press, 1993.

Brice, William R., and Silvia F. de M. Figueirôa. "Charles Hartt, Louis Agassiz, and the Controversy over Pleistocene Glaciation in Brazil." *History of Science*, vol. 39 (2001): 161–183.

Browne, Janet. "I Could Have Retched All Night: Charles Darwin and His Body." *Science Incarnate: Historical Embodiments of Natural Knowledge*. Edited by Christopher Lawrence and Steven Shapin. Chicago: University of Chicago Press, 1998. 240–87.

———. *Charles Darwin: The Power of Place*. Princeton: Princeton University Press, 2002.

Bruce, Robert V. *The Launching of Modern American Science: 1846–1876*. New York: Knopf, 1987.

Clark, Henry James. "Some Remarks upon the Use of the Microscope in the Investigation of the Minute Organization of Living Bodies." *American Journal of Science and Arts*, vol. 28, no. 82 (November 1859): 37–48.

———. "On the Origin of Vibrio." *American Journal of Science and Arts*, vol. 28, no. 2 (1859): 107–9.

———. "On Apparent Equivocal Generation." *American Journal of Science and Arts*, vol. 28, no. 82 (1859): 154–55.

———. *A Claim for Scientific Property*. Cambridge, MA: privately printed, 1863.

———. *Mind in Nature; or, The Origin of Life, and the Mode of Development of Animals*. New York: Appleton, 1865.

———. "Conclusive Proofs of the Animality of the Ciliate Sponges, and of Their Affinities with the Infusoria Flagellata." *American Journal of Science and Arts*, vol. 42 (1866): 320–24.

———. "Polarity and Polycephalism: An Essay on Individuality." *American Journal of Science and Arts*, vol. 49 (1870): 69–75.

———. "The American Spongilla, a Craspedote, Flagellate Infusorian." *American Journal of Science and Arts*, 3rd series, vol. 2, no. 12 (December 1871): 426–36.

———. *Lucernariae and Their Allies. A Memoir on the Anatomy and Physiology of Haliclystus Auricula, and Other Lucernarians, with a Discussion of Their Relations to Other Acalephae; to Beroids, and Polypi*. Smithsonian Contributions to Knowledge, 242. Washington: Smithsonian Institution, 1878.

Clark, William. *Academic Charisma and the Origins of the Research*. Chicago: University of Chicago Press, 2006.

The Complete Lincoln-Douglas Debates of 1858. Edited by Paul M. Angle. 1958. Chicago: University of Chicago Press, 1991.

Correspondence Between Spencer Fullerton Baird and Louis Agassiz, Two Pioneer Naturalists. Edited by Elmer Charles Herber. Washington, DC: Smithsonian, 1963.

Croce, Paul Jerome. "Probabilistic Darwinism: Louis Agassiz vs. Asa Gray on Science, Religion, and Certainty." *Journal of Religious History*, vol. 22 (February 1995): 35–58.

———. *Science and Religion in the Era of William James. Vol. 1: The Eclipse of Certainty, 1820–1880.* Chapel Hill: University of North Carolina Press, 1995.

Curtis, Caroline Gardiner. *Memories of Fifty Years in the Last Century: Written for Her Grandchildren.* Boston: privately printed, 1947.

Darwin, Charles. *Journal of Researches into the Geology and Natural History of the Various Countries Visited by the H.M.S. Beagle, Under the Command of Captain FitzRoy, R.N., from 1832–1836.* London: Colburn, 1839.

———. *On the Origin of Species: A Facsimile of the First Edition.* 1859. Cambridge, MA: Harvard University Press, 1964.

———. *The Descent of Man, and Selection in Relation to Sex.* 2nd ed. 1879. New York: Appleton, 1927.

Daston, Lorraine, and Peter Galison. *Objectivity.* New York: Zone, 2007.

Desmond, Adrian, and James Moore. *Darwin's Sacred Cause: How a Hatred of Slavery Shaped Darwin's View on Human Evolution.* Boston: Houghton Mifflin, 2009.

Desor, Édouard. "Account of the Development of the Embryo of the Starfish." *Proceedings of the Boston Society of Natural History*, no. 3 (1848–1850): 13–14 and 17–18.

Dexter, Ralph W. "The Salem Secession of Agassiz Zoologists." *Essex Institute Historical Collections*, vol. 101 (1965): 27–39.

——— "Agassiz on Zoological Classification and Nomenclature." *Bios*, vol. 50, no. 4 (December 1979): 218–22.

Di Gregorio, Mario A., with the assistance of N. W. Gill. *Charles Darwin's Marginalia*, vol. 1. New York: Garland 1990.

Dobbs, David. *Reef Madness: Charles Darwin, Alexander Agassiz, and the Meaning of Coral.* New York: Pantheon, 2005.

Donald, David Herbert. *Lincoln.* London: Cape, 1995.

Dupree, A. Hunter. *Asa Gray: American Botanist, Friend of Darwin.* 1959. Baltimore: Johns Hopkins University Press, 1988.

[Fields, Annie]. *James T. Fields: Biographical Notes and Personal Sketches, with Unpublished Fragments and Tributes from Men and Women of Letters.* Boston: Houghton Mifflin, 1881.

Fields, James T. *Ballads and Other Verses.* Boston: Houghton Mifflin, 1880.

Final Report of the American Freedmen's Inquiry Commission to the Secretary of War. New York, 1864. http://www.civilwarhome.com/commissionreport.htm.

Gladfelter, Elizabeth Higgins. *Agassiz's Legacy: Scientists' Reflections on the Value of Field Experience.* New York: Oxford University Press, 2002.

Gos, Charles. *L'Hôtel des Neuchâtelois: Un épisode de la conquête des Alpes.* Lausanne: Librarie Payot & Cie, 1928.

Gould, Stephen Jay. *Ontogeny and Phylogeny.* Cambridge, MA: Belknap Press, 1977.

———. "Agassiz's Later, Private Thoughts on Evolution: His Marginalia in Haeckel's *Natürliche Schöpfungsgeschichte.*" *Two Hundred Years of Geology in America.* Edited by Cecil J. Schneer. Hanover, NH: University Press of New England, 1979. 277–282.

———. *The Mismeasure of Man.* 1981. New York: Norton, 1993.

———. *The Flamingo's Smile: Reflections in Natural History.* 1985. New York: Norton, 1987.

———. *Bully for Brontosaurus: Further Reflections in Natural History.* 1991. London: Penguin, 1992.

———. *Hen's Teeth and Horse's Toes: Further Reflections in Natural History.* New York: Norton, 1993.

———. "Haeckel's 'Artforms of Nature': Either or Neither? Fused or Misused?" *The Hedgehog, the Fox, and the Magister's Pox: Mending the Gap Between Science and the Humanities.* New York: Three Rivers, 2003. 157–63.

———. *I Have Landed: The End of a Beginning in Natural History.* New York: Harmony, 2002.

[Gray, Asa]. "Review of *Explanations: A Sequel to the Vestiges of the Natural History of Creation.*" *North American Review*, vol. 52 (1846): 465–506.

Gray, Asa. *Manual of the Botany of the Northern United States, from New England to Wisconsin and South to Ohio and Pennsylvania Inclusive.* Boston: Munroe, 1848.

———. *How Plants Grow: A Simple Introduction to Structural Botany.* New York: American Book Company, 1858.

———. "Diagnostic Characters of New Species of Phaenogamous Plants Collected in Japan by Charles Wright, Botanist of the U.S. North Pacific Exploring Expedition." *Memoirs of the American Academy of Arts and Sciences*, New Series 6 (1859): 377–452.

———. *Darwiniana: Essays and Reviews Pertaining to Darwinism.* Ed. A. Hunter Dupree. 1876. Cambridge, MA: Belknap Press, 1963.

———. *Scientific Papers of Asa Gray.* Edited by Charles Sprague Sargent. 2 vols. Boston: Houghton Mifflin, 1889.

———. *Letters of Asa Gray.* Edited by Jane Loring Gray. 2 vols. Boston: Houghton Mifflin, 1893.

Haeckel, Ernst. *Ziele und Wege der heutigen Entwickelungsgeschichte.* Jena: Hermann Dufft, 1875.

———. *Das System der Medusen: Erster Theil einer Monographie der Medusen.* 3 vols. in 2. Jena: Gustav Fischer, 1879–1880.

———. *The History of Creation; or, the Development of the Earth and Its Inhabitants by the Action of Natural Causes.* Translated by E. Ray Lankester. 1868. 4th ed. 2 vols. London: Kegan Paul, Trench, Trübner and Co., 1899.

———. *Kunstformen der Natur.* 1904. Wiesbaden: Marix, 2004.

Hartt, Charles Frederick. *Scientific Results of a Journey in Brazil, by Louis Agassiz and his Traveling Companions: Geology and Physical Geography of Brazil.* Boston: Fields, Osgood and Co., 1870.

"Henry James Clark, 1826–1873." *General Catalogue of the Massachusetts Agricultural College, 1862–1886.* Amherst, MA: J. E. Williams, 1886. 103–7.

Hill, Thomas. "A Collecting Trip with Louis Agassiz" (1848). *The Harvard Book: Selections from Three Centuries.* rev. ed. 1953. Cambridge, MA: Harvard University Press, 1982. 54–58.

Holmes, Richard. *The Age of Wonder: How the Romantic Generation Discovered the Beauty and Terror of Science.* London: HarperPress, 2008.

Howe, Samuel Gridley. *The Refugees from Slavery in Canada West: Report to the Freedmen's Inquiry Commission.* Boston: Wright and Potter, 1864.

———. *Letters and Journals of Samuel Gridley Howe.* Edited by Laura E. Richards. 2 vols. London: John Lane, 1906–1909.

Howells, William Dean. *Literary Friends and Acquaintance: A Personal Retrospect of American Authorship.* Edited by David F. Hiatt and Edwin H. Cady. 1900. Bloomington: Indiana University Press, 1968.

Humboldt, Alexander von. *Voyage de Humboldt et Bonpland: Recueil d'observations de zoologie et d'anatomie comparée faites dans l'Océan Atlantique, dans l'intérieur du nouveau Continent et dans la mer du Sud pendant les années 1799–1803, 2ème partie zoologie.* 2 vols. Paris: Schoell, 1805–1809.

———. *Cosmos: A Sketch of the Physical Description of the Universe.* Translated by E. C. Otté. 2 vols. New York: Harper, 1858.

———. *Ansichten der Natur.* Edited by Rudolf Meyer-Abich. 3rd ed. 1849. Stuttgart: Reclam, 1969.

———. *Über das Universum: Die Kosmos-Vorträge 1827/28 in der Berliner Singakademie.* Edited by Jürgen Hamel and Klaus Harro-Tiemann. Frankfurt am Main: Insel, 1993.

Huey, Michael. "Medusa Man." *World of Interiors,* vol. 19, no. 8 (August 1999): 64–63.

Imbrie, John, and Katherine Palmer Imbrie. *Ice Ages: Solving the Mystery.* Cambridge, MA: Harvard University Press, 1979.

Irmscher, Christoph. *The Poetics of Natural History: From John Bartram to William James.* New Brunswick, NJ: Rutgers University Press, 1999.

———. *Music for the Worms: A Darwin Exhibit at Lilly Library, Indiana University Bloomington.* Bloomington, Indiana: The Lilly Library, 2009.

———. *Public Poet, Private Man: Henry Wadsworth Longfellow at 200.* Amherst: University of Massachusetts Press, 2009.

Isaacs, Gwyneira. "Louis Agassiz's Photographs in Brazil: Separate Creations." *History of Photography,* vol. 21, no. 1 (1997): 3–12.

James, William. "Louis Agassiz." *Science,* N.S. 5 (19 February 1897): 285–89.

———. *The Varieties of Religious Experience: A Study in Human Nature.* 1901–1902. London: Fontana, 1975.

Jordan, David Starr. "Agassiz at Penikese." *Popular Science Monthly* 40 (1898): 721–729.

———. *The Days of a Man: Being Memories of a Naturalist, Teacher, and Minor Prophet of Democracy.* 2 vols. Yonkers-on-Hudson, NY: World Book Company, 1922.

Kaeser, Marc-Antoine. *L'Univers du préhistorien: Science, foi, et politique dans l'oeuvre et la vie d'Édouard Desor (1811–1882).* Paris: L'Harmattan, 2004.

———. *Un savant séducteur: Louis Agassiz (1807–1873), prophète de la science.* Lausanne: Les Éditions de l'Aire, 2007.

Kirshenbaum, Sheril, and Chris Mooney. *Unscientific America: How Scientific Illiteracy Threatens Our Future.* New York: Basic, 2009.

Levine, George. *Darwin Loves You: Natural Selection and the Re-Enchantment of the World.* Princeton, NJ: Princeton University Press, 2006.

Lewes, George Henry. *Sea-Side Studies at Ilfracombe, Tenby, the Scilly Isles, & Jersey.* Edinburgh: William Blackwood and Sons, 1858.

Lindsay, Debra. "Intimate Inmates: Wives, Households, and Science in Nineteenth-Century America." *Isis,* vol. 89 (1998): 631–52.

Livingstone, David N. *Nathaniel Southgate Shaler and the Culture of American Science.* Tuscaloosa: University of Alabama Press, 1987.

Longfellow, Ernest Wadsworth. *Random Memories.* Boston: Houghton Mifflin, 1922.

Longfellow, Fanny Appleton. *Mrs. Longfellow: Selected Letters and Journals of Fanny Appleton Longfellow (1817–1861).* Edited by Edward Wagenknecht. New York: Longmans, Green, and Co., 1956.

Longfellow, Samuel, ed. *The Life of Henry Wadsworth Longfellow, with Extracts from His Journals and Correspondence.* 3 vols. Boston: Houghton Mifflin, 1891.

Louis Agassiz: Memorial Meeting of the Boston Society of Natural History, January 7, 1874. Boston: privately printed, 1874.

Lowell, James Russell. *The Complete Poems of James Russell Lowell: Cabinet Edition.* Cambridge: Houghton Mifflin, 1899.

Lurie, Edward. "Louis Agassiz and the Races of Man." *Isis,* vol. 45, no. 3 (September 1954): 227–42.

———. *Louis Agassiz: A Life in Science.* 1960. Baltimore: Johns Hopkins University Press, 1988.

Lyell, Charles. *Principles of Geology, Being an Attempt to Explain the Former Changes of the Earth's Surface, by Reference to Causes Now in Operation.* 3 vols. London: John Murray, 1830–1833.

Lyman, Theodore. "Recollections of Agassiz." *Atlantic Monthly,* vol. 33, no. 196 (February 1874): 221–29.

Machado, Maria Helena, ed. *Brazil Through the Eyes of William James: Letters, Diaries, Drawings, 1865–1866.* Cambridge, MA: Harvard University Press, 2006.

Marcou, Jules. *The Life, Letters, and Works of Louis Agassiz.* 2 vols. New York: Macmillan, 1896.

Mark, Edward Laurens. "Zoology." *The Development of Harvard University Since the Inauguration of President Eliot, 1869–1929.* Edited by Samuel Eliot Morison. Cambridge, MA: Harvard University Press, 1930. 378–99.

McSherry, Corynne. *Who Owns Academic Work? Battling for Control of Intellectual Property.* Cambridge: Harvard University Press, 2001.

Menand, Louis. *The Metaphysical Club: A Story of Ideas in America.* New York: Farrar, Straus, and Giroux, 2001.

Mettenius, Cecilie. *Alexander Braun's Leben nach seinem handschriftlichen Nachlass dargestellt.* Berlin: G. Reimer, 1882.

Morton, Samuel G. *Crania Americana; or, A Comparative View of the Skulls of Various Aboriginal Nations of North and South America.* Philadelphia: J. Dobson, 1839.

Norton, Bettina A. "Tappan and Bradford: Boston Lithographers with Essex County Associations." *Essex Historical Institute Collection,* vol. 114 (July 1978): 149–60.

Nott, Josiah C. "An Examination of the Physical History of the Jews, in Its Bearings on the Question of the Unity of Races," in *Proceedings of the American Association for the Advancement of Science. Third Meeting, Held at Charleston, S.C., 1850.* Charleston: Walker and James, 1850. 98–107.

Nott, Josiah C., and George R. Gliddon. *Types of Mankind; or Ethnological Researches, Based upon the Ancient Monuments, Paintings, Sculptures, and Crania of Races, and upon Their Natural, Geographical, Philological, and Biblical History: Illustrated by*

Selections from the Inedited Papers of Samuel George Morton, M.D. 2nd ed. Philadelphia: J. B. Lippincott, Grambo, and Co., 1854.

Oppenheimer, Jane M. "Louis Agassiz as an Early Embryologist in America." *Science and Society in Early America: Essays in Honor of Whitfield J. Bell Jr.* Edited by Randolph S. Klein. Philadelphia: American Philosophical Society, 1986. 393–414.

Packard, Alpheus Spring, Jr. "Memoir of Henry James Clark, 1826–1873. Read before the National Academy, 23 April 1874." *National Academy of Sciences, Washington, DC: Biographical Memoirs. Vol. 1.* Washington, DC: National Academy of Sciences, 1874. 317–28.

Paton, Lucy Allen. *Elizabeth Cary Agassiz: A Biography.* Boston: Houghton Mifflin, 1919.

Pierce, Sally, and Catharina Slautterback. *Boston Lithography, 1825–1880: The Boston Athenaeum Collection.* Boston: The Boston Athenaeum, 1991.

Preliminary Report Touching the Condition and Management of Emancipated Refugees, Made to the Secretary of War, June 30, 1863. New York, 1863. http://www.civilwarhome.com/prelimcommissionreport.htm.

Reichlin, Elinor. "Faces of Slavery: A Historical Find." *American Heritage,* vol. 28, no. 4 (June 1977): 4–11.

Repplier, Agnes. *J. William White, M.D.: A Biography.* Boston: Houghton Mifflin, 1919.

Roper, Laura Wood Roper. *FLO: A Biography of Frederick Law Olmsted.* 1973. Baltimore: Johns Hopkins University Press, 1983.

Royce, Josiah. "The Present Ideals of American Life." *Scribner's Magazine,* vol. 10 (1891): 376–88.

Ruiz-Trillo, Iñaki, Gertraud Burger, Peter W. H. Holland, Nicole King, B. Franz Lang, Andrew J. Roger and Michael W. Gray. "The Origins of Multicellularity: A Multi-Taxon Genome Initiative." *Trends in Genetics,* vol. 23, no. 3 (2007): 113–18.

Ruse, Michael. *Darwin and Design: Does Evolution Have a Purpose?* Cambridge, MA: Harvard University Press, 2003.

Sachs, Aaron. *The Humboldt Current: Nineteenth-Century Exploration and the Roots of American Environmentalism.* New York: Viking, 2008.

Sappol, Michael. *Anatomy and Embodied Social Identity in Nineteenth-Century America.* Princeton, NJ: Princeton University Press, 2002.

Schimper, Karl Friedrich. *Gedichte.* Erlangen: Ferdinand Enke, 1840.

Schwartz, Harold. *Samuel Gridley Howe, Social Reformer, 1801–1876.* Cambridge, MA: Harvard University Press, 1956.

Scudder, Samuel H. "In the Laboratory with Agassiz." *Every Saturday* 16 (4 April 1874): 369–70.

Senior [Dr. William Elder]. "Orthodoxy vs. Slavery." *The National Era,* vol. 6, no. 307 (18 November 1852): 185.

Shaler, Nathaniel Southgate. "The Negro Problem." *Atlantic Monthly,* vol. 54, no. 325 (1884): 696–709.

Slack, Henry J. "The Nature of Sponges (Researches of Clark and Carter)." *Popular Science Review,* vol. 11 (1872): 167–76.

Slotten, Ross A. *The Heretic in Darwin's Court: The Life of Alfred Russel Wallace.* New York: Columbia University Press, 2004.

Smith, David C., and Harold W. Borns Jr. "Louis Agassiz, the Great Deluge, and Early Maine Geology." *Northeastern Naturalist*, vol. 7, no. 2 (2000): 157–77.

Smyth, Thomas. *The Unity of Human Races Proved to Be the Doctrine of Scripture, Reason, and Science; with a Review of the Present Position and Theory of Professor Agassiz*. New York: Putnam, 1850.

Sollors, Werner. *Neither Black nor White Yet Both: Thematic Explorations of Interracial Literature*. New York: Oxford University Press, 1997.

Spitzka, Edward Anthony. "A Study of the Brains of Six Eminent Scientists Belonging to the American Anthropometric Society, Together with a Description of the Skull of Professor E. D. Cope." *Transactions of the American Philosophical Society*. New Series 21, no. 4 (1907): 175–308.

Stephens, Lester D. *Science, Race, and Religion in the American South: John Bachman and the Charleston Circle of Naturalists, 1815–1859*. Chapel Hill: The University of North Carolina Press, 2000.

Sumner, Charles. *The Question of Caste: Lecture by the Hon. Charles Sumner*. Boston: Wright and Potter, 1869.

Surdez, Maryse. *Catalogue des archives de Louis Agassiz, 1807–1873. Bulletin de la Société Neuchâteloise des Sciences Naturelles*, vol. 97 (1974).

Thackeray, William Makepeace. *Thackeray's Letters to an American Family*. New York: Century, 1904.

Tiedemann, Friedrich. *Das Hirn des Negers mit dem des Europäers und Orang-Outangs verglichen*. Heidelbrg: Karl Winter, 1837.

Tharp, Louise Hall. *Adventurous Alliance: The Story of the Agassiz Family of Boston*. Boston: Little, Brown, 1959.

——. *The Appletons of Beacon Hill*. Boston: Little, Brown, 1973.

Verrill, Addison Emery. "Revision of the Polyps of the Eastern Coast of the United States." *Memoirs Read Before the Boston Society of Natural History*, vol. 1 (1864): 1–64.

Voss, Julia. *Darwins Bilder: Ansichten der Evolutionstheorie, 1837–1874*. Frankfurt am Main: Fischer, 2007.

Wallace, Alfred Russel. "The Origin of Human Races and the Antiquity of Man Deduced from the Theory of Natural Selection." *Anthropological Review and Journal of the Anthropological Society of London*, vol. 2 (1864): clviii–clxxxvii.

——. "American Museums: The Museum of Comparative Zoology, Harvard." *The Fortnightly Review*, vol. 48 (1 September 1887): 347–59.

Wallis, Brian. "Black Bodies, White Science: Louis Agassiz's Slave Daguerreotypes." *American Art*, vol. 9, no. 2 (Summer 1995): 39–61.

Walls, Laura Dassow. "'Hero of Knowledge, Be Our Tribute Thine': Alexander von Humboldt in Victorian America." *Northeastern Naturalist*, vol. 8, no. 1. (2001): 121–34.

——. *Passage to Cosmos: Alexander von Humboldt and the Shaping of America*. Chicago: Chicago University Press, 2009.

Walsten, David M. "Darwin's Backwoods Correspondent: Letters Between Charles Darwin and Illinois Naturalist Benjamin D. Walsh." *Field Museum of Natural History Bulletin*, vol. 45, no. 1 (January 1974): 8–9, 9–15.

Whipple, Edwin Percy. "Recollections of Agassiz." *Harper's New Monthly Magazine*, vol. 59, no. 349 (June 1879): 97–110.

Wilder, Burt G. "Agassiz at Penikese." *American Naturalist*, vol. 32, no. 375 (March 1898): 189–96.

Wilder, Burt G. "Jeffries Wyman." *Leading American Men of Science*. Edited by David Starr Jordan. New York: Henry Holt and Company, 1910. 171–209.

Winsor, Mary Pickard. "Louis Agassiz and the Species Question." *Studies in History of Biology*, vol. 3 (1979): 89–138.

———. *Reading the Shape of Nature: Comparative Zoology at the Agassiz Museum*. Chicago: University of Chicago Press, 1991.

———. "Agassiz's Notions of a Museum: The Vision and the Myth." *Cultures and Institutions of Natural History*. Edited by Michael T. Ghiselin and Alan E. Leviton. *Memoirs of the California Academy of Sciences*. San Francisco: California Academy of Sciences, 2000. 240–71.

Wright, G. Frederick. "Agassiz and the Ice Age." *American Naturalist*, vol. 32, no. 375 (March 1898): 16–171.

Wyman, Jeffries. *Dear Jeffie: Being the Letters from Jeffries Wyman, First Director of the Peabody Museum, to His Son, Jeffries Wyman Jr.* Edited by George E. Gifford Jr. Cambridge, MA: Peabody Museum Press, 1978.

Index

Page numbers in italics refer to illustrations. Species names listed in
the index are those used by Agassiz and his contemporaries.